Shia Power

Geopolitical Affairs

Series Editor and Editor-in-Chief: Michel Korinman

Editor: John Laughland

This new books series will will cover global and regional geopolitics and current affairs. Each volume contains articles by commentators from all ends of the political spectrum, the goal being to present as many different points of view as possible. Geopolitics studies how geography and politics interact; *Geopolitical Affairs* aims to be the last word in what is happening on our planet today.

International Advisory Board

1. Shia Power: Next target Iran?
2. Migration in Europe and the Mediterranean
3. Russia, the Caucasus and Eastern Europe
4. The Americas

Geopolitical Affairs is published by the Daedalos Institute of Geopolitics in Cyprus in cooperation with OGENI, the Geopolitical Observatory for Nations and the World (*Observatoire géopolitique des espaces nationaux et internationaux*) at the Sorbonne in Paris.

Shia Power
Next Target Iran?

Editors

Michel Korinman

John Laughland

VALLENTINE MITCHELL ACADEMIC

LONDON · PORTLAND, OR

Daedalos Institute of
Geopolitics, Cyprus

OGENI
(Observatoire géopolitique des espaces nationaux
et internationaux), Sorbonne, Paris

First published in 2007 in Great Britain by
VALLENTINE MITCHELL ACADEMIC
Suite 314, Premier House, 112–114 Station Road,
Edgware, Middlesex HA8 7BJ

and in the United States of America by
VALLENTINE MITCHELL ACADEMIC
c/o ISBS, 920 NE 58th Avenue, Suite 300
Portland, OR 97213-3786

Website: www.vmbooks.com

British Library Cataloguing in Publication Data
A catalogue record has been applied for

ISBN 978 0 85303 750 7 (cloth)
ISBN 978 0 85303 751 4 (paper)

Library of Congress Cataloging in Publication Data
A catalogue record has been applied for

This group of studies first appeared in a special issue of
Geopolitical Affairs, 1/1 [ISSN 1753-5417],
published by Vallentine Mitchell Academic.

Typeset in 10.5/12pt Garamond by FiSH Books, Enfield, Middx
Printed in Great Britain by MPG Books Ltd, Bodmin, Cornwall

Contents

PART II. THE WAR TO COME

PART III. AHMADINEJAD,
THE SECOND REVOLUTION?

PART IV. SHIITE EMPIRE

PART V. PSYCHOANALYSIS AND GEOPOLITICS

Brzezinski, Kissinger and the Messianic School in the Middle East

Editorial
MICHEL KORINMAN

Jimmy Carter's former National Security Adviser, Zbigniew Brezezinski, has still not calmed down. This champion of the 'realists' thundered to his listeners at the New American Foundation on 20 July 2006 against the 'Zealots': Paul Wolfowitz, Bill Kristol, Richard Perle and their school of neo-conservatism. The United States, he said, had learned and was in the process of learning in Baghdad what Israel had learned from bitter experience in Lebanon: that peace settlements in the Middle East cannot be achieved by the force of arms. The United States' very capacity to lead the world is at stake. The next test, he said, was Iran which, unlike Iraq, is a serious country with which it will be necessary to negotiate, given the challenge launched by Tehran on its nuclear programme.[1]

Henry Kissinger has also crossed swords with the neo-conservatives in the columns of the *Washington Post*. He has said that the United Nations should not repeat the mistakes of the League of Nations in 1935–36, when the sanctions imposed on fascist Italy after the invasion of Abyssinia were so ineffective that the invasion was, *de facto*, tolerated. Kissinger wrote that the measures taken against Iran needed to be both fundamental and concrete: a 'geopolitical dialogue' could be no substitute for a solution. The former Secretary of State said that he could easily see Iran emerging as a factor of stabilization and progress in the region. But if Tehran insisted on combining in a single project based on nuclear arms the aims of the Persian Empire and the spirit of a crusade, then the collision with America (or rather the 5 + 1 Group composed of the permanent Security Council members plus Germany) would seem inevitable.[2]

For their part, the neo-conservatives like Richard Perle, former Assistant Secretary of Defense (1981–87) interpret Israel's intervention in Lebanon as an entirely legitimate response by a country whose very survival is under threat.[3] They claim to stand up to 'the establishment' which, behind Condoleezza Rice, and since 2003, has been arguing that an accommodation should be reached with the allies and the enemy – in this case a nuclear Iran – appeased.[4] Better still, they regard the Israeli campaign of the summer of 2006 as a dress rehearsal for a far more decisive action against Iran. Some in this camp probably would have preferred an inversion of the chronology: attacks first on the commanders in Syria and Iran, and then only later on their Lebanese clients. Some Israelis have the same idea.[5] In the same way, but obviously coming from the opposite perspective, the Arab press has analysed the 'Second Lebanese War' as a failed experiment by the US hawks. Their idea was first to test Hezbollah's capacity for resistance, then to encourage the Lebanese population to rebel against it, and finally to test the military option against Iran.[6]

Probably the rhetoric of the Iranian President Mahmoud Ahmadinejad has radicalized American and Israeli perceptions to the extent that many observers take him at his word. In other words, it is the Iranians who have set the agenda in at least one part of the world. They have done this by denying the Holocaust, which is presented as the latest brilliant manoeuvre by the Jews to legitimize the creation of a foreign state in the Middle East; by forging a millenarian and apocalyptic concept of a historic war for survival between martyr peoples, that is, the Shiites, and the Jewish state; and by announcing the imminent territorial eradication of Israel. As the researcher Eldad J. Pardo shows in this volume, this rhetoric was not invented by Ahmadinejad but is instead an integral part of the whole Iranian regime, starting with the Supreme Leader, Ali Khameini, who called for the destruction of Israel in 2000, and including the reformer Mohammad Khatami, president of the Islamic Republic from 1997 to 2005, who suggested that the 'racist and terrorist' Israeli regime be liquidated. According to Pardo, 'The destruction of Israel seems to be indeed a strategic priority for Iran, and cannot be judged as a tactic only.'

The very careful preparations made for the recent conflict, via Hezbollah and from 2000 to 2006, and about which the Israeli secret services evidently were very badly informed, is believed to go back to an undertaking which was anything but simply verbal.[7] In the words of an important religious conservative in Iran, Ahmed Khatami, 'They must be made to be afraid of the day when our missiles with a range of 2,000 km [Shahab-3] will hit the very heart of Tel Aviv.'[8] Pardo argues, however, that there is a tactical element in Iran's strategy: by focusing its rhetoric on Israel, it is distracting the West's attention from its true geopolitical project, which is to assume the leadership of all Shiites to the east of Egypt. The Iranians, moreover, have found the Israeli–Palestinian and Israeli–Lebanese conflicts to be excellent distractions from their nuclear programme and a good way of dividing the West.[9] The conclusion which many observers draw is that, once Iran has obtained a nuclear bomb, it will be impossible to exclude its use against Israel and Europe. The most plausible scenario is that of a crusade against the West under the cover of the nuclear umbrella.[10] In this context, economists' arguments about a rise in oil prices and military arguments about a blockade in the Strait of Hormuz or an Iranian attack on nearby oil fields seem rather irrelevant by comparison.

The Lebanese movement, Hezbollah, and its Iranian patron have made no mistake about this and have recoded their joint action in a very interesting manner. Hassan Nasrallah, the secretary-general of Hezbollah, who is the hailed in the Arab and Muslim street as the descendant of Nasser,[11] has suddenly discovered (for domestic consumption) that he did not expect the war which in any case he had not started but which Israel wanted at all costs.[12] This explains Hezbollah's proclamations of independence *vis-à-vis* Iran, which are indeed true, at least in this case: Iran, which is often under scrutiny for its overall strategy, was probably indeed faced *tactically* with a *fait accompli*.[13] Mojtaba Rahmandoust, adviser to the Iranian president for veterans of the Iran–Iraq War, has said categorically, 'In the current circumstances, Iran does not have any intention of attacking Israel.' For good measure, he added, 'But if Israel attacks us, then we will fight back.'[14]

It is certain that the Iranians are aware of the new map of the Middle East which is circulating on the Internet and which shows their territory amputated of its oil and gas fields (which go to a newly created Shiite Arab state in Iraq!); which establishes a 'Free Baluchistan' in the south-west of Iran and on Pakistani territory; and which 'compensates' Iran in Western Afghanistan by giving it numerous Persian-speaking Tajiks (from Herat) and semi-nomadic Aimaks (who like to call themselves Tajiks).[15] Is this geopolitical fiction, the product of the wild fantasies of military planners? Certainly, but will Tehran force the issue?

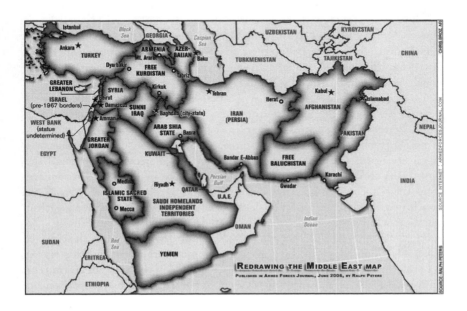

The Green Fourth International dominated by Iran is an old project of Ayatollah Khomeini's which was abandoned by his successors. It is not about to re-emerge. There was a clash at the Arab League summit in July 2006 over Iran's support for Hezbollah: Algeria, Sudan, Syria, Yemen and Qatar were in favour, Egypt, Jordan, Saudi Arabia and Kuwait were against. Some diplomats in the latter camp were happy to denounce the Shiites as 'worse than the Zionists' for their desire to create a crescent of radicalism from Tehran to Gaza via Damascus and South Lebanon. It has not escaped the attention of the Iranians that the intelligent and subtle Syrian Foreign Minister Walid Muallem was careful not to appear too intimately linked to the ayatollahs and that he preferred to join the Arab 'No' camp.[16] This is not even to include the competition from Al Qaeda which is concerned that it may find itself sidelined by the rise in the publicity given to the Shiites of Lebanon.[17] If there were a major crisis, Iran could find itself marginalized.

Will George Bush's crushing defeat at the Congressional elections on 7 November 2006 mark the beginning of a new policy? Observers in Washington are divided on the question. According to the very well-informed Seymour Hersh of the *New Yorker*, the hawks around Vice President Dick Cheney are still arguing in favour of pre-emptive strikes against Iran, possibly including tactical nuclear strikes, with or without the support of Congress.

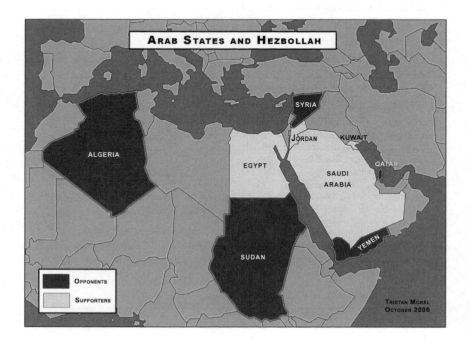

The aim would be not so much to destroy Iran's nuclear programme as to provoke regime change by force. The opponents of this project are the military top brass and the State Department who want first to exhaust all diplomatic means at their disposal.

Some agree with Karim Sadjadpour of the International Crisis Group that the appointment of Robert Gates as the new boss in the Pentagon means that strikes against Iran are now less likely.[18] The new Secretary of Defense was a co-signatory of a document in July 2004 which called for dialogue with Iran on certain well-defined subjects.[19] This anticipated the findings of the Iraq Study Group chaired by Lee Hamilton and James Baker which recommended engaging with Iran and Syria – which in any case is probably concerned at Iran's new hegemony in Lebanon – on stabilizing Iraq. The same report however also says that no concessions should be made to these two countries either on the nuclear issue or on Lebanon. Is this an attempt to square the circle?

Who is better placed to interpret his crushing defeat at the two elections held in Iran on 15 December 2006 – the elections for the Council of Experts and the local elections, at which the turn-out was 60 per cent – than President Ahmadinejad himself? 'The Iranian people have demonstrated their intelligence and dignity to the whole world,' he said.

Michel Korinman is Professor of Geopolitics at the Sorbonne, Director General of the Daedalos Institute of Geopolitics in Cyprus, and Editor-in-Chief of Geopolitical Affairs.

NOTES

1   <http://www.thewashingtonnote.com/archives/Brzezinski%20speech%207-20web.htm>.

2   'The Next Steps With Iran: Negotiations Must Go Beyond the Nuclear Threat to Broader Issues', *Washington Post*, 31 July 2006.

3   'An Appropriate Response', *New York Times*, 22 July 2006.

4   'Why Did Bush Blink on Iran? (Ask Condi)', *Washington Post*, 25 June 2006.

5   See Marc Henry, 'L'État hébreu tenté de frapper la Syrie', *Le Figaro*, 29–30 July 2006; Davide Frattini, '"Non sarà una guerra lampo" Prime previsioni: da poche settimane allo scontro totale con Siria e Iran', *Corriere della Sera*, 19 July 2006, who quotes Michael B. Oren, author of a major work on the Six Day War, in the weekly, *The New Republic*. The argument is that there can be no real ceasefire in Lebanon without Syria being taken out by a bombing campaign, for otherwise Damascus would remain faithful to its strategy of maintaining tensions, even to the point of provoking a regional conflict.

6   Cf. Hmida Ben Romdha, 'Test non concluant', *La Presse de Tunisie*, 18 August 2006, who examines the so-called 'Halutz plan'(named after the Chief of Staff of the Israeli Army) and who follows the line of the American commentators, especially Seymour Hersh .

7   Cf. Eldad J. Pardo, 'Race and the Nuclear Race: Anti-Semitism in Iran', in this issue of *Geopolitical Affairs*.

8   'L'Iran fête la "victoire" et menace l'État hébreu', Agence France Presse, *Le Figaro*, 16 August 2006.

9   Cf. 'Una domanda: Perché le classi dirigenti di Francia, Spagna e Italia stanno dalla parte di
    Hezbollah?', *Il Foglio*, 5 August 2006, concerning the positive results of these tactics in Southern
    Europe.
10 Cf. Pardo, 'Race and the Nuclear Race'.
11 Cf. Viviana Mazza, 'Nasrallah come Nasser: nuovo mito delle masse arabe In piazza, sul web,
    dall'Egitto a Gaza, lo sceicco diventa simbolo dell'orgoglio musulmano', *Corriere della Sera*, 30
    July 2006: 80 per cent of Christians and Druze and 89 per cent of Shiites approve of him,
    according to *The Times*. See also Hans-Christian Rössler, 'Panarabischer Aktionismus', *Frankfurter
    Allgemeine Zeitung*, 9 August 2006, who emphasizes the fact that Nasrrallah's support extends
    across all religions. On his triumph in the media, for example, *Al-Manar*, Hezbollah's TV station,
    see Giuseppe Zaccaria, 'Negli studi fantasma di Al Manar il verbo degli Hezbollah nell'etere', *La
    Stampa*, 6 August 2006 and Michael Borgstede, 'Die Märchen der Hizbullah', *FAZ*, 18 August
    2006.
12 'Un errore rapire gli israeliani non ci aspettavamo la Guerra. Nasrallah in tv: anche l'Italia media
    sugli ostaggi', *La Repubblica*, 28 August 2006.
13 Cf. Nikolas Busse, 'Weniger Einfluss auf die Hizbullah als oft vermutet. Die Rolle Syriens und
    Irans', *Frankfurter Allgemeine Zeitung*, 5 August 2006. There was an agreement in principle
    between the leader of Hezbollah and the Iranian leadership to capture the Israeli soldiers, but in
    the event Hezbollah acted with a particular objective: to exchange its hostages with Arab
    militants imprisoned in Israel.
14 Interview in Tehran with Delphine Minoui, *Le Figaro*, 28 August 2006: Rahmandoust did not
    answer the interviewer's questions about 'wiping Israel off the map'.
15 <http://voxnr.com.convergences/viewtopic.php ?p=23535&sid=587729196e3ecdd8534338891
    37a102c>. The names of Ralph Peters and Chris Broz are mentioned as sources. See also Andrea
    Nicastro, 'L'attacco a Beirut? È il piano di Bush per conquistare il mondo', *Corriere della Sera*, 1
    August 2006, who spoke to Mohammad Ali Mohtadi, a former adviser to the Iranian Foreign
    Minister and Director of the Centre of Strategic Studies for the Middle East: the American plan
    is said to be to create mini-states everywhere and it is supposed to start with Lebanon. The
    journalist notes perceptively that these kinds of ideas which circulate in the Arab or Muslim street
    are themselves often manufactured in think-tanks like this one.
16 Cf. Antonio Ferrari, 'Il mondo arabo si frantuma sul sostegno a Hezbollah', *Corriere della Sera*, 19
    July 2006. See also Pierre Prier, 'Guerre au Liban: l'Égypte et la Syrie s'accusent mutuellement
    de couardise', *Le Figaro*, 24 August 2006.
17 Cf. Arnaud de la Grange, 'Inquiète de l'aura du Hezbollah, al-Qaïda veut entrer dans le conflit',
    Le Figaro, 28 July 2006: Al Qaeda, as a Salafi Sunni organization, is 'naturally' anti-Shiite but the
    Iraqi and Lebanese conflicts have caused it to focus its attention on the global clash of
    civilizations.
18 Cf.Christiane Hoffmann, 'Aus Mangel an Beweisen', *Frankfurter Allgemeine Sonntagszeitung*, 26
    November 2006. The CIA, which on this occasion is not looking for a scapegoat, has refused to
    encourage any speculation on a secret report used by Hersh. See Seymour Hersh, 'The Next Act',
    The New Yorker, 20 November 2006, and Hersh, 'The Iran Plans', *The New Yorker*, 17 April 2006.
19 Cf. Philippe Gélie, 'Bob Gates nommé pour revoir la copie irakienne', *Le Figaro*, 6 December
    2006. Even Gates does not totally rule out strikes against Iranian nuclear installations although
    this is for him 'a very last resort' with 'very dramatic consequences'.

Maps

Iranian empires in history: four maps by Tristan Morel

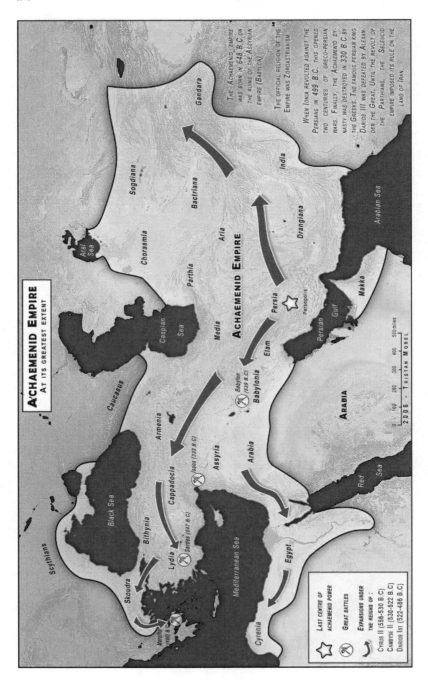

ACHAEMENID EMPIRE AT ITS GREATEST EXTENT

THE ACHAEMENID EMPIRE WAS BORN IN 648 B.C. ON THE RUINS OF THE ASSYRIAN EMPIRE (BABYLON)

THE OFFICIAL RELIGION OF THE EMPIRE WAS ZOROASTRIANISM

WHEN IONIA REVOLTED AGAINST THE PERSIANS IN 499 B.C. THIS OPENED TWO CENTURIES OF GRECO-PERSIAN WARS. FINALLY, THE ACHAEMENID DYNASTY WAS DESTROYED IN 330 B.C. BY THE GREEKS. THE FAMOUS PERSIAN KING DARIOS III WAS DEFEATED BY ALEXANDER THE GREAT. UNTIL THE REVOLT OF THE PARTHIANS, THE SELEUCID EMPIRE IMPOSED ITS RULE ON THE LAND OF IRAN.

Gandara

Aral Sea

Sogdiana

Bactriana

India

Chorasmia

Aria

Arabian Sea

Parthia

Drangiana

Caspian Sea

ACHAEMENID EMPIRE

Media

Elam Persia

Persepolis

Makka

Babylon (539 B.C)

Babylonia

Persian Gulf

Armenia

Caucasus

Arbela (333 B.C)

Assyria

Arabia

ARABIA

0 100 200 300 400 500 miles

2006 - TRISTAN MOREL

Black Sea

Cappadocia

Sardes (547 B.C)

Bithynia

Lydia

Red Sea

Mediterranean Sea

Egypt

Scythians

Skoudra

Marathon (490 B.C)

Cyrenia

LEGEND

☆ LAST CENTRE OF ACHAEMENID POWER

✗ GREAT BATTLES

⤷ EXPANSIONS UNDER THE REIGNS OF :
CYRUS II (556-530 B.C)
CAMBYSE II (530-522 B.C)
DARIUS IST (522-486 B.C)

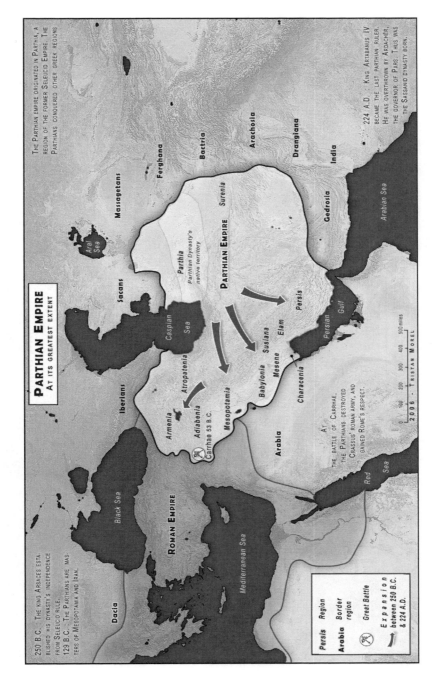

PARTHIAN EMPIRE
AT ITS GREATEST EXTENT

THE PARTHIAN EMPIRE ORIGINATED IN PARTHIA, A REGION OF THE FORMER SELEUCID EMPIRE. THE PARTHIANS CONQUERED OTHER GREEK REGIONS

224 A.D. : KING ARTABANUS IV BECAME THE LAST PARTHIAN RULER. HE WAS OVERTHROWN BY ARDACHER, THE GOVERNOR OF PARS. THUS WAS THE SASSANID DYNASTY BORN.

250 B.C. : THE KING ARSACES ESTABLISHED HIS DYNASTY'S INDEPENDENCE FROM SELEUCID RULE.
129 B.C. : THE PARTHIANS ARE MASTERS OF MESOPOTAMIA AND IRAN.

AT THE BATTLE OF CARRHAE, THE PARTHIANS DESTROYED CRASSUS' ROMAN ARMY, AND GAINED ROME'S RESPECT.

2006 - TRISTAN MOREL

0   100   200   300   400   500 miles

Persis   Region
Arabia   Border region
⊗   Great Battle
→   Expansion between 250 B.C. & 224 A.D.

Dacia

Black Sea

Mediterranean Sea

ROMAN EMPIRE

Iberians

Armenia

Adiabenia

Atropatenia

Mesopotamia

Carrhae 53 B.C.

Arabia

Red Sea

Caspian Sea

Aral Sea

Sacans

Massagetans

Ferghana

Bactria

Parthia
Parthian Dynasty's native territory

Surenia

PARTHIAN EMPIRE

Babylonia

Mesene

Susiana

Elam

Characenia

Persis

Persian Gulf

Arachosia

Drangiana

Gedrosia

India

Arabian Sea

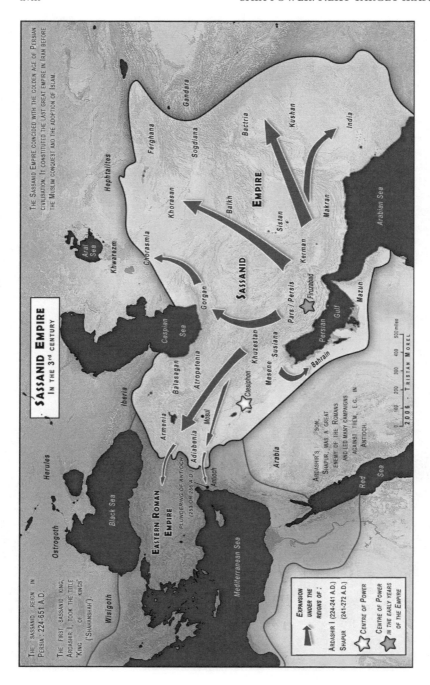

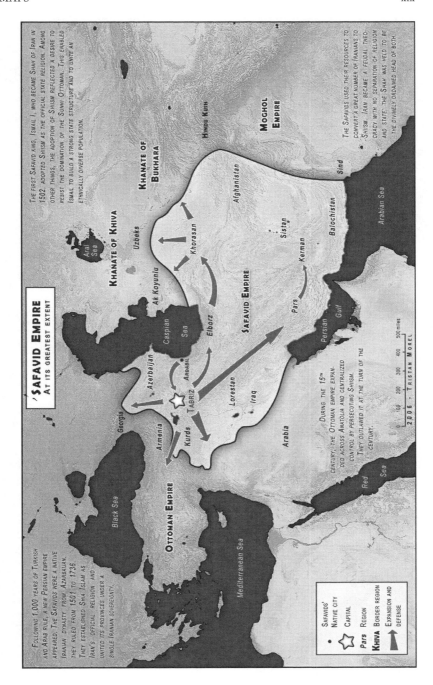

'SAFAVID EMPIRE
AT ITS GREATEST EXTENT

The first Safavid king, Ismail I, who became Shah of Iran in 1502, adopted Shiism as the official state religion. Among other things, the adoption of Shiism reflected a desire to resist the domination of the Sunni Ottoman. This enabled Ismail to build a strong state structure and to unite an ethnically diverse population.

The Safavids used their resources to convert a great number of Iranians to Shiism. Iran became a feudal theocracy with no separation of religion and state: the Shah was held to be the divinely ordained head of both.

Following 1,000 years of Turkish and Arab rule, a new Persian empire appeared. The Safavids were a native Iranian dynasty from Azarbaijan. They ruled from 1501 to 1736. They established Shia Islam as Iran's official religion and united its provinces under a single Iranian sovereignty.

During the 15th century, the Ottoman empire expanded across Anatolia and centralized control by persecuting Shiism. They outlawed it at the turn of the century.

MOGHOL EMPIRE

KHANATE OF BUKHARA

KHANATE OF KHIVA

SAFAVID EMPIRE

OTTOMAN EMPIRE

Hindu Kush

Sind

Arabian Sea

Afghanistan

Balochistan

Sistan

Kerman

Pars

Uzbeks

Khorasan

Ak Koyunlu

Aral Sea

Caspian Sea

Elborz

Persian Gulf

Azerbaijan

Ardabil

TABRIZ

Lorestan

Iraq

Arabia

Kurds

Armenia

Georgia

Black Sea

Mediterranean Sea

Red Sea

0   100   200   300   400   500 miles

2006 - TRISTAN MOREL

• Safavids' Native city

☆ Capital

Pars Region

Khiva Border region

Expansion and defense

PART I
Iran and the World

Iran's Global War Curriculum

ARNON GROISS

Introduction

Recent developments in and around Iran, and the accompanying contradictory declarations and messages emanating from it, have puzzled a great number of people who are genuinely interested in that country's political vision. Caught between fiery statements by current president Mahmoud Ahmadinejad and former President Mohammad Khatami's milder tone, they wonder what Iran really aspires to in this world.

The following is an attempt to present an outline of the Iranian worldview and agenda, based on a study of 95 school textbooks of all grades published in 2004 and 20 teacher's guides published mostly since 2000. This research, commissioned by the Center for Monitoring the Impact of Peace (CMIP) – a non-profit organization committed to investigating school books of Middle Eastern nations – focused on two main fields: the attitude to 'the other' and issues of peace and war.[1] The thousand or so pieces of text, maps, photographs and illustrations in these two fields, which were found in the books, surely represent the values and ideals Iran holds to more than other sources of information, since textbooks and teachers' guides in general provide a very clear idea of what an education system in any place would try to instil in the minds of the younger generations. The full report on the Iranian school books, with all the quoted references, is available on the organization's website: <http://www.edume.org>.

The general picture reflected by the Iranian school books does not bode well. The books reveal an uncompromisingly hostile attitude towards the West, especially the United States and Israel. In fact, the curriculum's declared goal is to prepare the students for a global struggle against the West[2] which bears alarming Messianic-like features to the point of self-destruction (see below).

This line of indoctrination, which is most apparent in the higher grades, is not a product of recent years. It was designed and developed by the founder of Revolutionary Iran, the late Ayatollah Khomeini, and has been implemented since the very beginning of the new regime, including during the term of former President Mohammad Khatami whose moderate appearance and pronouncements led people in the West to believe otherwise. One should bear in mind that, with one exception, the books and teachers' guides studied in this research were all issued under his presidency.[3]

Iran's war curriculum may be roughly divided into two main categories. One is the overall rationale presented in the textbooks. It shapes the students' perception of the world, of Iran's role within it and of the nature of the war to be fought. The other category is the actual preparation of the students for participation in this war, which involves hate indoctrination against the West, development of the spirit of military preparedness and, finally, encouragement of self-sacrifice.

Iran and the World

One can safely define the Islamic Revolution as the primary cause of Iran's war curriculum, for it was this Revolution which made Iran historically unique, imposed on it a unique mission, and also gave it a unique perception of the world. In this respect, Revolutionary Iran appears to be ideologically similar to the former Soviet Union.

As stated in one of the textbooks, the Islamic Revolution in Iran has created a peculiar phenomenon in history – the first Islamic rule in 14 centuries,[4] that is, since the Prophet Muhammad. As such, Iran's priorities should reflect Islamic goals, namely, pleasing God, leading the people to the real benefits of the Hereafter rather than to false mundane ones, propagating the religion of Islam in the world, and so on. One such goal set by Ayatollah Khomeini as a religious precept is fighting oppression:

> The martyrdom of the Commander of the Faithful [Ali] and also of Imam Hussein, and the imprisonment, torture, expulsion and poisoning of the [Shiite] Imams, have all been part of the political struggle of the Shiites against the oppressors. In one word, struggle and political activity are an important part of the religious responsibilities.
>
> (*Islamic Culture and Religious Instruction*, Grade 8 (2004), p. 96)

Indeed, the Islamic Revolution in Iran is seen as the culmination of the struggle against local oppression – the monarchy, which was supported by world oppression – the United States and the other powers. But victory in Iran is not enough. Islamic Iran has a religious obligation to globalize the Islamic Revolution against oppression and make the local victory universal:

> Now, in order to continue the Islamic Revolution, it is our duty to continue with all [our] power our revolt against the Arrogant Ones [a term mostly used now in reference to the United States, see below] and the oppressors, and not cease until all Islam's commandments and the spread of the redeeming message of 'there is no god except Allah' are realized in the whole world.
>
> (*Islamic Culture and Religious Instruction*, Grade 7 (2004), p. 29)

In accordance with this pattern of thinking, Iran views the world as comprising two opposed poles: the dominant and the dominated,[5] or the oppressors on the one hand and the oppressed on the other. This world dichotomy between 'good' and 'evil' is prevalent in the books.

While the oppressors in the historical period of the Shiite Imams were usually the Sunni caliphs, today's oppressors are the West in general, with the United States at its head, and all other powers and governments connected to it, such as Israel, the former Apartheid regime of South Africa, the Bosnian Serbs, the former Shah's government in Iran, Saddam's Iraq, etc. Czarist Russia and the former Soviet Union are also included in the oppressive West, but the Soviets look somewhat peripheral in the light of the huge number of references to the West's other components. Israel is referred to in the Iranian school textbooks far more extensively than Saddam's Iraq, which probably indicates its relatively higher position on the scale of 'oppressiveness'.

The oppressors' goal is 'to plunder the property of weak nations and enslave them'. They further 'make use of all the means they possess in order to demote the nations and make themselves the world's [sole] wielders of authority'. In order to strengthen their own rule, they use various ways – military, political, economic and cultural.[6]

The cultural dimension of the struggle against the West is emphasized a great deal in the textbooks. It is not Western culture itself which is rejected, though criticism of some of its aspects does exist, such as, for example, heedlessness of the otherworld and excessive concentration on mundane pleasures,[7] or permissiveness in the field of relations between the sexes.[8] Rather, it is the role played by Western culture against the oppressed which causes alarm. Western moral corruption, which is the result of the emphasis on material progress and mundane pleasures, has penetrated the Third World nations and caused social damage such as massive trade in narcotics and slave women and children, immoral behavior, and the like.[9] Western culture is also responsible, at least partially, for the UN's failure to protect human rights, because of the inadequate definition of such rights theWest has imposed on that organization.[10]

In the Iranian school textbooks, special emphasis is given to the danger posed by Western culture to Islam. According to the books, Western culture aims at misrepresenting Islam as illogical and as a factor of Muslim backwardness;[11] Western culture also endeavours to develop pessimism among Muslim women regarding their status in society and to draw them towards immorality,[12] tries to undermine the Muslim penal code,[13] etc. *The Satanic Verses* by Salman Rushdie is seen as part of 'a calculated plot on the part of the enemies of Islam'.[14] According to Ayatollah Khomeini, Western culture has even created a distorted kind of Islam which he styled 'American Islam' as opposed to 'Mohammedan Islam'. 'American Islam' is any kind of Islam influenced by Western culture which is rejected and considered totally negative in Khomeini's view: 'the capitalists' Islam, the Islam of the Arrogant Ones, the Islam of the untroubled well-to-do, the hypocrites' Islam, the Islam of the comfort-seekers, the opportunists' Islam and – in one word – American Islam... .'[15]

Moreover, Western culture is used as a tool in the hands of the oppressors to obliterate local cultures around the world which has negative implications on the local people's identity and consequently weakens their resistance to the Westerners' domineering efforts. Westernization, or 'Westoxication' [*Gharbzadegi*] – as it is called in the books, is a professed enemy of the Revolution.[16] Westernization is sometimes positioned as negating Muslim identity altogether. One of the accusations against the Shah's government is that it propagated Westernization and wiped out Islam,[17] and Ayatollah Khomeini attributes such an intention to the Great Powers of his time: 'The West and the East [he refers here to the Soviet Union] will not sit quietly, until they move you out of your Muslim identity.'[18]

On the other side of the global front stand the oppressed. They include the vast majority of the world's nations, adherents of various religions. But other than briefly mentioning them several times, the Iranian textbooks do not specifically define or describe the oppressed of other religions in any way, focusing solely on the Muslims among them. It is Muslims who are destined to bear the brunt of the war against the oppressors, saving the others from the oppressors' hold, and bringing about Islam's rule throughout the world. Muslims' special status among the oppressed stems from the fact that they are bound by their faith to fight oppression and – more importantly – from the fact that Islam gives them the power to do so. The Islamic Revolution is said to have made the Muslims in general aware of the power of Islam in this context, thus endangering the oppressive powers' interests in many places in the world.[19]

Calls urging Muslims everywhere to rise and fight the West appear in the textbooks several times,[20] the most dramatic being Ayatollah Khomeini's following call:

O Muslims of all countries of the world! Since under the foreigners' dominance gradual death has been inflicted on you, you should overcome the fear of death and make use of the existence of the passionate and the martyrdom-seeking youths, who are ready to smash the borders of unbelief. Do not think of keeping the status quo. Rather, think of escape from captivity, of deliverance from slavery, and of attack against the enemies of Islam. Glory and life are in fighting, and the first step of fighting is [the existence of] will. After that, there is the decision that you forbid yourselves to [submit to] the supremacy of world unbelief and polytheism, especially America.

(*Islamic Viewpoint*, Grade 11 (2004), p. 29)

Joining forces against the West requires unity, and the books try to spread the spirit of Muslim 'ecumenism' in this respect.[21] One reference by Khomeini states that more explicitly: 'The Muslims of the world, together with the regime of the Islamic Republic of Iran, should resolve to shatter the teeth in America's mouth to pieces.'[22]

It is obvious from the various references to this issue in the Iranian textbooks that Iran does not openly claim leadership of the Muslims in the global struggle against the West, probably because of the minority status of Shiites within the Muslim world. But it certainly emphasizes its unique position among the Muslims as far as the relations with the West are concerned. First of all, the Shiites are 'the oppressed' *par excellence*, as implied in a reference by Khomeini[23] who goes on to say: 'We are the permanent oppressed in history, deprived and barefoot. Other than God we have no one.'[24] Second, thanks to the Islamic Revolution under Khomeini's leadership, Iran has become relatively free of the phenomenon of Westernization[25] and that has made it more fit than others for the task of waging the war against the West. Third, Iran has already made the first steps on the road to war, by changing its status from a country cooperating with the West under the Shah to the West's fierce foe which found its expression in the occupation of the American embassy in Tehran in 1979[26] and the eight-year war with the West's ally, Saddam Hussein. With such arguments, Iran establishes in the eyes of school students its leadership role in the world's struggle against Western oppression.

The Global War

As already mentioned, world war against oppression is a religious obligation and an inevitable continuation of the Islamic Revolution in Iran.[27] In religious terms it is an 'initiative Jihad' [*Jehad-e Ebtedayi*] which is explained in the following way:

> If people are ignorant, live in poverty and deprivation, and the oppress-
> ors and the Arrogant Ones[28] plunder the product of their labour, the
> army of Islam knows its duty, which is to help the deprived and save
> them from the claws of the Arrogant Ones ... Initiative Jihad, then, is
> a kind of defence as well, defence of the deprived people's rights, defence
> of the people's honour, and defence of the rights of the oppressed.

> (*Islamic Culture and Religious Instruction*, Grade 8 (2004), pp. 69–70)

Being a form of jihad, the war should culminate in Islam's victory all over the world. The war's goals, as stated in one of the books, are: 'complete victory over the world of unbelief and arrogance, the eradication of any oppression, the appearance of the Master of the Age [the Shiite Hidden Imam], and the realization of the world government of Islam'.[29]

The inclusion of the Shiite Messianic idea of the reappearance of the Hidden Imam[30] in the list of the war's goals gives it an eschatological colouring, and makes of it a kind of Shiite Armageddon between the forces of good and evil. This notion is further emphasized by Ayatollah Khomeini's declarations which present the struggle as an all-out war of life or death to both parties.

Against this background it is quite astonishing to realize that the outcome of the perceived global war is uncertain. World victory of Islam is by no means guaranteed. It is Muslims' religious duty to fight oppression, but it is God's decision whether to grant them victory or martyrdom. In either case, they believe, victory is theirs. In Ayatollah Khomeini's words:

> I am decisively announcing to the whole world that if the World
> Devourers[31] wish to stand against our religion, we will stand against
> their whole world and will not cease until the annihilation of all of
> them. Either we all become free, or we all go to the greater liberty
> which is martyrdom ... Either we shake one another's hand in joy at
> the victory of Islam in the world, or all of us will turn to eternal life
> and martyrdom. In both cases, victory and success are ours.

> (*Islamic Viewpoint*, Grade 11 (2004), p. 29)

And again, on another occasion:

> If we are wiped out of the world's surface by the criminal hands of
> America and the Soviet Union and meet our God honourably and with

[our] red blood, it would be better than living a nobleman's comfortable life under the flag of the Red Army of the East and the black [flag] of the West.'

(Islamic Viewpoint, Grade 11 (2004), p. 26)

This ambivalent vision of the war's result is hardly encountered in similar historical cases, certainly not in the case of the Soviet Union which always showed its confidence in world victory for Socialism.

Although religiously based, the war against oppression does not target non-Muslims as such. Islam's victory does not necessarily mean the eradication of other religions, especially monotheistic ones. Islam has always been content throughout history with political dominance and did not usually impose itself on non-Muslims. The Iranian textbooks do not attack other religions – with the exception of Bahaism, which is considered a heretical offshoot of Shiite Islam nurtured by Western colonialism in order to shatter the unity of Iran's Muslims.[32] It is not that rivalries between Muslims and non-Muslims are not discussed, but the latter are not automatically regarded as enemies on account of their religion.

This is also the case with other cultures, including Western culture – as already mentioned.[33] In fact, there was an attempt by the former President Mohammad Khatami to introduce into the Iranian curriculum a new subject called 'Dialogue of Civilizations' in which an effort was made to reconcile between Western and Islamic civilizations on the basis of political and economic equality.[34] However, it is doubtful whether this subject with its accompanying textbook and teacher's guide is still taught in schools today, following the changing of the guard in the Iranian regime. In any case, the war on the West includes a cultural front against Westernization and other forms of attack by Western culture on Islam. One of the actions on this battlefield was Ayatollah Khomeini's pronouncement of the death sentence against the British writer Salman Rushdie, author of *The Satanic Verses*, a work which was regarded as an attack against Islamic beliefs.

Having analysed the overall rationale of the global war against oppression as it appears in the Iranian school textbooks, let us now turn to the actual preparation of school students for participating in this war, starting with the manner in which Iranian educators instil hatred for the enemy in the students' souls.

Hate Indoctrination

Hate indoctrination is a professed goal in the Iranian curriculum: 'The students should have a heart overflowing with hatred towards Arrogance,' says one of the textbooks.[35] Actually, one can discern three elements used in the Iranian school books as means for developing hatred towards the West, the United States and Israel: they are presented as *inherently evil*, as *enemies of Muslims* in general, and as direct *enemies of the people of Iran* themselves.

Inherent Evil

In the case of the West in general it is colonialism which serves to emphasize its evil nature, much the same as it is done in Marxist literature. Surprisingly, Czarist Russian and Soviet colonialism in Muslim Central Asia – an area in immediate proximity to Iran – is not discussed, while Western 'traditional' colonialism which never subjugated Iran is heavily emphasized. The conclusion one can draw is that Iranian educators do not really aim at Russia today and focus solely on the geographically 'Western' part of the West, though Czarist Russia and the Soviet Union feature to a certain extent as enemies of Iran and Ayatollah Khomeini sometimes mentions the Soviet Union as an enemy alongside the United States.

Colonialism is wholly evil:

> The plunder of the colonies, maritime piracy, the plunder of the natives, the establishment of completely unjust commercial relations with the people of the colonies, and [other] measures of this kind, enabled the European colonialist countries to enrich and strengthen themselves at the price of impoverishing others.

> (*History of Iran and the World {Humanities}*, Grade 11 (2004), p. 20)

Having explained that colonialism emerged in Europe under specific economic and technological circumstances, a guiding question is inserted: 'Was the phenomenon of Colonialism a unique product of Western civilization and culture?'[36] In the framework of this kind of indoctrination the same history textbook provides the student with abundant incriminating material about Western colonialism in various parts of the world.

Since the United States hardly has a colonialist past, the books concentrate, instead, on the attitude to Native Americans and African Americans in the past and at present.[37] But America has more evil to offer in world affairs:

> America is known as an Imperialist country, which embarks on military intervention wherever it sees that its interests are in danger. It does not refrain from massacring people, burying alive the soldiers of the opposite side and using weapons of mass destruction (as it did in Iraq). It makes use of atomic bombs (the bombardment of Japan). It

uses the weapon of human rights in order to suppress the justice seekers (as it does in its abuses against Islamic Iran). It creates the greatest dictatorships and the most violent and torturing security-oriented regimes, and defends them. Nor does it feel uncomfortable at all while human rights are violated (Iran at the time of the Shah after 1953). Its security system runs the largest smuggling networks, but it makes use of the pretext of drug smuggling in order to arrest those who oppose its policies in other countries (the case of Panama).

Such being the case, what would, and should, be your reaction to America?

(*Sociology {Humanities}*, Grade 11 (2004), p. 20)

As the leader of evil forces in the world today, America is given specific epithets, sometimes shared with other oppressors, such as 'World Devourers'[*Jehan Kharan*] and 'the Arrogant Ones' [*Mostakberan*], while the epithet 'the Great Satan' [*Sheytan-e Bozorg*] is restricted to the United States alone. In an assignment in a language textbook the students are required to write down an interpretation for some words, including the name 'America'.[38] The answer, given in the teacher's guide is: 'America – the Great Satan'.[39] Hatred for America is further enhanced by the slogan often heard in public events in Iran – 'Death to America', as seen in the following photograph of a demonstration.[40]

Iranian textbooks also include material intended to create feelings of antipathy towards ordinary American individuals and families, who are presented as a burden on world resources, compared to their Third World counterparts:

> The birth of one baby in the United States of America puts 100 times more pressure on the Earth's resources, and on the natural environment, than the birth of a baby in Bangladesh. Because the living of one American individual is linked to the consumption of more food and clothing, the possession of a private car, more communication and transportation, and the generation of more refuse and pollution, while the lifestyle in Bangladesh is such that it does not require great quantities of mineral resources and energy.
>
> One American family has an impact on the natural environment 40 times more than an Indian family, and 100 times more than a Kenyan family.
>
> (*Geography {Humanities & Islamic Sciences}*, Grade 10 (2004), p. 133;
> *Geography {General}*, Grade 10 (2004), p. 130)

In the case of Israel, hate indoctrination relies on three different foundations. First, there are the Jews. Although not considered an official enemy in Iran, they are never portrayed in positive ways. On the contrary, most references to Jews in the Iranian textbooks relate to their conflict with the Prophet Muhammad in Arabia in Islam's early years. One encounters in this context phrases such as 'confronting the Jews' plots', 'the Jews' pretext-seeking, hostility and treachery were exposed', 'a profit-seeking ethnic group'.[41] One can hardly expect school students of any age to easily differentiate between the Jews of Arabia in the seventh century CE and their modern co-religionists, especially when the latter are depicted as usurpers of Palestine.[42]

The second foundation is the Jews' national movement in modern times – Zionism, which is portrayed as a world organization with a great deal of influence in the West, America in particular. In addition to the establishment of 'the Jews' greater homeland' in Palestine, Zionism is said to aspire to the Jews' dominance over the world, very much in line with traditional anti-Semitic propaganda.[43] Zionism is accused of coveting all the Arab lands and of controlling most of Western news media.[44] The Iranian textbooks studied for the purpose of the present research do not contain many references to Zionism and the students are referred to the Persian translation of the pamphlet 'Caution, Zionism!' by the Soviet propagandist Yuri Ivanov. Recently released news refers to the introduction of a new program in Iranian schools in which special teams of instructors will teach the students about Zionism. In other words, intensification of anti-Israeli hate indoctrination is to be expected.

The third and mostly utilized foundation of anti-Israeli hate indoctrination is Israel itself. Israel is demonized in various ways: it is 'a base of America and other aggressive powers with the aim of taking over Muslim lands',[45] it turned the people of Palestine into refugees,[46] it occupies Jerusalem and the Muslim holy place of the al-Aqsa Mosque[47] and it oppresses and kills Palestinians under its occupation, including children.[48] Iranian textbooks contain literary material such as stories and poems which present this demonizing picture of Israel quite vividly:

> ... Then the Israeli officer pounded [three-year-old] Muhammad's head with his rifle butt and his warm blood was sprinkled upon [his six-year-old brother] Khaled's hands.

> (*Persian: Let's Read*, Grade 3 (2004), p. 113)

There is one instance where Israel, or the Jews, or both, are equated with garbage that should be removed. A picture story for third-grade students presents a clean and tidy town where the inhabitants suddenly discover a trail of garbage. They trace the contaminator who turns out to be a repugnant creature spreading garbage wherever he goes. They chase him away and clean up after him. In one of the pictures the Jewish-Israeli symbol of the Star of David is depicted as part of the garbage and in two other pictures this symbol is drawn on the creature's right arm.[49]

Enemies of the Muslims

Besides their inherent evil, all three entities are portrayed as enemies of Islam and the Muslims. Western colonialism in Egypt and Algeria, for example, is described in more detail than elsewhere in Africa. But the West's most dangerous attack on Islam is cultural, as already discussed. The United States is positioned in Khomeini's statements as the Muslims' arch-enemy,[50] and he further coined the term 'American Islam' for the non-revolutionary type of Islam he resisted. Israel's hostility to the Muslims is obvious due to the mere fact that the Palestinians are mostly Muslim. But the Iranian school books add the theme of the occupied al-Aqsa Mosque, in line with the importance accorded to this issue by Khomeini who introduced the annual 'Jerusalem Day' commemorating the occupation of that city by Israel.[51] In fact, the religious aspect of the conflict is emphasized in the Iranian school textbooks to such a degree that Israel is often mentioned by a specific epithet: 'the regime which occupies Jerusalem'.[52]

Enemies of the People of Iran

An obvious step in any effort of hate indoctrination would be to present the object as a direct enemy of the country the students belong to. Iran's modern history provides two such enemies: Czarist Russia and its Soviet successor on the one hand, and the British Empire during its presence in India and the Gulf on the other. Both are treated as such, but the emphasis in the books is on Britain, even though in certain periods Czarist Russia and the Soviet Union were in fact far more dangerous to Iran's territorial integrity. Britain is accused of having imposed the Pahlavi dynasty on Iran,[53] though at least some historians believe that this is not historically the case.

In contrast to Britain and Iran's northern neighbour, the United States has a record of friendly relations with pre-Revolutionary Iran. It is therefore presented as hostile to the Iranian nation on account of supporting the atrocities against the people attributed to the Shah's regime.[54] Later, when the Revolutionary regime took over – say the books – America came to the fore as Iran's primary enemy: it supported the armed opposition groups against the regime and, when they failed, incited Saddam Hussein to invade Iran.[55] When the Iraqis also failed, the United States saved them from military defeat by using its force against Iran, including a ferocious attack on an Iranian civil aircraft.[56]

The same approach is adopted regarding Israel, which also had good relations with Iran during the Shah's reign. Israel is accused of having helped to establish the Shah's secret services[57] and of sending torturers to Iran to teach torture techniques.[58] Ayatollah Khomeini presented Israel as an enemy of the Iranian nation from the early 1960s, completely demonizing it:

> Israel does not want the Koran to be in this state [Iran]. Israel does not want the Muslim clergymen to be in this state. Israel does not want the Islamic law to be in this state. Israel does not want scholars to be in this state. Israel pounded the Feyziyyeh [religious] College with the hand of its black agents. It pounds us. It pounds you, the nation. It wants to take possession of your economy. It wants to eliminate your commerce and agriculture. It wants to take possession of your wealth. Israel wants these things that are an obstacle to it, these things that are a barrier in its way, to be removed by the hand of its agents.
>
> (*History*, Grade 8 (2004), p. 76)[59]

Fighting Israel is thus given legitimacy in the framework of the general war against oppressors, for which Iranian school students are being prepared.

Military Preparedness

'The best form of defence is attack' says the proverb. In the case of the Iranian war curriculum the opposite is the motto. With a view to enhancing a sense of self- defence, students are presented with an array of dangers from enemies threatening Revolutionary Iran.[60] But a closer look at the arguments accompanying this thesis reveals the logic for this situation: it was Iran which started the offensive against world oppression and that triggered a counter-offensive. The Islamic Revolution 'shook the palaces of the Arrogant Ones and for this reason it became ... the target of the superpowers' hostility and conspiracy'.[61] 'The young Islamic Revolution', says another textbook, 'is never safe from ... the enemies ... because they see the life of the Revolution as their own death.'[62] This is, then, a struggle of life or death between Revolutionary Iran and world oppression headed by the United States.

Against such a formidable enemy a country like Iran should thoroughly prepare itself and muster all forces available. Ayatollah Khomeini had the idea of a general mobilization and military training for millions of men and women capable of carrying arms. That force, the nucleus of the planned 'army of twenty millions' was called 'the Mobilization of the Oppressed' [*Basij-e Mostaz'afan*][63] which now constitutes the regime's popular armed support within the Revolutionary Guards. Khomeini saw in this several-million-strong force the ultimate shield against any attack by the United States: 'If the agreeable melody of *Basij* thinking rings in a country, the coveting eye of the enemies and the "World Devourers" will stay away from it.'[64] According to one of the textbooks, the *Basij* is divided into sectorial units across the country such as that of physicians and engineers, trade unions, university and religious college students, city and town neighbourhoods, nomadic tribes, women, etc. One distinct unit is that of school students.[65] The *Basij* bases are usually situated in or near the mosques.[66]

School students of various ages are approached in this regard as follows:

> Boys and youth enrol in the Mosque *Basij*, and go through military training, so that they will be prepared for the defence of the Muslim country of Iran.
>
> (*Social Studies*, Grade 4 (2004), p. 119)

> In the light of Islam's directives and guidance, every Muslim youth should cast fear into the heart of the enemies of God and of His creatures with his own combat efficiency, and skilful shooting. He should always be ready to defend his country, his honour and his belief,

and employ all his ability and power in this direction. Are you also
ready to acquire combat arts in the *Basij* [units]?

(Islamic Culture and Religious Instruction, Grade 7 (2004), p. 60)

(Defense Readiness, Grade 8 (2004), p. 74)

As part of their military preparation, and alongside the actual training in the
Basij units, a subject titled 'Defence Readiness' is taught to school students
beginning in grade 8 (that is, 13–14 years old). The textbook for this subject
teaches basic military drills such as camouflaging, movement in battle
conditions, acquaintance with various kinds of weaponry and explosives, as
well as principles of civil defence, first aid, etc. The introduction in the book
for eighth-graders reads: 'This year, by reading the lessons of Defence
Readiness, you will become acquainted with the necessary preliminaries for
the acquisition of the techniques of defence and combat. In the coming years
in high school, you will learn… more comprehensive subjects in this regard.'[67]

In addition, the textbooks of this subject include warnings of the imminent
danger of attack by the enemies[68] and also verses from the Koran which urge
Muslims to be always on their guard and prepared for war.[69]

Within this context, the traditional Islamic ideal of jihad is utilized too.
Although jihad is also referred to by Khomeini and in the Iranian textbooks

as a spiritual effort,[70] or even used as a title for constructive projects in Iran,[71] a great deal is said in the books about jihad as a military effort. In this context, jihad is said to have been exercised by the early Muslims in order to preserve Islam and it is now 'our turn to fight the Jihad and make a sacrifice in the cause of religion. How are we to cope with the commitment to fulfil this great responsibility?'[72]

And again:

> Jihad and defence is an indispensable religious duty in Muslim society, and all should defend their country, dignity and belief with all [their] might. Therefore, we should always be ready to face the enemies.

(Islamic Culture and Religious Instruction, Grade 7 (2004), p. 58)

Self-Sacrifice (Martyrdom)

Jihad and martyrdom go hand-in-hand in Islam, as any jihad fighter is a potential martyr. Hence, the need arises not just to educate the school student to participate in jihad but also to prepare him for martyrdom, or, more correctly, to make him aspire to martyrdom as an integral part of his military training. This is done both directly and indirectly. The direct approach involves presenting to the students the value of martyrdom, supported by the relevant Koranic verses. A passage in one of the textbooks reads:

> Exalted God orders the Believers in many verses in the Holy Koran to fight the Jihad in the cause of God and kill the oppressors. He gives the glad tidings of forgiveness and eternal Paradise to anyone who becomes a martyr in the cause of God. He considers martyrdom a great victory.

(Islamic Culture and Religious Instruction, Grade 8 (2004), p. 72)

Developing this theme, the textbooks provide the students with sayings by martyr Shiite Imams, such as Hussein and Sajjad, describing death as a bridge leading from the miseries and unpleasantness of this world to the eternal life and happiness in the next. A guiding question is then inserted in the text: 'In the light of the words of Imam Hussein and Imam Sajjad about death, who is the good-doing Believer who would fear death and martyrdom and accept disgrace and humiliation?'[73]

Thus, welcoming death in God's cause, or martyrdom-seeking [*Shahadat-talabi*], in battle becomes a value: 'For those who believe in the Eternal World, life in this world has no value in itself. Its [real] value is dependent on the eternal life. Therefore, if a day arrives, on which the preservation of this life is nothing but disgrace, they return this Divine trust with utmost enthusiasm, and perform their duty before God.'[74]

The teachers on their part are encouraged to nurture in the students' souls the spirit of martyrdom-seeking through a variety of educational means. The following is a text taken from a teacher's guide which refers to a certain means for that purpose (the specific means could not be identified, as the student's textbook was not available to us):

> **Suggestion**
> This suggestion is intended to show the influence which the Divine insight regarding Paradise has on the creation of a martyrdom-seeking spirit and spiritual courage. It would be good for the teacher to stress the [necessity of] complying with this suggestion, encourage the students to [do] so, and to set up in class the assembled collection [of martyrs' wills, etc.].
>
> (*Religion and Life – Teacher's Guide*, Grade 10, Part 1 (2004), p. 162)

As for the indirect approach encouraging self-sacrifice, the Iranian curriculum deals with the issue of martyrdom to such an extent that the student may be said to be wrapped in an atmosphere of martyrdom glorification. 'Being immersed in the culture of martyrdom and martyrs'[75] seems to be the motto here. Indeed, the Shiite Imams who were mostly martyred by the Sunni caliphs in medieval times, as well as hundreds of thousands of martyrs in Iran's modern history – in the context of both the Revolution and the Iraq–Iran War – all provide the educational system with plenty of material to deal with in this framework, and so it does.

The culture of martyrdom and martyrs finds its expression in school through presenting the cases of selected martyrs, such as the Shiite Imams, anti-Shah activists, martyrs of the Islamic Revolution, leaders of the Islamic Revolution who were martyred by Iranian opposition groups and martyrs of the war with Iraq – chief among them being the school student Hossein Fahmideh who blew himself up under an Iraqi tank.[76] A related theme is the glorification of martyrdom and of martyrs. Poems equating the martyr with the sun, with a flower, a lamp, etc.,[77] or telling of the martyrs' voyage to God's presence[78] are found in the books, in addition to stories emphasizing their magnificence.[79] Wills of martyrs are reproduced in the books,[80] read in class and posted on the walls.[81] Families of martyrs are visited or invited to school, and the students are given homework and assignments with a view to instilling this value in their minds. For example, the students are requested to practice writing letters to official departments. One of the letters is a request to name a town square after one of the martyrs.[82] Another writing exercise is a letter of condolence to a relative of a martyred soldier.[83] In a third exercise the students are required to complete a story of which the beginning is: 'He was dying, but not of the mine's explosion, or even of the coup-de-grace fire of the Iraqis, but, rather, of gladness...'[84]. Students are also given the assignment to write down the names of martyrs of their own localities.[85] Exercises in mathematics mention schools named after martyrs.[86]

A special item in the school books in this context is the martyrs' blood: 'It is you [that is, the teachers], who can rise to guard the blood of the martyrs', says an introductory note in one of the textbooks.[87] The city of Qom, where Khomeini's oppositionist activity began in the early 1960s, is called 'City of Blood and Uprising' [Shahr-e Khun va Qiyam].[88] The black chadors of the martyr women massacred at the Zhaleh Square in Tehran on Black Friday during the Revolution were painted red by their blood.[89] An illustration of red drops of blood decorates a poem about martyrs in the war with Iraq.[90] A recurring motif in the books is the red tulip which symbolizes the martyrs' blood and is found on the Iranian flag too: 'I looked again at the [Iranian] flag and asked: "Dear father, what is the symbol in the middle of the flag?" My father said: "It is the word 'Allah' [God] ... in the form of a tulip. The tulip is the symbol of the martyrs' blood".'[91]

Red tulips appear with this meaning in poems [92] and also in art works, such as the following one:

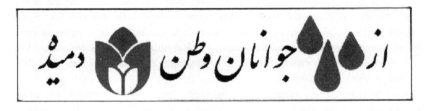

From the [drops of blood of] the homeland youth [tulips] sprout.
(*Art Instruction*, Grade 6 (2004), p. 68)

The result of this kind of education – as proudly presented in one textbook – is the following:

> During the eight years of Holy Defence [that is, the war with Iraq] more than 500,000 school students were sent to the fronts. 36,000 martyrs, thousands of missing-in-action, invalids, and liberated [prisoners-of-war] of this sacrificing section were offered to the Islamic Revolution.
>
> (*Defense Readiness*, Grade 10 (2004), p. 11)[93]

Conclusion

We have seen how the Iranian school curriculum instils in the souls of school students, especially in the higher grades, feelings of hatred towards the West in general and towards the United States in particular, and how it prepares the students for participation and self-sacrifice in a global war against these perceived enemies as a religious mission imposed on Revolutionary Iran by God Almighty in order to redeem the oppressed and bring about Islam's victory in this world. The books also emphasize the war's eschatological character as a life-and-death struggle between the forces of Good and Evil which is to culminate in the reappearance of the Shiite 'Messiah' (that is, the Hidden Imam). Such a curriculum presents a troubling picture of Iran's belligerent intentions which should sound the alarm to anyone who is committed to peace and stability in the world, first and foremost the international bodies, and also the countries and nations which might serve as targets for Iran's aspirations.

But this is not all. The core of this article started with a notion describing the Islamic Revolution as the primary cause of Iran's war curriculum and ended in a quoted sentence presenting it as a modern Moloch devouring its own children. Indeed, if one looks carefully into the curriculum of Revolutionary Iran one is struck by the systematic build-up of an educational environment leading the school students towards a violent future of which the result is bound to be disastrous for Iran itself in the first place. By sacrificing a very large number of school students and other young people in a planned world war, Iran is bound to lose its most important asset for future progress. It is one thing to encourage self-sacrifice in an ongoing struggle for existence, as was the case with the Iraq–Iran War. But preparing a whole generation for a global war of which the result might be – in Khomeini's own vision – collective martyrdom, is totally different and implies a dangerous inclination to self-destruction, not to mention the grave implications on the affected parts of the world. Even a professed religious country whose primary educational goal is 'pleasing God' should have some responsibility for its people's welfare in this world, and collective martyrdom is certainly not compatible with that. In short, this kind of curriculum, of which the logical foundations are questionable, poses a grave danger to the future of Iran itself.

What can one do about that? Not much, unfortunately. The Revolutionary regime in Iran appears to be confident enough to go on with such a curriculum which is further enhanced by other Iranian media of indoctrination such as the teachers in class, the state-controlled media – including politicised children's programs on television, religious sermons in local mosques all over the country, indoctrination practiced within the Basiji units which encompass thousands of children, etc. The change should come from the regime or through a massive popular movement against it, but none of these appears very likely in the foreseeable future. Other than that, the only thing which can be done is a world-wide outcry against this kind of indoctrination. But even that might have very little, if any, effect. It is high time for the world to realize that it is facing an entity which considers itself God's own instrument on earth and acts accordingly, away from what others would regard as ordinary logic. This is the real danger signalled by the curriculum presented here.

Dr Arnon Groiss is the Director of Research with the Center for Monitoring the Impact of Peace (CMIP). During the last seven years Dr Groiss authored eight reports issued by CMIP on school textbooks of Egypt, Syria, Saudi Arabia and the Palestinian Authority. The latest research on Iranian school books was co-authored with Mr Nethanel (Navid) Toobian.

NOTES

1   In all CMIP reports the same method of research is applied: any reference to the issues studied, whether text, photograph, map or illustration, is inserted in the report as is, in a specific chapter according to its subject, with minimum analysis – in order to let the material speak for itself. Clarifying comments are inserted in brackets within the quoted text or as footnotes. CMIP analysis is given in the conclusion of each report. CMIP's established method of research follows UNESCO's criteria for the content of textbooks (See: *A Handbook for the Improvement of Textbooks and Teaching Materials as Aids to International Understanding* Paris: UNESCO, 1949). Eight criteria were adopted from the UNESCO report:
     1   Are all data given accurate and complete?
     2   Are illustrations, maps and graphs up-to-date and accurate?
     3   Are the achievements of others recognized?
     4   Are equal standards applied?
     5   Are political disputes presented objectively and honestly?
     6   Is wording likely to create prejudice, misapprehension and conflict avoided?
     7   Are ideals of freedom, dignity and fraternity being advocated?
     8   Is the need for international cooperation, for the formation of common human ideals and the advancement of the cause of peace, as well as for the enforcement of the law, emphasized?

     Two additional criteria were added by CMIP:
     1   Is the 'other' recognized and accepted as equal, or presented in a stereotyped and prejudiced way?
     2   Do the school textbooks foster peace and reconciliation?

2   Introduction, *Religious Instruction*, Grade 5 (2004), page not numbered.
3   It might be true that a certain percentage of the school students, especially those who come from educated families of the higher classes in the large urban centers, are not totally affected by such indoctrination – as proven by the relatively large number of former school students who now form the core of the opposition to the regime in Iran. But they are still a minority compared to the rank and file of the student body who are influenced, as is the case with thousands of volunteers in the 'suicide bombing corps' against Israel.
4   *History of Iran and the World (Humanities)*, Grade 11 (2004), pp. 278–9.

5 *Economics {Humanities}*, Grade 10 (2004), p. 100.

6 *Islamic Viewpoint*, Grade 11 (2004), pp. 14–15.

7 *Religion and Life – Teacher's Guide*, Grade 10, Part 1 (2004), pp. 161–2.

8 *Sociology {Humanities}*, Grade 11 (2004), p. 25, and see lessons dedicated to criticism of Western culture in: *Religion and Life – Teacher's Guide*, Grade 10, Part 1 (2004), pp. 82, 161–2.

9 *Religion and Life – Teacher's Guide*, Grade 10, Part 2 (2004), p. 35.

10 *Acquaintance with Important Social Laws – Teacher's Guide*, High School Grades (2003), pp. 180–81.

11 *Lessons from the Koran*, Grade 11 (2004), p. 6.

12 *Islamic Viewpoint*, Grade 11 (2004), p. 37.

13 Ibid., p. 123.

14 *History of Iran and the World {Humanities}*, Grade 11 (2004), pp. 292–3.

15 *Islamic Viewpoint*, Grade 11 (2004), p. 30.

16 Ibid , pp. 14–15.

17 *History*, Grade 8 (2004), p. 81.

18 *Islamic Viewpoint*, Grade 11 (2004), p. 28.

19 *History*, Grade 8 (2004), p. 93.

20 See, for example, in *Islamic Culture and Religious Instruction*, Grade 7 (2004), p. 65; *Islamic Viewpoint*, Grade 11 (2004), p. 28.

21 *Islamic Culture and Religious Instruction*, Grade 8 (2004), pp. 99–100; *Defense Readiness 1 – Teacher's Guide*, High School Grades (2002), p. 3.

22 *Islamic Viewpoint*, Grade 11 (2004), p. 28.

23 *Islamic Culture and Religious Instruction*, Grade 8 (2004), p. 96.

24 *Islamic Viewpoint*, Grade 11 (2004), p. 29 (though Khomeini does not explicitly refer to the Shiites here, one should bear in mind that relatively many references to the Sunnite caliphs' oppressiveness in history exist in the textbooks, which excludes the Sunnites from the title of the 'permanent oppressed').

25 And see the piece about the purification of Iranian universities in: *History of Iran and the World {Humanities}*, Grade 11 (2004), p. 285.

26 See the references to this affair in: *History*, Grade 8 (2004), p. 93; *History of Iran and the World {Humanities}*, Grade 11 (2004), pp. 282 and further.

27 *Islamic Culture and Religious Instruction*, Grade 7 (2004), p. 29.

28 A term referring today to the United States mostly and see below.

29 *Islamic Culture and Religious Instruction*, Grade 8 (2004), p. 96 and see also p. 97.

30 The twelfth successor of Prophet Mohammad according to Shiite belief, Imam Mohammad al-Muntazar, who was born in 873 CE and disappeared at a young age to lead the Shiites from his hiding place throughout the centuries until his final return and triumph in the End of Days.

31 An epithet used by Ayatollah Khomeini to denote the United States and the former Soviet Union.

32 *History*, Grade 8 (2004), p. 37.

33 See the discussion above on the attitude to Western culture. It is Western culture's hegemony which is fought, not its mere existence, although it has certain negative aspects in Iranian-Muslim eyes.

34 See the relevant chapter in the CMIP report.

35 *Defense Readiness 1 – Teacher's Guide*, High School Grades (2002), p. 3, and see below the discussion of the term 'Arrogance'.

36 *History of Iran and the World {Humanities}*, Grade 11 (2004), p. 70.

37 *Geography – Teacher's Guide*, Grade 7 (1999), p. 84; *Persian Literature*, Grade 10 (2004), p. 65, followed by excerpts from *Uncle Tom's Cabin*, pp. 65–71.

38 *Persian*, Grade 7 (2004), p. 31.

39 *Persian – Teacher's Guide*, Grade 7 (2003), p. 76.

40 *Defense Readiness*, Grade 10 (2004), p. 7.

41 *History of Iran and the World*, Grade 10 (2004), p. 109.

42 *Geography {Humanities}*, Grade 11 (2004), p. 17.

43 *Social Studies {Humanities}*, Grade 12 (2004), pp. 41–2.

44 *History of Iranian and World Literature*, Grade 11 (2004), pp. 206–207.
45 *Geography {Humanities}*, Grade 11 (2004), p. 25.
46 *History of Iranian and World Literature*, Grade 11 (2004), pp. 195–6.
47 *Geography – Teacher's Guide*, Grade 7 (1999), p. 40.
48 *History of Iranian and World Literature*, Grade 11 (2004), pp. 204, 207; *Koran Studies*, Grade 3 (2004), p. 73.
49 *Gifts of Heaven – Work Book*, Grade 3 (2004), pp. 13–15.
50 *Islamic Viewpoint*, Grade 11 (2004) pp. 28, 29.
51 See the references to this issue in: *Geography – Teacher's Guide*, Grade 7 (1999), p. 40; *Social Studies*, Grade 3 (2004), pp. 56–7; *Mathematics*, Grade 3 (2004), p. 40.
52 *Social Studies {Civics}*, Grade 9 (2004), p. 59; *History of Iran and the World {Humanities}*, Grade 11 (2004), p. 282; *Geography {Humanities}*, Grade 11 (2004), p. 25.
53 *Persian*, Grade 8 (2004), pp. 6–7.
54 *Islamic Viewpoint*, Grade 11 (2004), p. 31.
55 *History of Iran and the World {Humanities}*, Grade 11 (2004), p. 286.
56 Ibid., p. 296.
57 *History of Iran and the World {Humanities}*, Grade 11 (2004), p. 251.
58 *Islamic Viewpoint*, Grade 11 (2004), p. 32.
59 The massacre of Feyziyyeh in 1963 by the Shah's security forces is referred to here. Khomeini tried to attribute that to Israel, though by proxy – the Shah's agents.
60 See, for example, the introduction in: *Defense Readiness*, Grade 10 (2004), page not numbered.
61 *History of Iran and the World {Humanities}*, Grade 11 (2004), p. 280 and see also p. 286; *History*, Grade 8 (2004), p. 93; *Defense Readiness*, Grade 8 (2004), page not numbered (Introduction); *Defense Readiness*, Grade 10 (2004), p. 3.
62 *Defense Readiness 1 – Teacher's Guide*, High School Grades (2002), p. 2.
63 *Islamic Culture and Religious Instruction*, Grade 7 (2004), pp. 60-61.
64 *Defense Readiness*, Grade 10 (2004), p. 6.
65 Ibid., p. 8.
66 *Social Studies {Civics}*, Grade 6 (2004), p. 66.
67 *Defense Readiness*, Grade 8 (2004), p. 3.
68 *Defense Readiness 1 – Teacher's Guide*, High School Grades (2002), p. 3.
69 *Defense Readiness*, Grade 10 (2004), pp. 3–4.
70 *Religion and Life*, Grade 9 (2004), pp. 59–60.
71 *Social Studies*, Grade 3 (2004), p. 48.
72 *Persian*, Grade 5 (2004), p. 134.
73 *Islamic Culture and Religious Instruction*, Grade 6 (2004), pp. 20–22.
74 *Islamic Viewpoint*, Grade 11 (2004), p. 47.
75 *Defense Readiness 1, 2 – Teacher's Guide*, High School Grades (2002), p. 2.
76 There are plenty of references to these cases of martyrdom and the following are just representative examples: for the Imams – *Islamic Culture and Religious Instruction*, Grade 8 (2004), p. 95; for the anti-Shah activists – *History*, Grade 8 (2004), p. 63; for the Revolution martyrs – *History of Iran and the World {Humanities}*, Grade 11 (2004), p. 266; for leaders assassinated by the opposition – *History of Iran and the World {Humanities}*, Grade 11 (2004), pp. 290–91; for martyrs of the war – *History*, Grade 8 (2004) p. 95; for Hossein Fahmideh – *Persian*, Grade 4 (2004), pp. 17–18.
77 *Persian*, Grade 7 (2004), p. 21.
78 *Religious Instruction*, Grade 5 (2004), p. 39.
79 See, for example, *Persian*, Grade 5 (2004), pp. 95–7.
80 *Defense Readiness*, Grade 10 (2004), p. 13; *Defense Readiness*, Grade 10 (2004), p. 12.
81 *Islamic Culture and Religious Instruction*, Grade 6 (2004), p. 22.
82 *Crafts and Techniques Instruction*, Grade 8 (2004), p. 96.
83 *Persian Language*, Grade 9 (2004), p. 113.
84 *Persian Language*, Grade 10 (2004), p. 64.
85 *Persian*, Grade 6 (2004), p. 26.

86 *Mathematics*, Grade 2 (2004), p. 156.

87 Introduction, *Religious Instruction*, Grade 5 (2004), pages not numbered.

88 *Social Studies*, Grade 3 (2004), p. 22.

89 *History of Iran and the World {Humanities}*, Grade 11 (2004), p. 266.

90 *Religious Instruction*, Grade 5 (2004), p. 39.

91 *Persian: Let's Read*, Grade 3 (2004), p. 98.

92 *Persian*, Grade 5 (2004), p. 42; *Persian: Let's Read*, Grade 3 (2004), p. 111; *Persian*, Grade 5 (2004), pp. 116–17.

93 According to testimonies from the battlefield, the children were given plastic keys symbolizing the keys to Paradise and sent to charge enemy positions through minefields in order to clear the way for regular forces.

Talking to Iran is a Better Idea Than More Sanctions

NORMAN LAMONT

The prospect of Iran acquiring nuclear weapons is undoubtedly alarming and the threatening remarks by President Mahmoud Ahmadinejad about Israel are unacceptable. But the west should be careful about embarking on an Iran strategy without an end-game. Both sides in this dangerous dispute risk finding themselves in a situation from which they cannot withdraw.

It is fashionable to decry the efforts of the EU3 – Britain, France and Germany – in their ongoing talks with Iran. I believe that the instincts of Jack Straw, British foreign secretary, are absolutely right and it is only common sense to seek a diplomatic solution before a potentially catastrophic confrontation.

Some commentators talk about Iran as though it were the old Soviet Union – a totalitarian state with no dissent. Iranian democracy is limited and chaotic but it is not the Soviet Union. The recent presidential election with a range of hardline and reformist candidates was more vigorously contested than the election in Egypt that was so lavishly praised by President George W. Bush. Mr Ahmadinejad has faced plenty of opposition from the Iranian parliament, which has been as energetic as the US Congress in rejecting nominations for office. And local newspapers have criticised the president's comments about Israel.

The constitutional position of the Iranian president is not comparable with that of his US counterpart. Both the nuclear issue and foreign policy in Iran are the prerogative of the supreme ruler, Ayatollah Ali Khamenei, not the president, and there have been reports of strains between the two leaders.

History plays an important part in US and Iranian attitudes. Americans remember the humiliating hostage crisis. For Iranians, the memory is of hundreds of thousands of dead in the Iran-Iraq war. They note that Saddam Hussein has been charged with using weapons of mass destruction against his own people but not against Iran. Older Iranians see parallels between western intervention on the nuclear issue and the overthrow in 1953 of Mohammed Mossadegh, then prime minister, in a US and British-backed coup, for daring to nationalise Iran's own oil.

For all that, Iran is neither as anti-American nor as religious as it appears. The most moving condemnation of the terrorist attacks of September 11 2001 that I read was from Mohammad Khatami, then president, who called them "an act of nihilism" with "no place in Islamic thinking".

Yet US strategy has been to drive Iran further into international isolation, even trying to stop Pakistan, India and Iran co-operating on a gas pipeline that would give Iran a vested interest in regional stability and bring economic benefits to all three countries. This policy makes no sense.

The west has generally been reluctant to recognise the reality of Iran as a regional power although Iranian influence has been considerably increased by the Iraq invasion. The US needed – and indeed received – help from Iran when it invaded Afghanistan. Although Iran did not oppose the Iraq invasion, Tehran has since been shut out of any economic role in the reconstruction of a country in which it has a natural interest.

Iran's co-operation will continue to be needed in Iraq. But there are strong emotions in Iran about its co-religionists. Two years ago when I visited Tehran, the city centre was dominated by massive photographs from western newspapers of Muslim prisoners being abused in Abu Ghraib prison.

There are already US sanctions against Iran; like the sanctions against Cuba, they have probably helped to prop up an unpopular regime. In both countries, the government has been able to demonise the threat from abroad. Every time an Iranian aircraft crashes, it is blamed on sanctions. America may be content to stop Iran selling gas to India but it is unlikely to want to hurt itself with an oil embargo. In any case it is difficult to see how further sanctions will change anyone's mind.

It may be that we are now past the point of no return. But it must be hoped that, even at this late stage, political dialogue will continue in an attempt to address Iran's genuine security fears. A better policy than sanctions would be to do the opposite:reopen the US embassy, drop all sanctions other than those involving military technology, and encourage investment in Iran and as much contact as possible with America. That strategy would please many Iranians and make the regime in Tehran really nervous.

Lord Lamont is chairman of the British Iranian Chamber of Commerce and a former Chancellor of the Exchequer (Minister of Finance).

This article was originally published in the *Financial Times* on 23 January 2006.

The Reality of Modern Iran

MICHAEL LEDEEN

The Islamic Republic of Iran was created by Ayatollah Ruhollah Khomeini's revolution in 1979 and remains a revolutionary regime, committed to the restoration of a universal Muslim Caliphate under the absolute rule of a clerical tyrant. The official website of the current Iranian Supreme Leader, Ali Khamenei, describes him as 'the leader of the Muslims', endowed with the authority of the ancient Caliphs to lead all Muslims, not just the Shiites alone.

Khomeini's revolution toppled not only the Shah, but traditional Shiite doctrine, according to which civil society must not be governed by clerics until the return of the 'Vanished Imam', whose reappearance would usher in the millennium. In contrast with Sunni doctrine, the Shiites had long insisted that the mosque was the rightful place for religious leaders, leaving government to secular power. Khomeini himself assumed power in Iran, and put in place a stern, oppressive system that drove women from public life, enforced puritanical regulations on the population, and carried out mass executions of those who challenged him. It was, and remains, a classic example of clerical fascism.

Those who protest have been systematically arrested, tortured or executed. More than a hundred Iranians were assassinated in Europe, the United States and the Middle East between 1979 and the beginning of 2001, in keeping with the straightforward pronouncement of Ahmad Janati, the secretary of the Council of Guardians on 15 June 2001: 'those opposing the regime must be killed.' Assassination is held in such regard that a street in Tehran was renamed after Khaled Istamboli, Anwar Sadat's killer.

In keeping with his conviction that all Muslims should follow his example, Khomeini soon challenged the Sunnis' control over the holy sites of Mecca and Medina, even backing an armed protest during the Haj. But he unhesitatingly worked with Sunnis against their common enemies, a practice that began nearly a decade before the revolution, when Yassir Arafat's (Sunni) Fatah trained the precursors of the Iranian (Shiite) Revolutionary Guards in Lebanon. In public tribute to this invaluable assistance, Khomeini invited Arafat as the first foreign guest of the Islamic Republic, and promised the PLO a royalty on every barrel of Iranian oil.

Khomeini's ambitions were not limited to the Middle East. From the moment of the overthrow of the Shah, the leaders of the Islamic Republic have declared, and waged, war against the infidels of the West, above all, the Americans and the Israelis. Their principal instrument has been the terrorist organization Hezbollah, which was created in Lebanon (where the Syrians provided safe haven) shortly after the revolution. In the 1980s, Hezbollah – operating in tandem with the PLO – organized suicide bombing attacks against the French and US Marine barracks, and the American Embassy in Beirut, as well as the kidnappings of US missionaries and military and intelligence officers who were then tortured to death. In the 1990s, Hezbollah conducted lethal attacks against Jewish targets in Argentina, for which leaders of the Iranian regime have been indicted.

Throughout this period, and contrary to a long-standing myth – according to which Sunnis and Shiites hate one another so much they cannot cooperate, even against a common enemy – Iran worked closely with Sunni terrorists. The most dramatic example is its close relationship with Osama bin Laden's Al Qaeda. The 1998 embassy bombings in East Africa – for which Al Qaeda took full credit – were in large part Iranian operations. Bin Laden had asked Hezbollah's operational chieftain, Imad Mughniyah, for help making Al Qaeda as potent as Hezbollah, and the original concept for the simultaneous bombings in Kenya and Tanzania came directly from Mughniyah. The Al Qaeda terrorists were trained by Hezbollah in Lebanon, and their explosives were provided by Iran. After the attacks, one of the leaders of the operations, Saif al Adel, took refuge in Iran, where he remains active today. Indeed, al Adel ordered a round of attacks in Saudi Arabia in 2003.

A US federal judge recently ruled that Iran was responsible for the 1996 Khobar Towers bombing in Saudi Arabia, in which 19 US Air Force personnel were killed and 372 wounded. The ruling was based in large part on sworn testimony from former FBI Director Louis Freeh, who had investigated the bombings at the time they took place. He found that two Iranian government security agencies and senior members of the Iranian government (including Khamenei and intelligence chief Ali Fallahian) provided funding, training, explosives and logistical assistance to the terrorists (who referred to themselves as 'Saudi Hezbollah', thereby explicitly confirming their ties to the mullahs).

This was only the latest in a long series of public statements about Iran's role in the Khobar Towers massacre and other terrorist attacks against Americans by top officials of the US Government. In the autumn of 1999, State Department spokesman James Rubin confirmed 'We do have specific information with respect to the involvement of Iranian Government officials [in the Khobar Towers bombing].' An indictment filed by the Justice Department in 2001 alleged Iranian direction of, and logistical support for, the attack – and noted that arrested conspirators confessed that the purpose of the attack was to strike the United States on behalf of Iran. Barely a week before the judicial finding, State Department Counsellor Philip Zelikow said that 'During the 1990s, Iran aided terrorist groups that were targeting Americans, Israelis, and Saudis. Agents of the Iranian government were involved in the attack on the U.S. Air Force barracks at Khobar Towers, in Saudi Arabia, in 1996.'

Iranian cooperation with Al Qaeda was not limited to the Middle East. In February 1996, British NATO forces in Bosnia found a manual for training terrorists that a British expert called 'the mother of all training manuals'. It was uncovered during an operation against a terrorist training camp in Pogorelica, during which Bosnian police arrested four Iranian 'diplomats' and eight Bosnian Muslims. The manual had been produced by the Iranian Intelligence Ministry, and had been earlier used to train Al Qaeda militants in Sudan. It was a thoroughly professional job, and included sections ranging from clandestine communications, to the creation of a 'secure' terrorist cell (including recruitment and maintenance of good morale), to staging simultaneous attacks, kidnapping, evading surveillance, and discourses on the anti-Western jihad.

The considerable sophistication of the training manual greatly surprised the British analysts, as it would the Americans with whom it was shared six years later, in 2002. The surprise was of a piece with the astonishment of the Israelis during the war with Hezbollah in the summer of 2006. The Israeli Defence Forces discovered that the terrorists were using highly advanced electronic surveillance devices, provided by the Iranian Revolutionary Guards at a cost of tens of millions of dollars. During the conflict, Hezbollah used two new listening stations to monitor Israeli communications, one on the Golan Heights and the other at Baab al-Hawa, near the Turkish border. Two others will become operational in the next couple of months.

The surprise derived from a common conceit: fanatics cannot be smart. Yet the leaders of the Islamic Republic are both. They have few peers when it comes to killing — thousands of political opponents have been murdered or executed, in Iran and abroad — and they excel at deception, as witness the secret nuclear programmem, which was kept secret for more than a decade.

No wonder, then, that the State Department invariably placed Iran at the top of its annual list of State Sponsors of Terrorism. And no one should be surprised that the 9/11 Commission found that Iran had enabled some of the terrorists who struck the United States to cross her territory en route to the US, and that many top Al Qaeda leaders had fled Afghanistan to Iran after the onset of the Coalition assault against the Taliban and associated terrorists.

In short, Iran has been at war with the United States, its friends and its allies for more than 27 years, and it is hard to imagine any basic change in Iranian behaviour. Tehran's war against the West is not based on a desire for territory, or on real or imagined grievances; it is rooted in the nature of the

Islamic Republic, it rests on ultimate issues. For the Iranians to negotiate a *modus vivendi* with us would be tantamount to abandoning the messianic vision of Khomeini and his successors. Thus, like the ideological wars of the twentieth century, this war will only end when one side has lost.

The war in Iraq, which so many take as the starting-point for their analysis of Iran's behaviour, has only an incidental role in this story of the Iranian war against the West; it provided another battlefield on which the Iranians have killed Western soldiers and civilians. But only the scale is new, the practice was already well established long before Operation Iraqi Freedom was even conceived.

None the less, the violence of the Iranian response, in tandem with their Syrian allies, surprised most Western strategists, because they failed to appreciate that, if Iraq followed Afghanistan on the path to freedom, the regimes in Tehran and Damascus would be mortally threatened. Indeed, the mullahs are openly challenged by mass demonstrations, strikes and protests on virtually a daily basis.

The Islamic regime in Tehran has long since lost any semblance of popular support, and has maintained power only through the systematic use of terror against its people. It cannot claim popular support on the basis of its accomplishments, because 23 years of theocracy have produced ruin and misery. Four million people have fled the Islamic Revolution, most of them well educated and highly skilled. The data on those trapped by the tyrants are startling:

- Sixty per cent of the population lives below the poverty line.

- One-third to one-half of all Iranians are malnourished.

- The average income for more than half the population is $1.40/day.

- The gross domestic product is less than half of what it was in 1978.

- The distribution of the shrinking wealth is firmly in the hands of the regime, and inequitably allotted. More than 80 per cent of the country's gross national product comes from the petroleum industry, which is entirely in government hands. The mullahs have effectively ruined this primary source of national wealth: oil production is currently 3.2 million barrels/day. It was 6.2 at the end of the Shah's rule. According to a study released on Christmas Day, 2006, by the National Academy of Sciences, oil exports are expected to decline by upwards of 10 per cent a year for the foreseeable future.

- Inflation has run wild. The exchange rate was 70 rials to the dollar in 1978, and it was more than 10,000 in late 2005.

- There are said to be more than 50,000 suicides per year.

Europeans shun the country. In the summer of 2001, *Newsweek International* proclaimed Iran the 'worst country in the world for journalists', and the French-led international organization, *Reporters sans frontières*, branded Ayatollah Khamenei one of the world's top enemies of a free press.

All of this might have been tolerated in the name of the true faith if the leaders had demonstrated a virtuous asceticism. But the regime is famously corrupt, and the tyrant has instituted a unique form of state theft. A percentage of most business deals, and even many elementary cash transactions, is deposited in an account known as the 'leadership's household', which is entirely at the disposal of the supreme leader, the Ayatollah Ali Khamenei. This tax ranges upwards from about 5 per cent to nearly 30 per cent on luxury items. The base price for a standard Iranian car – the Peykan – is roughly $6,250, but the actual cost is $8,125. The difference goes to Khamenei. The leadership is awash in money while the people starve.

Older persons may be unlikely to challenge a repressive regime (although Solzhenitsyn and the Sacharovs show this is not always true), but the young are the majority in Iran – well over half the population is under 25 years of age, and they have shown themselves willing to take risks. In 2001, hundreds of thousands of young people demonstrated against the regime, and in the spring and summer of 2003 large numbers again took to the streets, calling for a general strike. Leaders of the student movement, which, along with workers' organizations, is one of the few more or less open centres of anti-regime thought and action, are routinely rounded up, thrown in jail, and tortured. This was done, for example, shortly after President Bush's 'axis of evil' speech, when he branded Iran one of the terror states.

The regime is rightly nervous, since it knows its people would remove the theocracy if they had a chance. Public opinion polls conducted by the Ministry of Information three years ago showed that upwards of 70 per cent of Iranians disliked the system and wanted it changed. Students of revolution will see abundant signs of a brittle regime that knows its doom may be at hand, not least of all a massive smuggling of wealth outside the country.

Despite heavy-handed manipulation, even Iranian 'elections' have occasionally demonstrated the public's real mood: in 1997 more than 70 per cent voted for the most liberal candidate available, President Mohammed Khatami. They knew that Khatami was unlikely to change anything (if he tried, he, too, would occupy a cell in the Evin prison in Tehran), but a vote for Khatami was the only safe form of protest available to them. Khatami was the empty vessel into which the Iranians poured their contempt for the regime. Some Westerners, and a few of Khatami's supporters, convinced themselves that the 1997 elections marked a potential turning-point, and that a true reform of the mullahcracy might be effected by Khatami and his followers. But most Iranians recognized that the ruling ayatollahs would not tolerate reform.

Indeed, more than two hundred reformists were removed from the list of candidates by the dominant hardliners. Khatami was judged acceptable by the mullahs; otherwise his name wouldn't have been on the ballot. And in fact, no significant reforms were passed in nearly ten years in office, and an overwhelming majority of Iranian voters stayed away from the polls when he was re-elected, again choosing the only safe form of protest against the mullahs.

The election of Mahmoud Ahmadinejad in 2005 reflected both the regime's determination to crush all remaining domestic dissent with an iron fist, and its confidence that the United States would not directly challenge its domestic rule, or even its nuclear programme. By then, they had drawn the conclusion that the Bush administration, despite its harsh rhetoric about the 'Axis of Evil' and the president's repeated claim that the United States supported the Iranian people's 'legitimate desire to be free', was not going to do anything to support a revolution in Iran. In Bush's first term, Deputy Secretary of State Armitage proclaimed Iran 'a democracy', and secret talks were held throughout the first three years of the George W. Bush presidency – talks that were exploited by the Iranians to discourage their domestic opponents – and only suspended when it was discovered that the Al Qaeda terrorists who commanded the May 2003 suicide bombings in Riyadh, Saudia Arabia, were based in Iran. Even then, Secretary of State Colin Powell vowed that the talks would be resumed, and that there would be no change in Iran policy. Worse yet, the administration indulged in the same fantasy that brought ruin at the end of the First Gulf War.

Just as George W. Bush's father had convinced himself in 1991 that others would do the necessary dirty work in getting rid of Saddam Hussein, his son embraced the same illusion regarding the mullahs. Despite a near-constant rhetorical drumbeat from Bush and Rice against the Iranian regime, neither of them ever announced that the United States supported regime change in Iran. They seemed to hint at it from time to time, but they never quite said it. And in such matters, clarity is everything. The Iranian people were not inclined to risk their lives without clear signals, and manifest support, from the United States.

Moreover, the hardliners around Supreme Leader Khamenei were optimistic about their chances of driving the Americans out of Iraq and Afghanistan, and became increasingly brazen about supporting the terrorists in both countries. By the end of 2006, both Washington and London were saying publicly what had been known in military circles for a long time: that many of the most lethal roadside bombs and explosives used against coalition forces had come from Iran, courtesy of the regime's policies; that Iranian military intelligence officers were masterminding many of the attacks, and that a significant number of terrorists from Iraq, Afghanistan, Gaza and Palestine were trained, funded and armed by Iran.

Meanwhile, Khamenei and his cohorts believed they either had, or were on the verge of having atomic bombs and an effective delivery system for them. The Iranian nuclear programme had started under the Shah, and was elevated to an urgent project at the time of the First Gulf War, in 1991. The Iranians concluded that if Saddam had possessed atomic bombs, the Americans would not have dared to launch a massive military campaign against him. Ergo, Iran needed the bomb, to protect the regime against US armed forces.

But the geopolitical consequences of a nuclear Iran are not clear. It may well be that a successful Iranian nuclear test – and even more so a nuclear attack against Israel, which has been publicly promised by Khamenei and former President Hashemi Rafsanjani – would force the Bush administration to take drastic action. President Bush, after all, has repeatedly declared 'unacceptable' a nuclear-armed Islamic Republic. And in any event, nuclear weapons cannot protect the regime against its most likely doom, which is a popular uprising.

The mullahs' cheery reading of the international entrails may prove to be mistaken. After all, Saddam had extremely good grounds for believing in 1990 and 1991 that the United States had no objection to Iraqi occupation of Kuwait. And Osama bin Laden also had good grounds – very similar to the basis of Iran's current assessment – for believing that the United States would not respond violently to a direct terrorist attack.

Dictators have always had a particularly hard time understanding the ability of democratic societies to turn on a dime and spontaneously organize themselves to cope with serious problems. If the mullahs continue to kill Americans, they will eventually provoke a national response.

Even without a dramatic event, American support for a democratic revolution in Iran would be entirely in keeping with national tradition. Those who call themselves realists like to argue that the United States should not commit American power and prestige unless vital national security issues are at stake, but American history is full of actions undertaken because American leaders and the American people felt a moral obligation to do so. Thus, Corazon Aquino was supported against Ferdinand Marcos. Thus, we went to war in the Balkans to defend Bosnian Muslims. Thus, we moved against dictators in Haiti and Chile, and against the racist apartheid regime in South Africa. American national security was not at stake in any of those countries. That it is so directly threatened by the mullahs, and that they are on the verge of becoming a nuclear power, only adds urgency to the argument that we should finally respond to the twenty-year Iranian war against us, by helping the Iranian people rid themselves of their oppressors.

Michael Ledeen is Resident Scholar in the Freedom Chair at the American Enterprise Institute.

Iran, the Neo-Conservatives and Democracy

JOHN LAUGHLAND

Let us assume, for the sake of argument, that the neo-conservative view of the world is correct. The world contains a number of states dedicated to threatening US allies and perpetrating terrorist attacks. Although the war on terror has already involved the invasion of two major Muslim countries (Afghanistan and Iraq) a third country, Iran, has now emerged as a new threat. The proposed solution is the democratisation of the whole planet – in George Bush's words, "the ultimate goal of ending tyranny in our world".

During most of the Cold War, the hawks whom we now call neo-conservatives dismissed all talk of resolving international disputes through treaties or international organisations. They scoffed at the sight of Jimmy Carter leading the geriatric Leonid Brezhnev by the arm to sign the latest bilateral arms reduction treaty. They insisted that Soviet expansionism needed to be contained by military might. Even when Ronald Reagan and Caspar Weinberger proactively stepped full throttle on military spending to defeat the Soviets, no one suggested pre-emptively attacking their nuclear installations.

That belief was known as the doctrine of deterrence. Since the end of the Cold War it has been consigned to the dustbin of history. Today's neo-cons do not conclude from the possibility that Iran might obtain the bomb that counter-measures must be taken to deter her from ever using it. Instead, they bleat that Iran is infringing the terms of the Nuclear Non-Proliferation Treaty – one of the stupidest treaties ever to have entered the annals of diplomacy, because it elevates hypocrisy to a principle of international law by saying that only some states are allowed to have nuclear warheads – just as they alleged, falsely, that Saddam Hussein's gravest sin was to have violated some twelve-year-old and largely forgotten United Nations Security Council Resolutions.

In the academic jargon of international relations theory, therefore, the hawks have shifted from realism to idealism. Whereas previously they believed that the only reality in international relations was force, they are now drenched in that universalist ideology and faith in international institutions which is usually associated with the name of the arch-idealist, Woodrow

Wilson. To be sure, some neo-cons bluster against the UN, but President Bush's stated goal of liberating the whole of humanity is far closer to the one-world ideology which inspired the creation of the League of Nations than it is to the pessimistic *Realpolitik* of, say, Henry Kissinger.

The main difference from Woodrow Wilson and the neo-cons today is that the universalist ideology which they use to liquidate recalcitrant societies contains a double strychnine dose of one-world economic globalisation plus the homogenised trash culture of MTV and its associated vices of drugs and sex. Western opponents of the "evil empire" were right when they calculated that the slab-faced old Commies sitting behind desks in Moscow would be no match for the pony-tailed new Commies who sang with John Lennon, "Imagine there's no countries, It isn't hard to do, Nothing to kill or die for, No religion too." Just as the walls of Jericho were brought down by trumpets, and just as General Noriega was flushed out of the Papal Nunciature in Managua in 1989 by blaring rock music, so what remained of social conservatism behind the Berlin Wall was instantly dissolved by the hideous cacophony of Western postmodernism.

This abandonment of deterrence shows that political-ideological levelling out (what the Nazis called *Gleichschaltung*) is the key to the neo-con view of the world. Whereas deterrence assumed that the existence, somewhere in the world, of unfriendly and even evil regimes was as certain as death and taxes, and that a wise government consequently needed to keep such threats at bay, the neo-cons today believe that the very existence of hostile or even non-aligned regimes is a threat. Deterrence assumed a certain degree of political pluralism on the planet, whereas neo-cons believe with George Bush that "The survival of liberty in our land increasingly depends on the success of liberty in other lands." Today's neo-cons are the modern Athenians who told the inhabitants of Melos that their neutrality in the war against Sparta was intolerable.

Neo-cons believe, as George W. Bush said in 2002, that the great struggles of the 20th century have ended in the decisive victory of "a single sustainable model for national success". They welcome the end of the Cold War precisely because it overcame the division of the world into competing political systems, and seemed to create in its place the beginnings of a monolithic unipolar world system with America and American values (especially universal human rights) as its ideological core. Islam presents an obstacle to the full realisation of this goal and this is why neo-cons have now announced that they intend to "democratise" the whole of the Middle East as well.

Yet it is these underlying beliefs about the international system which give the lie to the neo-con claim to want to democratise the planet. Even if we leave aside the abuses committed in the name of democratisation – from 1953, when the CIA overthrew Prime Minister Mossadegh of Iran, to 2004, when spooky American technicians of regime change installed a friendly regime in Kiev – it is simply incredible that a plan for world-wide democratisation should now involve singling out Iran as an enemy. For the Islamic Republic of Iran is undoubtedly one of the most advanced democracies in the Muslim world.

Such a statement will doubtless surprise those who think of Iran as groaning under the yoke of a stifling theocracy, and who associate it with Hezbollah and Islamic Jihad. But there is no denying that the normal state institutions of the Islamic Republic are impeccably democratic. The President and the Legislature are directly elected by universal suffrage (including women); the political system is extremely vibrant, the latest presidential election having been far more hotly contested than the equivalent one in 2005 in Egypt; there is a basically free press, in which politicians including the president are frequently criticised; and the Iranian constitution gives equal rights to all citizens irrespective of race and sex, forbids the investigation of individuals' beliefs and the state inspection of letters or other forms of private communication, and guarantees *habeas corpus*, the presumption of innocence and equality before the law.

President Ahmadinejad may rail against Israel but this is perhaps the cry of frustration of a man who is less powerful at home than he would like to be: the Iranian President has had his nominees for Oil Minister rejected no fewer than four times by the Iranian parliament. The Islamic Republic's political system is at the very antipodes of the absolute monarchy which reigns in neighbouring Saudi Arabia, America's ally. There are no elements of democracy whatever in that country's national political life, which is why many Iranian leaders, including the fiery President, regard it as disgracefully backward.

To be sure, the Iranian constitution also contains peculiar elements found in no other state, most importantly the office of Supreme Leader who commands the armed forces, appoints the Council of Guardians (a theological body which scrutinises laws passed by the Legislature) and controls the state broadcasting network and the police. These powers are not wielded democratically. But all states contain constitutional elements which are specifically designed to mitigate the effects of direct democracy, the US Supreme Court being the best example of a powerful unelected body which intervenes actively in matters of public policy in the name of unchangeable principles. And, whatever the written provisions in the Iranian constitution, it is undeniable that the country's domestic politics are extremely fluid. Indeed one of the country's main failings is that the various factions battle it out so overtly that the rule of law suffers considerably: Iranian citizens often do not know which way state authority is going to strike next.

Finally, even the theocratic elements in the Iranian constitution themselves draw legitimacy – however bogusly - from the Islamic Revolution's claim to have been a democratic movement. I do not personally care for revolutions of any kind but there can be little doubt that the 1979 Iranian Revolution did in fact succeed because of popular hatred for a dictatorial foreign-backed regime. Add to all this the fact that the form of Islam preached in Iran is itself self-consciously progressivist – even conservative Iranian clerics dismiss the Islam of the Taleban or the Wahhabis as atavistic – and you have a country which American democratists ought to embrace as a model for the rest of the Muslim world.

More than that: Islam is itself a specifically democratic religion. In contrast to Catholicism, Islam has no coherent clerical hierarchy: it has no single ecclesiastical structure by which religious truth can be definitively established. This is why there are so many different sects of Islam: more or less anyone can interpret and teach the meaning of scripture. This is especially the case in Shiism. The holy Iranian city of Qom is home to as many competing schools of Islam as there are Ayatollahs to head them, and this is why our TV perception of huge crowds at Mecca or during the feast of Ashura accurately captures the essence of Islam as a religion of the masses.

As the horrified reaction to the election of Hamas in Palestine shows, the neo-con commitment to democratisation is as much about free choice as are the options offered to a shopkeeper when the Mafia comes round to collect the protection money. "It's up to you," the gangsters say as they crack their knuckles with a nonchalant smirk. "You can do what you like. But your sister over there, now she's a very pretty girl..." A commitment to democracy implies a commitment to pluralism, and to the possibility that people may make choices with which we do not agree. This is precisely why neo-conservatives are determined to prevent it.

John Laughland is Editor of Geopolitical Affairs.

This article was originally published in _The American Conservative_.

Iran and Russia: An Ambiguous Relationship

JULIA SNEGUR

After the Islamic Revolution of 1979, the end of the war with Iraq and the severance of its diplomatic relations with the United States, the Islamic Republic of Iran had to rebuild its armed forces. Since its military, industrial and technological needs would no longer be met by the United States, Iran turned to the USSR. Between 1989 and 1991 the two countries concluded four industrial and military accords, covering all types of armaments, for a total value of $ 5.1 billion. This was a unique opportunity for Moscow to strengthen its presence in the Middle East. Looking for new markets for its weapons remains a major objective of Russia's foreign policy, as is also the case for the US. By the first years of the twenty-first century, Iran had become Russia's third largest arms-importing country, after China and India.

The Relationship between Iran and Russia Since the Collapse of the USSR

Arms sales

After the collapse of the USSR, arms sales were seriously disrupted as a result of Western pressures on the Russian Federation. In May 1995, the US President Bill Clinton and the Russian Federation President Boris Yeltsin signed an agreement in which Russia committed itself to end its sales of arms and military equipment to Iran, by 31 December 1999. A secret protocol to this agreement (signed by Vice-President Al Gore and Viktor Chernomyrdin on 30 June 1995) detailed Russia's commitments and the financial compensation it was to receive in return. The United States, for its part, agreed to monitor American arms sales in the areas bordering Russia's eastern borders, and to develop industrial, technological and military cooperation with Russia: experts estimated that Russia lost between $2.2 billion and $4 billion in arms sales. In view of the considerable amounts of money at stake, one can imagine how annoyed Russia was at the secret agreement of 30 June 1995, since it was actually closing an important market for its industrial and military complex and wiping out a major source of income for its budget.

Basing itself on Articles 5 and 7 of the US-Russian agreement (which deal with a change in Iran's political situation, and with possible changes in the positions of other countries), and with a denunciation of the secret protocol during the election campaign of 2000, Russia considered it had the moral right to abandon its commitments and to resume its commercial activities, all the more so since the United States never ceased supplying Iran with arms itself, via other Middle Eastern countries, thereby simply recapturing the market abandoned by the Russians. The threat of economic sanctions against Russia was not meant at all to prevent Iran from getting military material; as a matter of fact, the Iranian Army is equipped with US-made missiles.

Russia's decision in November 2000 to resume arms sales to Iran aroused US protests: Washington argued that Iran was supporting terrorism via its links with Hezbollah. It was to no avail: very soon, in December 2000, a meeting with Iran's Defence Minister was organized in Moscow. After the attacks of September 11, whilst intense diplomatic activity was developing with a view to setting up an anti-terrorist coalition, Russia signed a military cooperation agreement with Iran on 2 October 2001, which provided for the acquisition of military equipment to an annual amount of $300 million for the next five years. Emboldened by the prospects of new sales, Russia hoped it could recapture the market it had lost. However, Russia was disappointed to note that the Iranians were reluctant partners, and was never able to compensate fully for the losses it incurred in giving up the previous deals.

The Iranians began to view Russia as an unstable and opportunistic partner, and to grasp that an important pillar of national power was industrial and technological autonomy. Iran has developed a solid infrastructure of technological research, covering all the different types of arms systems from interceptor fighter to submarines. The Iranian government has also prepared with Russia a 25-year-long rearmament programme, but Russia's participation deals mainly with technical support. In concrete terms, Iran is looking for cooperation in the following areas: developing an anti-aircraft defence system (against nuclear or conventional tactical missiles); setting up a military industry, producing under license materials for the army, the air force and the navy; modernizing its existing air force and setting up centres providing services, maintenance and training. In this context, the first Iranian satellite 'Sinah-1' (ZS-1) was launched on 27 October 2005, together with 'Kosmos-ZM', from the Russian Plesetsk base; a telecommunication satellite launch is planned for 2007. Today Iran and Russia are running a programme of scientific cooperation in the field of air and space as well as in the field of energy (nuclear and other). Therefore one can envisage a time when Iran would no longer be purchasing Russian armaments.

The United States' position is no less complex. Washington's foreign policy does not allow direct contacts with Iran in order to compete with Russia as an arms provider. Arms sales channelled through proxies cannot compete with those of the Russians. The United States is therefore losing an important market for its military industry, and one can better understand the irritation of those Americans who are watching the Russians' attempts to penetrate the Iranian market through military, scientific and economic projects. Obviously, Iran intents to regain its 'freedom', reinforce its position as regional leader and also assert its position in the world.

In spite of Western pressures, Moscow is therefore pursuing its military, industrial and technological cooperation with Iran, much to the detriment of the US. According to the CIA, Iran is looking to develop a ballistic arsenal, in cooperation with Moscow, in order to free itself from US pressures. Equipped with launchers of ABC (atomic, biological and chemical) weapons, Iran would be in a position to ensure its vital interests in the Gulf, and this, according to American criteria, represents a threat for the vital interests of the US, which is trying to put pressure on Moscow to stop its cooperation with Iran. For strategic and financial reasons, Moscow is sticking to its guns.

Regarding the nuclear question, Moscow is resolved to find a peaceful and negotiated solution, which it considers essential for the protection of its commercial and financial interests. The asymmetric nature of its nuclear cooperation with Iran ought to enable Moscow to remain in control if its Iranian partner starts to misbehave. Iranian diplomats were disappointed by the Russian vote in favour of handing over the problem to the Security Council. This is a clear indication of the limits of Moscow's readiness to support this 'rogue state', and of the importance Russia attaches to maintaining good relations with the West.

The Republics of Central Asia and the Caucasus

The Caucasus is obviously a matter of interest for Iran but it does not have the political means to take root in this region. Iran's concern at continuing Russian influence in the Caucasus combines with its desire to see US and Turkish influence reduced there as well. Iran fears regional destabilization resulting from territorial disputes, such as, in Nagorno-Karabakh, the conflict between Christian Armenia (an ally of Moscow *vis-à-vis* Azerbaijan), and Azeris, whose co-nationals are present in large numbers in Iran itself.

Central Asia – Turkmenistan, Uzbekistan, Tajikistan, Kyrgyzstan and Kazakhstan – is a very important area for Russia, the geopolitical heir of the USSR. It is Russia's strategic backyard, especially in view of the region's borders with China and the Middle East. The newly independent states of

Central Asia have separated Russia from its previous neighbours, Turkey, Iran and Afghanistan. Russia's objective today is to use this region not only as a buffer against negative influences from abroad, but also a means by which to preserve its relations with the countries of the Near and Middle East. This southern front, Russia's soft underbelly, is a space to be brought under control.

From a strategic point of view, Russia has no other wish but to maintain its territorial and military presence. Since 1994, Russia has concluded cooperation agreements with its southern neighbours. Such agreements contain provisions on the role of border guards and military integration. Neither Iran nor Afghanistan intends to invade the republics of Central Asia, but this is still a fragile area prone to a sudden deterioration of ethnic tensions, to civil wars, and arms and drugs trafficking. Preserving regional stability is therefore a common objective shared by Iran and Russia.

The Central Asian states themselves, however, have different and sometimes divergent strategies. This can be explained both by the different types of influence Russia has over them, and by the natural resources at their disposal. Russia wants them to export oil and gas through the traditional routes across Russia; the West – the US in particular – is encouraging them to use alternative routes, through the Caucasus, Turkey and Afghanistan.

The Caspian Sea

Geopolitically, the Caspian area encompasses not only the states whose borders share the Caspian Sea – Russia, Azerbaijan, Turkmenistan, Kazakhstan and Iran – but also the whole of the Caucasus region. Before the break-up of the USSR, there was no significant conflict around the Caspian Sea, since regional exploitation of oil was in the hands of Moscow. But since the dissolution of the Soviet Union, several factors such as the independence of the Soviet republics of Central Asia and the Caucasus, the definition of a new legal status for the sea (or its absence), the 'international' exploration and exploitation of hydrocarbons, have all made this area geopolitically very sensitive. Western oil and gas companies have taken a strong interest in the Caspian since access to new sources of hydrocarbons is vital for their future profits.

Since the dissolution of the USSR at the end of 1991, the five states which border the Caspian Sea have not concluded an agreement defining their maritime borders. This is slowing down the exploitation of the huge energy resources contained under this sea. The legal status of the Caspian Sea constitutes a serious bone of contention between its bordering countries: is it a sea or a lake? According to international law, the utilization of a lake's resources is to be decided unanimously by all the bordering countries. In the case of a sea, by contrast, each bordering state decides by itself areas which resources it is free to exploit at its convenience.

Consequently, Russia proposed the creation of a condominium for the legal exploitation in common of all the resources of the Caspian Sea, except those within territorial waters. This proposal was supported by Iran which owns a shorter coast length (1146 km for Iran, 825 km for Azerbaijan, 2320 km for Kazakhstan, 1460 km for Russia and 1200 km for Turkmenistan) and possesses therefore more limited hydrocarbon reserves. In the meantime, with the discovery of new hydrocarbon deposits, these positions have changed. After the discovery of reserves off its coastline, Russia again adopted the 'sea' option and signed bilateral accords with Kazakhstan in 1988 and Azerbaijan in 2001 on the division of Caspian Sea along a median line. Russia was *de facto* actually adopting the position of Kazakhstan and Azerbaijan. Russia also signed with these two countries an agreement in 2002 for the exploitation of several adjacent off-shore fields. Finally, on 14 May 2003, Moscow concluded a tripartite accord with its two partners on the sharing-out of the resources of the North Caspian according to the length of the coastline of the respective countries, namely 18 per cent for Azerbaijan, 19 per cent for Russia, and 27 per cent for Kazakhstan. Iran and Turkmenistan rejected this distribution and advocated an equal share, basing their arguments on the 1921 Treaty of Friendship between Russia and Persia, and on the Soviet-Iranian treaty of 1940.

The regulations to be adopted for the construction of pipelines both on the seabed and on the surface are another serious bone of contention between the Caspian states. The conditions for transporting the hydrocarbon resources of the Caspian Sea are at the core of rivalries between countries displaying interest in this area, since those who will control these supply lines will also exert influence on the production centres and their outlets.

Because of their hemmed-in position, the states of Central Asia (notably Kazakhstan and Turkmenistan, and to a lesser degree Uzbekistan) are confronted with the key problem of how to transport their gas and oil to the international market. This puts these states into a position of competition against rather than cooperation with one another. The republics of Central Asia are seeking an alternative to their traditional relations with Russia. The United States is the most active player in suggesting alternatives, because of their oil-oriented foreign policy and because of their ability to mobilize financial means and to bring under control the subtle political games played by the regional actors. This is a cause of much concern and trouble for Russia, which does not have sufficient means to counter the political and financial activity of the US, and cannot but lose its influence over the former republics of the USSR.

An analysis of Russia's geopolitical and economic position could lead to the conclusion that Moscow's interest is to prevent the opening up of Caspian hydrocarbon resources, because they will both compete directly with its products and lead to a greater autonomy of the new states. For these reasons, Moscow has attempted to slow down and even block some projects, or to determine at least that the exporting routes will pass through its territory.

The United States, for which Central Asia has become a 'strategic zone of interest', is also manoeuvring to promote its interests. Sticking to its policy of isolating the Iranian regime, the US government is strongly opposed to using Iranian territory for gas or oil transit. In order to avoid passing through the territories of Iran and Russia, Washington promoted the construction of the east–west pipeline from Baku in Azerbaijan to Ceyhan in Turkey. This pipeline has been in operation since the end of 2005. However, Russia has outflanked Washington and Ankara thanks to the Baku–Soupsa oil pipeline, active since 1999, as well as the Caspian Pipeline built by CPC (Caspian Pipeline Consortium) and active since November 2001, and the pipeline connecting Baku to Novorossiysk through Dagestan.

In other words, the Caspian Sea is today the hotspot of new Central Asian geopolitics. A fight for the control of its pipelines is raging, involving not only the bordering and neighbouring states but also big international actors interested in the use of hydrocarbons, such as the European states, China and notably the United States.

Conclusion

Iran and Russia have interests in common other than arms deals and regional stability. First, their interest is to prevent US military and political penetration in the zone of the Eastern States. Obviously they dislike the US concept of a 'Greater Middle East'. Besides, Moscow and Tehran, who possess respectively the first and second largest world natural gas reserves, are discussing the project of setting up a natural gas version of OPEC with a view to controlling its prices, avoiding financial risks and creating an Asiatic energy block.

The USSR and the Islamic Republic of Iran were two nations governed by a strong ideology which moulded the organization of their societies, as well as their strategic culture and foreign policy. The USSR was a power aiming at projecting its socialist ideology. The values of these two nations on the religious, economic and social levels were not opposite but divergent. Iran did not have a place in the Soviets' vision of socialist international relations. But geopolitical constraints forced Moscow to have a dialogue with Iran and to maintain stable relations with it. There were several options for 'controlling' this country:

- To absorb it. This is impossible, in view of the strong ideology of its regime.

- To weaken it. This may entail serious risks of Iran falling under foreign influence.

- To strengthen it. This may arouse feelings of revenge and a desire for power which could endanger the Russian zones of influence in the Caucasus and Central Asia.

- To drag it into cooperation, arouse its interest and even better to make it dependent. Russia's partners will dislike this option.

This sheds light on the USSR's (now Russia's) attitude to Iran, namely a delicate game aimed alternately at weakening Iran or strengthening it when it is in danger of coming into the American sphere of influence. In spite of allegations of an old and lasting strategic partnership, the relationship between Russia and Iran has actually developed thanks to the two historical upheavals triggered by the Iranian Islamic Revolution in 1979 and the collapse of the USSR in 1991. The latter event has changed the geopolitical map of the Caucasus, the Caspian area and Central Asia.

Since then, economic cooperation has been developing substantially between Iran and Russia. Western countries have been jealous of the political dialogue between them. But these two developments are not enough to ensure smooth relations between Russia and Iran. The character of this relationship is a matter of circumstance, probably enhanced by the presence of a third actor, the United States, often assuming a give-and-take pattern. Their relationship towards the United States remains ambiguous. Moscow and Tehran are striving to exclude the US from the region, but at the same time they are obliged to undertake a certain *rapprochement* with the US to ensure their development and even survival.

Once competing regional powers, Iran and Russia suppress their disagreements with a single aim in mind, namely to recover from setbacks and to let time heal wounds. Their relationship is based upon their ability to find areas in which to cooperate, and from which to get immediate benefits, often in the context of acts undertaken by third parties.

Finally, it is worth noting that, contrary to Russian and Iranian views on regional geopolitics, the United States is by its very presence a stabilizing factor, since it indirectly controls the balance of power between the two countries and actually brings Moscow closer to Tehran. This strategic understanding, based upon convergent interests and marked by asymmetry, makes it possible for Moscow not to automatically take sides with Tehran, and to continue playing an ambivalent role.

Julia Snegur is a PhD student in geopolitics at the Sorbonne.

India and Iran Today: Political and Strategic Implications

RONAK D. DESAI

Introduction

As the final session of the Republican-controlled US Congress came to a close in December 2006, one of its last acts as Congress before adjourning and ceding control to the Democrats was to pass legislation approving the US-India nuclear deal. One of President Bush's most important foreign policy initiatives, Congressional approval of the deal marked a new, unprecedented phase of relations between the world's oldest and largest democracies, and also seemed to have cemented the strategic partnership that both India and the United States have sought with one another.

Yet the US-India nuclear deal, which was formally announced in July 2005, also had the effect of thrusting another significant relationship under the international spotlight: that between India and Iran. Strengthening ties between the two countries suddenly came into focus as questions about the perceived New Delhi-Tehran partnership next began to surface.

The reality, however, is that close relations between India and Iran are not a new phenomenon and the countries have cooperated and continue to cooperate in a number of key areas. Since the September 11th attacks, the Indo-Iranian nexus adopted a strategic character, one that was formalized during former Iranian President Mohammad Khatami's visit to India in 2003. While New Delhi's increasingly strong relationship with the United States (as well as with Israel for that matter) will complicate an already complex foreign policy calculus, one thing that is clear is that any friendship between India and Iran is here to stay.

Background

Although Indian leaders regularly speak of 'civilizational ties' between the two countries due to the interactions of Persian and Indus Valley civilizations over a period of millennia, Indo-Iranian relations had not always been particularly warm. Even though both states had cast off the yoke of colonialism in the 1940s, relations between India and Iran quickly fell victim to Cold War politics and alignments and both nations found themselves on different sides of the superpower rivalry between the United States and the Soviet Union. Indo-Iranian relations were further complicated by improving relations between Iran and Pakistan, India's primary rival in the region. Tehran had maintained friendly ties with Pakistan since its inception, and it was the first nation to formally recognize Pakistan and establish diplomatic relations. Despite these difficulties, however, throughout much of the 1960s, 1970s and 1980s, India and Iran worked to overcome these barriers and become closer, cooperating in key economic and political areas. The period witnessed a number of high-level exchanges between the countries' leaders as a result.

The Post-Cold War Era

The sudden collapse of the Soviet Union and the unexpected end of the Cold War presented India and Iran with a new set of opportunities to strengthen their relationship and both states realized that they shared a number of interests and concerns. India and Iran grew uneasy when the United States emerged as world's sole superpower and the disintegration of the Soviet Union created many unstable arrangements in Central Asia, disconcerting both Tehran and New Delhi.

However, the most dangerous problem in Central Asia facing both India and Iran was the upsurge in Sunni Islamic extremist movements that spread throughout South and Central Asia in the early and mid-1990s.[1] The ascension to power by the Taliban, created and nurtured by Pakistan, was a major source of mutual concern both for New Delhi and Tehran and created strong tension between Iran and Pakistan. Moreover, India sought to pursue dynamic relationships with Iran and other Central Asian states to strategically outmanoeuvre Pakistan in the region. Tehran presented New Delhi with an attractive option of pursuing dynamic foreign relations with a critical Muslim state, in part to deflect Pakistan's rhetoric in international forums and to mollify India's large Muslim minority. Iran, on the other hand, saw in India a potential means to break out of its isolation caused in part by the containment policies of the United States.

The September 11 Attacks – Altering Security Environments

The terrorist attacks of September 11, 2001 brought to the region a number of far-reaching changes, which intensified activity between India and Iran and fundamentally altered the nature of their relationship. The US-led war on terrorism significantly altered the security environments of both India and Iran, perhaps the most important reason why the two nations recognized they had so much to offer one another.[2]

With the Taliban ousted in Afghanistan, New Delhi feared that remnants of the old regime and extremists' support of the Taliban would shift their jihadist activities to Kashmir. The global war on terror against Al Qaeda prompted Washington to resuscitate its relationship with India's nemesis, Pakistan. India watched with dismay as the United States made Islamabad a critical partner in the war against terror, and awarded Pakistan 'major non-NATO' ally status in late 2004.[3] From New Delhi's perspective, Washington has largely turned a blind eye to Pakistan's support for militancy in Kashmir, as well as Pakistan's illicit nuclear weapons proliferation activities.

Similarly, Tehran has a considerable reason to worry about this new security environment. While the United States has been a close neighbor due to its military presence in the Gulf since 1991, the US military footprint in the region has expanded dramatically since 9/11. The United States has a form-idable military presence in Afghanistan, Pakistan, Uzbekistan, and, obviously, Iraq. Iran is clearly concerned that the United States will promote regimes in these countries that are pro-American and hostile to Iranian interests in the region. Most importantly, with Iran's ambitions towards a nuclear weapons programme, Washington has pursued an aggressive policy of isolation in order to pressure Tehran to forfeit its nuclear ambitions. India's value to Iran in this regard has only increased recently as India has forged important relations with the United States, Israel, the European Union and the states of South East and North East Asia.

India and Iran Today: Areas of Cooperation

This altered security environment not only has had the effect of opening up a considerable number of opportunities for both India and Iran but also allowing them to recognize the several different areas in which they can cooperate. Strategically, both states are hoping that the demise of the Taliban, the US presence in Pakistan, and the enhanced international concern surrounding extreme Sunni Islamic movements will help arrest the spread of Sunni militarism.[4] Both states also share a key interest in rebuilding a stable, viable Afghanistan. The convergence of shared threats and perceived opportunities in this regard have encouraged Iran and India to move more swiftly on key areas that highlight their developing strategic relations. These include threats of terrorism (particularly from militant Sunni groups), security of the sea lanes of control (for example, the Strait of Hormuz), transfer and sale of select military technology, and integrity of energy supplies. This strategic and economic congruence of interests manifested itself during the January 2003 visit of former Iranian President Khatami to New Delhi. The state visit included the signing of the New Delhi Declaration and seven additional Memoranda of Understanding, and agreements which formally institutionalized India and Iran's strategic partnership.[5]

Yet the area of greatest cooperation between Tehran and New Delhi undoubtedly are to do with India's growing energy demands. Economic relations between India and Iran are dominated by Indian imports of Iranian oil and gas. Iran is endowed with one of the world's largest natural gas and oil reserves and India is one of the world's biggest oil importers.[6] This arrangement has truly reinforced Indo-Iranian relations. The potential for energy cooperation between the two countries is the clearest indicator that relations between Tehran and New Delhi go beyond a temporary congruence of interests. This is best exemplified through the unveiling of the Tehran–New Delhi gas pipeline proposal last year, which ties the two countries together for at least another half a decade. The proposed plan is significant because not only would the pipeline run through Pakistan, but also because leaders in New Delhi refused to abandon the deal even after Washington expressed its displeasure with the deal during negotiations with India over the nuclear deal.[7]

It is important to remember that any strategic partnership between India and Iran has profound implications not just for India and Iran but other global and regional players as well. Pakistan, Israel and the United States are all nations that warrant special attention.

The Pakistani Angle

While leaders both in Iran and India have explicitly stated that their strategic partnership is not aimed at any third country, any alliance between Tehran and New Delhi, military or otherwise, poses a serious threat to Islamabad. India is clearly eager to counterbalance Pakistan's influence in the Muslim world and the legitimacy Iran bestows on India by virtue of this alliance is likely to diminish Pakistan's traditional role as a torchbearer for the Muslim *ummah*.[8] India seems embarked on a policy of 'soft containment' against Pakistan. New Delhi has improved its relations with China and its other neighbours in the region, and with a strategic partnership growing between India and Iran (one with a possible military dimension), Pakistan finds itself encircled. The invigorated relationship between India and Iran has prompted strong calls within Pakistan demanding Islamabad improve its relations with Iran in order to neutralize Indian influence with Tehran. Ultimately, the best hope for Pakistan is that the Indo-Iranian relationship collapses under the weight of its own ambitions. Pakistan will undoubtedly seek to capitalize on two glaring contradictions in India's relationship with Iran: New Delhi's ties to Israel and the United States.

The Israeli Component

The increasing links between Tehran and New Delhi also have consequences for another important relationship that India is nurturing in the Middle East: one with Israel. Traditionally, India and Israel shared strained relations for over forty years, and New Delhi did not normalize relations with the Jewish state until 1992. Yet despite this fact, Indo-Israeli ties have flourished, with counter-terrorism and the sale of sophisticated weapons systems emerging as key elements in their partnership.[9] Needless to say, the two countries have made up for lost time, and cooperation between the two states has intensified to such a level that it has led officials in New Delhi to call Israel 'its most important strategic partner in the Middle East', and has similarly led Shimon Peres to describe India as 'Israel's best friend in the region'.[10]

Indeed India's growing strategic alliance seems contradictory to its strengthening ties with Iran, Israel's hostile enemy in the region. Israel regards Iran as a state sponsor of terrorism and has joined the United States in taking a harsh position against Tehran and isolating the country diplomatically, especially in wake of Iranian President Mahmoud Ahmadinejad calling for Israel to 'be wiped off the map'. Thus the question that naturally arises is how does India's relationship with Israel affect its relationship with Iran and vice versa. The answer lies within the fact that India is pursuing a twin track of bilateral relations with Iran and Israel, the region's two bitterest enemies. Indo-Israeli and Indo-Iranian ties operate independently of one another, and India's close ties with one country have not precluded New Delhi from pursuing a robust, strategic relationship with the other.

It is critical to note that Iran, obviously known for its anti-Israeli policies, has been surprisingly accommodating of India's new alliance with Israel. Indeed, when India normalized relations with Israel in January 1992, Iran was the only Middle Eastern country to express its disapproval. Since then, however, Israel has never been a factor in Indo-Iranian relations. Tehran has consciously avoided making its ties with New Delhi a hostage to the Israeli angle, perhaps because it is secure enough in the depth and strength of its relationship with India. On the other hand, however, Israel has expressed its concern and apprehension to New Delhi over India's growing ties with Iran, especially with regards to transfer of military technology.[11] India seems to have been able to effectively assuage Israel's concerns and the Israelis seem willing to also accommodate India cultivating ties with Tehran so long as New Delhi does not advance Iran's anti-Israel platform. Israel has instead begun to try to dissuade India away from Iran more subtly. Israel expressed no opposition to the US-India nuclear deal and the Jewish lobby's assistance in getting the deal. Congressional approval represented, at least in part, a carrot-and-stick strategy towards New Delhi with regards to Iran. How long India can continue balancing both Iran and Israel is still to be seen, yet the fragile complexity of India's foreign policy towards the Middle East was effectively illustrated this past summer following Israel's attack on Lebanon over the kidnapping of an Israeli soldier by Hezbollah in Lebanon.[12]

The Washington Angle

As mentioned above, the approval of the US-India nuclear deal by the US Congress heralds a new phase in US-India relations. Yet the shadow of New Delhi's relationship with Tehran loomed large over the negotiations of the deal, and even threatened to kill the bill within both chambers of Congress. Many US lawmakers wanted to make American approval on the deal contingent upon India severing its ties with Iran, or at the very least, upon assisting Washington in reining in Tehran's nuclear ambitions.[13] India explicitly rejected the first demand, making it abundantly clear that it would not permit its foreign policy to be dictated by the world's sole superpower. At the same time, New Delhi has made clear that it does not wish to see nuclear weapons in the Middle East and has aligned itself with international efforts to bring Tehran into compliance on the nuclear issue. As a result, in what many saw as a test of India's true loyalties, New Delhi voted with the United States on an International Atomic Energy Authority (IAEA) resolution finding Iran in noncompliance with its international obligations over its nuclear programme.[14] While Iran initially seemed to take offence at New Delhi's action, with some reports claiming Iran would cancel the pipeline deal, Tehran reversed its position, claiming plans for the pipeline remained unchanged. New Delhi once again voted against Iran in the UN in February 2006, but that vote was most likely motivated by New Delhi's desire to see the US-India nuclear deal move forward, especially after the US ambassador to India, Robert Mulford, explicitly linked India's vote to passage of the nuclear deal. But once again, shortly afterwards, India reaffirmed its friendship with Tehran, and the two countries even conducted joint naval exercises in March 2006, prompting criticism from many members of Congress and even from officials within the Bush administration.

The course New Delhi pursued during this period reveals two very critical facts about India's foreign policy directives. The first is that the India is unlikely to abandon its strong relationship with Iran for the United States or for any external power.[15] India's large energy needs, coupled with India's extremely sensitive perception of any possible encroachment on its sovereignty together makes this clear. Second, however, is that India's relationship with Iran will not, at least for now, adversely affect the deepening relationship between Washington and New Delhi. The Indian government seems to have so far been able to effectively ameliorate Washington's concerns in this capacity. There has been no clearer indication of this than the US-India nuclear bill. After several members of Congress threatened to kill the deal or drastically amend it to force India to change its relationship with Tehran, the Bush administration, led by Secretary of State Condoleezza Rice, sent a letter to lawmakers in both chambers of Congress urging them not to scuttle the deal over the Iran issue and assuring them that India stood with the United States with regards to Iran's nuclear programme. Every amendment that sought to force India to act against Iran was ultimately defeated and the only provision included in the legislation that addressed the India-Iran nexus was a non-binding resolution that stipulated that the president would have to give Congress an annual report on India's efforts towards curbing Iran's nuclear programme.[16] For now, Iran seems to be an issue upon which Washington and New Delhi agree to disagree. Whether or not India has a role to play as mediator between Iran and the United States is a possibility that has not yet been explored but one that could be potentially promising. Either way it is clear that Washington will be monitoring the growing Indo-Iranian alliance carefully; it will be interesting to see how the successful passage of the US-India nuclear deal affects this complex calculus over the coming months and years.

Conclusion

P.R. Kumarswamy observed that 'no other country in the world offers India the political and economic assets Iran does', and it is evident that the strengthening ties between New Delhi and Tehran are more than just an ephemeral alignment of interests.[17] As India and Iran continue their cooperation in a number of important areas, there is no doubt that the rest of the international community will continue to watch the growing relationship between New Delhi and Tehran with much interest. Plans for the proposed gas pipeline between India and Iran continue to move forward, with construction projected to begin by July 2007. Just two-and-a-half weeks before Congress gave the US-India nuclear deal final approval, Tehran once again reaffirmed its close ties with India.[18] The Indo-Iranian alliance has had far-reaching and significant implications for not only New Delhi and Tehran, but also for Washington, Jerusalem and Islamabad. India has done an effective job in manoeuvring between all these different countries, pursuing bilateral relationships with the United States and Israel while simultaneously engaging in a policy of soft containment against its regional rival, Pakistan. While it seems clear that the Indo-Iranian partnership is here to stay, what the future has in store for the friendship is yet to be seen. What is certain, however, is that any relationship between the world's largest democracy and most notorious theocracy will have a profound impact on not just South Asia and the Middle East, but the rest of the international community.

Ronak Desai is a recent graduate from Johns Hopkins University. He has written extensively on South Asia and the Middle East.

NOTES

1 Stephen Blank, 'The Indian-Iranian Connection and Its Importance for Central Asia', *Eurasianet.org* 12 March 2003.
2 C. Christine Fair, 'The New Delhi-Tehran Axis', *Atlantic Monthly Journal*, July/August 2003.
3 See Former Indian Ambassador to the United States Lalit Mansingh's speech at the George Washington University, Spring 2004.
4 Ibid.
5 Text of Declaration at <http://meaindia.nic.in/declarestatement/2003/01/25jd1.htm>.
6 Indian Ministry of Commerce and Industry, *Annual Report 2005–2006*.
7 'India-Iran Relations and U.S. Interests', *CRS Report for Congress*, 2 August 2006
8 Rizwan Zeb. 'The Emerging Indo-Iranian Strategic Alliance and Pakistan', *Central Asia-Caucasus Analyst*, 12 February 2003.
9 See also P.R. Kumaraswamy, "India and Israel: Prelude to normalization", *Journal of South Asian and Middle Eastern Studies*, vol. 19, No.2, Winter 1995
10 See Parag Khanna "The Axis of Democracy", *The National Interest* <http://www.inthenational interest.com/Articles/Issue16_17/vol1issue1617Khanna.html>.
11 P.R. Kumaraswamy, 'The 'Strategic Partnership' Between India and Iran', *Asia Program Special Report*, April 2004.
12 The conflict between Israel and Lebanon in the summer of 2006 put India in an awkward and precarious position. In order to reaffirm its ties with Israel, New Delhi condemned the abduction of IDF soldiers. Yet, as the violence escalated in the Middle East, the Indian government found itself under overwhelming domestic pressure and later condemned excessive Israeli violence in Lebanon. The conflict painfully exposed the delicacy and fragility of India's balancing act in the region.
13 'Lawmakers Concerned about US-India Nuclear Trade Deal', *Washington Post*, 15 November 2006.
14 'India Denies Iran Vote Pressure', *BBC News*, 25 September 2005.
15 'India-Iran Relations and U.S Interests', *CRS Report for Congress*, 2 August 2006.
16 Shortly after President Bush signed the bill into law on 18 December 2006, he attached a signing statement that said he reserves the right to ignore certain safeguards built into the legislation, further diluting the provision.
17 P.R. Kumaraswamy, 'The "Strategic Partnership" Between India and Iran', *Asia Program Special Report*, April 2004.
18 Iranian Foreign Minister Manouchehr Mottaki told reporters on 17 November 2006 that 'India is "indeed a big and great country" which will conduct its relations with other countries based on its national interest' and even went as far as saying 'we do not want to have good relations with India that will be against any third country.'

China's Ties with Iran and Its National Interests

FENG WANG

China and Iran have witnessed a stable and consistent improvement of their bilateral relations since the Iranian Revolution in 1979, especially in the post-Cold War era. The oil/gas trade and economic cooperation have become the key components between the two countries in recent years. China's need to meet its increasingly large energy needs is one of the main considerations for China to enhance its ties with Iran. Nevertheless, there are no pivotal national interests for China to pursue in Iran. China has thus to make a painful choice in the event there is no further room to mediate and negotiate over the Iranian nuclear issue in the future.

The Steady Improvement of Bilateral Political Ties

The People's Republic of China and Iran established diplomatic relations on 17 August 1971. Iran recognized the former as 'the sole legal government of China'. Since then, bilateral political ties between the two countries have grown steadily. During the 1970s, many high ranking Chinese and Iranian leaders exchanged visits. For example, Chinese Foreign Minister Ji Pengfei, Vice-Premier Li Xiannian, Foreign Minister Huang Hua and President Hua Guofeng visited Iran, while the then Iranian Empress Farah Pahlavi, Iranian Princess Ashraf Pahlavi and Iranian Prime Minister Hoveyda were welcomed in China.

With the establishment of the Islamic Republic of Iran in 1979, the political ties between China and Iran stepped into a new phase. From 1979 to 1988, important visits from some Iranian high-ranking officials took place. Among them, the landmark visit of Hojatolislam Hashemi Rafsanjani, then Iranian Majlis (Parliament) Speaker from 27 June–7 July 1985 laid the foundation for a stable and long-lasting cooperation between the two countries. His visit, accompanied by more than eighty religious and political figures, was the first visit to China by a senior Iranian leader since 1979. During his visit, a memorandum on economic, industrial, technological and scientific under-standing, an agreement on projects for the building of dams, cold-storage facilities, etc., as well as a two-year cultural agreement were signed. The two countries also agreed to cooperate in making peaceful use of nuclear industries.

From 1989 to the present day, political relations between Iran and China have been further strengthened. Many important exchanges have taken place between the highest-ranking officials. Six of these visits were particularly significant: the visit of Iranian President Ayatollah Syed Ali Khamenei to China in May 1989, the visit of Iranian President Rafsanjani to China in September 1992, the visit of Chinese President Yang Shangkun to Iran in October 1991, the visit of Prime Minister Li Peng to Iran in late October 1991, the visit to China paid by Iranian President Mohammad Khatami in June 2000, and the visit to Iran paid by Chinese President Jiang Zemin in April 2002. During these frequent visits, the two sides repeatedly recognized the necessity for further greater cooperation between the two countries in various fields, especially in economic and technological spheres.; Views on regional and international issues were exchanged, such as the need to establish a just and reasonable multi-polar international political and economical order, the opposition of the interference in the internal affairs of other countries by any country. Many Memoranda of Understanding and agreements in various fields had been signed, thus strengthening the bilateral ties between the two countries. For instance, during Khatami's visit to China, a 'Sino-Iranian Joint Communiqué' as well as five agreements concerning cultural exchange, invest-ment, tourism, energy and mineral cooperation were respectively reached. And during Jiang Zemin's visit to Iran, China and Iran signed another six agreements regarding energy, communication, sea transportation, cultural exchange and bilateral commercial spheres.

As well as the highest-level visits, many delegations on all levels and in various fields have been frequently exchanged, and the Shanghai Cooperation Organization (SCO), an intergovernmental organization established by China, Russia and four other countries in 2001, has become an additional mechanism for China and Iran to contact each other. Iran has been admitted into the SCO as an observer since June 2005. President Mahmoud Ahmadinejad hence attended the sixth summit of the SCO in the mid-June 2006 in Shanghai and then met with Chinese President Hu Jintao.

The Rapid Expansion of Mutual Economic Ties

With the joint efforts of the high-ranking visits and various delegation exchanges, the economic, trade and technological cooperation between China and Iran has greatly improved since 1971. In addition, the Ministerial Joint

Committee for Cooperation on Economy, Trade, Science and Technology, which was set up in 1985, has also been an important and effective motivating mechanism for China and Iran to expand their economic and trade ties. Up to the present, this committee had been convened for twelve sessions, in 1985, 1986, 1987, 1988, 1990, 1991, 1993, 1995, 1997, 1999, 2002 and 2004. During these sessions, many specific agreements on economic and technological cooperation have been signed. This committee has also made efforts to accelerate existing contracts' implementation.

Yet from 1971 to the end of Iran–Iraq War, the volume of trade between China and Iran was limited. In 1978, it reached $118 million from the minimal $5.98 million in 1971.[1] And the average trade volume between the two sides remained only about $200 million in the period 1971–88.[2]

Nevertheless, trade volume has grown rapidly ever since. It had risen from $178 million[3] to $1.347 billion between 1989 and 1999,[4] growing by over eight times within ten years. Chinese exports to Iran reached $663 million[5] from $131 million,[6] while Iranian exports to China reached $684 million[7] from only $47 million[8] during the same period, each increasing respectively by 5 and 14 times.

Furthermore, the two countries have witnessed an historical expansion of the bilateral trade from 2000 to 2005. The annual trade volume between the two countries reached $2.48 billion, $3.3 billion, $3.742 billion, $5.623 billion, $7.45 billion and $10.084 billion over that five-year period.[9] Exports from China to Iran were annually $0.713 billion, $0.889 billion, $1.396 billion, $2.316 billion, $2.555 billion and $3.297 billion from 2000 to 2005, while exports from Iran to China were $1.773 billion, $2.424 billion, $2.346 billion, $3.307 billion, $4.91 billion and $6.787 billion over the same period.[10] And during the period January–July 2006, the trade volume reached $7.918 billion.[11] China is thus ranked the No.2 importer of Iran (with Japan the No.1) and one of the main exporters to Iran.[12] The major commodity exports from China to Iran have expanded to electrical machines, complete sets of equipment, chemical and textile products, metals, cereals, oil foodstuffs and medicines, in return for Iran's crude oil, mineral products and rolled steel, etc.

The oil trade has remarkably become the key component among their mutual economic ties since the mid-1990s. From 1993 to 1999, China's import of crude oil from Iran rose from $95.13 million to $519.8 million.[13] That is to say, the oil trade made up nearly three-quarters of the total Iranian exports to China in 1999. And from 2000 to 2004, China's import of crude oil from Iran reached $1.464 billion, $2.069 billion, $2.04 billion, $2.636 billion and $3.536 billion respectively, which is over 80%, 85%, 86%, 80% and 72% of China's total import from Iran and 10%, 18%, 15.76%, 14% and 10.4% of China's import of total crude oil from the world during the same period of time.[14] Iran has thus become the No.1 crude oil supplier for China.[15]

In addition, in order to purchase more crude oil and natural gas from Iran, China not only welcomed Iran's investment and participation in its own domestic oil development, but also tried to participate in oil and gas exploration and development in Iran itself. In 1997, China agreed with Iran on a joint-venture project to upgrade a refinery in Guangdong Province in China to expand its capacity to process Iranian sulfa-containing crude. During Khatami's visit to China, the two sides agreed to further expand oil and gas cooperation. In January 2001, the two countries reached another agreement worth $13.252 million to explore oil in Zavareh, Kashan, 205 km south of Tehran. Meanwhile, a contract was also signed for an upgrading of refineries in Tehran and Tabriz , and for the Neka project to build an oil terminal port in the Caspian Sea.[16] And in 2004, China signed a $70 billion oil and natural gas agreement with Iran, which is China's biggest energy deal with the later. China accordingly will buy 250 million tons of liquefied natural gas over 30 years from Iran and develop the giant Yadavaran field, while Iran is also committed to export 150,000 barrels per day of crude oil to China for 25 years at market prices after commissioning of the field.[17] The oil and gas cooperation between the two countries is likely further expanded in the future.

Apart from the above, other aspects of economic and technological cooperation between the two countries have improved substantially. Project contracts totalling $1.804 billion[18] during 1984–99 were signed between Iran and China. The contracts signed in 1999 were valued at $114.08 million.[19] The contracted projects have covered thermoelectricity, hydroelectricity, dam designing, non-ferrous metals, geology and mining, light industries, fisheries, underground transport systems, etc. The following are some of the larger deals. One $573 million contract was signed in 1995 to build a subway and electrified railway in Tehran. Under this contract, Chinese companies undertook the project by supplying equipment and facilities such as cars, locomotives, signalling devices and electricity supply. Another big deal is a joint investment of $350 million to explore the Sungun Copper mines in the province of Eastern Azerbaijan in 1996. Until 2005, the number of Chinese enterprises invested in Iran in various fields including oil and gas has reached over sixty.[20]

Accompanying the project contracts is financial and credit cooperation between Iran and China. In 1996, Chinese banks and monetary institutions decided to provide a $270 million loan as buyer's credit for the Tehran subway system. And during President Khatami's visit, China agreed to allocate $500 million to construct the fourth line of Tehran metro system. During 1990–2000, China has placed a credit of $1.7 billion at Iran's disposal. However, Iran's direct investment in China is minimal. During 1992–99, the total volume of Iranian investment was valued at only $5.138 million.[21]

China's Policy Towards the Iranian Nuclear Issue

Since the exposure of Iran's secret nuclear sites in the middle of 2002, China's stance over this issue has three implications. First, China supports the maintenance of the international Nuclear Non-Proliferation Treaty (NPT) and opposes the proliferation of nuclear weapons, that is, China hopes Iran 'would not' develop nuclear weapons. Secondly, China agrees that Iran has the right to use nuclear energy for peaceful purposes according to the rules of the NPT. Yet, it is Iran's obligation to demonstrate that its nuclear technology will be used exclusively for civil purposes . Third, the Iranian nuclear issue should be peacefully solved through political and diplomatic efforts.

China has accordingly tried to play a proper role in resolving this issue, especially since Mahmoud Ahmadinejad was elected president and resumed Iran's uranium enrichment activities. China's endorsement of the six-nation package of proposals and the UN Security Council Resolution 1696, for example, which calls on Iran to stop its uranium enrichment activities and return to the negotiation table, is evidence of China's committment. China is also joining hands with the other four UN Security Council Permanent Members and Germany to consider whether or how to take additional measures since Iran has failed to comply with Resolution 1696. However, in the meantime China still calls upon, or mediates among Iran and all relevant parties, to resume as soon as possible dialogue and negotiations for the proper solution to this issue, and not to take any steps that will harm diplomatic efforts that may lead to complications or even loss of control.

However, as compared with other four Permanent Members and Germany, China has been able to play a limited and less important role in solving this issue. It is Iran and the US who has dominated the process of this issue, while Britain, France, Germany and Russia have played more positive and important roles than China.

China's Considerations Towards Iran

Iran is regarded by China as a regional power in the Gulf and the Middle East due to its strategic position in the oil-rich Gulf, as well as its size, its abundant oil resources and unique status in Muslim countries, hence it is important for China to realize some of its national interests. That's the main reason for China to persistently seek friendly ties and expand its economic and technological cooperation with Iran as mentioned before. The need to create a peaceful and stable international environment conducive to China's economic development through mutually friendly cooperation, the desire to establish a fair and reasonable multi-polar international political and economical order and counterbalance outside pressures, etc., are obviously some of the important interests that China has pursued in Iran.

In addition, the necessity to expand its overseas markets and suppliers of raw materials, in particular crude oil and natural gas suppliers, began to dominate China's consideration toward Iran around the middle of the 1990s. China has become a net oil importer since 1993 due to its rapid developing economy and its expanded domestic energy needs. Yet China has had more and more difficulty meeting this need by itself. And by the year 2010, the gap between China's predicted oil production and consumption would reach 90–177 million tonnes.[22] China's increasing reliance on oil imports is unavoidable in the future. As compared with the situations of oil and gas suplies from other likely sources, namely Indonesia, Malaysia, Mexico, Venezuela, etc., the oil and gas supplies in Iran and the Gulf have considerable advantages: they are the most abundant reserves, and relatively the cheapest, on the world oil market. Besides, there is a wider gap between these countries' oil output and consumption. Iran and the Gulf thus might be China's ideal long-term suppliers of crude oil and natural gas.

Compared with China, counterbalancing the Western powers, mainly the US, is Iran's primary objective in its considerations toward China. Alienation and confrontation have been the fundamental aspects of the relationship between Iran and the US since 1979. Although several attempts have been taken by both sides to approach each other, for example, President Khatami's initiative for the 'Dialogue between Civilizations', no genuine progress in a resumption of direct contacts between Iran and the US had been achieved in the past decades. Such hostility or tension has been detrimental to Iran's critical national interests. Iran thus must reduce such insecurity through seeking friendly relations with other countries, including China. The expansion of its energy exports to the rapidly emerging Asian-Pacific market, including China, may in some degree serve Iran's above political purpose.

Nevertheless, China has no vital national interests to pursue in Iran. The vital interests for China lie in, for example, seeking huge investment, advanced technologies and huge market essentials for its modernization, to safeguard its territorial integrity, to maintenance its stability and security, etc. These interests decisively drive China to place its highest priority on its relations with the developed countries including the US and its neighbours. It is also exactly the US and China's neighbours, instead of Iran, who have been the main trade partners with China.

The above considerations also determine the stance that China has taken concerning the Iranian nuclear issue. It is essential for China to maintain good ties with the developed countries as well as Iran in the meantime. Namely, China is not able to afford losing its ties with the developed countries in order to maintain a good relation with Iran. But China is obviously also reluctant to improve good relations with the developed countries at the expense of its profitable ties with Iran. However, in the event that there were no further possible room to negotiate over the Iranian nuclear issue in the future, there might be no choice for China but the endorsement of sanctions against Iran.

Feng Wang is a Research Fellow at the Institute of West-Asian and African Studies at the Chinese Academy of Social Sciences in Beijing.

NOTES

1   Deng-Ker Lee, 'Peking's Middle East Policy in the Post-Cold War Era', *Issues & Studies*, Vol. 30 No. 8, August 1994, p. 93.
2   Ibid.
3   Yitzhak Shichor, 'China's Economic Relations with the Middle East: New Dimensions', in P.R. Kumaraswamy (ed.), *China and the Middle East: the Quest for Influence*, New Delhi/Thousand Oaks, CA/London: Saye Republications Inc., 1999, p. 193.
4   *Almanac of China's Foreign Economic Relations and Trade*, 2000/2001, Beijing: China's Economics Publishing House, 2000, p. 541.
5   Ibid.
6   Shichor, 'China's Economic Relations', p. 183.
7   *Almanac of China's Foreign Economic Relations and Trade*, p. 541.
8   Shichor, 'China's Economic Relations', p. 183.
9   *Almanac of China's Foreign Economic Relations and Trade*, p. 502.
10 Xinhua News Agency, 18 April 2002, Tehran <http://www.china-drilling.com/vi.php?id=220 64>; <http://www.fmprc.gov.cn/chn/wjb/zzjg/-xybfs/gjlb/1444/default.htm>.
11 <http://www.fmprc.gov.cn/chn/wjb/zzjg/xybfs/gjlb/1444/default.htm>.
12 EIU: *Country profile, Iran, 2006*, p. 61.
13 *Almanac of China's Foreign Economic Relations and Trade*, various years.
14 Ibid. (2001/2002), p. 657; <http://www.china-drilling.com/vi.php?id=22064>. *China Commerce Yearbook*, 2005, *China Commerce and Trade Press*, Beijing, p. 831.
15 <http://english.china.com/zh_cn/news/china/11020307/20041101/11942873.html>.
16 FBIS-CHI, 13 January 2001; FBIS-NES, 12 January 2001.
17 <http://english.china.com/zh_cn/news/china/11020307/20041101/11942873.html>.
18 Shichor, 'China's Economic Relations'; *Almanac of China's Foreign Economic Relations and Trade*, 1998/1999, 1999/2000, 2000/2001.
19 *Almanac of China's Foreign Economic Relations and Trade*, 2000/2001.
20 <http://www.fmprc.gov.cn/chn/wjb/zzjg/xybfs/gjlb/1444/default.htm>.
21 *Lexis-Nexis*, 22 June 2000; *Almanac of China's Foreign Economic Relations and Trade*, 1998/1999, 1999/2000, 2000/2001.
22 Shichor, 'China's Economic Relations', p. 188.

A Pragmatic *Rapprochement*: Turkey and Iran after the Iraq War 2003

ASIYE ÖZTÜRK

In the last few years a remarkable *rapprochement* has taken place between Ankara and Tehran. Several Iranian ministers visited Turkey, while Prime Minister Erdoğan travelled to Tehran in July 2004 and December 2006. The opening of the Tabriz–Erzurum gas pipeline showed that both countries are seeking to extend their economic cooperation. The pipeline diplomacy is also of interest to Europe, as it will allow Iranian and Caspian gas to reach European markets and diversify European energy supply. Bilateral trade between Turkey and Iran doubled from $2.5 billion in 2003 to $5 billion in 2005. In addition to the steadily growing bilateral trade ties, a more or less strong political dialogue has evolved too.

The new geopolitical realities after the Iraq War 2003, and changing security perceptions on both sides, are some of the determining factors for the new relationship. This article will attempt to explain the new dynamics in the Turkish-Iranian relations after the Iraq War and argues that the growing political ties between Ankara and Tehran are an important asset for the European Union.

The 1990s: Confrontation versus Cooperation

Ever since the Islamic Revolution in Iran (1979), Turkish-Iranian relations have been described as 'controlled tensions'.[1] The main axis of Turkey's relations with Iran has been to downplay ideological differences and to emphasize pragmatism. In this sense, in the 1990s, Turkey pursued a double-tracked policy towards Iran: on the one hand, Turkey kept a distance from the mullahs' regime due to ideological concerns; on the other hand, economic ties were developed, particularly in the energy sector.

The main source of friction between Turkey and Iran was Tehran's support for the Kurdish separatists (PKK) and its alleged attempt to 'export' its brand of Islam in order to jeopardize Turkey's secular system.[2] Furthermore, Iran was one of the main opponents of the military cooperation between Turkey and

Israel, which deepened during the last decade and did allow Israel to use Turkish territory for military purposes.[3] In addition, an intense rivalry has grown up between the two states to fill the power vacuum in Central Asia and the Caucasus which has arisen after the collapse of the Soviet Union. Turkey tended to support the sovereignty of the newly independent states und to spread the secular 'Turkish model' promoted by the European states and the US. In addition, Turkey sought to gain access to the energy resources of the Caspian basin for boosting its own strategic importance, which must be seen in the context of increasing energy demands in Europe. Due to its limited political as well as economic capabilities, Turkey was made to cooperate with the US, which was facilitated due to their overlapping interests. Iran, also, wanted to profit from its geo-economic location and aimed to become the main export route between the world economies and the Caspian region. In the light of the Dual Containment strategy of the US, Iran was forced to ally itself with Russia.[4] At the end of the 1990s one could say that the predicted rivalry between Ankara and Tehran was much less volatile than expected. The main reason was Turkey's increasing domestic energy demand, which made her too dependent on Russia and which increasingly threatens the future of her security of energy supply. This resulted in a search for a considerable reduction of this dependency through cooperation with Iran, which coincided with Iran's desire for integration and participation in regional trade.

September 11th and New Strategic Realities

As mentioned above, the main rationale for the enhanced cooperation between Turkey and Iran was the new security environment created by the terrorist attacks on Washington and New York. After September 11th, the regional parameters in the 'Greater Middle East' changed fundamentally. The war in Afghanistan (2001) changed the balance of power and the regional dynamics in Central Asia in favour of the US and to the disadvantage of Russia.[5] The war in Iraq (2003) provoked nothing less than a geopolitical revolution, over-throwing the balance of power in the whole region.[6] With the occupation of Iraq, the US became a regional power and an adjoining neighbour of Syria, Turkey, Iran, Saudi Arabia and Kuwait. For the regional security system, this meant that in the medium term no other regional state could become a dominant regional hegemonic power. Furthermore, the arms race or the use of power politics to keep the status quo or to protect national interests was obsolete. In this sense, they were obliged to take political measures (or arm themselves with nuclear weapons) to preserve their regional positions and to keep the balance steady. As a consequence thereof, the security perceptions of Turkey and Iran changed, too.

Changing Security Perceptions after the Iraq War

The war in Iraq was a turning point in Turkey's regional politics. The year 2003 also became an *annus horribilis* in the Turkish-American relationship when Turkey refused to let US troops deploy from its territory during the Iraq War. For the first time since their close (military) partnership evolved in the early 1940s, the 'strategic consensus' between the two NATO allies was seriously put into question. The main reason was that their interests and their perception of threats with regard to Iraq were diametrically opposed to one other.[7] Turkey's main objectives were to preserve the territorial integrity of Iraq and to avert the emergence of an independent Kurdish state. Her main concern was instability in Iraq, because the US's war plans came at a time when South Anatolia was recovering from long-lasting sectarian violence between the PKK separatists and Turkish law enforcement forces. The PKK was disarming and Turkey was preparing new reforms to extend minority rights for the Kurdish population. Within this context, Turkey perceived the risk of an independent Kurdish state flourishing in northern Iraq as a threat to its social and territorial integrity. However, Turkey preferred to solve the problem in cooperation with Iraq's neighbours. For that purpose, she launched a diplomatic offensive and initiated several meetings in Istanbul to discuss ways of avoiding a potentially destabilizing war in Iraq with the foreign ministers of Iran, Saudi Arabia, Jordan, Egypt and Syria. At the same time, Ankara demanded the right to send troops into Iraq – officially to avert a humanitarian crisis in northern Iraq, to hold back a flood of refugees into Turkey, and to prevent terrorists crossing the border. In contrast to Turkey's interests, regime change in Iraq was the stated goal of US foreign policy. Washington, while officially rejecting the idea of an independent Kurdish state, was flirting heavily with the Iraqi Kurds – the only ally within Iraq on whose support the US could rely. Turkish demands for sending troops into northern Iraq threatened to open a 'war within the war' and hugely compli-cated the American military strategy. But from the viewpoint of Ankara, the US's policy neglected vital Turkish security concerns.[8]

Iran also opposed military action in Iraq. Like Turkey, Iran perceived an independent Kurdish state as a threat to its territorial integrity with regard to its own heterogeneous population and the Kurdish majority.[9] The toppling of Saddam Hussein in Iraq may have removed one security threat to Iran, but this has been replaced by the greatly increased US military presence. As mentioned above, Washington has became a neighbour of Iran. This fact must be seen in the light of the revived 'Axis of Evil' rhetoric of the neoconservative Bush administration, which included besides Iraq also Iran and Syria. The US accused Iran of financing international terrorism and acquiring weapons of mass destruction as well as pursuing a nuclear weapons programme. Iran was isolated and stigmatized as 'rogue state', while pressure on it increased steadily. This caused Iran to rethink its foreign policy strategy.[10] The new security environment forced Iran to search for regional partners and triggered a re-evaluation of its relationship with Turkey. The determining factor was the rationale of their Kurdish policy and their common goal to maintain a certain degree of regional stability. The security consultation between Turkey and Iran in course of the war acted as a catalyst and paved the way for deepening the economic and political dimension of the bilateral ties. In the political sense they found common cause in the fight against terrorism which means that Iran assured its support against the PKK and included the organization in its list of terrorist organizations.

It is obvious that this cooperation with Iran generated tensions in the Turkish-American relationship at a time when Turkey was trying to mend fences with its NATO ally. Turkey was aware of the fact that the US was the only power capable of preventing PKK terrorists along the Turkish-Iraqi border from penetrating the country. Washington held the sword of Damocles over Turkey and was able to play its 'Kurdish card' whenever it wanted to put pressure on Turkey.

The Iranian Nuclear Crisis and Its Impacts on Turkey

Although the origins of the Iranian nuclear programme date back to the 1970s, the crisis began in the year 2002, when Iran declared that it would resurrect its nuclear programme for peaceful purposes.[11] Iran signed the Nuclear Non-Proliferation Treaty which guarantees the right to use nuclear technology for civilian purposes. But Washington perceived the resumption of the nuclear programme as a threat to its vital own security interests, as well as to the security of its closest ally in the Middle East, Israel.. US politicians and Israel felt vindicated by the rising anti-American and anti-Israeli rhetoric and propaganda of Iran. Both accuse Iran of developing nuclear weapons – a charge Tehran denies.

In general, Ankara concedes every state the inalienable right to use nuclear energy for peaceful purposes. But Turkey shares European and US concerns regarding Iran's nuclear ambitions, being worried about a nuclear-armed Iran and also disapproving of the intransigent manner in which Iran seeks to solve the crisis. Certainly in the short run, Turkey is protected by the NATO umbrella. But a nuclear-armed Iran would unsettle the regional military balance, provoke a (nuclear) arms race and destabilize the whole region.[12] Furthermore, possession of nuclear arms would strengthen Iran's position in the Turkish-Iranian relationship and would be a serious challenge to Turkey's national security. On the other hand, the countries' bilateral relations are enjoying their best phase in political as well as economic terms since 1979. Turkey does not want to lose the Iranian market and sees Iran as a gate to the East (primarily Central Asia). Similarly, Turkey is Iran's gate to the West. As a neighbour, Turkey would derive much more benefit from a peaceful solution of the crisis, than any other country.

Therefore, in terms of political strategy, Turkey's thinking is more in line with the European policy of conditional engagement than the US, which is firmly convinced that the best way to deal with Tehran is through isolation and pressure. Like the EU, Turkey agrees that many aspects of Iran's behaviour are unacceptable, but does not believe that Tehran acts irrationally or that its behaviour is unchangeable. As a general rule, states seek to acquire a nuclear capability as a deterrent. Hence, the possible motives of the Iranian leadership have to been evaluated within the regional context and from an Iranian viewpoint. A closer look at Iran's security environment could maybe lift the veil of secrecy shrouding Tehran's nuclear ambitions: it feels encircled by US troops in the East as well as in the West and is stigmatized as 'rogue state'; it is faced with nuclear powers in the East (Pakistan and India) as well as in the West (Israel) and two of the currently main trouble spots, Iraq and Afghanistan, on its borders.[13] Iranian foreign policy seems to be a genuine nightmare.

Taking into consideration the new quality of Turkish-Iranian relations and also Iran's need for regional partners, Turkey's growing political as well as economic ties with Iran could be an asset for the EU, which wants to expand its influence and to persuade Iran to continue with the negotiations. In the last few years Turkey gained access to Iranian leaders and extended its communication capabilities. Even though Turkey is far away from playing the role of the major broker in the nuclear crisis between Iran and the West, it can serve as a facilitator and as a bridge – over the allegedly unbridgeable gap between the West and Iran.

Asiye Öztürk is a doctoral student at the University of Bonn.

NOTES

1   Cf. Bülent Aras, *Turkey and the Greater Middle East*, Istanbul, 2004, pp. 67–85. For an overview of the historic roots of the Turkish-Iranian Relations: Gökhan Çetinsaya, 'Essential Friends and Natural Enemies: The Historic Roots of Turkish-Iranian Relations', *Middle East Review of International Affairs*, Vol. 7 No. 3, September 2003, pp. 116–32.
2   Cf. Özden Zeynep Oktav, 'Changing Security Perceptions in Turkish-Iranian Relations', *Perceptions*, Vol. 9 No. 2, June–August 2004, pp. 103–17.
3   According to Noam Chomsky, before the Iraq War some 10 per cent of the Israeli Air Force was permanently based in Turkey; Mark Gaffney, 'Will Iran Be Next?', *Alternatives*, Vol. 2 No. 2, Summer 2003, pp. 196–216, 214.
4   The Dual Containment strategy of the Clinton-Administration led the United States to prevent

both Iraqi and Iranian expansion. The strategy was initiated in order to curb the economic development of both states. During this period, Iran strengthened its regional partnerships through a series of long-term bilateral and trilateral economic agreements, in particular with Russia, India and China.

5   Cf. Victor Mauer, ‚Die geostrategischen Konsequenzen nach dem 11. September 2001', *Aus Politik und Zeitgeschichte*, B 3–4/2004, pp. 18–25, 19.

6   Cf. Volker Perthes, ‚Geopolitische Grundlinien im Nahen und Mittleren Osten', *Blätter für deutsche und internationale Politik*, 6/2004, pp. 683–94.

7   Cf. Gökhan Çetinsaya, ‚Irak'ta Yeni Dönem, Ortado?u ve Türkiye', Ankara, 2006, pp. 38ff.

8   Cf. Henri J. Barkey and Ellen Laipson, 'Iraqi Kurds and Iraq's Future', *Middle East Policy*, Vol. XII No. 4, Winter 2005, pp. 66–76.

9   Cf. Oktav, 'Changing Security Perceptions', p. 111.

10 Cf. Bülent Aras, 'Turkey and the GCC: An Emerging Relationship', *Middle East Policy*, Vol. XII No. 4, Winter 2005, pp. 89–97, 90ff.

11 Cf. Bruno Tertrais, 'The Iranian Nuclear Crisis', in Ivo Daalder, Nicole Gnesotto and Philip Gordon (eds), *Crescent of Crisis. U.S.-European Strategy for the Greater Middle East*, Washington, DC, 2006, pp. 25–40.

12 Ian O. Lesser, 'Turkey, Iran and Nuclear Risks', *Turkish Policy Quarterly*, Vol. 3 No. 2, Summer 2004, pp. 81–98, 87ff.

13 Cf. Oliver Thränert, ‚Der Iran und die Verbreitung von ABC-Waffen', *SWP-Study*, August 2003, pp. 16–21.

PART II
The War to Come

Race and the Nuclear Race: Anti-Semitism in Iran

ELDAD J. PARDO

The *Shoah* was unprecedented. We hoped it would become a warning sign, not a precedent. Yet we have been proven wrong, it did become a precedent.[1]

Yehuda Bauer

It was with shock and disbelief that observers reacted at first to the brutal rhetoric employed by Iranian President Mahmoud Ahmadinejad towards Israel and the Jews. After all, the Islamic Republic aspires to become a nuclear power and is engaged in a nerve-straining tug-of-war with the international community, and especially the Western powers, on this matter. Arguably, the way to convince international public opinion that there is no room for alarm would be to project an image of a responsible, rational and peaceful power.[2] And yet, counter-intuitively, Ahmadinejad first calls to wipe off the map the State of Israel, a long-time member of the United Nations, and then denies that the Holocaust ever existed, suggesting, consequently, to transfer all Israeli Jews to Germany and Austria, whose peoples had perpetrated the Second World War bloodbath.[3] These and similar declarations and moves[4] soon became an effective argument for those considering Iran to be an irrational rogue state that should not be trusted with a nuclear weapon. The usage of such brutal anti-Semitic language is puzzling indeed. Not that the Iran of Khomeini, the founding father of the 1978/79 Revolution, had ever been pro-Israeli, or that Jew-hatred is absent of Iranian rhetoric. Indeed, Iranian animosity towards Israel springs from the core of the regime's worldview, according to which the conflict between the Islamic Republic and Israel is pivotal to the larger conflict between Islam and the imperialist West and its materialistic culture.[5] Not that a degree of anti-Semitism had not been a permanent fixture in the culture of pre-Revolutionary Iran, the golden age of Israeli–Iranian relationship, but the timing and the dramatic exacerbation of the rhetoric beg for an explanation.[6] Similarly, the central enigma, that of action rather than rhetoric, remains. Why, in the first place, does Iran go nuclear? Iran's straightforward answer is that it is none of anyone's business; Iran can become a nuclear power if it so wishes and this is enough by way of explanation. Moreover, the project is misleadingly represented as a civil enterprise having to do with economic considerations and scientific research.

And yet why? Why nuclear and why anti-Semitic? I will presently try to propose some answers to these questions and examine whether these answers amount to a coherent explanation for the Iranian policy.

Why Nuclear?

A quick look at the land of Iran reveals a country rich in energy resources in the forms of oil, natural gas and exposure to sun and wind. Iran does not need nuclear energy. It also does not need nuclear weapons. Why should it? With a territory more than three times larger than France and 73 times larger than Israel,[7] with huge annual income from oil and with a young, large population of 70 million, Iran should feel lucky, safe and secure. After all, most of the world's countries, including some owning cutting-edge technologies, do not even consider acquiring nuclear weapons. Take Canada or Indonesia, Mexico or Argentina, Sweden, South Africa, South Korea, Japan, Germany, Italy or Turkey as well as all the Arab countries – all are doing just fine without nuclear weapons. Here and there one can see the use of nuclear reactors for energy, but this will be in the most industrialized and energy-poor countries like Japan, a country committed to peaceful economic development, which does not even allow itself, officially at least, to hold a standing army.

The inconsistencies of the Iranian style of dialogue make the riddle of 'why nuclear?' even more intractable. A leading Middle East expert opined last year in a closed meeting that, in all likelihood, the Iranians themselves have no clue as to really why they are following this dangerous path.

I will presently propose a theory of the motivations lying behind the Iranian regime's determination to plunge into the nuclear race and then return to the anti-Semitic rhetoric, examining to what extent does it fit with Iran's nuclear policy.

Defending Iran

At its early stages, the program was probably meant to defend Iran. Naturally, there is no information available regarding the closed meetings leading to the fateful decision to launch Iran's nuclear program. One thing is clear: this decision was taken long before Ahmadinejad had become a household name around the world. In fact, it was probably around the time of Khomeini's death that Iran decided to become a nuclear power. Yet preparations began earlier. According to reports by Director General Mohammad ElBaradei to the International Atomic Energy Authority (IAEA) Board of Governors, Iran received drawings of a centrifuge sometime 'around 1987'. The source was probably Pakistan's Dr Abdul Qadeer Khan. Additionally, 'between 1985 and 1995 about 2000 components and some subassemblies had been obtained from abroad.'[8] The first known purchase of Chinese uranium shipment to Iran goes back to 1991. In 1995 Iran and Russia signed a contract to build again the Bushehr nuclear reactor.

Assuming that thoughts precede action, one must seek the initial motivation in the early stages of the Iran–Iraq War. Iranians invading into Iraq were facing stiff and effective resistance from the Saddam Hussein regime. The Iraqis, benefiting from Arab and international support and holding fast to their national cohesion and military spirit under their determined and ruthless leader, did not refrain using WMDs against Iranian fighters and Kurdish insurgents. Iran was locked into a state of mind of victimhood in an 'imposed war' (*jang-e tahmili*), yet clinging to a Shiite-*jihadist* spirit requiring the elimination of Saddam, the *Yazid* of the time. This re-enactment of Shiism's formative myth, the slaughter of Imam Hussein by Yazid's army on the plain of Kerbala in the year 680, provided the mental framework leading Khomeini to sacrifice Iran's youth, typically in their early teens, in suicide operations, by the hundreds of thousands. It was not until it became absolutely clear that there was no way to victory that Khomeini agreed to 'drink the cup of poison' in 1988 and accept a cease-fire.

This long traumatic war left a deep scar on the Iranian psyche. The decision of going nuclear should be evaluated against the background of this ordeal. Iran at the time began its long and arduous process of coming to grips with the after-effects of the multiple traumas of the previous years: the pre-Revolutionary crisis, the frenzy of the Revolution, including the public executions and the civil war, and, finally, the Iraqi invasion and the long, bloody and senseless prolongation of the war that ensued. Arguably, it was this war, alongside the Islamic Revolution's isolation in the international arena (albeit largely self-inflicted), that brought the Iranian leadership to conclude that weapons of mass destruction should form an essential component of the country's national security. The way Iraq ended the war, gaining the upper hand militarily, financially and diplomatically, after using WMDs with impunity, is especially important in this respect.

Iraq, however, soon squandered this hard-won achievement in the ill-calculated August 1990 invasion of Kuwait. The Kuwait War of 1991 ensued, leading to a humiliating Iraqi defeat at the price – from the Iranian point of view – of a more pronounced US presence in the Gulf. The Iranians did not focus on the bright side: the containment of Iraq and the American presence were probably factored in as one more reason for acquiring a nuclear deterrence. Likewise, the Middle East peace process was interpreted in Tehran as a curse rather than a blessing. Similarly ignored were sincere Israeli and American efforts to help Iran during the Iran–Iraq War in the covert operation which became famous as 'Irangate', or the 'Iran-Contra affair'.[9] This secret deal and the decision, by Tehran's hard-liners, to leak the story to the Lebanese newspaper *Al-Shira'*, constitute another example that Iran's security problems are typically self-induced.[10]

The Iranian security dilemma, then, includes a built-in paradoxical component. While the discourse is defensive, 'defending the revolution', 'defending Iran', 'defending Islam' and so on, what must be defended is the right to conduct jihad. Accepting weapons from the US, even in an emergency such as the Irangate example, entails the acceptance of limits on jihad. Iran sees itself as leading the world of Islam, as well as of the entire world of the underprivileged (*mostaz'afin*), in its struggle against America (the Great Satan) and Israel (the Small Satan). In that sense, Iranian ideology is similar to that of its Sunni rival, Al Qaeda. The latter's title means 'the Base', namely a safe place from which to launch *jihad*, a holy war to conquer infidel lands. The 'Holy Regime' (*Nezam-e Moqaddas*)[11] of the Islamic Republic of Iran with its affiliate groups, such as the Lebanese Hezbollah (Party of God), also considers itself as a 'base', without using this term, but for exactly the same cause. Hence, for example, in a recent speech Hasan Nasrallah, Hezbollah's leader, explains that the inclusion of Hezbollah in playing a role in Lebanese politics was meant by the Americans to distract his movement from its jihadist duties. Curtailing the right to conduct jihad, namely the right to attack others, is an act of aggression (*'udwan*, in Arabic), entailing the right for self-defence.[12]

Defending the Regime

What ensued is that defending Iran meant defending a specific policy, or, better still, defending the regime which conducts this policy. In other words, if defending Iran means defending the policy of keeping Iran, the 'base', from which jihad is to be launched, one in fact defends the regime and its jihadist policy and not the country and the people of Iran. This obviously makes sense also sociologically and politically. An Islamically fashioned never-ending conflict with outsiders keeps the Islamic regime relevant. The constant situation of emergency helps in confronting its growing unpopularity and allows the ruling class to stick to its prerogatives. Looking from the vantage point of today's rather-hated regime, then, a nuclear deterrent makes perfect sense, ideologically and pragmatically. It allows for an ongoing jihad, benefiting from its advantage as solidifying the system, without being exposed to a threat of a counter-attack. The nuclear weapons, alongside oil's easy cash flow, are two 'equalizers' allowing the unpopular regime of a basically weak country to retain power, without having to go through the necessary but dangerous ordeal of true reform.

Yet, going nuclear was not a simple decision. Khomeini, following Islamic law and being a believer in revolution brought about by God-fearing masses rather than by technological gadgets, never resumed the Bushehr Siemens nuclear project initiated by the Shah Mohammad Reza Pahlavi in the 1970s. Indeed, the death of Khomeini in 1989 signaled a sea change in the worldview of the Revolutionary leadership, previously partially planned ahead for by Khomeini.

Anticipating a legitimacy crisis emanating from his nearing death and the humiliation of accepting a cease-fire in the Iran–Iraq War (1988), Khomeini placed Iran in a controversial and antagonistic position with his *fatwa* (religious edict) calling for the assassination of British writer Salman Rushdie. The purpose of this move was probably to nip in the bud a possible moderation of the Revolution, when his own charismatic presence and religious authority were no longer extant. Other moves preparing the regime for an era of diminished legitimacy had been the massacre of thousands of political prisoners as well as the sacking of Khomeini's deputy and heir Ayatollah Ali Montazeri who objected to this atrocity.[13] Moreover, the constitution was changed to guarantee first, that Khomeini's successor would possibly be a cleric of lesser stature such as the current supreme leader Khamenei and second, that the actual powers given to the supreme leader would be much stronger as compared to the Majlis (parliament) so as to offset Khamenei's lack of charisma.

Khomeini was right. From the early 1990s on, the Iranian government suffered from a perennial legitimacy crisis at home.[14] In other words, the Iranian leadership of the early 1990s had to buy off the support of the people by showing palpable achievements, especially in the economic sphere. Power was valued more than spirit. Yet, this policy, epitomized by the business-oriented Rafsanjani, suffered from many a setback due to the never-ending tug-of-war between 'hard-liners' and 'pragmatists'. The early 1990s, with the collapse of the Soviet Union, and spread of democracy throughout Eastern Europe, Latin America and Africa, marked the beginning of a 'globalization' and the dawn of a semi-messianic Age of Wonder, bringing with it a belief in the 'End of History' and the 'New Middle East'. While Israel at the time was on the winning side, Iran was among the losers.[15]

At this point, the nuclear project changed its significance. No more threatened by the Iraqi enemy, it became part of a more pragmatic way of bolstering the embattled regime. Both 'hard-liners' and 'pragmatists' could share the quiet and slow nuclear dream, fully contracted to the Revolutionary Guards Corps. Similarly, the jihadi project, known as 'exporting the Revolution', continued at an unobtrusive pace, mainly through Iranian support of bodies such as Hezbollah and Hamas, but also through various propaganda and terrorist activities around the world.[16]

The victory of the reformist camp, beginning with the 1997 election of President Mohammad Khatami, enhanced this pragmatic line. Mending fences with the Arab world and Europe, getting even closer to Russia, China and Japan and, finally, exchanging winks with the United States, Iran also played rather supportive roles in facilitating the unilateral Israeli pullout from Lebanon and the US invasion of Afghanistan, while keeping international terrorism to the necessary minimum. In Iran itself a spring of comparative openness flourished.

Imperial Dreams: Leading the Islamic *Ummah*

Yet, the jihadist, and anti-Semitic, policy was neither buried nor forgotten. Many leading reformists subscribed to the destruction of Israel and were hesitant in getting close to the US. The hard-liners kept their grip on the real power positions. The Iranian educational system continued to teach millions of young Iranians that their country is a superpower destined to lead all the Muslims and the Third World against an 'arrogant West', led by the United States. Social and economic changes were effectively blocked by the hard-liners, using legal and illegal means alike. The nuclear project advanced in leaps and bounds far from the attention of public opinion. The general feeling remained that the Revolution had been a failure, the country's economy in a shambles, its leadership corrupt, its women, ethnic groups and religious minorities discriminated against, its opposition voices and free press steadily crushed and stifled, its people suffering from widespread unemployment, prostitution, drugs and AIDS. No spirituality or self-sacrifice could be traced among the ruling elite, whose legitimacy continued to plummet.

Hence, the Revolution, once seen as unstoppable, as destined to attract the masses of the Middle East, bring about the destruction of both the US and the USSR and rule the world, just did not deliver. While the USSR did disintegrate, it was clear by then that the spiritual power of the Revolution could not guarantee the survival of the regime. Freedom, equity and prosperity were distant as ever.

All these put together led to disillusionment from the reformist camp and the victory of Mahmoud Ahmadinejad in 2005, bringing in its wake a new revolutionary zeal and the revival of the concept of suicide martyrdom.[17] The pan-Islamic dream of a trans-national *Ummah* led by Iran as the centre of a prospective Muslim empire, resurfaced. Moreover, Ahmadinejad, a close ally of the Supreme Leader Ali Akbar Khamenei, managed to buttress the presidency like never before and become a true power broker.[18] Luck helped. Oil prices had been rising since 2000, the Israeli–Palestinian Oslo peace process had turned into an endless violent conflict, the post-9/11 United States struck Iran's enemies, first the anti-Iranian Taliban regime in Afghanistan and then Saddam Hussein's Sunni and secular regime in Iraq. While US forces surround Iran, their vulnerability, especially in Iraq, serve as a chip in Iranian hands. Moreover, US policy is directed at containing Iran's support for terrorism, especially its successful effort to scuttle the Middle East peace process, as well as its nuclear project. This policy is not directed against Iran or its regime *per se*, though a *rapprochement* with America, the 'World Arrogance', let alone with the 'abomination' of the Zionist Entity, may undermine the regime's *raison d'être*.[19] In other words, the enemy of the Iranian government is normalization, that is to say, cultural, political and legal freedoms. Iran has no real enemies, yet it has Islamically worded imperialistic ambitions. In former President Khatami's terminology, Iran strives to destroy the American plan of the 'Project of American Great Middle East' (*tarh-e khavarmiyaneh-ye bozorg-e amrika*) and replace it with a 'Project of Islamic [read Iranian] Great Middle East' (*tarh-e khavarmiyaneh-ye bozorg-e eslami*).[20]

Hence, the nuclear weapon, originally sought after as a means to defend the motherland, was later transformed into a tool to protect the regime and, as of late, has become part of an imperialistic/pan-Islamic design. While the exporters of the Revolution during the 1980s used ideological fervour alongside terrorist networks, the new Iranian hegemonic thrust relies on technology, know-how, intimidation and funding. Iran has shifted from 'Soft Power' to 'Hard Power'. Worshipping weapons and sophisticated technology goes hand in hand with the martial spirituality offered by these neo-Revolutionaries. This spirituality is bolstered by *redemptive anti-Semitism*, namely fighting the Jews as the source of all evil.[21]

Why Anti-Semitic?

The mounting attacks against Israel, and the Jews, since Ahamdinejad's election in May 2005, raises the question of whether the Iranian regime, in its core, subscribes to obscurantist-racist dictates. In other words, are we dealing with an irrational ideological commitment or is it a tactic intended to project an image of irrationality and defiance meant to sow fear and enhance deterrence?

Basics of Anti-Semitism

A typology of anti-Semitism is not easy to outline since the phenomenon is extremely wide in time and space. Yet, I will attempt here to propose a user-friendly framework that will allow us to come to grips with the phenomena we are dealing with. *Webster's Dictionary* defines the anti-Semite as 'one who discriminates against or who is hostile toward or prejudiced against Jews'. Lehrman, warning against confusing anti-Zionism with anti-Semitism, defines the characteristics of the latter as 'hate of Jews as such, a belief in a world Jewish conspiracy, a belief that Jews created Communism and control Capitalism, that they are inferior as a race and so on'.[22] To these one could add the blaming the Jews for the crucifixion of Jesus Christ, poisoning the Gentiles, using children's blood for rituals, as well as being greedy, stingy and evil.

This writer assumes that vilifying Zionism as such could be comfortably defined as a subcategory of anti-Semitism, namely an offshoot of hating the Jews as such. Zionism is the Jewish nationalism. One definition of national-ism is the '"devotion to the interests or culture of a particular nation'. Another is 'aspirations for national independence in a country under foreign domin-ation'.[23] Both definitions, and so Zionism, are rather widespread natural phenomena in the modern age, hence singling out Zionism for condemnation without the rejection of all nation-states and national movements is hardly distinguishable from hatred of Jews as such.

Moreover, Iranian and Arab propaganda is packed with 'classic' anti-Semitism of the Jew-hatred type as well.[24] Iranian anti-Zionism sees the Jews of Israel as thieves, stealing the lands of the Muslim Palestinians, an act that sits well with typical anti-Semitic stereotypes such as greed and trickery. In fact, Iranian Supreme Leader Ayatollah Khamenei describes the Israelis as group of evil thieves and robbers who gathered in Palestine to conduct their evil deed from there.[25] At times, as in Khatami's famous 1998 interview with CNN, Israel is attacked while criticism is directed to the 'adventurers' who joined the Great American Civilization, which was originally Puritan and religious.[26] On other occasions, such as the arrest of 13 Iranian Jews in Shiraz in 1999 falsely accused of espionage for Israel, the victims were non-Zionist Jews. Also, in 1994–95, the official newspapers, *Ettelaat* and *Jumhuri-ye Eslami*, published 150 chapters of *The Protocols of the Elders of Zion* and, in the year 2000, a special edition of the book was released with a special section connecting the Elders of Zion with Israeli policies.[27]

Why do people hate the Jews as such? Animosity toward different groups, especially minorities, and hostility toward others in general are widespread. Yet is there anything particular about Jew-hatred?

Two dimensions providing partial explanation for the anti-Semitism phenomenon will suffice for our purpose. The first is the 'structural dichotomy' of the Jewish condition and the second is the 'chosenness-related jealousy'.

The 'structural dichotomy' of the Jewish condition emanates from the simultaneous existence of two opposites. On the one hand, the Jews project power and high visibility and, on the other, their scant numbers and tiny territorial base suggest vulnerability. The high visibility flows from a disproportionate impact on world affairs exerted by a minority among the Jews traditionally attracted to fields related to the communication and transfer of knowledge. These fields range from banking to marketing to the media to politics to academia, in which Jews are active often with a cosmopolitan touch, coupled with a cultural drive for changing society (*Tikkun Olam*, the embetterment of the world). The success of Jews in these fields could be partially attributed to historical reasons such as existence through the ages as a 'global tribe', developing skills especially suited to an 'information age', and having an interest in systems limited in their ability to abuse the powerless and the 'other'.

Paradoxically, it is this high visibility of the few which feeds the image of all Jews as a conspiratorial group, scheming behind the scenes and controlling world powers for its hideous agenda. The vulnerability aspect of this 'structural dichotomy' derives from lack of a stable territorial base and low numbers: Jews form a fraction of a per cent of world population. The Zionist project generating a vibrant and very visible nation-state as an antidote to anti-Semitism did create miracles in adding security to the Jews. Still, the high-visibility attached to the Israeli success story has come with a pathetic size, territorially and demographically, and therefore invites aggression. The anti-Semite, then, antagonized by the highly visible 'other', identifies a weakness in the ranks of his demonized enemy and believes his prey can be attacked with impunity. What follows is that the same 'structural dichotomy' works for both anti-Zionism and anti-Semitism. Zionism created a state that is powerful and globally networked, and yet tiny, geographically and demographically, making Jew-hatred and Israel-hatred, phenomenologically parallel.[28]

The 'chosenness-related jealousy' has to do with Judaism's tenet according to which God has chosen the Jewish people, as His people. While almost every people or religion on earth share with the Jews the concept of being special, particular and better than others, only the chosenness of the Jews gained such fame. There are a number of reasons for this occurrence, including the Bible stories serving as a basis for Christianity, Islam and modern nationalism.[29] Also, the presence of Jews in the media and politics no doubt contributed to this awareness. Since the chosenness of the Jews appears to contradict the assumed chosenness of others, jealousy ensued. Jew-hatred is elicited by the inexplicable success in modern times of some Jewish individuals and projects. One such project is Zionism: the dramatic return to their original homeland in Palestine of millions of often-persecuted Jews from their diaspora in Christian and Muslim lands since the late nineteenth century. The establishment of Israel as a powerful state on lands 'belonging' to the Arab or Muslim nation unleashed similar feelings to those entertained by many Europeans in the nineteenth and twentieth centuries. In Europe, rage emanated from those who saw Jews shedding their discriminated status and occupying powerful positions 'belonging' to Christians. In the Sunni Middle East, rage was first directed toward local non-Muslims becoming full subjects with the help of European powers as well as toward European hegemony itself. The anger against Zionism followed with the post-First World War international decision to grant a homeland for the Jews in a territory 'belonging' to Islam.

Jealousy against the Jews is coupled by jealousy and hate of the West. The success of the Christian/secular world in the modern age is considered to be a source of shame to Muslim peoples. Israel is hated for its success as well as for the success of the West. The Holocaust, putting the Jews in the camp of the West's victims, breaks the paradigm. Therefore the Holocaust, or its actual significance, is so often denied. Doomed to oblivion are the role of Muslims, Arabs and Persians, in the Holocaust as well as their role in persecution of Jewish communities in Palestine and elsewhere.

To conclude this point, hatred of Jews is structural, them being 'powerful' and 'weak', dangerous and vulnerable. Jealousy emanating from a sense of failure is cardinal in hatred of the Jews and of the West. The Jews and Israel often symbolize the West and its values, either as its tool or as its controlling manipulator.

Iranian Anti-Semitism

Persians and Jews go back a long way together. Persia's Jewish community is the oldest diaspora on earth, if we include the Babylonian exile, turning, seventy years after the destruction of the first temple in Jerusalem in 586 BCE, into part and parcel of the Persian Empire. It was Cyrus the Great who allowed the Jews to come back to the Holy Land and it was in the Persian court that Jewish statesmen such as Ezra could operate. The story of Esther displays a fragile Jewish destiny oscillating between destruction and salvation, a recurring pattern in the history of Iranian Jews. To this day, the shrines of Mordechai and Esther serve as a site of pilgrimage for both Jews and Muslims. Jewish collective memory, focusing on the benevolent Cyrus and the Book of Esther's happy ending, ignores the persecution of the Sasanian period (246–651).

If we fast forward to the comparatively tolerant Muslim Iran, beginning with the seventh century CE, we encounter a civilization in which Jews and

Judaism have a defined place as protected (*dhimmis*), or the People of the Book (*Ahl al-Kitab*), meaning that they are discriminated against yet tolerated. Jews and the Israelites are described in Islamic texts in various shades of tolerance and intolerance.[30] In that sense, Islam is not different from other faiths characterized by 'the ambivalence of the sacred', in the sense that they include many traditions, which can be interpreted and applied as one chooses.[31] Hence, a famous Islamic tradition (*hadith*) confirms that the Jews will be massacred on Resurrection Day. If a Jew will hide that day behind a rock, that rock will call the nearest Muslim and exhort him to kill the hiding Jew.

Shia Islam tends to be traditionally less tolerant than Sunni Islam towards religious minorities, including Christians, Zoroastrians, Jews, Sunni Muslims and Bahais. With the advent of the Safavid dynasty (1501–1722), the suffering of the Jews in Iran, as well as that of other minorities, takes a turn to the worse.[32] Religiously, Shiism puts more emphasis on separation between believers and non-believers and connects them to rules of impurity. Hence, for example, a Shiite Muslim could marry a non-Muslim woman. A Jew, being impure (*najis*), could not drink water from a Muslim's cup and could not touch vegetables in the market. The Iranian clergy was often more independent from the government, some would argue, a genuine representative of the masses.[33] Hence, enforcement and persecution were stricter the central government was weaker and the power of the clergy rose. Cases such as massacres and forced Islamization, extremely rare elsewhere, were not uncommon in Iran and other Shiite-controlled countries.[34] The clergy spearheaded the campaign against granting equal rights to non-Mulims during the Constitutional Revolution (1906–11).

The reign of the Pahlavi dynasty (1921/5–1979) in Iran is considered the 'golden age' of Iranian Jewry, which, especially after the Second World War, enjoyed an unprecedented degree of security and prosperity. There were exceptions, however. Mainly, one should point to the *rapprochement* between Reza Shah and Nazi Germany, which brought Iranian Jewry to the verge of annihilation.[35] Iranians, considered Aryans by the Nazis, became a centre for German subversive and anti-Semitic activities throughout the Middle East. Anti-Semitism continued to exist also during the 'happy years' after the Second World War.[36] Some Iranian Jews told me that, on a personal level, hatred of Jews before the Revolution was greater than after it. Paradoxically, Israeli pro-Iranian policies, at times idealistic to the degree of naïveté, was taken as supporting the Shah's dictatorship and added fuel to Jew-hatred, and, of course, also to the continuing enmity of the Revolution to Israel.

Anti-Semitic utterances and calls for the destruction of Israel are a recurring motif in post-Revolutionary Iranian rhetoric. Ahmadinejad is not the first to call for the destruction of Israel. In fact, one may argue that he echoes his master's voice. Ayatollah Khamenei, the supreme leader of the

Islamic Revolution, called in 2000 in his own voice to destroy Israel.[37] The reformist President Mohammad Khatami said in 2001 that 'the presence of Israel in the region is the main stumbling-block to settlement of Middle East crisis.'[38] Objecting to the peace process, Khatami's idea of how to get rid of the Zionist 'racist terrorist regime' is through a vote that will dismantle Israel democratically with the votes of diaspora Palestinians.[39] The commitment to destroy Israel unites the reformists and the hard-liners. It is a cross-regime policy with no exception. One of the leading reformists, Hojatolislam Ali Akbar Mohatashemi-Pur, is considered a great supporter of Hezbollah and Hamas. He argues that Israel epitomizes the traits of pre-Islamic barbarism (*jahiliyyah*) as described by the Holy Koran, namely 'massacre, war, bloodshed and plunder'.[40]

The most well-known among these types of declarations is that of Ali Akbar Hashemi Rafsanjani, the head of the powerful Expediency Council, who had served twice as president as well as the speaker of the Majlis. Rafsanjani called Israel an artificial state, perpetrating numerous crimes, and suggested using a nuclear bomb to finish it off. While such a bomb will leave nothing on earth in Israel, he reasoned, a possible retaliatory attack on the Muslim world would cause nothing but a limited damage. Rafsanjani, speaking on the occasion of '*Qods* (Jerusalem) Day', 14 December 2001, warned of possible breakout of a Third World War between the Muslims and the 'powers of colonialism'.[41]

Rafsanjani's words are typically anti-Semitic in the way described above. While warning the Western powers, believed to be controlled behind the scenes by an international Zionist network, the threat is directed toward the territorially tiny Israel believed to be vulnerable to a nuclear attack. A closer look at Rafsanjani's words discloses a typical paradox one finds in Iranian argument. On the one hand, the world powers, the US and Britain, are seen as being manipulated by the Zionists. On the other hand, the State of Israel is in itself an 'artificial' being, created for guarding the colonial powers' interests in the post-colonial age. He also makes a distinction between Jews and Zionists, arguing that Zionism is harmful to the Jews. The invitation to a nuclear holocaust extended to the Israeli Jews and the anti-Jewish Iranian discourse, again, suggests that we are dealing indeed with anti-Semitism and not some political criticism of this or that aspect of Israeli policy.

Khomeini began his famous book *Velayat-e Faqih* (*The Guardianship of the Jurist*) with an attack on the Jews, although his main enemy is the secular West. Khomeini, albeit a high-level Shiite cleric, was inspired by the ideology of the Sunni Muslim Brothers, whose anti-Western ideology was imbued with the worst of European anti-Semitism, making Islamism to this day an anti-Semitic construct.[42] Anti-Semitic literature is popular in Iran. It is true, though, that Jews in the Islamic Republic, unlike the Bahai for example, are generally not targeted and do comparatively well as long as they know their place. Officially, Iranian enmity is directed to the 'abomination' of the State of Israel and not towards the Jews as such, who, evil by nature notwithstanding, should be tolerated as impure dhimmis.

Iran as a Persian-Shiite country has a number of other special sensitivities as regards Israel. The first is the question of victimhood. The Shiites see themselves as a victimized, tortured group. Their formative myth revolves around the suffering of Imam Hussein and his family, symbolizing the Shiite ordeal in history. In fact, in Shiite tradition the ancient Israelites, suffering slavery in Egypt, are seen as Shiites or proto-Shiites, a concept reminiscent of some aspects of the Catholic Church's theology.[43] The Jews, especially after the Holocaust, compete with the Shiites for the much-coveted title of the world's quintessential victims. A major ideological pillar of the Islamic Republic is to protect the 'downtrodden on earth' (al-mostaz'afin fi al arz). The Jews, with their diaspora and Holocaust, form an ideological competitor. Similarly, the question of chosenness: the Shiites see themselves as the chosen Islamic group, al-firqa al-najia, the only group to be saved and reach Paradise. Jews, and their concept of chosenness, are a nuisance.

Another cultural problem for Persians is the ability of Jews to handle Western cultural domination. For the Persians, the struggle with Western culture represents a second humiliation after their absorption and adoption of the religion and civilization of the invading Arabs. While Jews hold on to their original Scripture, written in Hebrew, Persians subscribe to the Arabic Koran. These cultural conflicts were never resolved and Persians continue humiliatingly to be attracted to their conquerors' culture. It is not far-fetched to assume that Arab–Jewish wars in which Arabs are killed provide a source of satisfaction for some sophisticated Persians. Finally, Iranians see Israel as much more dexterous than themselves in handling the West. The Holocaust is often seen in this context of the ability of the Jews, on the one hand, to keep their own culture and, on the other, to manipulate the West into supporting them by playing the guilt card. Iran, seeing itself too as a victim of Western imperialism should learn from Israel.[44] On another level, the economic success of Israel, like that of Japan and other non-Western countries, has been both a source of jealousy and a role model for imitation for Iranians. While Japan is now a role model for Iran, Israel served as such a role model in the 1960s.[45] For example, Israeli guardianship of the cause of world Jewry, an idea put forward by Theodore Herzl (the Roman negotiorum gestio),[46] may have served as a role model for Ayatollah Khomeini in assuming the role of guardian of the world's Muslims, a role now revived by Ahmadinejad. The Israeli success in combining Judaism and democracy is still a challenge to Iran, which has failed in its combination of Islam and modernity. The current solution, religiofascism, is facing, no doubt, a disaster.

The denial of the Holocaust, largely seen as a contribution of Ahmadinejad's to Iranian anti-Semitism, is in fact a major motif in Iranian propaganda in recent years. Litvak, who meticulously researched the topic, provides a wealth of references from Iranian media, beginning from 1998. Major outlets for Iranian Holocaust denial are the English-language newspapers, *Tehran Times* and *Kayhan International*, suggesting that Holocaust denial is instrumental and strives to drive a wedge between Israel and its Western allies, especially the Europeans who suffer from guilt. The historically wrong assumption there is that Israel was established on the basis of a 'Holocaust scheme' concocted during the Second World War by Jews and Americans. Hence, denial of the Holocaust is equivalent to denying Israel's right to exist and advancing the jihadi global campaign led by Iran. Litvak also sees Holocaust denial as meant to humiliate the Jews by ignoring their major tragedy and, moreover, by blaming them for worse behaviour than the Nazis, that is, worse than their own executioners. One can also add that over-emphasizing the Holocaust blurs the Middle Eastern origins and culture of the majority of Israeli society. Iran developed strong relations with Western Holocaust deniers, although there are two differences between the two parties. The first is that on the Iranian side one sees the most respectable figures denying the Holocaust – among them the Supreme Leader, the president, former presidents and so on – while the Holocaust deniers from the West are marginal racists. The other difference is that the Iranians, on the whole, rebuke the Nazis as cruel secular racists, while the Westerners, being racists themselves, strive to exonerate the Nazis. Still, the parties' shared hatred of Israel and the Jews helps them to cooperate.[47]

The *Shoah* is almost impossible to grasp. Similarly intangible is the revival of Jewish nationalism and the ingathering of the Jews to their historical homeland in Palestine. Both phenomena defy common wisdom and are often wrongly tied together in a simplistic cause-and-effect argument. While the horrors of the Shoah help Israel to explain its cause, the Jewish national movement was launched much earlier, in the late nineteenth century, as a culmination of decades-long historical processes invigorating the Jewish connection to Palestine. The Zionist project had been adopted by the international community already in 1920. Moreover, the destruction of European Jewry, the demographic hinterland of the Zionist movement, almost knocked dead the yet-to-be-born Israel. And yet, Israel and the Holocaust are tied together in people's imagination to this day in a cause-and-effect connection. The Iranians are no exception. Jalal Al-e Ahmad (1923–69), the most prominent Iranian publicist of the twentieth century who immensely inspired the leaders of the Revolution, visited Israel in the early 1960s, as a great admirer of the Jewish state. Al-e Ahmad argued, in an article following his visit, that Israel was miraculously created by prophet-like visionaries. As for the Holocaust, he points out that:

> [Israel] constitutes a coarse embodiment of the expiation for the crimes the Fascists committed during the war years in Dachau, Buchenwald, and the other furnaces. Note well: this is a crime, and the perpetrator of this crime is the Westerner, and I, the Easterner, have to pay the price. The Westerner exports the capital and I, the Easterner, provide the base. In this matter, too, I have much to say. Still, if we want to know the truth about all of this, Christianity made of Israel a curtain that it stretched out to separate itself from the world of Islam so that I would not see the real danger — that is how the Arabs were kept preoccupied.
>
> Another point is that, granted, I do see in this overly-displayed martyrdom of the Jews following the war massacres, the other side of the coin of Fascism, and basing [one's argument] upon a racism that has taken its place. And yet, I also see that if you are fated to become a base [for the West], you should learn from Israel for it has sold itself expensively! ...
>
> Israel is the quintessential example of how to do business with the West. With spiritual might of a martyrdom how can we milk Western industries, how can we collect reparations, and how can we use the West's investment monies for the development and prosperity of the country. Thus, for the price of few mornings of political dependency, we can consolidate our newly-established undertaking.[48]

The above text, written in 1964, suggests that the view of Israel taking advantage of the Holocaust for 'milking' the West is not a new one. Also, the belief that local Muslims pay the price for the Holocaust, a Western crime, and that Israel is a Western bridgehead serving the West to divert Muslims' rage away from itself are also not new. Similarly, the view of Iran as a victim of the West deserving reparations. Al-e Ahmad's conclusion was that the Muslims should learn from Israel the spirit of martyrdom (*shahadah*), how to make the best of a bad situation and then to adopt democracy and socialism with religious colouring. Khomeini and his followers, including current Supreme Leader Khamenei, read and hated this passage.[49] Khomeini's heirs use now similar analyses to rob Israel of its Holocaust 'asset', destroy it altogether and then move on to attack the West.

Litvak's well-documented findings suggest that the current Iranian Holocaust denial is part of a well-orchestrated campaign dating back at least to 1998. This campaign draws from ideas that had been circulating in Iran for at least four decades. I, therefore, reach the following two conclusions. The first is that Ahmadinejad's Holocaust-denial campaign is not new, and hence should be assessed as a well-thought-out Iranian policy aiming to achieve specific goals. My second conclusion is that we should treat on a similar basis the 'Wipe Israel off the Map' campaign as well as other moves. In other words, Ahmadinejad is neither a new Hitler nor a weirdo. He is a member of a sophisticated power group, most likely led by Supreme Leader Khamenei, and his anti-Semitic gambit should be seen as reflecting not personal eccentricity, but a well-calculated move.

The Tactical Dimension

The widespread presence of ideological rhetoric among Iranian leaders have often led observers to speculate whether these fiery declarations are just a mask covering pragmatic policies aimed at achieving national goals.[50] Indeed, a close look at Iranian policy in various domains betrays a commitment to the Iranian national interest at the expense of the declared 'Muslim' agenda. Some would even narrow down this agenda to that of Iranian Persians, forming 50 per cent of Iranian populace, or the ruling clergy.[51] One classic example is the support given during the 1990s to Armenia, a Christian state, and not Azerbaijan, a Shiite Muslim state, in the war between the two. Another example is the diplomatic umbrella extended by Iran to Russia to shield it from the wrath of Muslim states around the world for its power policies against the Muslim insurgents in Chechnya.[52] In both cases Iranian national interest took precedence, in the former, containing potential separatist tendencies in Iranian Azerbaijan and in the latter, maintaining good relations with Moscow, in the nuclear field as well as in various mutual interests, especially in and around the Caspian Sea.

Arguably, the animosity toward Israel remains the only domain in which a 'pure' Revolutionary policy is still possible and needed. It is possible, because Iran pays virtually no price in terms of damage to its national interests, especially if we assume that the Iranian-American chasm could have been bridged had there been a will for doing so in Iran. The loss of Israeli know-how in a variety of fields pertinent to Iranian needs should also be factored in, in light of the wealthy and multifaceted relations between Tehran and Jerusalem up to 1979 and Israel's reputation in supporting Third World countries. Yet, all in all, such a loss is negligible, assuming that the rampant anti-Israeli fervour in the rank and file of the ruling elite is genuine.

Accordingly, the Iranian anti-Israeli and anti-Semitic stance can be explained also as a pragmatically useful tactic. On the one hand, the price to pay for these policies is taken to be minimal. The benefits, on the other hand, are tangible. The first is enhancing the regime's legitimacy at home by continuing an endless state of emergency. Second, keeping the Arabs 'busy' with the Israeli front, hence offsetting a potential strategic danger, as was manifested during the Iran–Iraq War. Third, blocking the threat of regional waves of democracy, which could endanger the stability of the regime by raising the hopes for freedom at home by women, the youth and ethnic minorities, especially Arabs, Azeri-Turks, Kurds and Baluchis. There were a number of potential beginnings for regional democratic waves in recent years: the 1990s with the Oslo process, the post-9/11 American invasions of Afghanistan and Iraq and the American pro-democracy campaign, the rise of 'demo-Islam' in Turkey and the Syrian pullout from Lebanon. The US campaign for democracy in the Middle East, much ridiculed by many an analyst, continues to this day ignite the imagination and stir debates within Iran, even under Ahmadinejad and sometimes also on official media outlets.[53]

A fourth benefit for the anti-Zionist/anti-Semitic policy relates to advancing Iran's hegemonic ambitions by projecting the image of the defender of Islam in the Arab world. It is worth noting, however, that Iran has probably overplayed this card. The Sunni Arab countries, especially the regimes of Saudi Arabia, Egypt and Jordan, but also many elites across the Arab world, are genuinely worried of the prospect of a Shiite Iranian hegemony in the guise of pan-Islam. Contributing factors to these fears are Iranian persistence to become a nuclear power and its success in igniting recurring Israeli–Arab conflagrations most notably the last war between Israel and Hezbollah in July 2006. The magnitude of their military involvement in Lebanon, alongside their control of large sections of Iraqi Shiites, proves to be worrisome indeed.

Finally, the fifth potential benefit for the Iranian use of anti-Semitism is to drive a wedge between the West and Israel. The Iranians, as was manifested in Ahamadinejad's letters to US President George Bush and to Germany's Chancellor Angela Merkel, are trying to free the West from its guilt toward the Jews.[54] In other words, they deny the Holocaust in order to legitimize the revival of Western anti-Semitism by rejecting the dominant narrative of its horrible consequences. This policy is not unlike that of the original. Nazi Germany's Second World War propaganda successfully tried, on the one hand, to weaken the morale of the Western Allies by propagating that they are 'controlled by the Jews' who are solely to blame for the war. On the other hand, the Nazis executed the destruction of mainly European Jewry, following a genuine ideology of 'redemptive anti-Semitism', undisturbed by foreign criticism. Nazi propaganda managed to embarrass the Allies to such a degree that any aid to the Jews, in word and actions, was deemed counter-productive. Similarly, current Iranian anti-Semitism serves both to isolate Israel and to de-legitimize the effort to defend the West against a nuclear fascist-Islamic aggression by presenting it as another nasty Jewish trick.[55]

Similarly, driving a wedge between the West and Israel does not mean that either is not considered a real target. The extremely serious preparation of the Lebanese Hezbollah for a war against Israel in the years 2000–06 suggests a commitment which goes beyond mere lip service or even solidarity. The destruction of Israel seems to be indeed a strategic priority for Iran, and cannot be judged merely as a tactic.

Conclusions

The religious and racist dimensions of anti-Semitism in Iran are historically deep-rooted and substantially different from those of the Arab Sunni world. The jihadi radical-Islamic layer – directed towards the West, Israel and world Jewry – amounts to a fundamentalist global ideology seeking world hegemony, mainly through the humiliation of the arrogant and materialistic West.[56] The Islamic regime in Iran picked Israel and the Jews as a central target for hate and enmity within this anti-Western global worldview which it spearheads.

The Jews and Israel form a salient yet vulnerable global minority. The State of Israel, a democratic nation-state sitting on 'occupied land' and 'oppressing the Palestinian Muslims' in the heart of Islam fits into Iranian agenda. Israel's existence affirms the humanistic-secular world order on which it was established. The success of Israel in combining religion/heritage with prosperous democracy and the fact that this enterprise is run by Jews, is especially humiliating to Iranian Islam.

Pragmatically, anti-Semitism and anti-Israeli policy helps the Iranian regime, internally, to hold on to power by maintaining the atmosphere of a state of emergency, and externally, to gain consequence-free influence in the Arab world. In all likelihood, Iranian long-term strategy, backed by its nuclear build-up, aims at imposing Persian-led Shiite hegemony on the Middle East, east of Egypt, with or without Turkey. Anti-Israeli rhetoric helps weaken the Arab world's strength by dragging it into a perennial and taxing conflict with Israel, weakens Israel itself, and diverts attention from the Iranian nuclear build-up, both internationally and within the Arab world.

Current Iranian policy is reminiscent of that of pre-Second World War Nazi Germany in a number of ways. It has an anti-Western and totalitarian slant; it tries to mislead the West by describing the conflict as revolving around the Jews; it includes a component of redemptive anti-Semitism; it displays a built-in strand of pessimistic victimhood envisaging a doomsday of self-destruction[57] and is looking for a 'final solution' for millions of Israeli Jews. As with the Nazis, the Iranians begin by trying to drive the millions out by way of killing and terrorizing the population, with the full knowledge that mass-deportation will probably fail. Unlike Nazi Germany, however, Iran is not a formidable industrial and military power, the regime is unpopular and it typically does not persecute Jews as long as they 'behave'. Yet, also unlike Nazi Germany, Iran relies on a hinterland of the fantastically large number of Muslims around the world which it wants to lead as a 'Base' or 'Holy Regime'. Iran's immediate goals are to attain hegemony status over the Sunni Middle East, but, down the road, it may succeed in leading a Muslim coalition in a jihad against Europe or Russia.

The Islamic regime represents a small minority of Iran's population. Yet controlling a large country and benefiting from a handsome cash flow, an ambitious nuclear program, strong ideological commitment and much political, diplomatic and military savvy, it seems adamant on pursuing its imperialistic ambitions in the Middle East and beyond. Iran's nuclear build-up may have started in the 1980s as an answer to security concerns. Yet since then, and possibly from the beginning, it included an element of protecting the regime, against its own people, and as a springboard to aggressive adventures abroad.

Using the bomb will never be off the table once Iran acquires one and a passive-aggressive jihadi crusade against the West, under the umbrella of a nuclear threat, is a likely scenario. This article has shown that Iran's nuclear program and anti-Semitic/anti-Israeli agenda are not new but reflect a continuing and well-orchestrated policy. In recent years, and especially since the exposure of the Iranian nuclear program and the election of the millenarian Ahmadinejad as Iranian president, the rhetoric has gained a more global audience. Yet one should not dismiss it as reflecting a personal eccentricity. As hard facts show, in the nuclear build-up as well as in preparing Hezbollah to fight Israel, the actions behind the rhetoric have all along been serious, fully committed and right on target.

Hence, any future policy toward Iran's nuclear project should be clear and convincing. Clarity is imperative if one aspires to avoid a military confrontation or worse. The ideological dimension should also be tackled. Calls for the elimination of other nations should entail consequences.

Eldad J. Pardo is Young Truman Scholar at the Faculty of Humanities, Hebrew University, Jerusalem.

NOTES

1 In Shahar Ilan, 'A Genocide is not Much Less than a Holocaust', *Ha'aretz*, 12 May 2006, p. B6.
2 Dr Seyyed Ali Hosseini-Tash, Deputy Head of Iran's Supreme National Security Council, explains what Iran should do to deflect American pressure on the nuclear issue. It should 'display how good it is, to what extent it conducts its affairs legally, and why can it be trusted. At the same time, Iran must show it will not back off under pressure or threats and will protect its national interests' (*Persian TV, Channel 2*, 4 April 2006).

3   *MEMRI* Special Dispatch Series, No. 855, January 28, 2005, 'Anti-Semitism and Holocaust
    Denial in the Iranian Media"; *MEMRI* Special Dispatch Series, No. 1013, 28 October 2005,
    'Iranian President at Tehran Conference: "Very Soon, this Stain of Disgrace [i.e. Israel] will be
    Purged from the Center of the Islamic World and this is Attainable"'; *MEMRI* Special Dispatch
    Series, No. 1072, 18 January 2006, Iran TV Discussion on the Myth of the Gas Chambers and
    the Truth of *The Protocols of the Elders of Zion*; 'The Only Solution for the Cancerous Tumor [Israel]
    is Surgery'.
4   For example, the 'Holocaust Convention', held in Tehran, 14–16 April 2006.
5   Meir Litvak, 'Iran and Israel: The Ideological Animosity and its Roots' (in Hebrew), *Iyunim
    Bitkumat Israel*, 14 (2004): 367–92.
6   Sohrab Sobhani, *The Pragmatic Entente: Israeli–Iranian Relations, 1948–1988*, New York: Praeger,
    1988; David Menashri, *Post-Revolutionary Politics in Iran: Religion, Society and Power*, London and
    Portland, OR: Frank Cass, 2001.
7   The territory of France is 534,970 sq./km, while Iran's is 1,648,200 sq./km. The territory of larger
    Israel, including the Palestinian Territories and the Golan Heights (together 5,880 sq./km.) is
    21,940 sq./km. Taking away these territories would make Iran almost 103 times larger than
    Israel.
8   Christopher Clary, 'Dr. Khan's Nuclear WalMart', *Disarmament Diplomacy*, 76 (March/April
    2004), available from <www.acronym.org.uk>.
9   The deal was meant, on the Israeli side, to mend fences with Iran and then help the Americans
    free their hostages in Lebanon. The Reagan administration aimed at using the money earned from
    shipping military equipment to Iran to fund the Contras in Nicaragua behind the back of the US
    Congress.
10 Shahram Chubin, 'Iran's Strategic Predicament', *Middle East Journal*, 54 (1) (2000): 10–24.
11 Former President Mohammad Khatami in a speech to the military command, in daily newspaper
    Jamejam, 29 May 2005.
12 *Radio Damascus* (Arabic), 24 July 2006.
13 Ervand Abrahamian, *Tortured Confessions: Prisons and Public Recantations in Modern Iran* (Berkeley
    and Los Angeles: University of California Press, 1999), pp. 219–21. For a different take see Ali
    Akbar Mahdi's review in *International Journal of Middle East Studies*, 32 (3) (2000): 414–18.
14 Fariba Adelkhah, 'La Republique entre fauteuils et tapis: la société et le pouvoir', in *Thermidor en
    Iran*, eds Jean-François Bayart, Fariba Adelkhah and Olivier Roy (Paris: Editions Complexe,
    1993), pp. 53–89; Wright Robin, 'The Mullahs are Loosing the Grip', *Los Angeles Times*, 1994.
15 Eldad J. Pardo, 'The Age of Wonder and the Age of the Plumber: Iran and Israel in Global
    Perspective', in *Israel, The Middle East and Islam: Weighing the Risks and Prospects*, eds Oded Eran
    and Amnon Cohen, Jerusalem: Truman Institute, Hebrew University, 2003, pp. 51–74 .
16 The most blatant among the terrorist activities were the attacks on the Israeli embassy and the
    Jewish Community Center (AMIA) in Buenos Aires, in 1992 and 1994, as well as the
    assassination in September 1992 of four Kurdish Iranian opposition leaders at the Mikonos
    restaurant in Berlin. As for propaganda, an unknown dimension of it is the Iranian-Shiite
    campaign in Africa: Arye Oded, *Islam and Politics in Kenya*, Boulder, CO and London: Lynne
    Rienner, 2000.
17 Matthias Küntzel, 'Ahmadinejad's Demons: A Child of the Revolution Takes Over', *The New
    Republic*, 24 April 2006: 15–23.
18 Michael Slackman, 'Iran Chief Eclipses Power of Clerics', *The New York Times*, 28 May 2006.
19 Iran is seen as a combatant (*chaleshgar*) against American global hegemony: Mohammad Nasser
    Rabbani, 'hamszisti-ye iran va eraq dar sayeh-ye moteghayyerha-ye mantaqeh'i', *Khabargozari-ye
    Fars*, 6 June 2005.
20 Daily newspaper, *Jamejam*, 29 May 2005.
21 The term was coined by Saul Friedländer in his *Nazi Germany and the Jews: The Years of Persecution,
    1933–1939*, Vol. 1, New York: Harper Collins, 1997.
22 Anthony Lehrman, 'Resolute Policy against Anti-Semitism', letter to the editor, *Ha'aretz*, 22
    March 2006, p. B4.

23 Both, again, from *Webster's Dictionary*.

24 *MEMRI* Special Dispatch Series, No. 1053, 22 December 2005, 'Iranian TV Blood Libel: Jewish Rabbis Killed Hundreds of European Children to use their Blood for Passover Holiday and Discussion on Holocaust denial'; *MEMRI* Special Report, No. 11, November 1, 2002, 'Based on Qur'anic Verses, Interpretations and Traditions, Muslim Clerics State: The Jews are the Descendents of Apes, Pigs and other Animals'.

25 *Tehran Radio*, 20 July 1994. Quoted in Ephraim Kam, *From Terror to Nuclear Bombs: The Significance of the Iranian Threat* (in Hebrew), Tel Aviv: MOD Publishing and JCSS, 2004, p. 397.

26 *CNN* interview, 1 July 1998.

27 David Mensahri, 'Iran', in *Anti-Semitism Worldwide*, 1995/6 (Tel Aviv: 1996), p. 198; *'The Protocols of the Elders of Zion*, An Iranian Perspective', *MEMRI*, Special Dispatch Series, No. 98, June 2000. Quoted in Litvak, 'Iran and Israel', p. 379.

28 A classic example is Theodore Herzl, the founding father of Zionism. As a famous journalist he managed to convince three powers – Britain, Russia and Germany – to support his plans without any financial or political backing; yet he was unable to offer asylum to fellow Jews during the pogroms of 1903.

29 David Aberbach, 'The Poetry of Nationalism', *Nations and Nationalism*, 9 (2) (2003): 255–75.

30 Yohanan Friedman, 'Classification of Unbelievers in Sunni Muslim Law and Tradition', *Jerusalem Studies in Arabic and Islam*, 22 (1998): 163–95.

31 This term was coined by R. Scott Appleby who sees religious traditions as intrinsically wide and pluralistic, hence amenable to many a direction.

32 Mash-hoori, Délârâm, *Ragu-é Tâk: Du rôle de la religion dans l'histoire sociale de l'Iran* (in Persian) (Vincennes: Editions Khavaran, 1379 (2000)), pp. 48–83.

33 The actual role of clergymen in history, collaborators with the rulers or defenders of the masses, is a contentious and complicated topic. For a pro-clergy view see: Hamid Algar, *Religion and State in Iran, 1785–1906: The Role of the Ulama in the Qajar Period*, Berkeley: University of California Press, 1969. For another opinion see: Willem Floor, 'The Revolutionary Character of the Ulama: Wishful Thinking or Reality?', in *Religion and Politics in Iran: Shi'ism from Quietism to Revolution*, ed. Nikki R. Keddie, New Haven, CT: Yale University Press, 1983, pp. 73–97. For the clergy as a traditional class, at times pro-people, but intrinsically anti-democratic: Said Amir Arjomand, *The Turban for the Crown: The Islamic Revolution in Iran*, New York: Oxford University Press, 1988; Arjomand, 'The Ulama's Traditionalist Opposition to Parliamentarism: 1907–1909', *Middle Eastern Studies*, 17 (2) (1981): 174–90. A classic inside view of the clerics: Roy Mottahedeh, *The Mantle of the Prophet: Religion and Politics in Iran*, New York: Pantheon Books, 1985. Many clerics throughout history were responsible for persecution of religious minorities, especially, but not only, Bahais.

34 Amnon Netzer, 'Persecutions and Conversions in the History of the Jews in Iran in the 17th Century' (in Hebrew), *Pe'amim*, 6 (1980): 33–56; Netzer, 'The History of the Forced Converts of Mashhad according to Yaakov Daylamgan', *Pe'amim*, 42 (1990): 127–56; Jaleh Pirnazar, 'The Anusim of Mashhad', in *Esther's Children:Portrait of Iranian Jews*, ed. Houman Sashar, Beverly Hills, CA and Philadelphia, PA 2002, pp. 115–36; Ezra Spicehandler, 'The persecution of the Jews of Isfahan under Shah Abbas II (1642–1666)', *Hebrew Union College Annual*, 46 (1975): 331–56; Vera Basch Moreen, *Iranian Jewry's Hour of Peril and Heroism: A Study of Baba'i Ibn Loutf's Chronicle (1617–1662)*, New York and Jerusalem, 1987.

35 Amnon Netzer, 'Anti-Semitism in Iran' (in Hebrew), *Pe'amim*, 29 (1986): 5–31. Also based on interviews conducted by myself.

36 Michael Zand, 'The Image of the Jew in the Eyes of the Iranians after WWII (1945–1979)' (in Hebrew), *Pe'amim*, 29 (1986): 109–32.

37 Afshin Valinejad, 'Iran Leader Calls for Israel's Annihilation', *Boston Globe*, 1 January 2000, p. 4 (quoted in *RAND*, 2001, n. 80).

38 *IRNA*, 25 April 2001. In a meeting with the chairman of the Saudi Consultative Council (Shura), Sheikh Muhammed bin Ibrahim bin Jubair, at the eve of the Tehran conference in support for the Intifada. Earlier, in 1999, Khatami said Iran would never recognize the Zionist regime in Israel

because an administration based on seizing power illegally, aggression and murder, did not give
the Israelis the right to exist (*ArabMedia Summary*, 13 April 1999).

39   Interview with Christianne Amanpour, *CNN*, July 1, 1998.

40   <http://khabarnameh.gooya.com/politics/archives/009109.php>, 19 April 2004, quoted by
MEMRI and Litvak, 'Iran and Israel', p. 376 with other sources.

41   Rafsanjani's declarations from 14 December 2001 were reported the next day in the Iranian media
in Persian (*Kayhan*), Arabic (*Al-Vefagh*) and English (*Iran Daily*). No direct quotation exists.
Source: *MEMRI*.

42   Matthias Küntzel, *Djihad und Judenhass: Über die neuen antisemitischen Krieg* (Freiburg: ça ira Verlag,
2002).

43   Meir M. Bar-Asher, 'Les fils d'Israel, protoptypes de la Chîah: notes sur quelques traditions
exégétiques du chi'ism duodéimain', *Perspectives, Revue de l'Université Hébraïque de Jérusalem*, 9
(2002): 125–37.

44   For an early example see Jalal Al-e Ahmad's 'Safar beh Velayat-e Esra'il', published in Iran as *Safar
beh Velayat-e 'Azra'il* in 1984.

45   Ibid.; Eldad J. Pardo, 'Between East and West: Israel as a Role Model for the Iranian Left in the
1960s' (in Hebrew), *Iyunim Bitkumat Israel*, 14 (2004): 337–65. For an English summary and an
excellent discussion: 'Jalal Al-e Ahmad: the Dawn of the Islamic Ideology', in Hamid Dabashi,
Theology of Discontent: The Ideological Foundation of the Islamic Revolution in Iran, New York: New
York University Press, 1993, pp. 39–101.

46   Pardo, 'Between East and West'; Yoram Hazony, *The Jewish State: The Struggle for Israel's Soul*, New
York: Basic Books, 2000, pp. 104–107.

47   Litvak, 'Iran and Israel'.

48   Ahmad, 'Safar beh Velayat-e Esra'il'.

49   For a full analysis see Pardo, 'Between East and West'.

50   'Iran's ideology is often a mask for realpolitik. Iran still supports Shi'a radicals and other Islamists
throughout the world – and champions the anti-Israel front – but its motives and its priorities
are increasingly dictated by cold national interest concerns', quoted in Shahram Chubin,
Anoushiravan Ehteshami and Jerrold Green, *Iran's Security Policy in the Post-Revolutionary Era*,
Washington, DC: RAND, 2001.

51   Brenda Shaffer, 'The Formation of the Azerbaijani Collective Identity in Iran', *Nationalities Papers*,
28 (3) (2000): 449–77.

52   Brenda Shaffer, *Partners in Need: The Strategic Relationship of Russia and Iran*, Washington, DC: The
Washington Institute for Near East Policy, 2001.

53   See for example the debate on Channel 4 TV (6 March 2006, *Gostareh-ye Siyasat*) on the principle
of democracy (*mafhum-e demokrasi*) and whether there can be an 'Islamic' democracy that is
fundamentally different from the 'liberal' one. While detractors of the US pointed to the
American support of the Shah, the answer was that Iran cooperates with dictatorships such as
China, North Korea and Cuba. See also Adel Haddad, the Majlis' Speaker, 'The Islamic
Revolution is the result of the love of freedom and democracy of the Iranian nation', *Frasnews*, 2
June 2005.

54   'Missive from Tehran: Merkel Rebuffs Ahmadinejad's Letter', *Spiegel Online*, 21 July 2006. The
10-page letter, following a similar 18-page one to Bush, denied Israel's right to exist and that the
Holocaust ever happened, provoking the Chancellor to repeat Germany's position that 'Israel's
right to exist is a key part of our state's policy.'

55   In dubbing Iranian-Islamism as fascist, I follow Iranian Muslim philosopher Abdolkarim Sorush:
Siyasat-Nameh (Tehran: Mo'asaseh-ye Farhang-e Sirat, 1999/1378), pp. 215–17. Abrahamian and
others see Khomeinism as a populist regime: Ervand Abrahamian, *Khomeinism: Essays on the Islamic
Republic* (London and New York: I.B. Tauris, 1993). The militaristic dimension, however, makes
it more and more look like fascism and worse. See, for example, a photograph of Lebanese
Hezbollah fighters giving a Nazi-style salute: *Arab Insider*, 25 May 2006 <www.arabinsider.com/
h/315/450.htm>.

56   Martin Kramer, 'Islam is the Power of the Future', in *Arab Awakening and Islamic Revival: The*

Politics of Ideas in the Middle East, ed. Martin Kramer (New Brunswick, NJ and London: Transaction Publishers, 1996), pp. 141–59.

57 For the Nazi case see Saul Friedländer, *Reflections of Nazism: An Essay on Kitsch and Death*, trans. from French by Thomas Weyr (New York: Harper and Row, 1984). As for Iran: martyrdom and being slaughtered by the father in major defeat is a mainstay of the culture, both as it looks back at pre-Islamic Heroism and as reagards to Shiism and its major myth, the martyrdom of Imam Hussein. See Michael C. Hillmann, *Iranian Culture: A Persianist View* (Lanham, MD, New York, London: University Press of America, 1990).

The Need To Block A Nuclear Iran

EFRAIM INBAR

A nuclear Iran constitutes a serious threat, not only to the Middle East, but to the entire world. Diplomatic efforts have failed to halt Iran's nuclear programme. As the Iranian acquisition of a nuclear bomb nears, the threat of using force – and even actual use of force – seem the only viable preventive measures. Middle Eastern states can hardly establish a nuclear 'balance of terror' with Iran, and there is no fool-proof defence against nuclear-tipped missiles. Military action against Iranian nuclear installations involves many risks and complications, but the difficulty is exaggerated, and inaction is bound to bring about far worse consequences.

With each day, Iran grows closer to acquiring nuclear weapons. Tehran has evaded the International Atomic Energy Agency (IAEA) safeguards and has built a militarily significant nuclear programme. Iran has resisted all diplomatic pressure to discontinue this programme and seems intent on producing highly enriched uranium (HEU), which constitutes the final and critical stage in the construction of a nuclear bomb. In mid-January 2006, Iranians decided to break the IAEA seals on some of their nuclear facilities, signalling Tehran's determination to proceed with its centrifuge uranium enrichment programme. Indeed, Iran announced formally on 11 April 2006 that it has completed the experimental stage of uranium enrichment on its way to fissile material.

Official statements by the leaders of Western countries indicate growing exasperation with Iran's behaviour on the nuclear issue and unwillingness to bow to demands that the country abandon its plans to produce fissile material.[1] US Ambassador to the UN John Bolton expressed a 'sense of urgency' on this issue.[2] Even Mohammed ElBaradei, director general of the IAEA, said that the world is losing patience with Iran.[3]

Within the international community, Israel seems most concerned about the prospects of a nuclear Iran. In December 2005, Meir Dagan, the chief of the Israeli secret service Mossad, warned that Iran's strategic decision to acquire the technological basis to become a nuclear power would be realized within a few months.[4] The Chief of Staff of the Israel Defense Force (IDF), Lt Gen. Dan Halutz, offered a similar evaluation on 4 December 2005, while a few days earlier the Chief of the IDF Intelligence Department, Maj. Gen. Aharon Zeevi (Farkash) had warned that March 2006 constitutes the 'point of no return', indicating that after such a date, any diplomatic efforts to curtail the Iranian nuclear programme would be pointless. No explanation of the term 'point of no return' was offered, leaving it unclear, although it probably refers to a certain measure of nuclear technological ripeness.

This article initially reviews Iran's nuclear programme and presents its strategic rationale. It subsequently analyses the nature and the magnitude of the Iranian nuclear threat. The article ends with a review of the available options for halting the country's nuclear programme, including the wisdom of a military strike aimed at curbing Iran's nuclear effort.

The Iranian Nuclear Programme

The Iranian nuclear programme began during the reign of the Shah, reflecting Iran's perception of itself as a great power and an ancient civilization with hegemonic aspirations in its region.[5] After a period of suspension by the Islamic Republic, the programme was resumed. Despite the cover-up attempts, a great deal of Iran's nuclear infrastructure is known. Many known Iranian nuclear activities are suitable for military nuclear applications, and some activities have little or no suitability for any other purpose.[6] Iran has been constructing a reactor at Arak moderated by heavy water and fuelled with natural uranium, a type highly suitable for producing weapons-grade plutonium. This fissile material comprises the core of any nuclear bomb. Iran has also built a uranium conversion facility at Isfahan, to convert uranium core concentrate (yellowcake) into the uranium hexafluoride ($UF6$) gas suitable for enrichment at the centrifuge enrichment plant in Natanz. Highly Enriched Uranium (HEU) is also fissile material.[7]

There are additional indications that Iran has worked on plutonium separation and on a bomb design. Technology transfer from China, Russia, and especially Pakistan, complemented by purchases of nuclear-relevant components in Western Europe, provided the technical and engineering know-how for the Iranian nuclear scientists to make progress along the nuclear path. While Iran's rate of progress is disputed among intelligence services, it could clearly become a nuclear power in the near future. The timetable for assembling a nuclear device is influenced by Iran's capability to cross two thresholds: the production of a sufficient amount of fissile material for the bomb's core and the bomb design itself. Work on the two enterprises can be undertaken concurrently.

The Islamic Republic of Iran has invested tremendous political capital and vast resources in going nuclear. This behaviour has added strain in its relations with the United States. The tense relationship was reinforced by the hostility displayed by radical Islamic elements of the regime. Tehran's overall anti-American foreign policy has resulted in the inclusion of Iran by President George W. Bush, in January 2002, on his 'Axis of Evil' list.

The Iranian sense of vulnerability and threat perception increased following the US military presence in Afghanistan, on Iran's eastern border, and the US invasion of Iraq, on its western border. The two invasions caused Tehran to feel encircled by the United States and more exposed to a potential American attack. Tehran's assiduous attempts to augment its deterrence stem from its fear of attacks on the part of an imperially disposed United States and/or its Middle Eastern allies. In addition, Iran shares a border with Pakistan, a nuclear-armed nation since 1998. These factors provide Iran with an additional strong incentive for walking the nuclear path.

From an Iranian perspective, the North Korean example is also a compelling one. While the United States did not hesitate to invade Iraq, which it believed to be striving towards weapons of mass destruction (WMD), it refrained from attacking North Korea despite the fact that it abrogated the 1994 Agreed Framework with Washington, defiantly withdrew from the Nuclear Proliferation Treaty, and announced its possession of a nuclear deterrent. The fact that North Korea was much closer to producing a nuclear bomb than Iraq seemed to have constituted a critical difference that moderated the American response to a similar challenge.[8] North Korea's more developed nuclear programme provided a modicum of deterrence. While the regional context, that is, the proximity of great powers such as China, Russia and Japan, probably played no less of a role in determining the US reaction, Iran may have learned the lesson that the nuclear bomb can serve as a good insurance policy against outside intervention.

Accelerating its nuclear programme seems the most appealing option for Iran. The country has admitted that it has clandestinely produced small amounts of fissile material (plutonium). It might succeed in acquiring sufficient weapons-grade plutonium or HEU, and probably has worked for some time on assembling a deliverable nuclear weapon – though it may stop short of actually testing a nuclear device. Iran could, therefore, rely on inter-ested intelligence agencies and attentive observers to surmise that a weapons capability exists or could quickly be realized. Nuclear opacity , which is not an Iranian invention, has its strategic benefits.[9]

It is highly unlikely that Iran will adopt a policy of nuclear reversal reminiscent of South Africa, Argentina, or Brazil.[10] Its security predicament is very different from the strategic environments of Sub-Saharan Africa or Latin America that allowed nuclear abstinence. Moreover, the stakes of the ruling elite in Iran in the nuclear programme are inextricably connected to its political and even physical survival, with an infinitely greater intensity than in the other states mentioned. The regime in Tehran may well have come to the conclusion that the speedy and successful conclusion of nuclear efforts could serve as a guarantee to its future at home. Destabilizing the regime of a nuclear state, which may lead to chronic domestic instability, civil war, or disintegration, is a more risky enterprise than undermining a non-nuclear regime.

In light of the growing widespread concern about its nuclear aspirations, Tehran's best option is to continue negotiations with various representatives of the international community. Even after the Iranian matter is brought to the UN Security Council (UNSC), diplomatic negotiations are likely to continue in order to determine the reaction of the UNSC. This amounts to a temporary stalemate. Tehran will try to buy time as discussions drag on or are temporarily suspended between rounds to allow for additional consultations. Hassan Rowhani, who headed the Iranian negotiating team with the Europeans, revealed how Tehran played for time to dupe the West after its secret nuclear programme was uncovered by the Iranian opposition in 2002.[11] Such an Iranian strategy of 'talk and build' capitalizes on European and American reluctance to escalate. Deciding that negotiations are useless requires alternative action, which is not an enticing option.

Essentially, inconclusive talks preserve a status quo, a tense standoff in which Iran can go on with its opaque, though no longer clandestine, nuclear programme. Indeed, a strategy of 'talk and build' accompanied by temporary concessions postpones diplomatic and economic pressures and, most importantly, preventive military strikes by the United States. Tehran is undoubtedly watching the developments in Korea, and insufficient American determination to put an end to the Korean nuclear programme will encourage Iranian procrastination. Moreover, Iran's sense of vulnerability is accompanied by an evaluation that a US embroiled in Iraq is weak, while the higher energy prices enhance the Iranian hand in international negotiations.

Iran's nuclear programme was initiated with the intention of acquiring hegemony in the region and the ability to play the role of a great power in world affairs. Nowadays, it also seems to be designed to provide a strategic response to US political and cultural hegemony in world affairs. Tehran wants to be able to continue to oppose American policies and to deter possible American action against the radical Islamic regime. Similarly, it wants to block the influence of American culture, which is perceived as decadent and particularly dangerous.[12] Yet Iran's current nuclear appetite also stems from theological motivations. Some ayatollahs also view an Iran armed with nuclear weapons as an instrument in Allah's hand to impose Islam upon the entire world, believing that they, the ayatollahs, have been chosen by Allah to carry out His mission.[13] President Mahmoud Ahmadinejad reported having a vision when defending Iran's right to master nuclear technology at the UN General Assembly in the autumn of 2005. This ideological dimension of the Iranian nuclear rationale is quite troubling. Indeed, a stalemate that permits Iran to move forward with its nuclear programme would pose grave threats to regional security as discussed below.

The Nature of the Threat

The Islamic Republic of Iran is the greatest, most urgent threat to regional order in the Middle East and a challenge to US hegemony in world affairs. Iran is a revisionist state trying to export its Islamic Revolution, a mission intertwined with the nationalistic aspirations for grandeur rooted in a historic awareness of being an ancient civilization. In its behaviour, revolutionary Iran largely conforms to what Yehezkel Dror termed a 'Crazy State'.[14] Such a state is characterized by far-reaching goals in its foreign policy, a propensity for high-risk policies, intensive commitment and determination to implement these policies, and unconventional diplomatic style. If Iran becomes nuclear, these foreign policy features will probably be even more pronounced.

Iran actively supports the insurgency in Iraq against the establishment of a stable, pro-American regime. Tehran encourages radical Shia elements in Iraq in order to promote the establishment of another Islamic republic and foments trouble in the Shia communities in the Gulf States. It opposes a more liberal regime that could potentially serve as a catalyst for democratization in the area. Iran is allied with Syria, another radical state with an anti-American predisposition, and seeks to create a radical Shia corridor from Iran to the Mediterranean. Moreover, Tehran lends critical support to terrorist organizations such as Hezbollah, Hamas and Islamic Jihad.[14] According to the US State Department, Iran is the most active state sponsor of terrorism.[15]

Iran's nuclear programme, coupled with long-range delivery systems in particular, threatens regional stability in the Middle East. Iran possesses the Shehab-3 long-range missile (with a range of 1,300 km) that can probably be nuclear-tipped and is working on extending the range of its ballistic arsenal. American allies, such as Israel, Turkey, Saudi Arabia and the Gulf States, are within range, as well as several important US bases. The chief of the IDF Intelligence Department, Maj. Gen. Aharon Zeevi (Farkash) reported that Iran has also acquired twelve cruise missiles with a range of up to 3,000 km and with an ability to carry nuclear warheads.

Further improvements in Iranian missiles would initially put most European capitals, and eventually, the North American continent, within range of a potential Iranian attack. Iran has an ambitious satellite launching programme based on the use of multi-stage, solid propellant launchers, with intercontinental ballistic missile properties to enable the launching of a 300 kg satellite within two years. If Iran achieves this goal, it will put many more states at risk of a future nuclear attack.

The nuclear ambitions of the Islamic Republic of Iran are, of course, a challenge to the international nuclear non-proliferation regime (NPT). A nuclear Iran might well bring an end to this regime and to American attempts to curb proliferation in the Middle East and in other parts of the world.

Indeed, the emergence of a nuclear-armed Iran would have a chain-effect, generating further nuclear proliferation in the immediate region. Middle Eastern leaders, who invariably display high threat perceptions, are unlikely to look nonchalantly on a nuclear Iran. States such as Turkey, Egypt, Saudi Arabia and, of course, Iraq would hardly be persuaded by the United States that it can provide a nuclear umbrella against Iranian nuclear blackmail or actual nuclear attack. US-extended deterrence is very problematic in the Middle East.[16] Therefore, these states would not resist the temptation to counter Iranian influence by adopting similar nuclear postures.

The resulting scenario of a multi-polar nuclear Middle East would be a recipe for disaster. This strategic prognosis is a result of two factors: a) the inadequacy of a defensive posture against nuclear-tipped missiles, and b) the difficulties surrounding the establishment of stable nuclear deterrence in the region.

Missiles are the most effective means of delivering nuclear weapons. While the United States is developing a Ballistic Missile Defence (BMD) system and Russia claims to have a missile intercept capability with its S-300 missile system, only Israel possesses a serious capability to parry a nuclear missile attack. Israel has developed a defensive layer around the Arrow-2 anti-ballistic missile, which is designed to intercept the family of Scud missiles. This programme, which began in the late 1980s, benefited from generous US funding and amounts to the only deployed operational anti-ballistic missile system so far in the world.[17] Since 2000, Israel has deployed several operational batteries of Arrow missiles. The interception range is about 150 km away from Israel's borders. Yet no defence system is foolproof. The Arrow-2 provides a certain measure of protection, but it is a first-generation weapon system, and even its developers do not claim a flawless interception rate. Moreover, it is not clear how the Arrow would function if enemy missiles were equipped with countermeasures or if the enemy were to use saturation tactics.[18]

Israel has hitherto had the upper hand in the regional technological race, but there are no assurances that this will always be so. The difficulties that Israel faces in dealing with Katyushas, Qassams and tunnels show that Israeli ingenuity may not come up with immediate adequate responses. This is true of the United States as well. Even if defensive solutions are eventually devised, there may be windows of vulnerability, which could be of catastrophic dimensions in a nuclear scenario.

All Middle Eastern states are so far defenceless against Iranian missiles. Indeed, as the Iranian nuclear programme progresses, one can clearly detect a rise in threat perception on the part of most Arab states in the region. Several states within Iranian range, such as Turkey and India, have shown interest in purchasing the Israeli BMD system, whose export requires US approval. However, at present, while Israel is partly protected from Iranian nuclear missiles, the rest of the region remains vulnerable to such a threat.

The Iranian nuclear threat is also to be taken seriously in light of the difficulties of achieving a stable deterrence with Tehran.[19] Unfortunately, there are scholars who belittle such fears by releasing optimistic evaluations regarding a potentially stable 'balance of terror' between Israel and Iran, modelled on the relationship between the two superpowers during the Cold War. Such a bilateral relationship, where the two sides deter each other, cannot be easily emulated in the Middle East. A 'balance of terror' between two nuclear protagonists is never automatic, and could not be taken for granted even between the United States and the Soviet Union. Unfortunately, the situation in the Middle East is even less stable.

A second-strike capability, which allows a state to respond in kind after being subjected to a nuclear attack, is critical in establishing credible deterrence. During the Cold War, submarines constituted the platform for any second-strike capability; the difficulty in locating them underwater rendering them less vulnerable to an enemy first-strike attack. Indeed, the Soviet Union and United States relied on the survivability and mobility of their submarines, characteristics that would enable them to carry out a second-strike with nuclear-tipped missiles. While the superpowers possessed large submarine fleets, it is doubtful that any Middle Eastern power owns enough submarines equipped to do the job. Israel's current fleet includes three Dolphin-class submarines, to be augmented by the end of the decade by two additional vessels recently purchased in Germany. However, it is not clear whether Israel's submarines carry enough punch to deter adversaries. In this context, it is important to note that no fleet can ever be fully operational. Some vessels are in port for maintenance, while others are en route to the designated area of operations or on their way back to the homeport. Furthermore, the most appropriate launching area in the Indian Ocean is far away from Israel.[20]

More significant is the fact that maintaining a second-strike capability is an ongoing process requiring continuous improvement, which depends to a large extent on the adversary's actions. Such a process is inherently uncertain and ambiguous. Moreover, before an initial 'effective' second-strike capability is achieved, a nuclear race may create the fear of a first-strike nuclear attack, which might in itself trigger a nuclear exchange. This is all the more probable because adequate warning systems cannot be erected when the distances between enemies are so small, as is the case in the Middle East. The influence of haste and the need to respond quickly can have extremely dangerous consequences.

The discussion above has focused on the problems of establishing bilateral nuclear deterrence between Iran and Israel. In a nuclear multi-polar environment, achieving stable deterrence would be even more difficult. Deterrence may work in part because a threat is transmitted correctly and not misread by the enemy. Yet, Middle Eastern countries have not established any hotlines or special communication links with Iran and/or each other, which could have serious consequences in a nuclear crisis. In the Middle East, communication is not only a technological problem, but is also a political problem, as several states have refrained from establishing diplomatic links with a number of regional capitals. Middle Eastern powers would also have to establish early warning systems searching in all directions. Moreover, the requirements for an 'all directions' second-strike force are very complicated. In addition, the rather rudimentary nuclear forces in the region would be likely to be prone to accidents and mistakes. The newly acquired nuclear arsenals would lack the sophisticated technology of the great powers, which reduces such mishaps through devices for locking, fusing, remotely controlling and releasing nuclear warheads from afar. Nuclear arms in the hands of several Middle Eastern powers would actually increase the possibility of pre-emptive strikes and catalytic wars.

While it can be argued that Middle Eastern leaders behave rationally, many of them engage in 'brinkmanship', leading to miscalculation. Even of greater consequence, their sensitivity to costs and their attitudes to human life hardly conform to Western values. Iranian leaders have said that they are ready to pay a heavy price for the destruction of the Jewish state. For example, on 14 December 2001, the Ayatollah Ali Akbar Hashemi-Rafsanjani declared that the use of a nuclear bomb against Israel would destroy the Jewish state, producing only 'damages in the Muslim world'.[21] Moreover, while Arab leaders issued similar statements in the past, the historical animosity between Persians and Arabs could also produce motivations to use nuclear weapons under extreme circumstances. Strong mutual mistrust, a basic feature of Middle Eastern political culture, creates a psychological environment that is conducive to rigidity and inflexibility. These are highly dangerous qualities in a nuclear situation, where it is important to leave the enemy a way to retreat – what Thomas Schelling calls the 'last clear chance'.[22] The 'dialectics of the antagonists'[23] in the Middle East can hardly turn a 'balance of terror' into a 'balance of prudence', in which each adversary exerts maximum caution and consideration, permitting coexistence. Nuclear deterrence is probably harder to achieve than deterrence theorists had believed, because there is great variation in how people calculate their interests and react to threats.

Furthermore, as the nuclear taboo is eroding at the interstate level, Iran, or a faction, or even individual officials in the government may decide to pass a nuclear device to a terrorist organization, such as Hamas or Hezbollah, to be used against Israel or a 'heretic' (either Muslim or Christian) regime.[24] This possibility is intensified by the fact that the weapons are apparently institutionally under the control of hardliners even in the context of the Iranian government, such as the Islamic Revolutionary Guard. The 'crazy state' posture may be conducive toward Iranian nuclear largesse to other radical Islamic groups operating outside the Middle East. The Iranians have used proxies to carry out attacks against their enemies in the past. An indirect mode of operation would put many capitals in the world in danger and make Iran a somewhat less likely subject for retaliation. In any case, a nuclear Iran might provide emboldened global jihadist terrorist groups a haven where they think they are immune to Western reach.

A nuclear Iran would also enhance Iranian hegemony in the strategic energy sector, by its mere location along the oil-rich Persian Gulf area and the Caspian Basin. These two adjacent regions form the 'energy ellipse', which holds over 70 per cent of the world's proven oil and over 40 per cent of natural gas reserves.[25] Giving revolutionary Iran a better ability to intimidate the governments controlling parts of this huge energy reservoir would further strengthen Iran's position in the region and world affairs. Such a position would also make Iran's containment even more difficult and would necessarily embolden Islamic radicals everywhere.

For Israel, a nuclear Iran constitutes an existential threat. The tripartite combination of a radical Islamic regime, long-range missile capability, and nuclear weapons is extremely perilous. Due to its small and dense population, Israel is exceedingly vulnerable to a nuclear attack. In December 2005, Israel's Prime Minister Ariel Sharon termed the Iranian programme 'a grave threat' stressing that Israel 'cannot accept a nuclear Iran'.[26] This statement is a reflection of a long-held high-threat perception of a large part of Israel's strategic community. Indeed, Prime Minister Yitzhak Rabin (1992–95) already perceived Islamic Iran, which was engaged in acquiring a nuclear capability and in sponsoring terror, as Israel's arch-enemy,[27] while all of his successors maintained this assessment. While Israel was pleased with the change of tone in Tehran toward the United States after Ayatollah Mohammed Khatami was elected as president in 1997, Tehran continued to retain its anti-Israeli policy.[28]

Iranian President Ahmadinejad, elected in June 2005, has contributed to Israel's fears by issuing a series of inflammatory statements. On 26 October 2005, he called for Israel 'to be wiped off the map'. On 14 December 2005, in a speech that was televised live, Ahmadinejad denied that the Holocaust had ever happened, suggesting that Israel's Jews be relocated to Europe or even to

Alaska. Such statements from high-ranking officials cannot be dismissed as pure rhetoric; they reflect a policy preference. An Iran strengthened by a nuclear arsenal may pursue such a policy.

In summary, an Iranian nuclear bomb would bring about additional nuclear proliferation in the region, enhance the power of a 'crazy state', and embolden Islamic radicals elsewhere. In addition, the technological uncertainties of a defensive system and the possibility of establishing stable nuclear deterrence lead to the inescapable conclusion that regional security is best served by denying Iran a nuclear bomb.

Blocking Iran's Nuclear Aspirations

There are several ways to deal with the Iranian nuclear challenge. These options are discussed below.

Diplomacy

For many years, Iran deceived the IAEA, violating the safeguards agreement and failing to report the full scope of its nuclear activities. Finally, Iran was asked to freeze its uranium enrichment programme, and to sign the Additional Protocol to the safeguards agreement with the IAEA, allowing for more intrusive international supervision. An October 2003 high-profile visit by the foreign ministers of France, Germany and the United Kingdom (EU-3) signalled the European attempt to apply heavy diplomatic pressure. For two years, the Europeans conducted negotiations with Iran in attempt to reach an agreement. The European approach, which Washington decided to go along with for a while, was to create a political atmosphere that delegitimized the Iranian quest for a nuclear bomb and to provide incentives for Iran to cooperate on the nuclear issue.

Yet, after several suspensions in the talks with the Europeans, the Iranians have rejected the European 'carrots' offered to them. In all probability, the West has nothing to offer that can dissuade Iran from going nuclear, particularly since the nuclear programme is viewed as the best insurance policy for the current leadership and is probably the single most popular policy associated with this regime. Iran is a clear case where all means of persuasion, short of the use of force, are ineffective. 'Soft power' has its limitations.[29]

The United States probably decided to go through the motions required by the Europeans in order to secure European support for a tougher approach when diplomacy has run its course. The United States even lent its support to the Russian offer to conduct the enrichment of Iranian uranium on its soil for the same reason. Washington preferred to raise the issue of Iran at the UN

Security Council (UNSC) in order to impose economic sanctions and eventually secure international legitimacy for military action against the nuclear installations.

Iran's intransigent behaviour and growing impatience on the part of the international community, combined with US pressure, convinced the IAEA to finally recognize Iran's non-compliance with its treaty obligations in September 2005, although the Board of Governors of the IAEA that met again in November 2005 postponed the referral of the Iranian case to the UNSC in order to allow more time for negotiations. This postponement served Iranian interests in gaining time within its 'talk and build' strategy. Only in February 2006 did the United States finally win approval from all key players in the IAEA, especially Russia and China, to send the issue of Iran's highly suspect nuclear programme to the UNSC Yet, the UNSC took no real action. In an attempt to galvanize an international coalition in favour of sanctions, Washington announced at the end of May 2006 its new readiness to enter negotiations with Iran on the nuclear issue, on the condition that Tehran suspends uranium enrichment.

Economic Sanctions

As the diplomatic option is being exhausted and in the absence of a clear unequivocal nuclear reversal on part of Iran, the United States will try to prod the UNSC into eventually imposing a strict set of sanctions against Tehran that include economic and political isolation combined with a military quarantine, tightly controlling what flows in and out of Iran. While the Europeans may join the United States in mandating and applying sanctions, China and Russia, which have veto power in the UNSC, are less likely to cooperate in engineering an US-sponsored campaign against Iran. They have their own economic interests in Iran and want to play a role in the region rather than defer to American leadership. Eventually, the UNSC may decide on sanctions, whose content effectiveness is primarily dependent upon the need to forge an international consensus.[30] Clearly, China and Russia have no strategic interest in a nuclear Iran and would eventually join the sanctions, but they prefer Iran to respond to their proposals rather than to American initiatives.

There are also a number of specific factors discouraging countries from supporting sanctions against Iran, ranging from fear of Tehran's sponsorship of terrorism to economic costs, or desire to gain Iranian cooperation on other issues. US sanctions against Iran have also long been in place without forcing Tehran to change policy.

While economic sanctions would certainly hurt the Iranian economy, which is much dependent upon refined oil products,[31] economic pressures are not the best means to stop Iran from going nuclear. The international studies literature displays serious scepticism regarding the effectiveness of economic sanctions. Often, such sanctions merely serve to make a point and to keep an issue alive in the absence of the political will to take military measures to remedy the situation. Moreover, in the past, societies and regimes have demonstrated great resilience and capacity to withstand pain in the face of economic sanctions.

Islamic Iran, which seeks a nuclear bomb primarily to gain regional hegemony and to allow it to oppose a Pax Americana, is ready to pay a high price for its foreign policy orientation. Actually, external pressure has been used more than once as a focal point for rallying domestic support for the embattled regime. Another major problem with economic sanctions is that it takes time to put them in place and to make them felt in the target country. In the case of Iran, time is of critical importance, particularly if Iran wants to present the world with a nuclear *fait accompli*.

Indirect Pressure on Iran

The Iranian challenge could also be dealt with by adopting an indirect strategy. This might require focusing on Syria – the weak link in Iran's strategic outreach – possibly even leading to the demise of that regime – and on Iran's client Hezbollah group in Lebanon. The Baathist regime is under increasing international and domestic pressure. Cornering Tehran's regional allies will weaken and isolate Iran, possibly making the Islamic Republic more susceptible to Western pressures.

Another aspect of the indirect approach on the nuclear issue, though in this case dealing with Iran itself, would be to encourage regime change in Tehran. This is particularly difficult in police states, such as Iran, where suppression is effective in paralysing any meaningful political opposition. Nevertheless, such situations are not stable, and Iran has a history of popular uprisings.[32] If it is true that human beings prefer to live in freedom than in fear and that many are ready to take personal risks to realize this dream, Iran could be ripe for removing the yoke of the mullahs. Being more advanced than Arab states according to almost every socio-economic criterion, Iran could be a better candidate for democratization. US diplomacy aimed at strengthening the dissenting voices in Iran might be successful in fostering an effect similar to the one that brought about the Soviet empire's disintegration.[33]

The indirect strategy is advantageous, as it rests on regional and domestic dynamics while minimizing a popular Iranian antagonism towards the American activist approach. Yet even if it were to be successful, such a strategy may again take too much time. International procrastination and past diplomatic failures to delay the Iranian programme may leave no other choice but the military option to prevent a nuclear Islamic Republic of Iran.

Coercive Measures

Covert operations to block the Iranian nuclear programme, if ever used, have clearly failed. US Ambassador John Bolton declared on 30 October 2003, when serving as under secretary of state for arms control and international security, that the United States was actively seeking to curb proliferation. 'Rogue states such as Iran, North Korea, Syria, Libya and Cuba, whose pursuit of weapons of mass destruction makes them hostile to US interests, will learn that their covert programmes will not escape either detection or consequences', he warned. 'While we will pursue diplomatic solutions whenever possible, the United States and its allies must be willing to deploy more robust techniques, such as the interdiction and seizure of illicit goods, the disruption of procurement networks, sanctions, or other means.'[34]

While Israel was more taciturn about the issue, as threat perception increased, Prime Minister Sharon decided in November 2003 to place the responsibility for an integrated strategy to prevent the nuclearization of Iran in the hands of Mossad.[35] Its head, retired Maj. Gen. Dagan, who has a rich history in combating terror, was appointed in September 2002 to hone the skills of this organization in covert operations. The declarations of Israeli senior officials in the winter of 2005–06 indicated greater alarm than before, meaning, *inter alia*, that whatever means were taken failed to achieve the intended results.

One variant of covert operations is to focus on the highly skilled elements of those working for the Iranian programme. The Iranian nuclear programme has a limited number of scientists whose contribution is critical to its successful completion. The interested intelligence services have probably already identified the key scientists who keep it moving. Removing these scientists would also affect the possibility of renewing the nuclear efforts in case a freeze of the Iranian programme were to take place. Therefore, serious offers of refuge and a professional career in the West should be extended to these scientists. Alternatively, they should be intimidated from further cooperation with the Iranian nuclear programme. It would not be impossible to organize a well-orchestrated campaign to do so against those who prefer the patriotic option of continuing to serve their state. In fact, the mere beginning of such a campaign of carrots and sticks may deter others from cooperating with the Iranian nuclear programme and hasten their exit from Iran.

Another coercive option is a blockade on Iranian oil exports to signal to Iran that the United States and the West mean business. With oil selling at over $60 per barrel (as of February 2006), oil exports are the source of enormous wealth used by the ayatollahs to buttress the regime and pursue its nuclear programme. Denying a hefty income constitutes a threat to the regime. A blockade may indeed escalate into a tanker war as witnessed in the last years of the Iraq–Iran War, which ended in Iran backing down.[36]

In the first decade of the twenty-first century, the US Navy and Air Force can police the Strait of Hormuz in order to prevent Iranian oil from reaching the market. While smuggling oil would still be possible, most Iranian oil exports would be affected. Concern about the overall effect on oil markets and supply would be a major factor deterring such a strategy, but this approach may well be the only alternative to either a direct attack or accepting Iran's possession of nuclear weaponry.

The final option is the use of force. Presumably, the United States already has contingency plans and training assets for an attack against Iran's nuclear facilities.[37] Israel conducted such a strike in 1981 against Iraq's nuclear reactor, which effectively ended Saddam Hussein's nuclear potential. In a similar fashion, prior to concluding the 1994 Agreed Framework with Pyongyang, the Clinton Administration contemplated surgical strikes to end the North's nuclear weapons programme.

While it is probably true that intelligence services cannot provide military planners with a full and comprehensive picture of the Iranian nuclear programme, what we know seems to be enough to allow identification of the main targets. The military capability to hit all targets is important, but a partial destruction would be enough to cripple Iran's ability to build a nuclear bomb in the near future. Moreover, no large-scale invasion is needed in order to do the job, but only a sustained bombing campaign with commando strikes.

While Iran has spread out its nuclear facilities and built a large part of the nuclear complex underground in order to protect it from conventional air strikes, technological advances in penetration of underground facilities and increased precision might allow total destruction. The difficulties in dealing a severe military blow to the Iranian nuclear programme are generally exaggerated.[38] A detailed analysis of the military option is beyond the scope of this paper, but the US military definitely has the muscle and the sophistication needed to perform a pre-emptive strike in accordance with its new strategic doctrine, as well as the capability for a sustained air campaign, if needed to prevent the repair and reconstruction of the facilities targeted.

American declarations on this issue indicate a willingness to consider all options. In January 2005, US Vice-President Dick Cheney expressed concern that Israel might attack Iran: 'Given the fact that Iran has a stated policy that their objective is the destruction of Israel, the Israelis might well decide to act first, and let the rest of the world worry about cleaning up the diplomatic mess afterwards.' This statement actually legitimized such action and subtly indicated to the Iranians that the US might not be able to stop Israel from acting unilaterally. In August 2005, on the eve of a trip to Europe, President Bush insisted that he wanted a peaceful, diplomatic solution to the Iranian nuclear problem but refused to rule out military action. On several occasions,

Bush repeated this viewpoint. Several US senators also recognized that a military strike on Iran must be a foreign policy option.[39]

Despite the difficulties faced by the administration with regard to its Iraq policy, American public opinion could conceivably be enlisted to back a military strike on Iran if a clear-cut case is made that all other options have been exhausted in the quest to prevent a very dangerous development, especially in the period following a US withdrawal from Iraq. The changing atmosphere toward Iran in Washington's corridors of power affects the national mood. Indeed, a *Los Angeles Times* poll of 27 January 2006 indicates that 57 per cent of Americans back an attack on Iran if defiance persists. A Pew Research Center poll released on 7 February 2006 (see table below) showed that public concern over Iran's nuclear programme has risen dramatically in the past few months. Today, 27 per cent of Americans cite Iran as the country that represents the greatest danger to the United States. In October, just nine per cent pointed to Iran as the biggest danger to the United States, while there was far more concern over Iraq, China and North Korea. Nearly two-thirds (65 per cent) believe that Iran's nuclear programme is a major threat to the United States, placing it on a par with North Korea's nuclear programme, and far ahead of China's emerging power among possible threats to the United States. Overwhelming numbers believe that if Iran were to develop nuclear weapons it would likely launch attacks on Israel (72 per cent), and the United States or Europe (66 per cent). There is even greater agreement that a nuclear-armed Iran would be likely to provide nuclear weapons to terrorists (82 per cent). Even if these trends do not hold for long, second-term presidents such as Bush are less susceptible to the vagaries of public opinion. The personality of the current president and his worldview well suit such an approach.

American perceptions of Iran reflect a global phenomenon. A major BBC World Service poll exploring how people in 33 countries view various countries found not a single country where a majority has a positive view of Iran's role in the world (with the exception of the Iranians themselves). Indeed, the United States is not alone in considering the use of force. British Prime Minister Tony Blair warned that the West might have to take military action against Iran after worldwide condemnation of Iranian President Ahmadinejad's call for Israel to be 'wiped off the map'. France also seems to realize that use of force may be necessary.[40] Washington has been trying to gain Ankara's support for US policy toward Tehran's nuclear programme. By one report, CIA Director Porter Goss visited Ankara in December 2005 and asked Turkey to help the United States deal with the Iranian nuclear issue. As the threat perception in Turkey increases, the country is more likely to cooperate.

What country represents the greatest danger to the US?

	Mar. 1990 %	Feb. 1992 %	Sept. 1993 %	Aug. 2001 %	Oct. 2005 %	Feb. 2006 %
Iran	6	4	7	5	9	27
China	8	8	11	32	16	20
Iraq	*	12	18	16	18	17
North Korea	*	*	1	1	13	11
The US itself	4	3	*	2	7	5
Al Qaeda/terrorists	–	–	–	*	2	4
Russia/USSR	32	13	8	9	2	3
Japan	8	31	11	3	1	1

If military action is to be taken, the timing of an attack must be sensitive to collateral damage, particularly after the nuclear programme has reached a stage where nuclear radiation and contamination might occur. Moreover, it would be preferable for the attacks to precede the consummation of the Russian sale of 30 Tor-M1 air defence systems to Iran (to be delivered in the 2006–08 period), as well as upgrades of the Mig and Sukhoi fighter jets used by Iran. This $1 billion arms deal will bolster Iran's capabilities to exact a higher price from the adversary's pre-emptive strike.[41]

However, in reality, military action may not prove necessary. An ultimatum that includes an unequivocal American threat to use force might be enough to convince the Iranians to freeze their nuclear programme and wait for a better time to complete it. Such an ultimatum could be accompanied by force concentration along the borders of Iran (in Afghanistan and in Iraq), naval manoeuvres in the Persian Gulf and Indian Ocean, and reconnaissance flights over Iranian air space. The threat of military force should be preceded by intensive American efforts to explain the danger of a nuclear Iran and active public diplomacy to gain international approval for military action. Israel and Turkey can add to this atmosphere by actions such as conducting civil defence and military drills. Since Iran practices brinkmanship as a regular part of its policy, only the threat of imminent US military action will define the boundary that the Iranian leadership does not want to cross.

This series of steps is exactly what most Arab states in the region expect. None of them wants a nuclear Iran, as it threatens them and their interests. It is worth remembering the support most Arab states lent to Baghdad during its long war with Tehran (1980–88). Indeed, the danger to the Arab world is more immediate than it is for the United States or perhaps even Israel. Only the actual use of nuclear weapons by Iran would endanger Israel or American forces, while the mere possession of such weapons – and their use for leverage and intimidation – could force Arab countries to submit to Tehran's demands. Consequently, most Arab leaders – except for those in Syria – hope to see the hegemonic superpower take a resolute stand on the matter. Whatever public reaction may surface in the region, in private the majority will savour such an American demonstration of leadership and determination in obstructing the Iranian nuclear programme.

If the United States does not act in accordance with its international responsibilities as a superpower, Israel will have to face the difficult choice of how to respond. Since June 1981, Israel's position has been that a military nuclear programme implemented by a hostile state constitutes a *casus belli* warranting pre-emptive action. With more to lose if Iran becomes nuclear, Israel would have more incentive to strike than the United States.

Israel can undertake a limited pre-emptive strike.[42] Israel certainly commands the weaponry, the manpower, and the guts to effectively take out key Iranian nuclear facilities. Capable of carrying as much ordnance as a Second World War heavy bomber, the F-15I can also deploy precision-guided munitions and penetrate enemy air space at low levels and high speeds. Israel's submarines can launch cruise missiles at long distances, and its commandos have a very good record of operating at great distances from home.

The air strike route is of course problematic, as Israeli airplanes would have to fly over Arab airspace. Although Israel and Turkey have a well-developed strategic relationship, it is unlikely that an AKP-ruled Ankara would allow the use of its airspace in an attack on Iran, but damaged Israeli aircraft or gunned-down Israeli air crews would have a chance of landing or surviving in Turkey or in the Kurdish areas of Iraq.[43] While it would be very difficult for Israel to carry out a sustained air campaign, creative solutions could be devised to increase Israeli projection of power at distances of over 1,000 km. Israel's leaders are likely to enjoy domestic support in the event that Israel decides to launch military strikes against Iranian nuclear facilities. Such support may erode, however, if the military operations are unsuccessful and if the toll of casualties is very high.

Any decision to use force must take into consideration the Iranian reaction to a military strike and prepare for it. The Iranians can interfere with the flow of oil from the Gulf, and launch a counter-attack with ballistic missiles (probably using conventional warheads) against its neighbours and Israel. They can also instigate Shia revolutions in the Gulf States and use proxy terrorist organizations to attack the United States and its allies, in particular Israel. The Gulf States are likely to prefer facing any Iranian challenge before it goes nuclear. Probably, the West can bear the limited cost likely to be exacted by Iran. The cost issue is not really relevant for Israel, because it will suffer the wrath of Iran even if the United States alone bombs the Iranian installations.

Conventional missile attacks on America's allies are unlikely to cause much damage, although they could partly paralyse their economic activities. The results would probably resemble those of the Iraqi missile attacks on Israel and Saudi Arabia in 1991. Acts of terrorism could create greater damage, although more intensive intelligence efforts and higher alerts of the internal security forces could limit the effectiveness of such operations. In any case, military strikes against Iran need to be accompanied by pre-emptive measures against terrorist cells and Iranian personnel involved in supporting and activating terrorist activity.

Damaging oil fields and installations in the Gulf, as well as interfering with the oil flow, is a major affront to the well-being of the international community and would put Iran in conflict with most of the world. Interruptions in the export of Iranian petroleum would also negatively affect the Iranian economy and subsequently the regime survivability. In any case, an Iranian decision to attack the oil routes, before the state has acquired the bomb, might be deterred by a clear commitment from the US to use its military power to assure the security of these routes. However, even without such a commitment, the US would act if confronted by Iranian attempts to block the Strait of Hormuz. While revolutionary Iran may become bold and adventurous with a nuclear arsenal at its disposal, before acquiring such awesome weapons it is unlikely to estrange the whole international community by causing serious damage to the supply of a critical commodity such as oil. The determination of the West, displayed by the use of force against Iran's nuclear installations, might even have a paralysing effect on the regime. In any case, to counter a scenario where Iran brings about serious supply shortages in oil supply, the US can exploit its Strategic Petroleum Reserve, as well as the oil strategic reserves of its allies to allow for replacement of the Iranian crude oil output in the world oil markets for some time.

Conclusion

A nuclear Iran poses a serious threat to the Middle East. Moreover, a nuclear bomb in the hands of such an extremist regime may have widespread repercussions, far beyond the region. Iran's deeply rooted ideological hostility towards Israel coupled with its emerging military capabilities puts the Jewish state in a particularly vulnerable spot. Diplomacy is doomed to fail and economic sanctions are usually ineffective, leaving only the threat to use force and the actual use of force as viable options to delay the completion of the Iranian nuclear programme. Resolute action against Iranian nuclear installations involves many risks, but inaction, it seems, will have far more serious repercussions.

If the United States refrains from action, Israel will face the difficult decision of whether to act unilaterally. While less suited to do the job than the

United States, the Israeli military is capable of reaching the appropriate targets in Iran. It remains to be seen whether Jerusalem will be forced to act in accordance with its strategic doctrine. If, despite local and/or international efforts, the Islamic Republic of Iran succeeds in emerging with a nuclear arsenal, however, it will not be the end of the current crisis, but rather the beginning of a new and far more dangerous one.

Efraim Inbar is Professor of Political Science at Bar-Ilan University and the Director of the Begin-Sadat (BESA) Center for Strategic Studies. The author appreciates the research assistance of David Leitner and Tamara Sternlieb. A version of this article appeared in English in the electronic journal MERIA (Spring 2006).

NOTES

1   See, inter alia, Ian Cobain and Ian Trainor, 'Secret Services say Iran is trying to assemble a nuclear missile', *Guardian*, 4 January 2006, http://www.guardian.co.uk./iran.story/0,12858,1677542,00. htm; Hillary Leila Krieger, 'Vienna Envoy: EU could impose Iran sanctions if UN doesn't', *Jerusalem Post*, 1 January 2006, p. 1; 'Alpogan: Turkey against Iran obtaining nuclear weapon capability', *New Anatolian*, 26 January 2006, p. 3; 'Stop Iran', *Defense News*, 16 January 2006, p. 20. See also: <http://www.rferl.org/featuresarticle/2006/02/FA989EBF-4EE0-43BD-9C68-C42A5338D385.html>; <http://www.forbes.com/business/manufacturing/ feeds/ap/2006/02/18/ap2537453.html>; <http://www.jpost.com/servlet/Satellite?cid=1139395436735& pagename =JPost%2FJPArticle%2FShowFull>; <http://www.cbsnews.com/stories/2006/01/12/world/main 1203654.shtml>.

2   'Sense of Urgency Cited by Bolton on Iran A-bomb', *Sun* (New York), 12 April 2006.

3   Uzi Mahnaimi and Sarah Baxter, 'Israel Readies Forces for Strike on Nuclear Iran', *London Times*, 11 December 2005. see also http://www.usatoday.com/news/world/2005-12-09-iran-nuke_x.htm?csp=34; http://msnbc.msn.com/id/10858243/site/newsweek/.

4   'Dagan: Iran will be become independent in its nuclear programme within months', *Haaretz*, 28 December 2005, p. A12.

5   For the Islamic Republic's quest for nuclear weapons see Patrick Clawson and Michael Rubin, *Eternal Iran. Continuity and Chaos*, New York: Palgrave Macmillan, 2005, pp. 139–46; for background and chronology of the nuclear programme, see <http://www.nti.org/e_research/ profiles/Iran/1819.html>.

6   For a comprehensive review of the nuclear programme, see Joseph Cirincione, Jon B. Wolfsthal, and Miriam Rajkumar, *Deadly Arsenals: Nuclear, Biological and Chemical Threats*, Washington, DC: Carnegie Endowment for International Peace, 2005), 2nd edn, pp. 295–314. See also the fact sheet at <http://www.armscontrol.org>; and Douglas Frantz, 'Iran Closes in Ability to Build a Nuclear Bomb', *Los Angeles Times*, 4 August 2003.

7   Natural uranium consists mostly of the uranium-235 isotope, with about 0.7 per cent by weight of uranium-235. The uranium-235 isotope is fissionable material. Enriched uranium is uranium whose uranium-235 content has been increased through a process of isotope separation. The fissile uranium in nuclear weapons usually contains 85 per cent or more of uranium-235, known as weapons-grade.

8   For estimates of Korean capabilities, see Jonathan D. Pollack, TITLE??'The United States, North Korea, and the End of the Agreed Framework', *Naval War College Review*, Vol. 56 (Summer 2003),

pp. 11–49.

9   For such a posture, see Benjamin Frankel, ed., *Opaque Nuclear Proliferation: Methodology and Policy Implications*, London: Frank Cass, 1991.

10 For an analysis of denuclearization, see Ariel E. Levite, 'Never Say Never Again: Nuclear Reversal Revisited', *International Security*, Vol. 27 No. 3 (Winter 2002/03), pp. 59–88.

11 Philip Sherwell, 'How we duped the West, by Iran's nuclear negotiator', *Daily Telegraph*, 5 March 2006.

12 For the roots and character of anti-Western ideologies, see Ian Buruma and Avishai Margalit, *Occidentalism. The West In the Eyes of Its Enemies*, London: Penguin Books, 2004.

13 Mordechai Kedar, 'Nucleotheism', *Jerusalem Post*, 14 December 2005, p. 13.

14 See Yehezkel Dror, *Crazy States*, Lexington, MA: Heath Lexington, 1973, Chapter 2. For an early reference to 'rogue states', see Anthony Lake, 'Confronting Backlash States', *Foreign Affairs*, Vol. 73 No. 2 (March/April 1994).

15 For the rationale of state-supported terrorism and for Iran's links to the Hezbollah, see Daniel Byman, *Deadly Connections. States that Sponsor Terrorism*, Cambridge: Cambridge University Press, 2005, pp. 21–52; 79–116.

16 US Department of State, 'Patterns of Global Terrorism – 2003', 29 April 2004, <http://www.state.gov./s/ct/rls/pgtrpt/2003/31644.htm>.

17 'Ze'evi: US-Iran diplomatic process stuck in the mud', *Jerusalem Post*, 21 December 2005, p. 2.

18 Uzi Rubin, the father of the Israeli Arrow missile programme, noted that Iranian capability to launch a satellite – an ability that Iran is aggressively pursuing – amounts to the country's possession of intercontinental missiles. See Julie Stahl, 'Iran's Space Launch Programme May Put US at Nuclear Risk', *CNS News*, 9 December 2005,<http://www.cnsnews.com/ViewForeign Bureaus.asp?Page=\ForeignBureaus\archive\200512\FOR20051209e.html>.

19 Kathleen J. McInnis, 'Extended Deterrence: The US Credibility Gap in the Middle East', *Washington Quarterly*, Vol. 28 No. 3 (Summer 2005), pp. 169–86.

20 For the Arrow programme, see Uzi Rubin, 'Meeting the "Depth Threat" in Iraq – The Origins of Israel's Arrow System', *Jerusalem Issue Brief*, Vol. 2 No. 19, Jerusalem Center for Public Affairs, 5 March 2003). The United States and Israel have also shown interest in the Boost Phase Intercept option (BPI), when missiles are slow and have a big electronic signature. This option is of particularly appeal if the missile carries a nuclear warhead that could explode immediately after launch in the vicinity of the launcher. This weapon system is still in a development stage, and it is not clear if it will be operational by the time Iran goes nuclear.

21 For US difficulties in erecting a missile defence system, see Jeremy Singer, 'MDA War Game Highlights Missile Defense Complexity', *Defense News*, 6 February 2006. p. 18.

22 For the formative argument that nuclear deterrence is context-dependent, see Albert Wohlstetter, 'The Delicate Balance of Terror', *Foreign Affairs*, Vol. 36 No. 1 (January 1959), pp. 211–34. For an application of this argument to the Middle East, see Yair Evron, 'Nuclear Weapons in the Middle East', in Asher Arian (ed.), *Israel: A Developing Society*, Assen: Van Gorcum, 1980, pp. 105–26. For a similar argument about the Indian subcontinent, see S. Paul Kapur, 'India and Pakistan's Unstable Peace: Why Nuclear South Asia Is Not Like Cold War Europe', *International Security*, Vol. 30 No. 2 (Fall 2005), pp. 125–52. The counter-argument that nuclear proliferation might bring stability is extremely problematic. For a recent formulation of this thesis, see Kenneth N. Waltz, 'For Better: Nuclear Weapons Preserve an Imperfect Peace', in Scott D. Sagan and Kenneth N. Waltz (eds), *The Spread of Nuclear Weapons: A Debate Renewed*, New York: W.W. Norton, 2003.

23 One reason for the Israeli interest in cooperation with India is to facilitate a naval presence in the Indian Ocean. See Efraim Inbar, 'The Indian-Israeli Entente', *Orbis*, Vol. 48 No. 1 (Winter 2004), pp. 99–100.

24 <http://www.iran-press-service.com/articles_2001/dec_2001/rafsanjani_nuke_threats_141201.htm>.

25 Thomas C. Schelling, *The Strategy of Conflict*, 4th edn, Cambridge, MA: Harvard University Press, 1970, p. 37.

26 Raymond Aron uses this phrase to emphasize that the dialogue between the participants in a

conflict establishes the meaning of the action. See his *War and Peace: A Theory in International Relations*, Garden City, NY: Doubleday, 1966, p. 167.

27   The author thanks Steven David for bringing this point to his attention. For a balanced discussion of nuclear terrorism, see Robin M. Frost, *Nuclear Terrorism After 9/11*, Adelphi Paper No. 378, London: IISS and Routledge, December 2005.

28   The term 'energy ellipse' was coined by Geoffrey Kemp and Robert E. Harkavy, *Strategic Geography and the Changing Middle East*, Washington, DC: Carnegie Endowment for International Peace, 1997, p. 113.

29   *Jerusalem Post*, 1 December 2005, p. 1.

30   'Interview with PM Rabin', *Bamahane*, 23 September 1992,p. 9. For Rabin's attitude toward the introduction of nuclear weapons in the Middle East, see Efraim Inbar, *Yitzhak Rabin and Israel's National Security*, Washington, DC: Wilson Center and Johns Hopkins University Press, 1999, pp. 118–24.

31   For Iranian attitudes toward Israel, see David Menashri, 'Iran, Israel and the Middle East Conflict', *Israel Affairs*, Vol. 12 No. 1 (January 2006), pp. 107–22.

32   For the notion of 'soft power', see Joseph S. Nye, *Soft Power. The Means to Success in World Politics*, New York: Public Affairs, 2004.

33   See Farah Stockman, 'US and Allies Eye Sanctions on Iran', *Boston Globe*, 21 February 2006.

34   Mel Levine, Alex Turkeltaub and Alex Gorbansky, '3 Myths About the Iran Conflict', *Washington Post*, 7 February 2006, p. A21.

35   See Robert A. Pape, 'Why Economic Sanctions Do Not Work', *International Security*, Vol. 27 No. 3 (Fall 1997), pp. 90–136; Jean-Marc F. Blanchard and Norrin M. Risman, 'Asking the Right Question: When Do Economic Sanctions Work Best?', *Security Studies*, Vol. 9 Nos 1/2 (Autumn 1999–Winter 2000), pp. 219–53.

36   Clawson and Rubin, *Eternal Iran*, p. 158.

37   Natan Sharansky, *The Case for Democracy*, New York: Public Affairs, 2004.

38   See Abbas Milani, 'US Foreign Policy and the Future of Democracy in Iran', *Washington Quarterly*, Vol. 28 No. 3 (Summer 2005), pp. 41–56.

39   <http://www.state.gov/t/us/rm/25752.htm>.

40   *Haaretz*, November 24, 2003, p. A. 5.

41   Barry Rubin, *Cauldron of Turmoil. America in the Middle East* (New York: Harcourt Brace Jovanovich, 1992), pp. 102-109.

42   Seymour M. Hersh, 'The Iran Plans – Would President Bush go to war to stop Tehran from getting the bomb?', *The New Yorker*, 17 April 2006 <http://www.newyorker.com/fact/content/articles/060417fa_fact>.

43   Inter alia, see Edward N. Lutwak, 'In a Single Night', *Wall Street Journal*, February 8, 2006.

44   'Cheney: Iran at 'top of list of Trouble Spots' asks' Israel to carry out the Attack', Centre for Research on Globalisation, January 12, 2005. Available at: <http://globalresearch.ca/articles/501A.html>.

45   'Bush declares solidarity with Europe on Iran', *MSNBC*, 18 February 2005. Available at: <http://www.msnbc.msn.com/id/6992154/>.

46   '"All options are on the table", President George W. Bush on Iran', *Disarmament Diplomacy*, 12 August 2005. From Yaron Deckel, 'Interview of the President by Israeli Television Channel 1', Israeli TV Channel 1, at the Bush ranch, Crawford, Texas, 11 August 2005. <http://www.acronym.org.uk/docs/0508/doc04.htm>.

47   Carol Giacomo, 'US Senators say military strike on Iran must be an option', *Reuters*, 15 January 2006.

48   '57% Back a Hit on Iran if Defiance Persists', *LA Times*, 27 January 2006, based on *LA Times* poll <http://www.latimes.com/news/nationworld/nation/la-na-fornpoll27 jan27,0,5687029.story?coll=la-home-headlines> (and another presentation of BBC poll results: <http://www.globescan.com/news_archives/bbcpoll06-3.html>).

49   See <http://people-press.org/reports/display.php3?ReportID=269>.

50   See <http://www.globescan.com/news_archives/bbcpoll06-3.html>.

51 Philip Webster, 'Blair hints at military action after Iran's "disgraceful" taunt', *Times Online*, 28 October 2005 <http://www.timesonline.co.uk/article/0,,251-1846793,00.html>.

52 Interviews of the author with senior French officials, February 2006.

53 *Cumhuriet*, 13 December 2005.

54 Lyubov Pronina, 'Russian Arms Sale to Iran Draws US Scrutiny', *Defense News*, 12 December 2005, p. 6.

55 Nathan Guttman, 'Yaalon: Israeli Can Hit Iran's Nuke Sites', *Jerusalem Post*, 10 March 2006, p. 1.

56 See Efraim Inbar, *The Israeli-Turkish Entente*, London: King's College Mediterranean Programme, 2001, Chapter 2.

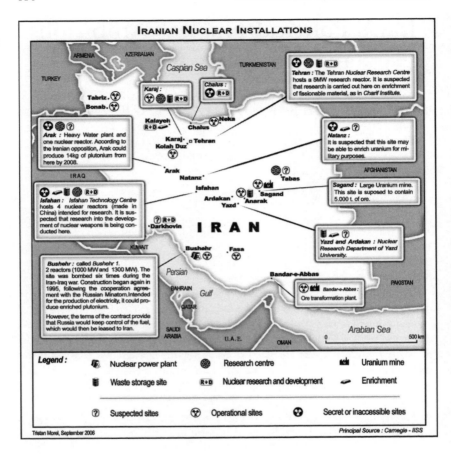

IRANIAN NUCLEAR INSTALLATIONS

Tehran : The *Tehran Nuclear Research Centre* hosts a 5MW research reactor. It is suspected that research is carried out here on enrichment of fissionable material, as in *Charif Institute*.

Arak : Heavy Water plant and one nuclear reactor. According to the Iranian opposition, Arak could produce 14kg of plutonium from here by 2008.

Isfahan : Isfahan Technology Centre hosts 4 nuclear reactors (made in China) intended for research. It is suspected that research into the development of nuclear weapons is being conducted here.

Natanz : It is suspected that this site may be able to enrich uranium for military purposes.

Sagand : Large Uranium mine. This site is suposed to contain 5.000 t. of ore.

Yazd and Ardakan : Nuclear Research Department of Yazd University.

Busehr : called Bushehr 1. 2 reactors (1000 MW and 1300 MW). The site was bombed six times during the Iran-Iraq war. Construction began again in 1995, following the cooperation agreement with the Russian Minatom.Intended for the production of electricity, it could produce enriched plutonium.

However, the terms of the contract provide that Russia would keep control of the fuel, which would then be leased to Iran.

Bandar-e-Abbes : Ore transformation plant.

Legend :

Nuclear power plant	Research centre	Uranium mine
Waste storage site	Nuclear research and development	Enrichment
Suspected sites	Operational sites	Secret or inaccessible sites

Tristan Morel, September 2006

Principal Source : Carnegie - IISS

Iran's Political/Nuclear Ambitions and US Policy Options

KARIM SADJADPOUR

**Testimony Before the US Senate Foreign Relations Committee
18 May 2006**

Mr Chairman and Senator Biden, thank you for allowing me, on behalf of the International Crisis Group, the privilege to discuss before you the fate and relationship of the two countries which I care most deeply about, the United States and Iran.

Mr Chairman and Senator Biden, I fear we are on a collision course with decidedly devastating consequences for the future of the US's international standing, nuclear non-proliferation, Middle East peace and security, and Iran's evolution toward a society which respects the human rights and civil liberties of its citizens. What was once described as a game of chess has evolved into a game of chicken: The United States and Iran are like two cars moving head on with increasing velocity. Most concerning is that neither side believes that it serves its interests to slow down or get out of the way.

The policy stances of both sides have the merit of being clear: Washington sincerely doubts that Tehran's intentions are peaceful, and refuses to 'reward bad behaviour' or 'confer legitimacy' on the Iranian regime by talking to it. Tehran, meanwhile, believes that the nuclear issue is simply a pretext used by the US to cover its regime change ambitions, and that agreeing to compromise on its 'legal NPT rights' would not allay US pressure, but on the contrary be perceived by Washington as a sign of weakness that would only invite further pressure. Operating under this premise, Iran's leadership believes it must not relent from its position, especially when oil prices soar, its hand in Iraq is strong, and there is still no indication that a more conciliatory Iranian approach would beget a more conciliatory US response.

I do not believe that a nuclear-armed Iran is inevitable. Nor do I believe that a firm decision has been made in Tehran to pursue the acquisition of a nuclear weapon.

Despite current ominous trends I remain hopeful that the Iranian people's aspirations to live in a more open society at peace with the outside world is a worthy goal which will one day be realized. But I believe the probability of achieving either of these two salient goals – preventing a nuclear-armed Iran and forwarding the cause of Iranian democracy – is highly unlikely in the context of current US policy toward Iran.

Over three decades of US attempts to change Iranian behaviour by isolating it politically and economically have borne little fruit: 27 years after the 1979 revolution, Iran continues to sit atop the State Department's list of the world's state sponsors of terror, continues to play an unconstructive role in the Israeli-Palestinian conflict, continues to expand its military arsenal, and continues to repress its own population. If US policy toward Iran were a business model, it would have been scrapped long ago for failing to achieve its bottom line.

Tehran's Calculations: The Internal Nuclear Debate

Iran's senior leadership has always attempted to project a unified mindset regarding the nuclear issue, but in reality the country's ruling elites are divided into three broad categories: those who favour pursuit of the nuclear project at all costs; those who wish to pursue it without sacrificing diplomatic interests; and those who argue for a suspension of activities to build trust and allow for a full fuel cycle down the road. Understanding and exploiting these differences should be a key component of any diplomatic approach.

The first group, sympathizers of President Mahmoud Ahmadinejad, comprises ideologues and confrontationists who romanticize the defiance of the revolution's early days. They believe that former President Mohammed Khatami's 'détente' foreign policy projected an image of weakness while achieving little for Tehran other than membership in the 'Axis of Evil'. In contrast, they favour an uncompromising approach, in some cases going as far as to advocate that Iran withdraw from the NPT, unequivocally pursue its nuclear ambitions, and dare the international community to react. This group advocates measures such as withholding oil exports and cutting diplomatic ties with countries that side against Iran, confident that 'the West needs Iran more than we need them'. While two to three years ago such views were on the fringe, with the recent elections they have gained increased relevance and credibility.

Like the confrontationists, the second group is highly cynical of Western (particularly US) intentions, and argues that Iran is 'bound by national duty' to pursue its 'inalienable' right to enrich uranium. Unlike them, however, they favour working within an international framework. Iran's lead nuclear negotiator Ali Larijani is perhaps the best representative of this group, arguing simultaneously, perhaps inconsistently, that Iran must neither succumb to 'Western double standards' nor abandon diplomacy. 'The West wants two classes of nations,' Larijani frequently says. 'Those that have nuclear technology and can be advanced, and nations that must be restricted to produce only tomato juice and air conditioners ... [But] a country's survival depends on its political and diplomatic ties. You can't live in isolation.'

The third, more conciliatory group, arguably most representative of popular sentiment, is currently the least influential. After months of silence, however, they are increasingly beginning to make their voices heard. Former President Khatami and former lead nuclear negotiator Hassan Rowhani have criticized their successor's disregard for diplomacy, and the country's largest reform party recently urged the government to voluntarily suspend all nuclear fuel cycle work. Believing the costs of nuclear intransigence to be greater than its benefits, they argue that Iran should freeze its enrichment activities in order to build confidence and assuage international concerns. This group welcomes diplomacy and has consistently backed direct talks with the US, convinced that the Europeans are incapable of providing the political, economic, and security dividends Iran seeks.

Signing off on all major decision in Iran is Supreme Leader Ayatollah Ali Khamenei, whose 17-year track record suggests a leader who wants neither confrontation nor accommodation with the West. Yet decisions in Iran are made by consensus rather than decree, and at the moment Ayatollah Khamenei appears more influenced by advisors who argue - with some plausibility - that nothing short of regime change will satisfy the US, and that retreating on the nuclear question will only display weakness. If there is to be a clash with the US, Tehran's hard-liners want it to occur on their terms, when oil prices are high and the US is bogged down in Iraq.

Ahmadinejad and the Struggle for Power

If Mahmoud Ahmadinejad's election proved anything, it is that the Iranian regime is far from monolithic and Iranian politics are far from predictable. While his triumph last June was widely viewed as a consolidation of power by the nation's conservatives, differences among conservatives have never been greater than today. And though it was widely assumed that he would focus on domestic economic affairs and have minimal influence over Iran's foreign policy, in the nine months since his inauguration Ahmadinejad's impact on Iran's foreign relations has been nothing short of monumental.

Ahmadinejad's assertiveness and outspokenness has surprised many. During his election campaign he criticized Iran's previous nuclear negotiating team for being 'frightened', and as president he disbanded it in favour of his own. He is said to have personally authored the provocative speech he delivered at the UN Security Council last September, and to have penned his recent 18-

page letter to President Bush. Ahmadinejad also has repeatedly issued provocative, bellicose statements on Israel that go beyond what the Supreme Leader or others in the leadership have pronounced.

By most accounts, the president's style has irked the country's entrenched political elite. Senior officials have complained that he 'doesn't play by the rules', and displays a surprising lack of respect for the Islamic Republic's protocols and hierarchy. Rather than defer to the elders of the revolution on matters as significant as the nuclear issue or US-Iran relations, he has tried to present himself as a force that cannot be bypassed. Indeed, political rivalries once kept under wraps are now playing out in the open. Last month, for example, Ahmadinejad's eagerly anticipated announcement that Iran had successfully operated a centrifuge cascade was pre-emptively leaked by Rafsanjani to the Kuwaiti press. More recently, when news came out that he had written an unprecedented letter to President Bush, former lead nuclear negotiator Hassan Rowhani quickly countered by releasing a concise, two-page compromise proposal to *Time* magazine – seemingly sending a message to the West that he is an alternative messenger with an alternative message.

Ahmadinejad's behaviour can be explained on two counts. To some extent, it is a function of his ambiguous relationship with Ayatollah Khamenei. The two men have decidedly different post-revolution experiences and respon-sibilities: Ahmadinejad and his peers' most salient experience was fighting in the battlefields during the Iran-Iraq war whereas Ayatollah Khamenei was serving as president, and faced with the day-to-day dilemmas of governing a country embroiled in a full-blown war and facing near total political, economic, and diplomatic isolation. Wary of repeating this experience, the Supreme Leader has more than once publicly downplayed Ahmadinejad's fiery pronouncements. Yet, at the same time, there is evidence that Khamenei appreciates Ahmadinejad's anti-corruption campaign and his com-mitment to revolutionary ideals, and finds comfort in working with a junior president who is seemingly loyal to him and at the same time makes him look like a moderate. Moreover, Khamenei judges various government officials by their results: in this case, he may well consider that during his relatively short tenure Ahmadinejad has accomplished more progress on the nuclear file than in the previous two and a half years of negotiations with Europe.

While Ahmadinejad's behaviour has caused disquiet among the political elite, his standing on the Iranian street is more difficult to assess. On one hand he has failed to deliver on his core electoral promise, namely that he would 'put the oil money on people's dinner tables'; since his inauguration last August the country has experienced massive capital flight, foreign investment has dropped precipitously, and Tehran's stock exchange has lost nearly a third of its value. Most noticeably for the Iranian people, inflation has increased dramatically, and unemployment has also risen.

Still, Ahmadinejad continues to enjoy some backing, a result of his populist rhetoric, pious ways, humble lifestyle, and fiery nationalism. Aware that he lacks support among the urban middle and upper classes, he instead has courted economically disenfranchised Iranians in smaller towns and far-off provinces, promising loans and debt-relief. Realizing that he lacks favour among the country's top elite—technocrats, business mangers, journalists, academics and even senior clerics – he curries favour with the country's paramilitary groups, such as the *basiji*; has attempted to co-opt the country's military forces by providing numerous projects in the construction and development sector to Revolutionary Guard commanders; and has formed close alliances with powerful hard-line clerics in Qom, such as Ayatollah Mesbah Yazdi. All in all, he has managed through his nationalist rhetoric and postures to set the tone for Iranian foreign policy in a way that few had anticipated beforehand.

Iran's Domestic Evolution

Despite concerns about Ahmadinejad and his team's desires to return to the early days of the revolution, societal reform in Iran is a train that has left the tracks. While it may be slowed down at times, and will certainly face delays and obstacles, it is a process that will be near impossible to reverse, for sheer demographic reasons: Two-thirds of Iranians are under 33-years-old; they increasingly are connected to the outside world via satellite television and the Internet; and they have no special affinity for a revolution they did not experience and a revolutionary government which has not been able to meet their economic expectations.

Indeed, for the vast majority of Iranians the priority is economic rather than political deliverance. This is not to say that democracy and human rights are not important concerns, but that for a majority of Iranians they come second. As a Tehran labourer once explained to me, 'When your stomach is empty you don't cry for democracy, you cry for bread!'

While throughout the country Iranians' sense of alienation *vis-à-vis* their leaders is palpable, despite these socio-economic discontents people have become increasingly disillusioned with politics. In 1997, 2000, and 2001 they went to the polls in overwhelming numbers, twice to elect President Khatami and once to elect a reform-minded parliament, yet saw insufficient returns on their civic investments. As a Tehran-based intellectual once told me, 'People's political frustration is to be expected. It's like exercising every day for six years and not seeing any results. Soon you are going to stop going to the gym.'

What's more, without a clear alternative model or alternative leadership, the deep-seated desire for economic, political, and social reform among many Iranians is tempered by a strong aversion to unrest, uncertainty, and insecurity. Having already experienced one tumultuous revolution (or in the case of Iran's youth, the aftermath of one tumultuous revolution) and a brutal eight-year war with Iraq, Iranians have few concrete ideas as to how change should take place other than it ought to occur *bedun-e khoonrizi* – 'without bloodshed'.

The post-war turbulence and insecurity in next-door neighbour Iraq has made Iranians even wearier about the prospects of a sudden political upheaval or a quick-fix solution. As opposed to the aftermath of the US removal of the Taliban in Afghanistan, when some Iranians could be heard naively romant-icizing about the prospects of a swift US intervention in Tehran, today it is rare to find any Iranians who see Iraq as a model for change, or look to their Western neighbour with envy. In the widely echoed words of one middle-class, middle-aged Tehran resident, 'When we look at what's going on in Iraq, it seems that the real choice is not one between democracy or authoritarianism, but between stability or unrest. People may not be happy in Iran, but no one wants unrest.'

Implications for US Policy

1   *To effectively counter Tehran's confrontationists, the US must simultaneously strengthen its pragmatists.*

While the US should make clear that a bellicose Iranian policy will not reap rewards, it should also clarify that a conciliatory and compromising Iranian stance would trigger reciprocal steps. A broader diplomatic accommodation – Iran forsaking domestic uranium enrichment and modifying its objectionable domestic and regional behaviour in exchange for improved bilateral relations, security assurances, and a lifting of sanctions – is the preferred option. But given the depth of mutual mistrust and ill will, it may not be possible to achieve this at the moment.

A smaller bargain proposed by the International Crisis Group would be to offer Iran a 'delayed, limited enrichment scheme', acknowledging its eventual right, after several years of a total freeze, to operate a small-scale uranium enrichment facility under an intrusive inspections regime, making clear that a military program would not be tolerated.

In both instances the logic is similar: to strengthen the hand of Iranians who are pressing for a more accommodating foreign and nuclear policy, they need to have a realistic and appealing alternative to point to.

2   *Dialogue does not equal appeasement and certainly not indifference to human rights abuses.*

It is important that we disabuse ourselves of the notion that dialogue is tantamount to appeasement, or would be 'selling out' the Iranian people's aspirations for a more representative government. Quite the contrary: opinion polls suggest that upwards of 75 per cent of Iranians want their government to have relations with the US. Iranian democratic activists like female former MP Fatemeh Haghighatjou – currently a fellow at MIT – have long argued that a U.S-Iran diplomatic accommodation is crucial for domestic change to take place in Iran. Embarking on a comprehensive dialogue with Iran would provide the US with the opportunity to match its rhetorical commitment to Iranian democracy and human rights with action, instead of ineffectively, and at times counterproductively, trying to promote it from afar.

Greater economic and cultural contacts with the outside world, combined with continued international insistence on political reform and respect for human rights, would strengthen Iran's burgeoning civil society not weaken it, and dilute the conservatives' hold on power rather than fortify it.

3   *A sudden upheaval or abrupt political change in Iran is unlikely to be for the better.*

John Limbert, the erudite Iran scholar and talented former US diplomat (taken hostage in Iran for 444 days) once reflected on the 1979 Iranian revolution that his liberal-minded Iranian friends 'who could write penetrating analyses and biting editorials' lacked the stomach to 'throw acid, break up meetings, beat up opponents, trash opposition newspapers, and organize street gangs … .and engage in the brutality that wins revolutions'.

Today we should be similarly sober about the realities of a short-term upheaval in Iran. There currently exists no credible, organized alternative to the status quo whether within Iran or in the diaspora. And despite the fact that a majority of Iranians are in favour of a more tolerant, democratic system, there is little evidence to believe that in the event of a sudden uprising it would be Iranian democrats who come to power, especially in a country with nearly 150,000 Revolutionary Guardsmen and two million members of the *basiji*, whose livelihood, in many cases, depends on the continuation of the status quo.

4   *The US should make it clear that it has no intention of undermining*
     Iran's territorial integrity.

While a diversity of opinion exists among Iranians regarding the country's nuclear ambitions, the maintenance of the country's territorial integrity is an issue which unites the vast majority of countrymen of all ethnic, religious, and political persuasions. Amid widespread concern and rumours in Iran that the US is flirting with a strategy of supporting ethnic Iranian separatist groups, Washington should do its utmost to reassure the Iranian people that such concerns are unfounded.

Mr Chairman and Senator Biden, I believe there are two equally plausible visions for Iran's future. One is a hostile, backward-looking nation increasingly isolated from the international community, but with enough oil wealth to fund military and paramilitary groups which repress popular demand for change. Despite popular discontent, such a situation could be sustainable in Iran for years if not decades; an Islamic Cuba, with, potentially, a nuclear weapon.

The second scenario is of a country which has made amends with the United States, is re-integrated into the international community, experiences large flows of foreign investment, a strengthened middle class, a burgeoning private sector, and a free flow of tourists and members of the Iranian diaspora visiting freely. It is this scenario which will provide fertile ground for Iran's transition to a more tolerant and democratic system at peace with the international community.

Karim Sajadpour is an analyst with the International Crisis Group.

The Iranian Nuclear Programme: Process and Legitimacy

ALI RASTBEEN

Iran as a nuclear power is now the central concern of international diplomacy. There is an irrational debate about the real nature of Iran's project to acquire civil nuclear technology. Many, especially the United States, contest Iran's right to develop civil nuclear technology, even though this right is enshrined in the Nuclear Non-Proliferation Treaty (NPT). Since the break-up of the Soviet Union, the concept of nuclear deterrence has changed and this has thrown international relations into confusion. This change has especially altered relations between the United States and the former Soviet Union towards third countries. A chasm has opened up between the notion of nuclear energy for civil and military purposes. Attention is focused on the need to prevent the use of 'weapons of mass destruction'. According to this policy, the United States and the Western powers are trying to hold back the capacities of countries which either have or are about to have nuclear power, all in the name of the risks of nuclear proliferation and of nuclear terrorism.

It is important to understand the nuclear question in all its different aspects. These include the fact that many states want to have nuclear energy and that states which have signed the Nuclear Non-Proliferation Treaty have a right to do so. Nuclear militarization is not a priority in the development of modern energy policy. Today, this problem has arisen with respect to a unique and interesting case, that of Iran. The Iranian nuclear programme does not date from the time of this crisis. Instead, its origins lie in cooperation with the United States and France. However, an understanding of the origins of this crisis does not change the classic doctrines of nuclear strategy. These doctrines evolve in a completely different manner according to regional geopolitical plans and according to the emerging powers.

The Genesis of the Iranian Nuclear Programme

In 1961, the Shah visited General de Gaulle and inspected the French nuclear installation at Sarclay. As such, nuclear cooperation with Iran was therefore an energy policy supported by the Western powers. From the 1950s, the United States claimed strategic control over nuclear energy and sought to determine the choices of its allies and their own access to it. President Eisenhower made it clear that this was a form of pre-emptive cooperation when he declared in 1959, 'Whenever a president of the United States decides the it is in the security interests of the US, the US will improve the nuclear capacity of the chosen allies. According to what is appropriate, this will occur through exchanges, the provision of information and materiel, or even through the supply of nuclear weapons, with the appropriate arms controls measures.'[1] The emergence of Iran's ambition to acquire nuclear energy corresponded to socio-economic development which modified the political and strategic landscape of the country.

Indeed, the economic factors which are necessary for the development of the energy sector became for Iran a launching-pad for the elaboration of an energy policy which was both carefully planned and implemented in cooperation with Western powers. Income from oil exports allowed the Shah to undertake a process of major political, economic and social transformation in Iran. Land belonging to the Crown and the state was distributed to the people in 1958, and this was a prelude to the 'white revolution' of 1963. The maximum size of a land holding was fixed at 10–15 hectares according to irrigation. In 1966, more than 2 million families (more than 11 million individuals) benefited from this agrarian reform which, in less than ten years, saw the disappearance of the class of large landowners which had previously been all-powerful. More than one-third of fertile land had belonged to this class, which represented 0.2 per cent of the population. In parallel, education for the masses was developed with the creation of a body of teachers whose task was to educate illiterate people in villages. Between 1954 and 1970, a period in which the population rose by more than 50 per cent,[2] the number of children in primary schools rose by a factor of 3.7, the number in secondary schools by a factor of 7, and the number of people at college by a factor of 8.[3] In the space of thirty years, the proliferation of schools, especially in the countryside, completely changed the social landscape of Iran. Iranian society was transformed from an illiterate one to an ever more educated one.[4] This evolution is explained by the very nature of the white revolution, whose whole purpose was to change the way traditional Iranian society functioned.

However, oil production increased at a vertiginous rate, reaching around 293 million tonnes in 1973 and making Iran the fourth largest producer of oil in the world (after the US, the USSR and Saudi Arabia). Iran became the second largest exporter of oil, just behind its rival in the Persian Gulf, Saudi Arabia. On 24 May 1973, Iran gained control of its oil production via a new agreement signed with the oil consortium. At the beginning, the nationalization of the oil industry by Prime Minister Mossadegh in March 1951 demonstrated that Iran wanted to abandon its status as a 'peripheral' state in order to achieve independence and control over its natural resources. Mossadegh's strategy was based in part on the weakening of British power in the Middle East after the Second World War. The nationalization cancelled the terms of the contract with the Anglo-Iranian Oil Company in 1933, in spite of numerous attempts to find a compromise which Mossadegh rejected because he knew that the British presence in Iran kept the country in a state of energy dependency. According to Ramazani, the British government had indicated its readiness to conclude another contract on the basis of 'an equal share of profits' after nationalization.[5] Britain and the US tried to find a diplomatic solution to the question of nationalization and of how to exploit Iran's natural resources.[6] The affair was a source of concern for the United States because the new arrangements affected the West's oil supplies. The nationalization set an example for other peripheral states, the exploitation of whose hydrocarbons and other strategic sites was in the hands of Western powers.

The departure of British forces from the south of Iran should not, however, be interpreted as a reduction of Western influence in the region. On the contrary, the United States was well aware of the risk that the Tudeh Party might take power in a communist coup.[7] George McGhee, US Under-Secretary of State for the Middle East, South Asia and Africa, wrote in July 1951:

> What is at stake in Iran is far more than oil. One can be sure that the Kremlin will take the opportunity to fish in the 'troubled oil' of Iran because, quite apart from its oil, Iran would be a superb strategic gain. The control of Iran, which has a surface area as large as the United States to the East of the Mississippi, would put the Soviet Union on the communications route between the free nations of Asia and Europe.[8]

After the nationalization of oil, Iran championed the rise in the price of 'black gold' within OPEC. The Tehran agreements of February 1971 caused a 40 per cent increase in Iran's revenue from oil. Income from oil in the following years was $5 billion in 1973 and $20 billion in 1974. Iran had not only large oil reserves (9 billion tonnes) but also large reserves of natural gas (7.6 billion tonnes), and had embarked on a rapid process of strengthening its economic, political and military power. By 1974 the annual growth rate had been 12 per cent for five years. Annual per capita income went from $400 to $650 between 1970 and 1973 and it was predicted to double by 1982. Faced with such change in the energy sector, however, the Shah was not prepared to give in to the illusions of oil, in spite of the excellent economic perspectives which oil offered Iran. Why was there such interest in developing nuclear energy? What was the Iranian strategy for developing nuclear power in the Middle East?

The Shah spoke in terms of the energy of the future, saying that important projects would be launched on the basis of nuclear power, and that this would change the situation in the Middle East. This economic expansion did not impact only on regional and international politics; on the contrary, the economic growth of Iran took place within a political system which became more and more authoritarian even though it did seem to have the support of the majority of the population (notwithstanding violent opposition by certain student, intellectual and religious circles). In addition to the repression of the opposition (there were more than a hundred executions between 1971 and 1974) political parties were dissolved in 1975 and a single organization was put in place, the 'Iranian Renewal'. However, Iranian foreign policy was heavily based on the armed forces, which had the most modern weaponry, supplied by the United States and Britain.

The introduction of nuclear energy in Iran, as in the majority of Western states, started at the end of the 1950s with the US 'Atoms for Peace' programme.[9] This was an initiative whose purpose was to prevent states outside American influence from obtaining access to nuclear technology. This meant preventing new states from becoming nuclear, other than the USSR and the US.

It was at the 'Atoms for Peace' exhibition in Tehran in 1957 that the Shah announced the signature of an agreement, proposed by the US, on research into the peaceful use of nuclear technology. The cooperation was initially limited to technical assistance and to the 'lease' of several kilogrammes of enriched uranium. A year later, the centre for nuclear research, which operated in Baghdad under the auspices of the Central Treaty Organization (CENTO),[10] was transferred to Tehran. Nuclear energy cooperation was not limited to this regional alliance but instead also included European states.

Before 1964, most of the electricity-generating stations in Iran were small diesel units which operated for local private businesses. In 1963, an 'electricity authority' was created which later became the Ministry of Water and Electricity. A dozen regional electricity enterprises were constituted to coordinate the existing network of small private stations spread around the country. The majority of these stations were nationalized.

At the international level, conference on the peaceful use of nuclear energy were held in Geneva in 1955 and 1958. These produced documentation on technical information on the peaceful use of nuclear energy by the states that had it, including the Soviet Union. Dozens of countries launched nuclear programmes and the first international sales of reactors for commercial use of scientific research took place. For the most part these were not American stations using enriched uranium but instead stations built by the British, French or Canadians which used natural uranium.[11]

In 1956, France decided to train Iranian physicists through a programme of scientific cooperation. It should be recalled that the Americans had a monopoly over the supply of nuclear technology to Iran, as it did in cooperation with its European allies: the Americans decided in 1970[12] to start building uranium enrichment plants in Europe. Iran, associated with this programme of cooperation with France and the US, became an actor behind the scenes in the development of Western nuclear programmes. Two consortia were created, firstly Eurodif in 1973 – the European Gaseous Diffusion Uranium Enrichment Consortium which included France, Spain, Italy, Belgium and Iran. This was a programme to build a gigantic uranium enrichment plant in Europe. Iran's financial participation in this consortium was significant and helped it to enrich uranium. This agreement in turn gave rise to the creation of two companies incorporated in France, Sofidif and Coredif. Iran's share was 40 per cent of Sofidif and 20 per cent of Coredif. Through this form of shareholding Eurodif became the largest commercial uranium enrichment facility in Europe, and third in the world after the US and the Soviet Union. Iran had a blocking power in the consortium, being the largest shareholder, which gave it a power of control and decision on 'sensitive' production lines, in particular those of enriched uranium for military use.[13] According to this agreement, Iran had the right to take 10 per cent of the uranium enriched by Eurodif, which permitted it to have a sufficient quantity to power ten nuclear stations. The same agreement provided, in its juridical section, for the financial support of Iran via a loan. Tehran lent France a billion dollars through the Commissariat for Atomic Energy, which was a support fund for setting up the facility. Iran's shareholding in Sofidif also gave it 10 per cent of the plant's production. It was a simple agreement: 'The whole agreement was extremely clear and written on a single page.'[14] After the signature of this agreement in 1974 in Tehran[15], the sale of these nuclear stations was shared out between France and Germany. The cooperation between the nuclear powers went beyond the Franco-Iranian agreement, but the new Eurodif factory set the stage for a more structured cooperation with the Americans. The United States had had an Iranian programme since the 1960s[16] in parallel with the agreement with France. Henry Kissinger's visit in 1974, before the Franco-Iranian agreement had been signed, opened the perspective of a new cooperation with the US. The communiqué issued at the end of this visit spoke of launching an Iranian-American cooperation programme in nuclear matters, but also of the integration of Iran – as the only non-Western country – into the new structure of nuclear powers. Kissinger confirmed these agreements at the beginning of August 1976.[17] The agreements concerned the provision by the United States of more than six nuclear reactors in addition to those sold by France and Germany. The Shah's goal was to develop several nuclear stations on Iranian soil in cooperation with the powers of the nuclear club. For him, the shareholding in Eurodif, together with American aid, was to enable Tehran to develop new nuclear technology, while he always emphasized that the nuclear bomb was completely excluded from his programme. The Shah declared in 1976:

> We will be the fifth military power in the world in five, perhaps six years. Today, we are not yet in a position to possess a nuclear weapon. However, since we are going to build nuclear power stations, people will always say that we are able to do so with enriched uranium. But then, why pick on Iran, since the same thing would also be true of many other countries as well?[18]

In 1974, the Shah set up the Iranian Atomic Energy Organization, reflecting Iran's genuine undertaking to develop a nuclear programme in the long term and which planned for the construction of 23 nuclear power stations by 1994.[19]

However, the Iranian nuclear programme did not follow the regular rhythm suggested by the different agreements concluded with France and the United States. Energy policy, and particularly oil, changed the situation and modified the political landscape of the Middle East. The Shah started to renegotiate the oil agreements which had been signed with Western companies. This led to a rise in the price of oil by the OPEC countries. The oil crisis was aggravated by the Yom Kippur War and by the support given by the US to Israel. The politics of 'oil at its true value', as the Shah liked to say, had consequences for his nuclear policy and for its development and infrastructure programmes. Iran's development was driven by its new riches and its military power; it was accompanied by the prospect of having a nuclear potential as well.

The ambitions for regional development were part of this prospect of alliances in the Persian Gulf. The different Iranian ambitions supported by the Shah concerning economic and financial development in different sectors, in particular in the Middle East and in Central Asia, were not at all welcome in the US administration. Henry Kissinger declared, 'The United States will oppose all attempts by any country to attain a dominant position in the world or in the region.'[20] However, the central issue of the period was how to put in place a buffer zone to prevent Soviet influence in the Middle East. When Iran had a long northern frontier with the Soviet Union, the US's fears concerned a possible Soviet seizure of Iranian oil fields. Later, after the Soviet invasion of Afghanistan in 1979, the Carter administration feared the creation of a pro-Soviet political movement in Iran. This is one of the reasons why the US supported nuclear power stations in Iran, in response to an increase in the Soviet presence.[21]

The Americans did not want to supplant a regional economic and nuclear power. Nuclear cooperation with Iran continued after 1975. Purchase and construction contracts were signed for two 1,240 mega-watt nuclear stations with the German society, Kraftwerk Union, a subsidiary of Siemens, at Bushehr in the South of Iran.[22] There were therefore four companies in cooperation with which Iran could constitute its nuclear potential: Framatome (France), Siemens/Kraftwerk Union (Germany), and Westinghouse and General Electric (United States). The small TRIGA ('Training, Research, Isotopes, General Atomics') nuclear reactor was conceived and produced by the US company General Atomics. TRIGA reactors can be built and used without a nuclear isolation chamber. Consequently, these reactors are principally used by scientific and university organizations for activities such as teaching, private research for commercial purposes, or for the production of isotopes.

US control over nuclear activity persisted throughout the troubles which the Iranian political system underwent. The US was always concerned about the nuclear capabilities of developing countries. The Islamic Revolution and the arrival of Ayatollah Khomeini to power dramatically changed the cooperative relationship with the US and overturned the civil nuclear programme.

During his reign, the Shah played off the American and the Soviet superpowers against each other, and his military and industrial purchases in the Soviet Union had been a cause of concern for the US. However, the rise of left-wing factions in Iran reached an unprecedented level. The inflexion of Iran policy towards a pro-Soviet position represented a major risk for the Americans. Ultimately the Shah, twenty years after being re-established in power, did not fulfil the Americans' expectations. A 'regime change' could occur, and the idea gained ground in the US that a new regime could be acceptable, providing that it would be anti-communist.

The changes of US policy in the region, in particular the change of alliance and the beginning of the war between Iran and Iraq, considerably weakened Iran's nuclear potential. However, China entered the game from 1985 onwards, when a bilateral agreement was signed for the training of 15 Iranian nuclear engineers in China with the intent of building reactors. It was again the difficulty of dealing with foreigners – a cooperation the Islamic Republic had denounced five years previously – which led Iran to develop its internal competences. Israel and the United States continued to supply arms necessary for the Iran–Iraq War. In August and September 1985, Israel sold 504 TOW missiles to Iran. In November of the same year, 18 anti-aircraft HAWK missiles were delivered to Iran directly by the CIA, but they were sent back for technical reasons. On 17 February 1986, the US sent a further 500 TOW missiles to Iran, via Israel again, then 500 more on 27 February, 508 in May, another 500 in October.

This cooperation culminated in the fact that none of the companies – besides Eurodif which was riven by dissent from the beginning of the 1980s – was in a leading position in nuclear development and cooperation. Germany signed a contract with Argentina in 1987, and the company of which Germany's KWU owned 25 per cent of the capital was itself Iran's partner in the nuclear power station at Bushehr. France and the United States reacted strongly against this new agreement. Tehran's objective was to finish the station at Bushehr: it wanted Argentina to provide uranium, and it wanted the training of technicians and the transfer of technology. This type of partnership in which the principal provider hides behind the cooperation of a third state was to continue until the 1990s. Germany's participation behind that of Argentina reactivated American cooperation under Reagan behind China, and France signed an agreement with Pakistan, thereby relaunching a triangular relationship between Paris, Islamabad and Tehran.

The West's abandonment of support for Iranian civil nuclear power is one of the elements which was to characterize the relations between a closed nuclear club and a state whose policy depends on the different political components of its political system. In the 1990s, Pakistan and India became nuclear powers with India, conducting nuclear tests which again caused a change in alliances. The states of the region went beyond the framework of merely civil nuclear power. Israel had no civil nuclear programme and was able to development a significant military nuclear programme.

American Strategy: A Game on Two Levels

This series of issues arising out of the Iranian nuclear question represents today a game at two levels.[23] The negotiations led by the Europeans and then by the Group of Six continue to aim at the complete cessation of Iranian nuclear activities. However, the war in Iraq, and the fragility of the Bush administration following the 2006 mid-term Congressional elections which overturned the Republican majority in Congress,[24] have disoriented US policy in the Middle East. In the minds of the neo-conservatives, the imbalance of power in the world was to provide a chance to pursue a wholesale remodelling of the 'Greater Middle East'. But how will US foreign policy modify its strategy in the Middle East if the neo-conservative vision is no longer dominant?

The project of the 'Greater Middle East' is aimed at a region in which there is a strong imbalance of power and where, under the guise of 'democratization', the Middle East is to be remodelled by an increased American presence. However, the nuclear question is not a question of democracy but a question of strategic power. A remodelling of the regional cannot take place for numerous reasons. On the one hand, the nuclearization of Iran and the unshakeable support of the population for this project remains an obstacle to deploying the Iraqi method, namely military intervention. In this double game, the weight of internal factors is taken seriously in international negotiations. Washington is aware of the popular support inside Iran for the civil nuclear energy programme. There is also increasing opposition to

American foreign policy both within the US and in the Arab-Muslim world, in particular following the patent failure of the military intervention in Iraq. The strategic weight of Iran's nuclearization has numerous geopolitical consequences in the region, in particular the emergence of politico-religious factions and the changing of geostrategic alliances with which the US is confronted. The Israeli–Lebanese war of July 2006 changed the balance of power, which means that the US must revise their strategy towards Iran.

In a study published in 2005, when the Iraq war was continuing to undermine US strategy in the Middle East, a report was published entitled 'Getting Ready for a Nuclear-Ready Iran'.[25] In this report, the researchers came to the nearly unanimous conclusion that targeted strikes could succeed if the following conditions are met:

- To have precise information on Iranian installations. This is partly the work of the United Nations inspection teams, complemented by the information provided by US and Israeli spy satellites.

- To ensure that the take-off and refuelling points of the aircraft taking part in the attack are not too far away from the targets. However, given that the Iranian nuclear installations are about 1,500 km from Israel, this represents a problem for the Israelis and indeed we will see below that this is not necessary a workable solution.

- The attackers would have to have the capacity to surprise Iran's air defences, which are less sophisticated that that of the US and Israel. Without this, the aircraft could theoretically be shot down. This could give the Iranians valuable time to respond and to move the mobile parts of their nuclear programme.

- There would need to be international approval for such an attack, which does not exist at the present. This could change if China and Russia, traditional supporters of Iran, decide to stick to their economic interests alone which are infinitely more important in the West than in Iran.

However, there are many reasons why targeted strikes might not succeed. First, the Iranian nuclear installations are numerous and dispersed all over the country. Some of the installations are subterranean fortresses. If strikes are decided by the US or Israel, there will have to be not merely one strike but a series of continuous intensive ones lasting several days. Israeli General Shlomo Broum, who took part in drawing up this study, has declared that 'Any strike against Iran's nuclear installations would require numerous intensive strikes at a relatively high number of well-fortified sites.' Such an operation is much more difficult and complicated than the strike against the Iraqi nuclear reactor in 1981, which required one single attack. The effect of surprise at which all Israeli military strategy excels would disappear after the first strike, and this would give the Iranian air defences the time to save what could be saved. Secondly, in the case of attack, Iran would not wait to react. Israelis fear an immediate response from Hezbollah in Southern Lebanon, which is already well armed by Iran with 'Fajr' rockets, already a permanent threat against Northern Israel. Iran could also use its 'Shebab 3' missiles which can reach Israel, but the response would be far more serious if the strikes showed traces of radioactivity. A response with chemical or bacteriological weapons is more likely, a nightmare for Israelis. The Iranians could also respond by attacking Israeli targets around the world, using the various small groups which are linked to them. For this reason, many Israeli strategists have come to the con- clusion that it is no easy matter to attack Iran's nuclear capability militarily because success is not guaranteed and every attempt therefore represents a high risk. This is without even taking account of the disastrous consequences of such an initiative.

Given the internal pressure to which the US administration is subject, as a result of the Iraqi disaster and the rise of terrorism in that country, this conclusion is being reached at various levels. Moreover, the participation of the Europeans in the negotiations with Iran constitutes a form of homogenization of the strategy to be adopted towards Iran. The evolution of the Iranian question since the report of the International Atomic Energy Authority (IAEA) on 31 August 2006 to the Security Council, in virtue of Resolution 1696, emphasizes that Iran has not suspended its uranium enrichment. This deadline was decided by the Ministers of Foreign Affairs of the five members of the Security Council of the United Nations and Germany – the Group of Six – who met in Paris on 12 July 2006 to examine the possibility of new sanctions against Iran. The Security Council refrained from adopting sanctions immediately, and decided instead to pursue a diplomatic solution to the crisis. This constitutes a new stage of the Iranian nuclear crisis whose right to the peaceful use of nuclear energy is defended and affirmed by Tehran. The Iranian government has suggested 'serious negotiations' on the nuclear question with the Group of Six.

The proposition of diplomatic negotiation was submitted by the European Union's High Representative for Foreign and Security Policy, representing the Group of Six, last June. The Group suggested two stages in which it would impose sanctions on Iran. The first phase would consist of a resolution passed quickly by the Security Council to demand the suspension of all sensitive nuclear activity. There would be a first decision based on the response of the Iranian government, for if Tehran refuses to stop its nuclear activity, the Group of Six will work towards a resolution imposing sanctions on the basis of Article 41 of Chapter 7 of the Charter of the United Nations:[26] 'We have decided to work towards a resolution of the Security Council of the United

Nations which would oblige Iran to suspend its uranium enrichment, as demanded by the IAEA. If Iran refuses to comply, we will work for the adoption of measures on the basis of Article 41 of the Charter of the United Nations.'[27] It seems likely that there will be an escalation of the crisis behind the opaque management of it. In spite of the IAEA inspections which have been continuing since 2003, no proof has been found of any military nuclear programme in Iran.

In order to bring matters to a head, the United States is currently encircling Iran by military deployment in neighbouring states. Washington is also attempting to stem the influence of the Islamic Republic beyond its frontiers, working towards its political and diplomatic isolation. It has undertaken a strategy of direct and indirect destabilization of Iran. There has been a convergence between US and European strategy against Tehran's entry into the nuclear club. This resembles the alliance which came together after the Iraqi invasion of Kuwait in 1990. In both cases, the aim was to prevent the emergence of a Muslim power which would be able partially to redress the imbalance of power in the region which is currently very favourable to Israel. In spite of the convergence, considerable differences persist between Europe and the US on the goals to be attained. The Europeans would be satisfied if Iran abandoned its military nuclear ambitions, and they would be prepared, in return, to normalize their relations with Tehran. The United States, meanwhile, believe that if Tehran backs down, this should reinforce the determination of the 'international community' to act in order to accelerate the downfall of the Iranian regime.

But what would the emergence of an Iran with nuclear weapons mean for Middle Eastern strategy? Not only is the country surrounded by nuclear powers but also its leaders believe, rightly, that the 2003 war against Iraq had as a consequence – and perhaps even as an aim – the encirclement of Iran by the United States, which now has a military presence in the ex-Soviet republics of Central Asia, Afghanistan, Pakistan, the Gulf, in Iraq and even in the Caucasus. The only response to this would be the use of force in a conflict with Israel, for example from Lebanon or from the Palestinian territories, or by groups which Iran could rally or recruit and equip in neighbouring states. If this happened, however, Iranian leaders fear an American intervention in favour of Israel, whence the interest for them of an adequate capacity for nuclear deterrence. Such a capacity would serve only to prevent possible nuclear attacks from the region: it would need only medium-range missiles like the Shehab 3, which has a range of 1,300 km, capable of reaching Israel.

What form would a conflict between Iran and the United States take? It is very difficult to envisage the US launching a war analogous to that waged against Iraq: with its surface area, its population and its natural resources, Iran is a country of a quite different dimension and any occupation of it would require far more troops. Besides, the position of Russia is that Moscow considers itself to be 'a historic and stable' partner of Iran. It is understandable if Russia draws on the recent history of cooperation between the Soviet Union and Iran. Traditionally, Russia has always been prudent – or suspicious – towards Iran's nuclear intentions. The arrival of Putin to power in 2000 centralized Russian foreign policy and reduced the chaos which had characterized the Yeltsin presidency. Russia became more and more convinced that Iran would emerge as a key actor in the region. For Russian diplomacy, Iran should not be subjected to double standards. Russia considers that nuclear cooperation, and more generally cooperation in high technology, is a key element in its strategic relationship with Iran. This attitude can be explained by the US's policy, which is driven by the aim of ejecting Russia from the lucrative energy market. This school of thought continues to guide the majority of the Russian elite on the Iranian question, including President Putin himself.

Iran's right to develop a civil nuclear capability is enshrined in the Nuclear Non-Proliferation Treaty. The council of governors of the International Atomic Energy Authority has refused to agree to Iran's request for authorization for the project of creating a reactor at Arak, fearing that this could be used for military purposes. The decision taken by the IAEA, which was arrived at after many days of discussion by industrialized countries and developing countries, leaves open the possibility that Iran might make the same request in the future. It is difficult to know what the IAEA will do in such a case, since the decision was only to delay an examination of the request and not to refuse it.

Between law and the legitimacy of the negotiation process, the actors of this international crisis are trying to adapt a national policy favourable to negotiation and a foreign policy which implies the use of force and sanctions. The military hierarchy of nations remains a central political and economic factor in international negotiations. The relaunch of negotiations with Tehran and the participation of the US might be a good lesson in what not to do when one is trying to prevent the emergence of a new geopolitical arrangement in the region.

Ali Rastbeen is President of the International Institute of Strategic Studies, Paris.

NOTES

1   National Security Council 5906/1, 'Basic National Security Policy,' 5 August 1959, declassified in 1996 (White House Office, Office of the Special Assistant for National Security Affairs:

Records, 1952–1961, NSC series, Policy Papers subseries, box 27, Dwight D Eisenhower Library, Abilene, KS), p. 9. Quoted in the thesis by Grzegorz Kostrzewa-Zorbas, *American Response to the Proliferation of Actual, Virtual, and Potential Nuclear Weapons: Lessons for the Multipolar Future,* Johns Hopkins University, MD, 1998.

2   Cf. Habibollah Zandjani, 'Evolution de la population iranienne à travers les recensements', in *Population,* 32ème année, No. 6, November–December 1977, pp. 1277–83.

3   Daniel Poneman, *Nuclear Power in the Developing World* London: George Allen & Unwin, 1982, p. 84.

4   Marie Ladier-Fouladie, 'La Transformation sociale en Iran: une approche démographique', *Etudes du CERI-Sciences Po,* February 1999.

5   Ramazani Rouhollah, *Iran's Foreign Policy 1941–1974: A Study of Foreign Policy in Modernizing Nations,* Charlottesville: University Press of Virginia, 1975.

6   Numerous suits were brought by the British government against Iran in the International Court of Justice and the issue was raised in the Security Council. Averill Harriman, President Truman's special envoy, made several trips in July 1951 which achieved no result either. See Mark D. Skootsky, 'U.S. Nuclear Policy. Towards Iran', *Nonproliferation Analysis,* Vol. 1, No. 1 (July 1995).

7   Cf. My article, 'Les Eléments étatiques en Iran,' in *Géostratégiques,* No. 10, December 2005.

8   US State Department, Bulletin 25, No. 630, 23 July 1951, quoted in Skootsky, 'U.S Nuclear Policy towards Iran', p. 243.

9   In 1995, an 'Atoms for Peace' conference was held in Geneva on nuclear power. The title recalled President Eisenhower's speech in 1954. It was followed by three further meetings with the same name. 'Atoms for Peace' was a programme which was supposed to control the nuclear sector which was otherwise not being properly controlled.

10   This treaty governing military relations in the Middle East, also knows as the Baghdad Pact, was signed on 24 February 1955 by Iraq, Turkey, Pakistan, Iran and the United Kingdom. The treaty was renamed CENTO after Iraq withdrew from it on 21 August 1959. The alliance lasted theoretically until 1974 when Turkey invaded Cyprus.

11   Eden Anthony, *'Full Circle,'* Boston, MA: Houghton Mifflin, 1960, pp. 217–44.

12   This was the year in which Iran ratified the Nuclear Non-Proliferation Treaty, having signed it on the day when the treaty was first presented, in 1968.

13   Yves Girard, *Un Neutron entre les dents,* Paris: Rive Droite, 1997, p. 52.

14   Ibid., p. 60

15   *Considering the Options: US Policy toward Iran's Nuclear Program,* Washington Institute for Near East Policy, Washington, DC, No. 305, October 2003.

16   Cf. US Congress, Senate, Committee on Foreign Relations, US Military Sales to Iran, Staff Report to the Subcommittee on Foreign Assistance, 94th Congress, 2nd Session, Government Printing Office, Washington, DC, 1976, p. 12.

17   Ibid., p. 37

18   Chris Quillen, 'Iranian Nuclear Weapons Policy: Past, Present and Possible Future,' *Middle East Review of International Affairs, (MERIA),* Vol. 6 No. 2, June 2002.

19   Ibid.

20   *Nucleonics Week,* 8 July 1976, pp. 4–5.

21   For more details see the thesis by Nadir Barzin, *'L'Economie Politique de Développement de l'Energie nucléaire en Iran (1957–2004),'* Ecole des Hautes Etudes en Sciences Sociales, 2004.

22   David Albright and Mark Hibbs, 'Is Iran going nuclear?', *Bulletin of the Atomic Scientists,* March 1992, Volume 8, No. 2.

23   In the sense of Robert Putnam's 'two-level' game theory.

24   On 10 November 2006, it was confirmed that the Democrats had taken control of the Senate. Following the close result in Virginia, where the Democrat Jim Webb was finally declared the winner, the upper chamber of the American Congress fell to the Democrats, with 51 seats (including two independents) to 49 for the Republican Party. The Democrats gained a comfortable majority in the House of Representatives.

25   The report was published in October 2005 by the Strategic Studies Institute, a body within the

Pentagon. Sixteen strategy specialists from the US, Israel and Europe participated in the study. See <http://www.strategicstudiesinstitute.army.mil>.

26 The Security Council can decide what measures should be taken to give effect to its decisions. It can invite members of the UN to apply these measures, which can include the partial or complete interruption of economic relations, rail, sea, air , postal, telegraphic and radioelectric communications, as well as the breaking-off of diplomatic relations.

27 Statement by the French Foreign Minister, Paris, 12 July 2006.

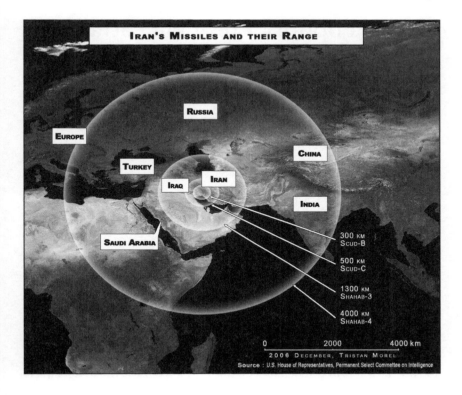

Iran's Populist President, Strategic Foreign and Nuclear Policy: The Influence of Domestic Politics on the Current Iranian Nuclear Stand-Off

JALIL ROSHANDEL

Iran's interest in nuclear technology pre-dates the 1979 Revolution, as it began work on acquiring nuclear energy under the Pahlavi regime in the 1960s. Although Tehran is a signatory to the Nuclear Non-Proliferation Treaty (NPT), Iran has been developing nuclear capabilities since the mid-1980s. The controversy over Iran's nuclear programme intensified since the early 2000s, as the Islamic state has maintained a defiant principled resistance in response to increased external pressure for abandoning its uranium enrichment programme, claiming its inalienable right to develop civilian nuclear energy infrastructure. Recent revelations about Iran's expanded nuclear capabilities, followed by Iran's decision to stop the International Atomic Energy Authority's (IAEA) additional inspection and formally resume its uranium enrichment programme on 9 January 2006,[1] created an immediate and ongoing international crisis.

In consideration of motivations underlying the quest for nuclear capability in any given country, conventional wisdom may perceive the drive within a national interest-national security paradigm – in fact within a realist framework. While nationalism can better explain the motivations of Iran's nuclear programme, one may also argue that domestic factional politics in Iran significantly influence nuclear policies. However, after examining Iranian political power structures, despite outside appearances, factionalism has limited influence on nuclear politics. Finally, as some may point out, nationalism must be considered not only as an underlying motivation for nuclear arms development everywhere, but more importantly as a highly significant domestic element influencing Iran's nuclear policy today.

With a focus on factors motivating foreign policy and the nuclear development programme particularly since Mahmoud Ahmadinejad was elected president on 24 June 2005, we will explore to what degree Iran's foreign and nuclear policy depends on the 'president' among a whole host of other factors in general and on the personality of Ahmadinejad in particular.

Understanding Motivations Underlying Nuclear Proliferation

Eisenstadt (1999) argues that, after Iran's costly war with Iraq (1980–88), deterring Iraq became the principle rationale for pursuing a nuclear programme (p. 125).[2] Iran's hostile perception of Israel has also been cited as a security factor motivating Iran's nuclear programme: 'Iran, under the Shah, opposed the Israeli nuclear asymmetry in the Middle East and Israel's refusal to sign the NPT. Accordingly, the Pahlavi regime sought to establish its own nuclear programme and called for the creation of a Middle East Nuclear Free Zone' (Bahgat, 2006: p. 129). From this viewpoint, Iran has developed nuclear capabilities to deter potential Israeli attacks.

Iran's perceived vulnerability to US possible aggression is most commonly presented as inspiring Iran's nuclear ambitions, given Iran's controversial history with the 'Great Satan'. The US played a vital role in the aftermath of the Islamic Revolution of 1979; most Iranians believe the US has rescued Iraq in its war with Iran, ignoring its use of chemical weapons; the US invaded Afghanistan in 2001 and Iraq in 2003, and branded Iran as a member of the 'axis of evil' with North Korea and Iraq in 2003, while persistently supporting Israel's continual occupation of Muslim lands.

Some Iranians believe nuclear capability is the only guarantor of the nation's independence from US domination (Chubin and Litwak, 2003: p. 106). This notion was reinforced by the US's more benign and less confrontational response to North Korea's nuclear activities than to Iraq's, which did not possess weapons of mass destruction (Pollack and Takeyh, 2005: p. 23).

Iran's nuclear ambitions traditionally have been understood within what is known as the 'security model': the security threats posed by many neighbours, including more significantly, conflicts with Iraq, Israel and the United States, are considered fundamental factors underlying Iran's nuclear ambitions. The security model (the 'realist' model) has a simple answer to the proliferation question: 'states will seek to develop nuclear weapons when they face a significant military threat to their security that cannot be met through alternative means' (Sagan, 1997: p. 54). However, closer examination of these views fails to provide adequate understanding of Iran's motivations in the current nuclear stand-off.

A rational analysis of Iran's nuclear programme, however, clearly reveals that Iran's nuclear capabilities would prove of little value against Israel or the US. As Perkovich (2003) aptly states, 'Acquiring a small handful of nuclear weapons would not reduce decisively US and/or Israeli motives or capabilities to attack Iran. Rather, Iran's effort to acquire a nuclear arsenal increases the threat of attack' (p. 5). Iranians recognize that use of nuclear weapons against Israeli or US interests would be suicidal. Moreover, Sagan insightfully argues, 'Realist history depends primarily on the statements of motivation by the key decision-makers, who have a vested interest in explaining that the choices they made served the national interest' (1997: p. 63). Although Iranian leaders may justify the nuclear programme by pointing to real security threats, rational analysis of these explanations suggests that the security model cannot comprehensively explain Iran's nuclear motivations; other factors must be considered: 'Nuclear weapons, like other weapons, are more than tools of national security; they are political objects of considerable importance in domestic debates and internal bureaucratic struggles and also serve as international normative symbols of modernity and identity' (p. 55).

To better understand Iran's nuclear motivations, a consideration of domestic politics is warranted. The 'domestic politics' model focuses on the domestic actors who encourage (or discourage) governments from pursuing nuclear capabilities (Sagan, 1997: p. 64).[3] According to Sagan, domestic actors (such as politicians in states in which individual parties strongly favour nuclear weapons acquisition) 'create the conditions that favour weapons acquisition by encouraging extreme perceptions of foreign threats and promoting supportive politicians' (ibid.), an observation which begets the consideration of nationalist sentiment as a potentially significant factor motivating Iran's nuclear programme. Theoretically, nationalism may be incorporated in the 'symbolic' model, which perceives nuclear decisions as serving important symbolic functions domestically, both shaping and reflecting a states identity (p. 73); according to this perspective, the decision to initiate a nuclear weapons programme is not motivated solely by perceived regional and international security threats, but also by the search for prestige, status and respect (Bahgat, 2006: p. 126).

The influence of nationalism domestically can provide a better understanding of Iran's nuclear motivations than can the security model. In reality, nationalist sentiment, more than realist security concerns, has been a primary motivation for Iran's nuclear programme, and the predominant force influencing Iran's current nuclear policy position. Since the reign of Reza Shah prior to the Second World War, Iranian foreign policy has continuously aimed to restore Iran to its 'rightful' place as a Great Power in the Middle East and beyond (p. 130). This vision has not materialized, and Iran may have developed something of an inferiority complex, especially after the revolution in 1979. Alienated from the international landscape, Iran views nuclear weapons as 'an almost magical source of national power and autonomy'(Perkovich, 2004: p. 4). Academics such as Michael Kraig (2005) and Bahgat (2006) agree that nuclear capability would serve as an expression and guarantor of self-reliance, independence, regional power, and at the global level, equality with other great powers – effects that would feed Iran's collective image of itself. In fact Iran is over-obsessed with this latter factor of equality and justice in international relations as emphasized by Ahmadinejad in his talks at the UN or letters he has sent to President Bush.

It is likely that Iran fears a military attack by the US or other adversaries, but this hard security argument is simply not adequate to explain Iran's nuclear motivations. Iran is more concerned about the threat from the US, challenging its self-identity as an Islamic Republic. Kraig elaborates: 'In this perception or worldview, all US critiques of specific actions in the nuclear, missile, or terrorism issue areas are actually window dressing for the true issue: the character of the Iranian government as a whole' (2005: p. 1). US response to Iran's nuclear programme – particularly condemning Iran as part of an 'axis of evil' and 'an outpost of tyranny', threatening regime change, and imposing economic sanctions – make even Western-minded reformers in Iran proudly resist the US (Perkovich, 2004: p. 9).

Because the question of Iran's nuclear programme has been masked in a language of 'nuclear technology', the government has not had to defend domestically its motivations: the sheer fact that the US has made outright attempts to prohibit Iranian access to any nuclear technology makes an ample case that the programme must be undertaken. Thus, 'In arguing that the nuclear energy programme seeks to make Iran a modern state with access to advanced technology, the regime strikes a sensitive chord' (Chubin and Litwak, 2003: p.105).

This dynamic allows those who support the nuclear programme to portray international objections as attempts to keep Iran backward and dependent, and as an indication of hostility toward an independent Iran. However despite the emphasis on the principle of independence in the Iranian constitution, Iran had to depend on external assistance (Russia, Pakistan, etc.) in its pursue of nuclear capabilities, most significantly, because it operates from a world-view that conceives the programme as necessary to protect its very identity.

The Influence of Factional Politics on Nuclear Policy

The 'domestic politics' model holds that politicians in states in which individual parties strongly favour nuclear weapons acquisition can significantly influence nuclear policy. Defenders of this model and many academics recognize the potential influence of factional politics on nuclear policy. However, the influence of Iran's many political factions on the state's nuclear policy has been highly debated. Iran's ruling elites are divided into three broad categories: those who advocate pursuing the nuclear project at all costs; those who defend pursuing it without sacrificing diplomatic interests; and those who argue for suspending activities to build international trust and approval (Sadjadpour, 2006: p. 2). The latter constitute the ideological reformists, while the two former comprise the ideological conservatives. Bitter disagreements between these groups characterizes Iran's domestic political environment.

The reformers, empowered by the election of President Khatami in 1997 and parliamentary victories in 2001, tried to ameliorate international relations, and are still very sensitive to the political costs of nuclear proliferation. Conservatives, on the other hand, continue to define their foreign policy in opposition to the US and often resort to belligerent methods to achieve their aims (Pollack and Takeyh, 2005: p. 20). Recent parliamentary and presidential elections have replaced reformists with a conservative majority in all branches of government – legislative, executive and judicial.

In addition to the ideological rift between the reformer and conservative parties, there exists a major division within the conservatives between the hard-liner and the pragmatist factions, which fundamentally centers on foreign policy issues including nuclear proliferation (Pollack and Takeyh, p. 21). Influential pragmatists include Iran's lead nuclear negotiator Larijani, former President Rafsanjani, and Secretary of the Supreme National Security Council Rowhani. Like reformists, 'Pragmatists believe the regime's survival depends on a more judicious international course' (p. 25). However, they remain highly cynical of Western (particularly US) intentions, and maintain the state's inalienable right to enrich uranium. They emphasize the economic dimension of nuclear diplomacy, and unlike the hard-liners, favour working within the international framework (p. 22). Hard-liners, grounded in the nation's domestic political history – 'revolution, war, sanctions, and alienation from international society – share a sense of embattlement in a hostile environment, leaving little scope for debate' on the nuclear issue (Chubin and Litwak, 2003: p. 100). The most ardent of Khomeini's followers, hard-liners perceive independent nuclear capability as necessary for the survival of the Islamic Republic. Current President Ahmadinejad and his cohorts advocate an uncompromising pursuit of nuclear capability, including withdrawal from NPT commitments if necessary (Sadjadpour, 2006: p. 2).

Many scholars insist that the ideological rifts and factions in Iran's domestic political arena can only significantly influence the state's nuclear programme. In line with the domestic politics model, Eisenstadt maintains that regime factionalism causes radical departures from established patterns of behaviour as different factions work at cross purposes, subverting their rivals, and pressing the government to act inconsistently with general policy (1999: p.

136). 'Domestic politics are likely to influence any decision to cross the nuclear threshold. Some members of Iran's clerical leadership might believe that they could stand to gain *vis-à-vis* political rivals if Iran were to declare itself a nuclear-weapons state, or conduct a nuclear-weapons test' (p. 131). In other words, political elites with extreme agendas can leverage their power – relative to opposition – to influence nuclear policies. More specifically, academics recognize the power of conservatives (especially hard-liners) to advance nuclear programmes.

Given the purported influence of these factions on nuclear policy, many scholars have emphasized the importance of understanding factional political dynamics for non-proliferation strategies and negotiations. Chubin and Lutwik, for example, argue that the gap between the hard-line conservatives in Iran and the rest of society presents an avenue for influencing the country's decisions regarding its nuclear programme (2003: p. 100). One conceivable non-proliferation strategy could involve 'strengthening the hand of Conservative Pragmatists, who could then argue for slowing, limiting, or shelving Tehran's nuclear programme in return for trade, aid, and investment that Iran badly needs' (Pollack and Takeyh, 2005: pp. 20–21). Arguments touting the influence of ideological and factional rifts on Iran's nuclear programme are not convincing, however, as the following arguments shall demonstrate.

A fundamental factor negating the influence of factional domestic politics on Iranian nuclear policy can be demonstrated by the experiences of both reformist President Khatami and current hard-liner President Ahmadinejad. Despite authentic aspirations of liberal reform in the domestic and international arena, and a reformist majority in the executive and legislative branches, very little progress was realized under Khatami. The US, under the Clinton administration, repeatedly offered comprehensive deals with substantial incentives in order to build a cooperative relationship with Iran; but Khatami's evident receptivity to these offers triggered a conservative backlash that ultimately debilitated Khatami's government: 'Conservative ideologues in Tehran repeatedly quashed the efforts of any Iranian who attempted to take up the United States' conciliatory offers' (Pollack and Takeyh, 2005: p. 25).

Khatami wielded little political influence on foreign affairs. Real power has been monopolized by the Supreme Leader, Ayatollah Khameini since 1989; the military, judiciary, the Iranian Revolutionary Guard Corps (IRGC), the intelligence and security services, among others, all answer to the Supreme Leader. This aspect of Iranian governmental structure significantly minimizes the influence of factional politics on Iran's nuclear programme. Consider, for example, when in a 1998 interview with CNN, Khatami dramatically called for the 'wall of mistrust [between Iran and the US] to be torn down' (in Buchta, 2000: p. 134). Khameini responded days later emphatically warning of the dangers of normalizing relations with the US, which effectively forced Khatami to dismiss further talks with the US (p. 135).

More recently, with the election of current hard-liner president, Ahmadinejad, international players feared that Iran would fervently pursue nuclear proliferation. Although Iran has acted more boldly of late with regard to its nuclear programme, this is not attributable to the president's influence on nuclear policy. The reality is that the Iranian presidency is mostly a visible and ceremonial office that lacks decision-making power. The president does not determine policies, even though Ahmadinejad − 'belligerent, naïve, at once a fundamentalist and nationalist, and a dark genius at mobilizing Iranian public opinion' (Moaveni, 2006) − pretends he does. The general guidelines of Iranian domestic and foreign policy are determined by the leader and, since the president does not have command over the armed and security forces (Khatami didn't even have any command over domestic security), he cannot change the course of action. One of the characteristics of Ahmadinejad's presidency has been his 'mobocratic' policy of mobilizing the public opinion, in other words, a hue-and-cry policy that lacks international support and power, but brings the mob into the streets to trumpet what they have been instructed to say.

Traditionally, no Iranian president has had the power to go against the nuclear option. Even Khatami was by no means close to such a decision to forgo nuclear option. All Ahmadinejad has done since 2005 is to keep the furnace hot by pushing the mob to the streets and wrapping the nuclear issue it in a more nationalistic dress. At the same time he has not missed a moment to create a new subject for the international media's attention, with the latest Holocaust denial conference in Tehran.

People around Ahmadinejad have either emerged from a section of the ruling elite that has little or no expertise on foreign policy issues or they are a resurging part of the system that was pushed back more than two decades ago by the pragmatists who thought they may not serve their interest. A shift of role −usually from the bottom to the top −− is not unusual in the Iranian power structure and this is exactly what is happening under Ahmadinejad.

The presidency and other governmental institutions are not entirely devoid of power and in fact they have some room to manoeuvre to show their power, though more often they play an advisory role in decision making and participate in a loose system of checks and balances. The reality is that the Supreme Leader is the most important political actor in terms of influencing policy making and in our case the nuclear policy. Khamenei, the conservative leader −ideologically somewhere between the pragmatist and hard-liner camps − has aimed to balance factional interests, especially concerning the nuclear issue: 'In his years as supreme leader, Khameini has attempted to balance the ideologues and the realists, empowering both factions to prevent either from achieving a preponderance of influence' (Pollack and Takyeh, 2005: p. 22). As president, Ahmadinejad has alarmed international actors in recent months by his reactionary and hasty statements concerning Iran's nuclear policy; Khameini has acted to restore some balance again: 'The creation of a Foreign Policy Council ... to carry out the Supreme Leader's foreign policy – rather than Ahmadinejad's slogans – is another sign the real decision-making circles in Iran are located beyond the inexperienced president's office of the foreign ministry' (Roshandel, 2006: p. 1). Khameini appointed Kamal Harrazi, (the man Ahmadinejad had removed as foreign minister after taking office in 2005), as the panel's chairman, which amounts to limiting the hard-liner president's powers (Vick 2006). Essentially, the political power structure in Iraq largely inhibits the potential influence of factionalist politics on nuclear policy.

Additionally, political power structure in Iran can explain the highly unpredictable and seemingly irrational policy positions and responses of the Iranian government with regards to the state's nuclear programme: 'Iran has reacted hastily and conveyed messages from different and uncoordinated sources of power within the regime' (Roshandel, 2006: p. 1). Competing pressures between the moderates and conservatives have resulted in inconsistent government positions: Even as Iran agreed to suspend efforts to acquire nuclear capabilities in 2003, signing the NPT's Additional Protocol, the government has insisted that it would never give up its nuclear programme (Pollack and Takeyh, 2005: p. 24). More recently, when news came out that Ahmadinejad had written an unprecedented letter to Bush, the former leading nuclear negotiator Rowhani quickly countered by releasing his own compromise proposal to *Time* magazine (Sadjadpour, 2006: p. 3). This is just one of many instances in which the Iranian government has spoken with more than one voice in foreign policy. Iranian leaders – whether conservatives, hard-liners, or reformists – are all guilty of voicing differing, and at times, contradictory opinions. In early 2005, former president Khatami, who usually denied Iran's nuclear intentions, implied that Iran could be forced to withdraw from the NPT under diplomatic pressure (Saikal, 2006: p. 195), while today the Iranian Foreign Minster Mottaki (Deputy Foreign Minister under Khatami) claims that this major international treaty should not be weakened and Iran will stay within the treaty. The lack of coordination between governmental entities, and the extreme polarization of ideological views among political actors in Iran, can account for the unpredictable and seemingly contradictory positions on nuclear policy. A better understanding of this phenomenon requires a reconsideration of the role of nationalism as influencing (not just motivating) nuclear programmes.

Revisiting Nationalism and Nuclear Policy

Support for the acquisition of advanced nuclear technology in Iran crosses ideological and factional lines. The resonance of nationalist sentiments with Iranians, and by extension the salience of nationalism for nuclear policy, is evident. From this perspective, Iran's nuclear weapons programmes serves a symbolic function demanding respect and fostering national power, pride and prestige. However, scholars recognize that when such symbols are contested (as they often are) the resulting norms are spread by power and coercion and not by the strength of ideas alone (Sagan, 1997: pp. 75–6). This principle is perhaps manifested in Ahmadinejad's manoeuvring with nuclear policy issues. Wolfsthal (2006) explains, 'Domestic political considerations are a major factor in Iran's decision to resume its nuclear activities. President Ahmadinejad has gained power on a nationalistic platform and increasingly vitriolic rhetoric, and Iran's uranium enrichment efforts are increasingly cast in terms of its national sovereignty and prestige' (p. 4). This observation implies that, although political factions in and of themselves may not have the clout to influence nuclear policy decisions – largely due to structural limitations – the invocation of nationalism within the existing political structure by factionalized individuals can certainly influence and significantly influence nuclear politics.

Populist President, Strategic Decisions

As mentioned earlier, Ahmadinejad does not determine Iranian strategic decisions. He is perhaps the weakest link in the decision-making circle. But, his trumpet makes louder noises.

The core value of the people around Ahmadinejad's group is to use the mob to demonstrate to what extent their power has the support of the nation. While Ahmadinejad himself does not tolerate the slightest opposition to his policies, he praises Hezbollah for opposing Lebanese government and he sends a message to the 'American people'. It would be interesting to ask him if he would tolerate similar messages coming from other leaders of the world to the 'Iranian people'. It seems as though Ahmadinejad is just creating a gloomy environment where the Persian cliché of 'fishing in murky waters' applies best.

Former Louisiana state representative, and ex Ku Klux Klan leader, David Duke, was one of the participants in the Holocaust conference in Tehran. In an interview broadcast live from Tehran, Duke claimed 'the Iran conference was a conference for freedom of speech' (CNN Transcripts). If this is true, then it must be a big step forward because Ahmadinejad has no reputation for honouring freedom of speech; just a few months before, a major Iranian daily *Shargh* was shut down for publishing an ambiguous caricature that implicated Ahmadinejad.[4]

In his domestic policies he is often blamed for promising too much and delivering too little. Ramazan Ali Sadeghzadeh, member of the Islamic Majlis (Parliament) accuses him of using rhetoric and slogans espousing 'loving and justice', the results of which cannot be measured and evaluated. He believes the president's achievement and decisions since 2004 lack scientific and experts' support, or were not coordinated with different sectors of the state. Sadeghzadeh believes Ahamadinejad's governmental decisions are often contradictory and inefficient.(*Aftab Yazd*, 3 December 2006)

On his government's policies he is accused of Machiavellian tactics. According to the Iranian daily *Aftab Yazd*, the government dedicated a budget of five billion rials (roughly fifty million US dollars) to organize an international conference in support of Palestinians. Meanwhile, many university students and political activists (known as 'marked with stars') have been denied the opportunity to pursue their studies. This and similar policies are often criticized in both private and public circles. Most recently, Emad Afrough, head of the Majlis' cultural committee, criticized Ahmadinejad's government in a parliamentary speech, and recommended that the government should avoid taking 'Machiavellian decisions'.

Conclusion

While conventional analysts would argue that strategic security issues have motivated Iran's nuclear weapons development, closer examination suggests the implicit rationale for the nuclear programme lies in the worldview of conservative hard-liners, who regard nuclear capability as the ultimate guarantor of Iran's influence. By invoking nationalism in defence and nuclear policy, national history and common identity, Iranian nuclear policy receives some support from the people.

This line of thinking suggests that empowered reformists would have the capacity to influence the direction of the nuclear programme; closer examination of the nature of factional politics, and its limitations within the political power structure (specifically the Supreme Spiritual Leader) suggest that any attempted reforms that could be conceived as potentially harmful to Iran's national interests would likely be derailed by conservative political elites and the Iranian population at large, sensitive to anti-US propaganda.

This understanding of the current Iranian nuclear stand-off has serious implications that should be considered in strategies for achieving non-proliferation cooperation. Perhaps most significantly, increased international pressure (especially from the US) will only heighten nationalist sentiment and solidify domestic public favor for nuclear development programmes. Given that Iran is well on its way to nuclear capability, and has already invested a great deal in the programme, it will be unlikely to relinquish its efforts altogether; as such, international actors concerned with this situation will need to work to include Iran in the international playing field, where Iran may let down its nationalist guard, and embrace further international cooperation.

Works Cited

Bahgat, Gawdat (2006), 'Nuclear Proliferation: The Islamic Republic of Iran', *International Studies Perspectives*, Vol. 7 No. 2: 124–36.

Buchta, Wilfried (2000), *Who Rules Iran?: The Structure of Power in the Islamic Republic*, Washington, DC: Washington Institute for Near East Policy.

Chubin, Shahram, and Robert S. Litwak (2003), 'Debating Iran's Nuclear Aspirations', *The Washington Quarterly*, Vol. 26 No. 4: 99–114.

CNN, 'The Situation Room', Aired 13 December 2006. Transcripts available at <http://transcripts.cnn.com/ TRANSCRIPTS/0612/13/sitroom.01.html>.

Eisenstadt, Michael (1999), 'Living with a Nuclear Iran?', *Survival*, Vol. 41 No. 3: 124–48.

Kraig, Michael Ryan (2005), 'Policy Analysis Brief: Realistic Solutions for Resolving the Iranian Nuclear Crisis', *The Stanley Foundation*, 1–7 April <http://www.stanleyfoundation.org/reports/GSI05pab.pdf>.

Moaveni, Azadeh (2006), 'Mahmoud Ahmadinejad, Iran's High-Stakes Nuclear Gambler', *Time* magazine online version, 30 April <http://www.time.com/time/magazine/article/0,9171,1186909,00.html>.

Perkovich, George (2003), 'Dealing with Iran's Nuclear Challenge', Washington, DC: *Carnegie Foundation for International Peace*: 1–16 <http://www.ceip.org/files/projects/npp/pdf/Iran/iraniannuclearchallenge.pdf>.

Pollack, Kenneth, and RayTakeyh (2005), 'Taking on Tehran' *Foreign Affairs*, Vol. 84 No. 2: 20–26.

Roshandel, Jalil (2006), 'No real change in policy', in *Middle East Roundtable Online Forum*, Vol. 25 No. 4, 6 July: *Bitterlemons-international.org* <http://www.bitterlemons-international.org/inside.php?id=567>.

Sadjadpour, Karim 18 May (2006), 'Iran's Political/Nuclear Ambitions and U.S. Policy Options', *International Crisis Group*, 18 May <http://www.crisisgroup.org/home/index.cfm?id=4143&1=1>

Sagan, Scott D. (1997), 'Why Do States Build Nuclear Weapons?: Three Models in Search of a Bomb', *International Security*, Vol. 21 No. 3: 54–86.

Saikal, Amin (2006),. The Iran nuclear dispute', *Australian Journal of International Affairs*, Vol. 60 No.2: 193–9.

Vick, Karl (2006), 'Ayatollah's Moves Hint Iran Wants to Engage', *Washington Post*, 5 July.

Wolfsthal, Jon B. (2006), 'Understanding Iran's Nuclear Maneuvers', Washington, DC: *Center for Strategic and International Studies*, 11 January <http://www.bits.de/public/documents/iran/060112_wolfsthal.pdf>.

Jalil Roshandel is Associate Professor and Director of Security Studies programme at Political Science Department, East Carolina University.

NOTES

1   Iran had voluntarily frozen its uranium enrichment programme for two years as a confidence-building measure.

2   The primary motivations presented were to achieve self-reliance, to transform the nation into a regional power capable of projecting influence beyond the Middle East, and to strengthen deterrent capability against various perceived threats.

3   Sagan includes three primary domestic actors in the domestic politics model. In addition to politicians, the state's nuclear energy establishment and important units within the professional military are listed. In this piece, we have considered the politicians' influences on nuclear motivations only.

4   The caricature showed a chess table with a donkey, instead of horse with a halo above its head. Allegations indicated that it resembled Mahmoud Ahmadinjad when he claimed he was covered in a glow of light as he addressed the United Nations General Assembly.

Interview with
Professor General Isaac Ben-Israel

What is Iran's missile capability?

The facts are well known. Iran has a missile capability which goes from short-range rockets to Shahab-3 and 4 missiles. The Shahab-3 has a range of between 1,200 km and 1,500 km, which means that it can reach Tel Aviv. This missile is operational. Iran received help to construct it from experts from Russia and North Korea. The Shahab-4 missile will have a range of between 2,000 km and 2,500 km, which means that it could reach Europe.

These missiles are not particularly accurate: 50 per cent of the warhead would fall within a 2–3 mile radius of the target. The flight time of these missiles is ten minutes for the full range. This is quite enough time for people to take shelter, as happened when Iraq fired missiles at Tel Aviv during the 1991 Gulf War. There was not a single fatality from Saddam's Scud missiles in 1991 because there was adequate warning before the missiles fell. The same thing would happen in the event of a Shehab-3 attack. In other words, the construction of these missiles makes no sense unless the Iranians plan to use them for non-conventional warfare. This is what I assume they intend to do.

What is Iran's nuclear capability?

Again, the facts are clear. The Iranians are building a nuclear capability but they do not have it yet. Their programme is running on two tracks: enriching uranium with centrifuges, and producing plutonium. They currently have neither enriched uranium nor plutonium. It will take them from three to six years to achieve this, unless they are interrupted.

Is it possible to strike at Iran's nuclear installations using conventional weapons?

Yes. These are sensitive facilities – centrifuges for enriching uranium, a reactor for producing plutonium. Israel has already carried out a conventional attack on a nuclear installation, when it attacked Iraq in 1981. A successful attack depends on the right intelligence. I assume that the United States, the United Kingdom or Israel have such intelligence. Nuclear installations are very difficult to hide. So there is no problem from a military point of view. The question is whether it is wise, not whether it is possible. In recent years, the United States, the United Nations Security Council, the European Union quartet have all been trying to apply diplomatic pressure on Iran to abandon its nuclear programme. Only at the end of December [2006], the Security Council decided on sanctions. Maybe this approach will work; maybe it will not. It is difficult to predict what will happen. Rationally, the Iranians have no reason to want a nuclear capability but I do not know whether the regime is open to rational argument, especially in view of the role that religion plays in the Iranian regime. It is difficult to predict what will happen. There may come a time when the world says, 'Enough is enough.'

Can Israel alone take out Iran's nuclear installations?

Yes – Israel could, Britain could, the United States could. The reason why people are reluctant to do this lies in the fact that Iran controls much of the world's oil. People fear the consequences if Iran stops exporting its oil or prevents its neighbours from doing so. This is why China and to some extent also India (net importers of oil, including from Iran) are not cooperating very enthusiastically with the international community on Iran. Furthermore, Iran could retaliate, including by means of terrorism. So you have to balance the potential gains against the costs.

The gain would be to delay Iran's nuclear programme. You cannot liquidate it completely because Iran would simply start again. It is not practical to liquidate the whole of Iran. But you can gain time, putting the project back by as much as five years. Some say that five years is not enough. But others think that five years is a lot of time, especially since you could do the same thing again after five years. We can learn from the Iraqi precedent. After Israel's attacks in 1981, the Iraqis abandoned their plutonium production and started to enrich uranium instead. In 1991, the United States found that Iraq was close to being able to enrich uranium but its capacity was destroyed in the 1991 Gulf War and kept under subsequent control by the UN weapons inspectors. In 2003, Saddam Hussein was overthrown and is now awaiting execution. In 1981, one could have said that we had only delayed Iraq's nuclear programme. But other events came along, and today there is no nuclear Iraq. If we gain time in Iran, there might be a revolution against the Islamic regime. After all, the world's objection to Iran's nuclear programme is itself a result of the particular nature of the Iranian regime. If the regime changed, then the world might object less, or not at all, to a nuclear Iran.

Professor Ben-Israel is a professor at Tel Aviv University, and is the former head of Research and Development for the Israeli Defence Force.

Geopolitical Affairs interviewed Professor Ben-Israel on 23 December 2006.

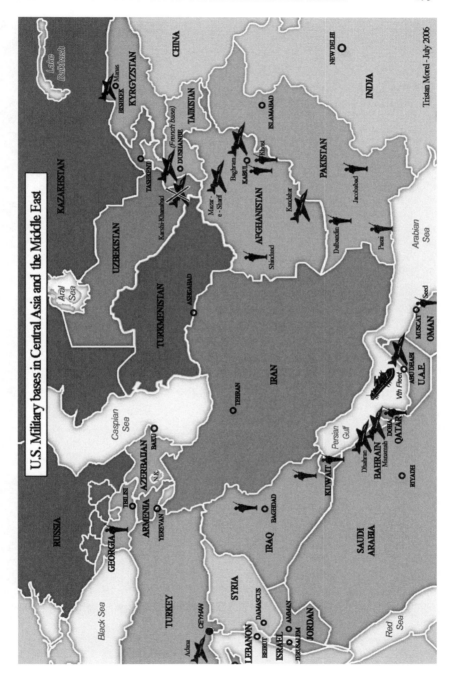

U.S. Military bases in Central Asia and the Middle East

Tristan Morel - July 2006

PART III
Ahmadinejad, The Second Revolution?

The Rise of the
Neoconservatives in Iran[1]

ANOUSH EHTESHAMI
and MAHJOOB ZWEIRI

Introduction

Without giving in to a deterministic view of modern Iranian political history, against which Gheissari and Nasr strongly argue, it is still possible to discern a certain pattern in the reform process in Iran.[2] Indeed, five patterns of political discourse can be said to have dominated politics in modern Iran in the twentieth century: 'the traditional patrimonialism of the Qajar era, democratic parliamentarianism of the constitutional era, modernizing autocracy of the Pahlavi era, revolutionary ideology of the Islamic Republic, and the end of the democratic pluralism of the reform movement'.[3] The latter ended officially with the election of President Mahmoud Ahmadinejad as the sixth Iranian president. This paper will analyse how the reform movement played a significant role in helping in the rise of Iran's neoconservative forces – who are ideologically Islamist, revolutionary in character, and populist in application and policy terms – to the heart of Iran's political institutions. This forms the basis of our definition of neoconservatism in Iran, which is a largely non-clerical force and is dominated by the security actors.[4]

Unpredictable change is how some commentators summarized developments in Iran after 1997. As we said earlier, what has become known today as the Islamic Republic's reformist movement acquired international prominence in the wake of Hojatolislam Mohammad Khatami's overwhelming victory in the May 1997 presidential poll. Against all the odds and expectations, this mild-mannered cleric's election victory promised to usher in a new era in revolutionary Iran. It is apparent from his first term in office that this former close confidant of Ayatollah Khomeini and former cabinet minister's electoral commitments to reforming the system and opening it up to public scrutiny and accountability were very real indeed. As evidence of this, we can point to the fact that by the end of his first term Khatami had not only managed to change and reshape the country's political agenda and introduce new and controversial dimensions to the national debate, but actually shifted the geography of the debate to the public arena, allowing the population to evaluate and form informed judgements about the very nature of the country's Islamic system of governance. While perhaps his administration proved less successful in actually implementing the wide range of social and political reforms promised, none the less his reformist agenda set the benchmark by which the Islamic Republic was to be judged by Iranians themselves as well as by an ever-attentive international community.

President Khatami unashamedly championed reform of the governing system in Iran, proposed comprehensive changes to the country's civil-state relations, and sought to make the Islamic system more in tune with the aspirations of the people. Observers of modern Iran cannot help but be struck by the historical parallels between Khatami's 'revolutionary' agenda for reform and the two earlier occasions in which the desire for political change had become the country's defining force. The first of these was the 1905–06 Constitutional Revolution, which gave Iran its first taste of 'modernity' and, in the process, brought to an unceremonial end to the Qajar Dynasty. The second was Iran's 1979 revolution against the Pahlavi regime and its Westernized system of governance. Looking at the two revolutions, despite its early successes the Constitutional Revolution did not manage to institutionalize the aspirations of Iran's modernizers and early democrats. The 1979 Islamic Revolution, on the other hand, having given birth to an altogether new and unique political order, was said to be the embodiment of the Iranian people's historic and spiritual aspirations. Yet, barely twenty years after the Islamic Revolution, we find yet again Iran in the grips of another period of rapid change and fundamental transformations, facing the same fundamental questions as in 1905. In this context, it is pertinent to raise the question, of how much socio-political progress did Iran really make in the intervening years through the course of the late twentieth century? To answer this question adequately, one needs to trace the origins and nature of the reform process today and consider some of its consequences.

The evolution of Iran's political system in the 1990s, marked by some key constitutional reforms in 1989, following the end of the Iran–Iraq War and the death of the founder of the new republic, Ayatollah Khomeini, can be divided into two distinct periods: the pragmatist-reconstructionist Rafsanjani presidency (1989–97); and, the pragmatist-pluralist Khatami presidency (1997–2005). President Rafsanjani, a seasoned politician, close ally of Ayatollah Khomeini and a central figure in the Islamic revolutionary elite since the revolution itself, became Iran's first executive president in 1989, winning 13.5 million out of the 14.2 million votes cast in that year's presidential poll. Despite the customary level of horse trading in appointments to senior posts, the make up of Rafsanjani's cabinet largely reflected his administration's core objectives: reconstruction of the shattered country and reform of the economy and the bureaucracy. To this end, he assembled a team of largely Western-educated technocrats and social reformers. He established what he himself dubbed 'the cabinet for reconstruction', with Khatami as one of its key social reformer members.

By any measure then his agenda was a reformist one, albeit largely limited to the reform of the economy and creation of the right conditions for growth. His proposed reforms, which won praise from the conservative forces who later came to oppose President Khatami's political and social reforms, hinged on the introduction of sweeping market reforms, privatization and structural adjustment. So comprehensive was his brief that his economic reform strategy won the approval of the IMF for its thoroughness and depth.

Rafsanjani gained the support of the Faqih (Ayatollah Khamenei), as well as the Majlis' backing. The Majlis (parliament) was gradually won over as Rafsanjani slowly dropped his social reform agenda (including Khatami himself from his cabinet) in favour of practical measures which would move the economy towards the free market system. Support from the Majlis, however, had to be 'engineered', and a pro-economic reform majority from the ranks of the conservative and right-wing forces had to be found. Thus, in the course of the early 1990s, Rafsanjani led a successful campaign against the so-called étatist and Islamic leftist and populist forces, which led to their wholesale exclusion from the Fourth Majlis, which began work in 1992, at a particularly critical time in the reform process. Once in place, the conservatives supported most of the Rafsanjani administration's economic programme, but continued their opposition to the liberalization of foreign trade and unhindered foreign investment, and their support for the maintenance of subsidies on certain foodstuffs and primary inputs, despite their removal of the architect of the economic reforms, Mohsen Nourbakhsh, from the cabinet. In this fashion, the conservative forces gained control of the Majlis, and were to keep it until the Sixth Majlis elections in February 2000.

The price for the Rafsanjani-conservative partnership was the wholesale removal of political and social reforms from Rafsanjani's reform agenda. To put this in context of the shift in Rafsanjani's agenda, suffice to note that Rafsanjani himself entered the Majlis race with the conservative camp and against the Khatami reformers in the Sixth Majlis elections. This is testimony to the relationship which he had struck with the conservative forces in the early and mid-1990s and the gap which had now appeared between him and his reform agenda and that of President Khatami's. Even more telling was the very low support that he and his family received from the electorate; his daughter, who had been a close ally of the reformers, was not elected, his brother was not elected and Rafsanjani himself abandoned the chase after it was made clear that his presence in the Majlis would not be welcomed. This is perhaps the sorry end of the first phase of reform in Iran since the late 1980s.

The Development of the '2nd Khordad' Reform Movement

The 2nd Khordad movement's aims are clear: to overhaul the Islamic Republic, modernize its structures, rationalize its bureaucracy, and put in place a more accountable and responsive system of government. In short, and not intending to be uncharitable in any way, the movement was looking to turn Iran into more of a 'normal' state, and a force for positive change in the international system. While different groups of the 2nd Khordad coalition pursued slightly different priorities, on the whole they were committed to the process of change championed by Khatami.

In a striking fashion, the team assembled by the president reinforced the reformist nature of his government. Of the 22 cabinet members he presented to the Majlis for ratification in 1997, no less than seven had PhDs, eight were engineers (*mohandes*), and all three clerics had advanced theological degrees. Moreover, one of the three clerical members of his 1997 cabinet, Hojatolislam Nouri, was one of the most outspoken members of the new team on social reform.

The 2nd Khordad movement consolidated its May '97 gains with victories in the February 1999 municipal elections and the February 2000 elections for the Sixth Majlis. In the former elections, they secured control of virtually every major city and a majority of towns as well. The municipal elections marked the first time that the Iranian people had directly elected their mayors and other local representatives. As such, the municipal elections were the reformists' first stab at the decentralization of power in a highly centralized state. Through this election victory they took control of the country's key constituencies.

Meanwhile in the Majlis elections, the pro-Khatami list won over 60 per cent of the seats. The 2nd Khordad coalition candidates, representing some twenty parties, organizations and groups, took almost all of Tehran's 30 seats – arguably the most important constituency in the country – and the majority of seats in a host of other towns and cities. As this was perhaps the Islamic Republic's most openly contested parliamentary election, we can perhaps draw some lessons from it. First, despite the coalition nature of the reform movement, its candidates were disciplined and all followed the same agenda in their campaigns. Secondly, the reformist candidates scored highly across the country, sometimes replacing popular candidates who had allied themselves too closely with the centrist list which also supported the former president

Rafsanjani. The problem for the technocratic centrist camp was the close association of one of their leaders, Rafsanjani, with the conservatives. For this association, the electorate punished the centrist front, despite the fact that many of its members had very close and long-standing links with the leaders of the 2nd Khordad movement. The elections for the Sixth Majlis, thus, provide anecdotal support for the contention that for the first time in their history the Iranian electorate discovered the true meaning of tactical voting, and took great care to ensure that its true spokespeople entered the new Majlis.

One final observation is linked to the fact that a remarkably small number of clerics actually entered the Sixth Majlis. After a long period of monopoly control of the parliament, over time their numbers have shrunk from over 150 in the first and second Majlises in the early and mid-1980s to fewer than half a dozen in early twenty-first century. Whether this trend indicates a 'de-religioization' of the key elected offices of the Islamic Republic, or the regime's total, and therefore passive, control of the political system remains to be seen. But the clerics' growing absence from such important bodies as the legislature must be indicative of a still changing and evolving political topology in an avowedly Islamic state.

The 2nd Khordad movement's other major achievement was its ability to modernize and liberalize the media. With over forty newspapers, weeklies and other papers in circulation until the conservative backlash of the late 1990s, newspaper kiosks across the country were a hub of activity and debate after the May '97 elections. The reformist newspapers shouted the loudest, raised the most important issues in a challenging manner, engaged in debate, and dared to criticize authority. Through their sheer audacity, they managed to break many of the taboos in this largely patriarchal Muslim society. Many of Iran's recent cultural openings owe much to the efforts of these newspapers. Despite the reformist press' recent setbacks, we can conclude that the print media has managed to establish its place as perhaps the most important source of ideas, and an unrestricted forum, for wide-ranging and free debate in the country.

Electoral Defeat: Catalyst for Action

The four harsh defeats which the right wing suffered in less than a decade, in the seventh presidential elections 1997, eighth presidential elections 2001, local elections 2003, and sixth Majlis 2004, seemed to have permanently changed the political landscape of the country. Together, they marked the growing imbalance of power between the traditional conservatives, 'neoconservatives', and the reformists. The dynamism generated by the reform movement reflected the desire within Iranian society for change. Although

President Khatami in his eight years in office may have failed to achieve in policy terms the desires and aspirations of his electorate, none the less, it is interesting that the groundswell of support for his reforms were such that between 1997 and 2004 he and his allies dominated the national scene. But despite the rise and overwhelming presence of the reformists in many institutions of the Islamic Republic, the traditional conservative forces kept control of several of key instruments of power, namely: the armed forces, the media, the judiciary, and the major economic organizations such as the *Bonyads* (foundations).

At the same time, the same timeline shows that alongside the electoral successes of the reform front, a more profoundly neoconservative force was also emerging, fearful of change and of the long-term consequences of the reform movement for the survival of the republic in its existing form. This group included those individuals who remained loyal to the ideals of the Revolution and the sacrifices made in the long and bloody war with Iraq in the 1980s.

Thus, there was real conflict on the ground between reformists and neoconservatives, a conflict in which all tools of power were ultimately deployed. To shed further light on the political situation post-1997, we will review the conservatives' strategy towards the reform camp at the height of the latter's political successes. Through this investigation we attempt to analyse how the so-called neoconservative forces emerged, what strategies they finally adopted to win back the support of the masses for their cause, and who finally led them back to power.

The Ninth Presidential Elections: The Rise of Ahmadinejad

Since the first-term election of President Khatami in 1997, pundits and students of Iranian affairs took for granted that Iranian society was steadily undergoing political transition and was retreating from its revolutionary politics. At the heart of this reform movement, it was believed, lay the easing of social restrictions and a host of secular liberal rights such as freedom of expression, movement and association.[5] Although this reformist agenda remained far from realization, during his two terms President Khatami championed the expansion of the institutions of civil society and the transformation of Iranian political discourse towards democratic pluralism. But while he may have succeeded in transforming the political discourse, he ultimately failed to introduce the real changes that might have made the process irreversible. Ultimately, the failure to deliver led to public dissatisfaction and alienation.[6] This was exacerbated by the chronic economic problems facing Iran prior to the oil boom of the mid-2000s. It is worth noting that well before the presidential elections, the reform coalition that had brought Khatami to power had concluded that Khatami had lost much of his popular support due to his inability to improve socio-economic conditions, and for failing to stand firm against the conservative factions and an antagonistic judiciary.[7]

Ironically, the idea of social and economic reform had become so well entrenched in the Iranian political landscape that it provided the golden opportunity for potential candidates of the rightist persuasion to speak to pertinent social and economic issues in the 2005 presidential elections without surrendering their core beliefs. This election was to be about values and the means to the realization of a good life while remaining committed to the founding principles of the Islamic Revolution. The election itself, sadly, proved to provide another example of a cynical manipulation of the electoral system than the politics of values so warmly promised by the messages of potential candidates in the race.

In the end, only eight presidential candidates were authorized to run by the Guardian Council from the list of over a thousand registered candidates. The vast majority of the candidates had been disqualified by the body. Amongst the list of eight candidates, Mahmoud Ahmadinejad appeared amongst the least competitive and was in fact an unknown political quantity to the Iranian electorate.[8] Until a week prior to the election, he had barely surfaced in opinion polls and due to lack of enthusiasm surrounding him, he was continuously denying rumours of withdrawing from the electoral race. Indeed, even in the last week of the campaigning, most surveys were predicting a three-man race between a centrist (former president Hashemi Rafsanjani), a conservative (former national police Chief Mohammed Bagher Qalibaf), and a reformist (former Minister of Higher Education Mostafa Moin).[9] There was no sign of Ahmadinejad in the national coverage of the electoral debates.

Moreover, every major presidential candidate spoke in terms of the need to enhance social and economic reforms in the country, which not only indicated the success of Khatami's ability to change the discourse of the nation, but also showed blanket support for the chosen path of the country by the candidates. Even Mohsen Rezaei, the former head of the Revolutionary Guards, and Bagher Qalibaf, wrapped themselves in the rhetorical cloak of social and economic reforms. Tehran's police chief even went as far as sending his advisers to seek guidance from Prime Minister Tony Blair's campaign managers on how to target the affluent middle classes of Tehran and succeed in repackaging himself as a pro-reform candidate.[10]

Among reformers, media attention focused on Moin, who called for democratization and greater respect for human rights. Moin started slowly but appeared to finish strongly, igniting at least some enthusiasm among the young and the more well-to-do reformers alike. Among the Right, eyes were on Qalibaf and Ali Larijani – a close adviser to Supreme Leader Ayatollah Khamenei. Weeks prior to the poll itself, newspapers considered close to

Khamenei even urged Qalibaf to withdraw in favour of Larijani as a means of strengthening the conservative faction in the race; in conservative strongholds such as Qom, Larijani's presence was the most visible. But most of the focus, domestic and international was on Rafsanjani. People close to Khamenei signalled a lack of enthusiasm for him, viewing him as a potential counter-weight and a threat to the Supreme Leader's authority. Broadly disliked and perceived as corrupt,[11] he none the less appeared to be the default candidate, a potential bridge between neoconservatives and reformers, and a gateway for the West.

In short, compared with the others Ahmadinejad was little more than a dark horse, seemingly lacking important financial, institutional and popular support. Few appeared to have given serious thought to his candidacy until shortly before the vote itself. Nor was he noticed as a serious competitor by Rafsanjani, Qalibaf or Moin. Their advisers failed to even mention Ahmadinejad as a serious contender for presidency. With attention on Rafsanjani and Moin, neoconservatives appeared worried and divided.

The Iranian presidential elections of 2005, the ninth presidential election in Iranian history, took place in two rounds, first on 17 June 2005, and then as a run-off on 24 June.[12] This in itself was a new development, forcing the former President Rafsanjani to battle twice in the same race against a little-known foe. The surprise remains that the election led to the victory of Ahmadinejad, the conservative mayor of Tehran, with 19.48 per cent of the votes in the first round and some 61.69 per cent in the second.[13] Ahmadinejad is believed to have won the second round because of his populist views, especially those regarding the poor and their economic status. The election saw a turnout of over 60 per cent of eligible voters, seen as a strike back by Iran at the United States' initial allegations that many in Iran would be restricted from voting. The first round of the election was a very close race with minor differences in the number of votes won by each candidate.

As already noted, this was the first presidential run-off in the history of Iran. Before the run-off took place, it was compared to the 2002 French presidential elections, in which the splintering of the left-wing vote similarly led to a run-off between the moderate Jacques Chirac and the far right Jean Marie Le Pen. The comparison was made because of the unexpected votes of Ahmadinejad, the very close race, and the comparability of the political standings of Rafsanjani and Ahmadinejad to those of Chirac and Le Pen. But after the results for the run-off were out, the comparison was considered void because of the higher standing of Ahmadinejad and the inability of his opponents to form a majority alliance against him. While pre-voting polls mostly favoured a run-off between Rafsanjani and Mostafa Moin, the actual vote count from the Ministry of Interior unexpectedly put Ahmadinejad and Mehdi Karroubi in second and third places. Rafsanjani and Ahmadinejad led with respectively 21.0 per cent and 19.5 per cent of the vote, and were followed by Karroubi (17.3 per cent), Qalibaf (13.9 per cent), Moin (13.8 per cent), Larijani (5.9 per cent), and Mehralizadeh (4.4 per cent).[14] This was the result of 29,317,042 votes, which amounts to a turnout of 62.66 per cent, as there were 46,786,418 eligible voters. While Rafsanjani had secured the first place in the first round, he failed to win the second round, by failing to attract the people who had voted for the reformist candidates and who were expected to support him in the second round. Ahmadinejad won with 61.7 per cent of the vote, while Rafsanjani only secured 35.9 per cent. There was a total of 27,959,253 votes cast in the second round, slightly lower than the first round. Considering that the number of eligible votes was raised by about 150,000 people, the turnout was about 59.6 per cent.

Mahmoud Ahmadinejad has presented himself as a politician who wants to serve the Iranian nation, in particular those who have been forgotten by previous governments. There is no doubt that his social and religious background are behind every move or statement. Using religious phrases about the hidden Shia Imam, speaking extensively about social justice, redistributing wealth, bringing new but inexperienced faces to politics, ignoring the political role of women and limiting it to family affairs, and finally presenting the government as a representative of the people rather than their master, continue to dominate his strategy. It is for the combination of religion and new-style politics that Ahmadinejad is being referred to as a real phenomenon in modern Iranian politics.

He does however represent a far more radical shift in the social structure of the country's elite than is immediately apparent, and his agenda presents a more radical agenda compared even with the first revolutionary generation. He hails from those who inherited the country from the Pahlavis and thus formed the country's new emerging urban-based social classes.[15] The bulk of this group had emigrated from different Iranian cities to the capital, swelling its population to 12 million today. The interests of these internal migrants were inextricably linked to that of the Islamic regime and many of them joined the Islamic Republic's Revolutionary Guards (Sepah) for ideological reasons and also for defending their new power base. They are religious to the extent that religion dominates their lives. Mahmoud Ahmadinejad is a child of this same social environment and his presidency reflects the same.

These social groups associated with the revolution were adversely affected by the reform policies of President Mohammad Khatami, and they felt that their hard-fought-for revolutionary aims had been undermined by Khatami's reforms. They felt a real sense of isolation and alienation in what they regarded to be 'their' Islamic Republic. The reform movement – in their eyes – focused on political change, forgetting the role of these social groups in establishing the Islamic state and in protecting its ruling regime. In one word, they felt that they had been betrayed, and that the regime had been 'kidnapped' by liberals, intellectuals and irreligious people. Perceptions, even, of the reform movement amongst various social classes has played an important part in the divisions emerging between the political elite itself. In the last analysis, fear of the reforms helped in mobilizing the traditional urban masses in support of the neoconservatives, especially Mahmoud Ahmadinejad.

The Iranian neocons are in power precisely because they 'rediscovered' the traditional lower and middle classes and also because they separated themselves from the traditional conservatives, who were seen as not having done enough to protect the masses. The masses were also angered by the level of corruption of Iranian politicians who were busy protecting their own interests, and using their political vantage point for personal gain. Ahmadinejad used hatred of corruption to great effect in his election campaign, arguing that such individuals were not only unclean morally but also untrustworthy for they had also abused the religion of the people. Only he, Ahmadinejad claimed, could rid the republic of these unworthy politicians. He was, he said, 'the people's man', and the only man who could lead Iran's 'third revolution'.

Factionalism and the Struggle for Power in Iran

In many ways Ahmadinejad's victory reflects the transformation of the political struggle in Iran from one between the conservatives and the reformists, to one within the powerful conservative faction itself. The new guard represents the rise of the military in Iranian politics. The old guard, however, remains at the heart of power, occupying many of the unelected offices of the system. Such figures as Ayatollah Rafsanjani, representing pragmatic conservatism, remain powerful actors in Iranian politics. In his case, not only because of his role as head of the Expediency Council, but also because of his strong patrimonial network of political support, which he has been able to develop over the decades. On the other hand, there is Ahmadinejad, a man of humble origins with support among the lower classes and strong links to the Sepah, the Basiji and to cliques such as the Hojjatieh Society. It has become clear since the election that Ahmadinejad has been manoeuvring to create political space for ideologues close to him and to dominate state institutions with like-minded individuals. Ahmadinejad represents a close-knit network of factions populated by ideologues who display a strong sense of entitlement to power as the revolution's true sons.

The harsh reality of the ongoing power struggle is clearly visible in Iran. Rafsanjani, for example, has on more than one occasion openly attacked Ahmadinejad and accused him of undermining national unity and elevating incompetent cronies to positions of power and influence. Not to be outdone,

Ahmadinejad in turn has hinted that he would seek to bring Rafsanjani and those who benefited excessively under his tenure of presidency to trial for corruption.[16] If the president were to actually act on this threat then he would more than likely open a major fault-line amongst the elite, perhaps irrevocably ending any pretence of union amongst the political elite. In the midst of this ensuing power struggle, the position of the Supreme Leader Ayatollah Khamenei has remained somewhat ambivalent. Although Ahmadinejad had originally been Ayatollah Khamenei's protégé; there were rumours that Khamenei would have little choice but to realign himself with Rafsanjani to protect the old guard in the middle of its struggle with the new guard. This is an outcome that Ayatollah Khamenei would not relish, given the tense relations between he and the Rafsanjani camp.[17]

Given the potential gravity of the situation, the victor of this conflict is likely to be the old guard. Ahmadinejad and his advancements are likely to be blocked by the old guard, because Ahmadinejad threatens their political and economic power in Iran. Whatever the outcome of the political struggle, the old guard would still have to deal with the pressing social and economic crisis besetting Iran. The reformist movement may have been defeated politically and without the momentum it had during the late 1990s, but those who supported it continue to exist in Iran, and the discourse of the reform movement continues to resonate. As the door to state institutions is locked to them, so these individuals have looked to alternative ways of political engagement, whether through the expansion of civil society or through the use of the internet.[18] The chance that the conservative old guard would emerge from its struggle with Ahmadinejad seriously weakened always exists; providing an opportunity for the reformists to re-emerge.

At stake in this political infighting is not only pride but the economic spoils of political power. The formal Iranian economy is worth about $500 billion, but there is also a vast informal economy; much of which is actively encouraged by the political system and managed by religious foundations and other networks that link the market with different parts of the power structure.[19] Despite a number of internal social and economic problems, economic development has occurred and this has been fuelled by oil income. The main beneficiaries have been the elite business factions linked to the old guard. These factions have in turn used their wealth and influence to engage in speculation on the stock market and in real estate and to reinforce their economic and political power, in particular strengthening their ties within the economic elite. However, in the first year after the election of Ahmadinejad, the economic situation deteriorated. Foreign investors have fled to surrounding Arab countries, the stock market has plummeted and confidence in the banking system has weakened.[20] Most of this has been due to a lack of confidence in the economic policies of Ahmadinejad by foreign investors and the appointment of ministers with little known economic and political management experience. The poor handling of the economy is a strong reason for the old guard in combination with the business faction to rein in Ahmadinejad and his clientele.

Ahmadinejad's ideological leanings are also a liability for the old guard. Islamist ideology has been exploited by the old guard to entrench their status and power in the hierarchy of politics in Iran. This can explain why the old guard have maintained and consolidated their strength; even not reversing Khatami's policy of liberalism. However, Ahmadinejad has spoken of a necessity to roll back secular liberalism to protect the Islamic identity and principles of Iran. This is likely to be seen as a threat by the old guard, adding another source of conflict in the collision between the two camps. Therefore it can be seen that a number of factors are responsible for this power struggle. From the militarization of politics to mishandling of the economy – the struggle is likely to continue.

Governance under Ahmadinejad

We have argued that the election of Ahmadinejad represents a major turning point in Iranian politics. Broadly speaking, the reasons for Rafsanjani's defeat, and Ahmadinejad's success, fall into two categories; namely, Rafsanjani's failure to gain the support of Khamenei and his coterie of advisers, and Rafsanjani's failure to convince the people of his sincerity and the soundness of his policy priorities. At a broader level, the reformists and even dissidents failed to understand the possibility of a regressive revolution taking hold in the country. They assumed that their slogans in support of political development, multi-party politics and integrating Iran into the international system would guarantee their place at the centre of power, giving them perpetual victory in elections. More than anything, Ahmadinejad's victory demonstrated that Iran remains a deeply polarized society some 26 years after the victory of the revolution. In the same way that Khatami's victory in 1997 and 2001 demonstrated that there was grass-roots support for reform and Iran's integration into the international community, Ahmadinejad's victory has shown that a large number of Iranians strongly support the neoconservatives and believe in their slogans regarding the redistribution of wealth, eliminating poverty, rooting out corruption and protecting the Islamic nature of the state.

Time will tell whether Ahmadinejad can deliver on the promises he made during his electoral campaign and convert the slogans into tangible outcomes. However, what is for certain is that Ahmadinejad is in the process of revolutionizing Iranian politics by introducing and exposing the neoconservatives to mainstream Iranian politics. With them, however, has also come military baggage, resulting in the political establishment acquiring a more militaristic face for the first time in over a generation. These changes by Ahmadinejad have not gone unnoticed internally, or indeed externally. Internally the old guard are fearful of the road on which Ahmadinejad may be leading Iran, with fear of their economic and political status being diminished by the new revolution launched by Ahmadinejad. Externally, the military character of the Iranian regime has raised alarm bells and has intensified the stand-off between Iran and the West. The debates about Iran's nuclear programme have also increasingly been articulated around these same issues since 2005.

The internal challenges to Ahmadinejad have begun not from the reformists but from the old faction of the conservatives who feel that they are being pushed to the side by the ascent of the new guard in Iranian conservatism. This power contest is likely to characterize politics in Iran into the future, even possibly feeding into the external pressure being talked about over the republic's stated and unstated nuclear ambitions. The manner in which Ahmadinejad handles and manages both challenges will determine his support base in society and importantly his longevity in power. It seems therefore that the division within the ruling conservatives is serious, and is likely to increase over Ahmadinejad's economic and social policies. As we saw, he has been under increasing pressure from clerics in relation to some of his social policies (allowing women's presence in football stadiums, for instance), and for his efforts to tackle social corruption in a public manner. He has also been accused of following a populist agenda in economic policy and foreign relations for short-term political gain[21].

What the consequences of these tensions might be for the remainder of his presidency will become apparent in the next twelve to eighteen months. However, an early indicator was the December 2006 elections for the Khobregan Majlis, which as a constitutional body is charged with 'electing' the Faqih. The final list of candidates which was announced by the Guardian Council at the end of November 2006 showed that the struggle is indeed between the neoconservatives and the tradition Right. This conclusion is based on our assessment of the final 'shortlist' of candidates, in which a number of the neoconservative candidates (and also 'neoreformers') were disqualified.[22] This led to the 'neoreformers' boycotting the elections and it also gave the traditional Right more of a chance to win a majority of seats. The Majlis elections of 2008 also will more than likely bring an open struggle between the neoconservatives, the traditional Right and the reconstituted 'neoreformers'. The positioning of the traditional Right will be the main story of this round of Iranian electoral politics, we suspect.

Despite all that the new president may have done, his election victory has not changed the structures of power, nor the relationship between the institutions of power, which continue to be dominated by the conservative hierarchy which has been in place since the 1979 Iranian Revolution. Ahmadinejad's devotion to the Leader is legendary and he does not, for a moment, entertain ideas of changing the balance of power between the various institutions of power away from the Leader's office. Furthermore, despite his neoconservative leanings, President Ahmadinejad must govern a modern, complex and wayward state, as well as rule over a restless population which no longer responds positively to pressures from above, who is at the same time desperate for its fair share of Iran's bounties. We would submit that the president will find moving the goal posts, in terms of the national agenda, a lot harder than even delivering on his lofty election promises. We did suggest earlier that the weight of geopolitical realities today, as well as 16 years of constructive/reform-oriented policy making at home, have their own policy momentums, which cannot easily be dismissed or bypassed. None the less, we still believe that it should be asked how far a post-revolutionary state can be run by a neo-revolutionary president? This is a question that merits further investigation. Our suspicion is that in the medium term it will probably have to be the neo-revolutionary who must change, given Iran's shifting demographic balance, its economic difficulties, its role in the international political economy as a major hydrocarbons producer, and the pressures associated with geopolitics. Nevertheless, the dawn of post-détente in Iran's regional policies is unlikely to be warmly received by its neighbouring countries, despite continuing exchange of niceties between the new administration and its neighbours, and high-level visits by the president and his emissaries to neighbouring Arab states. The real irony is that Iran's radicalizing tone is taking place just as Iraq may finally be emerging from the dark shadows of the 2003 war. The return of the political process to Iraq, we argue, will further complicate relations of the Gulf Co-operation Council states with Iran, with the latter being perceived by the neighbours as making strategic gains in Iraq. None of this provides a recipe for happy coexistence, particularly under the leadership of Iran's neoconservatives.[23]

Since 9/11, the securitization of international politics and the grand geopolitical developments in West Asia have had such a dramatic impact on the Iranian polity that today it has an administration dominated by the security spirit of the revolution, if not indeed many of its personnel. Foreign policy in Iran is not shaped in a vacuum and we would venture to suggest that it is still the wider context that determines the national agenda. To follow President Ahmadinejad's policies we must therefore appreciate the domestic backdrop as well as the regional realities in which they take form. Ultimately then, it could be argued that unlike any other time in the life of the Islamic Republic, while the main threats to its national security may have been eliminated, its own policies and political priorities are such that it could now be generating such potentially huge security challenges for the future that it may have little alternative but to embark on the building up of its defences in anticipation of external attack. At no other time in recent history of the region has the danger of a self-fulfilling prophecy of militarization coming to pass been greater than the present time. When the Iranian president spoke of his election victory as a 'second Islamic revolution' in the country, he would have had the domestic situation in mind, but in reality he may well have forced Iran to relive the tense and lonely period of the 'First Republic' in the 1980s, when friends and allies were in short supply and when defiance of the international community was the republic's *modus operandi*. The costs of isolation today, however, could be incalculable in terms of opportunities lost, pressures endured and the high price to be paid by the next generation for the country's rehabilitation. The ruling conservative hierarchy have certainly recognized the dangers of an imbalanced foreign policy, and as a result Ayatollah Khamenei commissioned the creation of the non-partisan Foreign Relations Strategic Council in the summer of 2006 in order to seek advice of experts in relation to international affairs and the formation of Iran's foreign policy. It will be interesting to see to what extent the advice which is given is actually taken on board by the ruling neoconservative elite gathered around the presidency and in the Majlis. A key test of the direction of Iranian foreign policy will be the ruling elite's reaction to the ongoing nuclear negotiations converging around the EU package which was tabled in Vienna on 1 June 2006. It is our view that Iran might agree to the suspension of its uranium enrichment programme only to be able to test the credibility of the EU and US in terms of what is actually being offered, but beyond that a clear resolution is not yet in sight. It is likely therefore that the nuclear issue will not be solved under the present US administration, making it interesting to see how a new US administration will deal with Iran. It is for this reason that the prospects of a military confrontation of sorts cannot yet be ruled out.

If the neoconservatives fail to invest in this historical moment, it is likely that there will be no more real incentives from the West, which would in turn enable the reformist camp in Iran to review its own strategy in order to dislodge the neoconservatives from power. Again, domestic and international have become hopelessly tied together to generate yet more complexities in the case of the Islamic Republic of Iran.

Professor Anoush Ehteshami is Head of the School of Government and International Affairs, University of Durham.

Dr Mahjoob Zweiri is Teaching Fellow at the School of Government and International Affairs, University of Durham.

NOTES

1   This article is based on our major study of post-Khatami Iran, published as *Iran and Rise of its Neoconservatives: The Politics of Tehran's Silent Revolution*, London: I.B. Tauris, 2007.

2   A. Gheissari and V. Nasr, *Democracy in Iran: History and the Quest for Liberty*, Oxford: Oxford University Press, 2006.

3   F. Jahanbakhsh, 'Religious and Political Discourse in Iran: Moving Toward Post-Fundamentalism', *The Brown Journal of world affairs*, IX (2), Winter/Spring 2003, p. 243

4   I. Berman, 'Understanding Ahmadinejad', *The American Foreign Policy Council*, June 2006.

5   'Round 12 for Iran's Reformists', *Middle East Report Online*, 29 January 2004.

6   'His first 100 days', *Al Ahram*, 1–7 December 2005, issue No. 771.

7   B. Ghammari, 'How the reformists lost the presidency – What's the matter with Iran', 5 July 2005 <www.Iranian.com>.

8   'Iran: What Does Ahmadinejad's Victory Mean?', *International Crisis Group*, 4 August 2005.

9   Most of whom were disqualified by the Guardian Council, which holds veto power over all political candidates in Iran.

10 B. Ghammari, 'How the reformists lost the presidency'.

11 'Iran's Presidential Coup', 27 June 2005 <www.opendemocracy.net>.

12 'Iran Hardliner Sweeps to Victory', *BBC News*, 25 June 2005.

13 Ibid.

14 Ibid.

15 <http://roozonline.com/02article/012435.shtml>.

16 T. Porteous, 'Reading Iran', *Prospect*, No. 118, 22 January 2006.

17 M. Khalaji, 'Iranian President Ahmadinezhad's Relations with Supreme Leader Khamenei', Washington Institute for Near East Policy, *Policy Watch*, No. 1147.

18 Porteous, 'Reading Iran'.

19 Ibid.

20 Ibid.

21 A. Savyon, 'Iran's 'Second Islamic Revolution: Fulfilled by election of Conservative President', *The Middle East Media Research Institute*, 4 July 2005, *Aftab-e Yazd* (Iran), 22 June 2005, *Iran* (Iran), 22 December 2005.

22 <http://www.isna.ir> 29 November 2006.

23 'Saudis Fuming over Iran President's Holocaust, Israel Comments', 10 December 2005 <http://www.newsmax.com> ; 'Ahmadinejad draws ire of Saudis, Iranians, West over Israel remarks', 10 December 2005 <http://www.dailystar.com>; 'Iran: Holocaust remarks misunderstood', 16 December 2006 <http://www.cnn.com>.

The Enigma of
President Ahmadinejad

MANSOUR FARHANG

The emergence of President Mahmoud Ahmadinejad of the Islamic Republic of Iran as a threat to international peace and security calls to mind Hegel's famous remark that 'the real is absurd but the absurd is rational.' It is indeed absurd that Mr Ahmadinejad inaugurated his presidency by proclaiming that 'the wave of the Islamic revolution' would soon 'reach the entire world',[1] and then proceed to organize an international 'conference' to prove that the Holocaust is a myth.[2] Yet, this absurdity appears to have its own rationality when placed in the context of Iran's domestic politics and viewed as a response to the Bush administration's delusional approach to the entanglements of the Middle East region.

Every successful revolution seems to produce a political order that is more influenced by the native culture or the society's settled habits than by the idealistic claims of the revolutionaries during their oppositional struggle. The Iranian Revolution is the latest example. It began with the promise of dismantling the incumbent absolute monarchy and transforming Iran into an open and lawful society. Instead, the revolution devoured many of its children and reincarnated the autocratic rule of the past in a theocratic form. A novel feature of this new governing system is the regularly held elections that are undemocratic but competitive. They are undemocratic because only candidates with submission to clerical supremacy are allowed to run, but they are nevertheless competitive and consequential. Campaigns for presidential and parliamentary elections in the Islamic Republic reveal some differences among the Islamists about national economic policies and disbursement of funds or financial privileges by the state. The dramatic increase in oil revenues (estimated to exceed $60 billion in 2006) have enabled the regime to feed a growing system of nationwide patronage that includes the businesses allied with or controlled by ruling clerics, as well as the elite of the Revolutionary Guards and the country's vast security apparatus. In the June 2005 presidential elections, in spite of widespread disappointment about the ability of 'elected' officials to fulfil their promises, 27 million people, nearly 60 per cent of eligible voters, cast ballots and the results introduced the enigmatic President Mahmoud Ahmadinejad.

Candidate Ahmadinejad ran on a populist platform and hardly mentioned anything about his foreign policy positions. He campaigned among the poor and the lower-class sectors of the population, proclaiming that poverty, corruption, nepotism and the deepening gap in the distribution of wealth and income were betraying the promises of the revolution. He repeatedly said to his audiences that he could solve these problems if they chose him as their president. An uninitiated observer might get the impression that Mr Ahmadinejad was condemning the regime. After all, who was responsible for the miseries he wanted to remedy? The reigning ayatollahs who had been in charge of public policy for 25 years? Shortly after taking office, Ahmadinejad realized that the 'elected' president has little power to change the country's economic policies. He quickly learned that he could not do much about the growing poverty, corruption and nepotism in the Islamic Republic without exposing the self-serving practices of the high-ranking clerical clique, a group of men who have arrogated to themselves the permanent right to rule Iran. Former President Mohammad Khatami learned the same lesson when he tried to push for political reform after his surprise victory in 1997. Thus, Ahmadinejad abandoned his anti-poverty rhetoric and, instead, chose to increase state support for charitable activities and to shift the focus of his speeches from fighting poverty and corruption to the defence of Iran's nuclear programme and the moral urgency of confronting Israel. Virtually all the high-power clerical cliques encouraged him to pursue his new agenda without openly associating themselves with his rhetoric. He was also cheered by the state's security forces and the most fanatical elements of the regime's popular base

To understand Mr Ahmadinejad's behaviour and motives, we need to keep the following facts in mind: 1) the Iranian political order is factionalized and the ruling elite openly compete with each other for power and perquisites; 2) Islamic Iran, like Iran in other periods in its history, wants to be a serious player in the geopolitical games of the Persian Gulf region, and 3) the Islamic Republic and the United States have been antagonistic toward each other since the 1979 revolution but their security interests and regional ambitions converged in the overthrow of the Taliban in Afghanistan and Saddam Hussein in Iraq. The implications of these facts can lead to diverse and competing interpretations, but no serious analyst or policy maker should minimize their significance for the Iranian state and US-Iranian relations.

During the first decade of the Islamic Revolution, Ayatollah Khomeini was the uncontested leader of the country and his power was rooted in his ability to mobilize millions of intensely devoted supporters with simple declarations. His successor, Ayatollah Ali Khamenei, had no such power and lacked the capacity to develop a significant following of his own. Yet, the clerical regime needed an ultimate arbiter for its factional and personality clashes, and Ayatollah Khamanei was chosen to play the role. In this sense, Khamenei is the most powerful individual within the regime, but he cannot afford to be oblivious to the demands and expectations of competing leaders and factions. In other words, since Ayatollah Khomeini's death in 1989, Iran has not had an absolute leader – a virtually unprecedented situation in the modern history of the country.

Another recent occurrence in Iran is a significant increase in the number of former Revolutionary Guards' commanders in positions of power in the organs and agencies of the state. This development is due to the fact that the Guards' central role in the Iran–Iraq War enabled them to build direct popular support in the social base of the regime. Moreover, as public disillusionment with the regime's poor economic performance, social strictures and political repression increases, the clerical rulers are compelled to view the coercive apparatus of the state as an indispensable force for their survival. This reality has motivated a growing number of the Revolutionary Guard officers to give up their uniform and enter the national or local political scene. It was under such circumstances that a number of former Revolutionary Guard commanders began to use the Martyrs Foundation (a welfare organization that helps the veterans of the Iran–Iraq War and the families of soldiers killed or wounded in the conflict) and the *basiji* or militias, the largest volunteer force established during the war, as instruments of electoral campaigns for parliamentary or presidential races. In the presidential elections of 2005, Ahmadinejad managed to utilize the resources of the *basiji* and the Martyrs Foundation in a surreptitious manner with astonishing effectiveness.

The Islamic Republic and the United States have been obsessed with each other since the 1979 fall of the Pahlavi Shah, America's close ally for a quarter of a century. Thus once Ahmadinejad was elected to high office, it was simply a matter of time before he and his counterpart in Washington would lock horns. Ahmadinejad fired the first shot by sending President Bush an 18-page letter, challenging him to a debate and urging him to be righteous in his conduct. President Bush ignored the letter, behaviour which provided sufficient evidence for Ahmadinejad to prove the correctness of his positions on a cluster of abstract issues he had raised in his letter. This was not the first time that President Bush had ignored invitations of dialogue from Iran. Since 9/11, Iran has used a variety of channels to announce its readiness for direct talks with Washington.[3] Such failed attempts have convinced Iran's leaders across the factional divides that President Bush's refusal to engage them is due to pressure from Israel and its Washington lobby. Flynt L. Leverett, who has served in senior positions at the National Security Agency and the Central Intelligence Agency reveals that 'in the spring of 2003 we received through this Swiss channel a one-page document, which basically laid out an agenda for a diplomatic process that was intended to resolve on a comprehensive basis all of the bilateral differences between the United States and Iran.'[4] According to Leverett, President Bush regards the Iranian regime as 'fundamentally illegitimate' and, therefore, 'has deliberately ruled out direct negotiations with Iran either over the nuclear issue or over the broad range of strategic issues that you would need to talk to Iran if you were going to get a real diplomatic settlement on the nuclear issue'.[5] The fact that the administration resists suggestions from most foreign policy experts and many former officials, both Republicans and Democrats, to begin direct contact with Iran reinforces the official Iranian suspicion that Washington and Tel Aviv are adamantly opposed to a peaceful settlement of the nuclear issue. It appears that Iran's rulers are convinced that the United States and Israel are seriously considering bombing Iran's nuclear and military facilities before the Bush administration finishes its term in office.

One way that Iranian leaders are trying to prevent such an attack is to attract support for their position in the Arab world. Such support could only come from the Arab masses, not governments, and the most effective way to cultivate that support is to attack Israel and champion the cause of the Palestinians. It is in this context that the repugnant 'conference' on the Holocaust was used to demonstrate Iran's resolve to confront Israel. The idea of holding the 'conference' must have been approved by Ayatollah Khamenei and other ruling clerics, but it took a character like Ahmadinejad to become the public promoter of the show. The 'conference' could also be used to neutralize the bizarre Arab perception concerning Iran's role in the invasion of Afghanistan and Iraq. Before 9/11, two of Iran's six neighbours, Afghanistan and Iraq, were hostile to Iran's ruling clerics, but the overthrow of the Taliban and Saddam Hussein enabled them to establish good relations with both of them. The ironic convergence of interests between Iran and the United States in the ousting of the Taliban and Saddam Hussein has persuaded many people in the Arab world that the Bush administration and Iran's reigning ayatollahs are actually in cahoots. In March 2006, the host of a popular talk show on Al-Jazeera television, *The Opposite Direction*, asked viewers whether they considered Iran an enemy or an ally of the United States in Iraq. Over 70 per cent of the 1,374 respondents called Iran an ally.[6]

When Ahmadinejad says he wishes to see Israel 'wiped off the map', his intended audience is the populace of the Arab Middle East. He hopes to rekindle the extinguished fire of the Islamic Revolution and return the Islamic Republic to the time when Ayatollah Khomeini could demand human and material sacrifices from the Iranian people to confront the 'Great Satan', fight a war against Saddam Hussein's Iraq and prepare for the liberation of Jerusalem. Ahmadinejad's attacks on Israel and advocacy of Islamic militancy have some appeal to the poor and hopeless in Arab countries, particularly among the tormented Palestinians. But in Iran, where political repression, social strictures and double-digit unemployment and inflation plague the country, most people view Ahmadinejad's rhetoric with contempt and ridicule. As long as the United States supports, diplomatically and financially, the Israeli occupation of Palestinian land and Jewish settlement expansion on the West Bank, Middle Eastern politicians can use anti-Americanism as a rallying cry for their domestic or regional agendas. This is exactly what Iran is doing. It wants to transform its dispute with the United States over the nuclear issue into a confrontation between the region's Muslims and Israel; the Holocaust 'conference' was intended to serve this purpose. The price Iran will pay for whatever advantage it might have gained from this outrageous 'conference' among the Arab masses will be a marked increase in the Western fear of its nuclear programme. Yet as long as the United States threatens to take military action against Iran, the Iranian regime will try to use a mixture of religious and nationalistic rhetoric to rally most of the population around the state. The discontent of Iranians with their theocratic government should not be confused with lack of support for the integrity of the country. Iran's rulers are first and foremost focused on the ways and means of remaining in power. They are passionate advocates of martyrdom, but they do not wish the honor for themselves. The vast majority of a nearly million Iranian dead or wounded in the Iran–Iraq War came from the rural and urban poor sectors of the population.

The Bush administration insists on suspension of Iran's uranium enrichment as a precondition for negotiation; the Iranian regime continues to reject the idea of any precondition for such talks. The Iranian leaders are doubtful that the Bush administration is interested in a negotiated settlement of the dispute. They seem convinced that the neo-conservatives decide US policy concerning the Middle East, and their goal is regime change in Iran. Press reports and Bush's public statements about Iran clearly suggest that the option of air strikes against Iran is under serious consideration. In September 2006, President Bush quoted Osama bin Laden and Mahmoud Ahmadinejad to argue that they posed a totalitarian threat as great as that from Nazism and Communism. And for the first time, he claimed that Iran and Hezbollah are as dangerous to US security as Al Qaeda.

President Bush's position on Iran's nuclear programme is a symptom of the US's policy toward the Islamic Republic since its inception – a policy that rejects engagement and uses exclusion, sanctions and threats to isolate and pressure the country. This policy has failed and nearly all area experts believe that a movement toward normalization of relations between Washington and Tehran would serve the national interests of both countries and create a secure environment in the Persian Gulf region. Survey research reveals that the overwhelming majority of the Iranian people wish to see an end to their nation's antagonism toward the United States. There is a sea-change in Iran's public opinion about the US. However, it would be a grave mistake to conclude from this reversal of Iran's popular attitude that the Iranian people are ready to see their country, once again, become a client of Washington. US policy makers should be sceptical about what they hear from Iranian exiles. They would be well served to recall the rosy scenarios they heard from Iraqi exiles prior to the ousting of Saddam Hussein.

Iran is a despotic state, but only Iranians living within the country can develop appropriate strategies for challenging their rulers. The US threat against Iran can only make life more difficult for the human rights activists and pro-democracy forces who live under constant restriction and threats. Political and cultural repression has worsened since Ahmadinejad was sworn into office. All independent newspapers have been banned and censorship of books has reached an unprecedented severity. Militia organizations have come to control the universities. Ahmadinejad has called upon students to demand the expulsion of secular or liberal professors. There is a growing aspiration for democracy among the middle class, particularly the young, but it is yet to produce a viable opposition to the regime. Moreover, Iranians are fearful of violent encounter with the security forces and seem to hope for incremental change toward moderation in the apparatus of the state.

The 15 December 2006 elections for city councils around the country resulted in a decisive loss for the candidates associated with Ahmadinejad, but it is unrealistic to expect the new city council members to be significantly different, politically or culturally, from their defeated rivals. For the council elections represented a struggle for local control between two factions equally committed to the theocratic order. The leader of the winning faction is the mayor of Tehran, Mohammad Bagher Qalibaf, a former Revolutionary Guard commander who was one of the five approved candidates in the 2005 presidential elections. So long as the competing factions within the regime accept the rules of the undemocratic but competitive elections and remain submissive to the superior authority of the ruling clerics, the electoral process can be a source of strength for the regime. Iran's leaders and official comment-ators interpret the 61 per cent turn-out of the 44 million eligible voters as evidence of popular legitimacy for the Islamic Republic. The elections for the 86-member Council of Experts that took place on the same day shifted the number of votes cast for the candidates; but unlike the 233,000 men and women who ran for the local councils, members of this exclusively clerical body were all the self-appointed 'viceroys of God on earth'.

Ahmadinejad has little influence on Iran's foreign policy and his sensationalism is a passing phenomenon. Moreover, Iran's military capability is too weak to pose a challenge to the US or Israel in the foreseeable future. What should be treated as a serious threat to international security is the continuation of the face-off between Washington and Tehran, because it could lead to another catastrophic outbreak of violence in the Middle East region. The only way for the United States and Iran to break the deadlock in their 27-year-old estrangement is a genuine effort toward reconciliation. It is imperative that the United States accepts the Iranian leaders' repeated call for direct talks and test the possibility of a comprehensive bargain at the negotiating table. The US ought to reassess its policy on Iran and stop being swayed by right-wing Iranian exiles and their neo-conservative promoters who claim to have the capacity to change the Iranian regime and turn the country, once again, into an instrument of US hegemony in the Middle East region. If the Bush administration wants to help the prospects for democracy in Iran, it should begin direct and transparent dialogue with the Iranian government and pave the way for a gradual move toward normalizing diplomatic, commercial and cultural relations between the two countries. The vast majority of Iranians would welcome such a development. The struggle for democracy must be a native project. International promotion of human rights can inspire the struggle for democracy in Iran, but coercive interference from without is bound to result in massive death and destruction for the Iranian people and make it more difficult for them to challenge their tyrannical rulers.

Mansour Farhang, Professor of Politics at Bennington College, served as revolutionary Iran's first ambassador to the United Nations. He resigned his position in protest when his efforts to negotiate the release of the American hostages in Tehran failed.

NOTES

1   *The Times* (UK) online, 30 June 2005.
2   *New York Times*, 13 December 2006, p. A10.
3   <http://www.mideastweb.org/iranian_letter_of_2003.htm>.
4   Bernard Gwertzman, 'Q&A: Iran: Bush Administration "Not SeriousAbout Dealing With Iran"' <www.nytimes.com/April 4, 2006>.
5   Ibid.
6   Jalal Ghazi, 'News Analysis', *Pacific News Service*, 15 March 2005.

SHIITEISTAN

PEPE ESCOBAR

> With one stroke, a world which billowed with fertility was laid
> desolate, and the regions thereof became a desert, and the greater part
> of the living dead, and their skin and bones crumbling dust; and the
> mighty were humbled and immersed in the calamities of perdition.
>
> *Persian historian Juvaini, on the Mongol invasion of Khorasan*

A *ziyarah* – a pilgrimage to Mashhad – is a key event in the life of a Shiite. As a
pilgrim to Mecca receives the honorific title of 'Haji', a pilgrim to Mashhad
receives the title of 'Mashti'. For some Shiite scholars the pilgrimage could even
assure a place in Paradise. As gateways to Paradise go, the Astan-e Qods-e
Razavi – housing the holy shrine of Imam Reza - is one of the most dazzling
religious complexes in the world. We are totally immersed in a celebration
caravan featuring elaborate minarets, blue domes, an unequalled Golden Dome,
a Timurid mosque, a kaleidoscope of calligraphic and floral motifs, museums,
breathtaking iwans (two of them entirely coated with gold), madrassahs,
courtyards, libraries, stalactite stucco decorated with multicoloured glass and
marvels like the 30-million-knot Carpet of the Seven Beloved Cities.

At sunset – lost in the multitude of black chadors and white turbans
occupying every square inch of this huge walled island – the power of the
Shiite faith strikes us like lightning, as powerful as Buddhism when we
circumambulate the Jokhang in Tibet. The shrine complex was built by Shah
Abbas at the beginning of the seventeenth century – and enlarged ever since.
Imam Reza's shrine itself – where pilgrims from all over the Shiite world
touch and kiss and weep and cling to a silver cage – is absolutely off-limits to
non-Muslims.

The public relations officers who care for foreign pilgrims tell us 'your holy
host is in fact Imam Reza', the eighth Shiite imam, born in Medina in 765
AD and martyred by the Abbasid caliph Mamoon in 818. Mashhad means
literally 'the burial place of a martyr'. It also means big business. The foundation that manages the complex is now an enormous conglomerate that
includes nearly sixty companies. Most of the foundation's funds come from

donations, bequests and the selling of gravesites beneath the shrine: being buried next to Imam Reza is an invaluable honour. The foundation is heavily involved in charity, runs pharmacies and hospitals, provides housing, builds mosques and develops poor areas in the Iranian province of Khorasan.

***

A spectre is haunting the Middle East – at least in the minds of selected Sunni Arabs (especially Wahhabis), as well as members of a collection of right-wing American think-tanks. That spectre is a Shiite crescent, spreading from Mount Lebanon to Khorasan, across Mesopotamia, the Persian Gulf and the Iranian plateau. Yet facts on the ground are much more complex than this simplistic formula whereby, according to Riyadh, Amman and Kuwait City, Tehran remote-controls its allies Baghdad, Damascus and southern Beirut.

Seventy-five per cent of the world's oil reserves are in the Persian Gulf. Seventy per cent of the Gulf's population is Shiite. As an eschatological – and revolutionary – religion, fuelled by a mix of romanticism and despair, Shiism could not but instil fear, especially in hegemonic Sunni Islam. But for more than a thousand years Shiite Islam has been in fact a galaxy of Shiisms. It's as if it was a Fourth World, always cursed with political exclusion, a dramatic vision of history and social and economic marginalization.

Historically, the Christian West has always trembled when faced with the passion of Islam. But since the Crusades there has never been a challenge like this: Islam not only denounces the West's arrogant economic and cultural imperialism, but also condemns its lifestyle. The problem is that the alternative, Ayatollah Khomeini-created, post-1979 Iranian model essentially did not deliver. So in a sense the true Islamic Revolution is only beginning.

Shiites finally won political power in Iraq. They have conquered it in Lebanon, and are actively claiming it in Bahrain. They are the majority in each of these countries. Shiism is the cement of their communal cohesion, and essential in fuelling their political action to change their historically inferior socio-economic status. That's demography fuelling political power. But that does not mean that all Shiite political roads lead to Tehran. And it does not mean that Beirut or Damascus are clones of Tehran.

Ayatollah Mohammad Hussein Fadlallah, the top Lebanese Shiite cleric, is extremely independent from Iran. Hezbollah, being a movement founded in a multi-religious country, could never impose Khomeini's concept of *velayat-e-faqih* – the ruling of the Islamic jurisprudent – to Lebanon as a whole. Hezbollah's Sheikh Nasrallah – who studied in Iran as well as in Iraq – juggles the cloaks of religious leader and pragmatic political leader.

With the Islamic Revolution, for the first time in history the Shiite clergy was able to take over the state – and to govern a Shiite-majority society. No wonder this is the most important event in the history of Shiism. It's a totally different story in Saudi Arabia, where Shiites are a minority of 11 per cent, repressed as heretics and deprived of their rights and fundamental freedoms by intolerant Wahhabis. Not for much longer. Shiites are concentrated in the eastern province of Hasa, Oil City *par excellence*; as the majority of the skilled workforce they are itching to control their oil wealth as much as their Iraqi brothers may have finally managed to. These are Arab Shiites who constantly go on pilgrimage to Iran's holy sites in Tehran, Qom and Mashhad.

The tension between Tehran and Qom is at the heart of Iran's future. Whenever I go to Qom I'm reminded that as far as major ayatollahs are concerned, their supreme mission is to convert the rest of Islam to the original purity and revolutionary power of Shiism – always critical of the established social and political order. But as a nation-state at the intersection of the Arab, Turk, Russian and Indian worlds, as the key transit point of the Middle East, the Persian Gulf, Central Asia, the Caucasus and the Indian subcontinent, between three seas (the Caspian, the Persian Gulf and the Sea of Oman), close to Europe and at the gates of Asia, Tehran on a more pragmatic level simply cannot go on preaching: it must conduct an extremely complex foreign policy.

Olivier Roy, expert on Islam and a director of the CNRS (Centre National de la Recherche Scientifique) think-tank in Paris, characterizes Tehran's thinking as 'pan-Islamist', always emphasizing anti-imperialism, Arab nationalism and anti-Zionism. Diplomats in Tehran never admit it explicitly, but what it boils down to in terms of *realpolitik* is a counter-encirclement foreign policy. And not only because of the post-9/11 US military bases which today almost completely encircle the country. Iran rivals Turkey for influence in Central Asia and rivals Saudi Arabia for hegemony in the Persian Gulf – with the added complexity of this being a bitter Sunni–Shiite rivalry as well. Rivalry with Pakistan – again for influence in Central Asia – subsided after the Taliban were chased out of power in Afghanistan. But basically Tehran regards Pakistan as a pro-American Sunni regional power, thus not exactly prone to be attentive to Shiites. This goes a long way to explain the Iran-India alliance.

There's a fierce competition going on, with different civilizations like Turks, Persians and Russians placing all bets on future trade routes in Central Asia. In the early twenty-first century Iran is positioning itself as a bazaar-State, set on becoming the unavoidable player in an oil and gas-fuelled New Silk Road and thus recovering the pre-eminence it enjoyed in the era of Darius, the King of Kings.

But how to get there? Way beyond spin, 'diplomacy' and manufacture of consent, the heart of the matter is that the US President Bush ('all options are on the table') won't stop seriously considering a nuclear first strike against Iran before he leaves power in early 2009.

Due to the opacity of Iran's theocratic nationalism, outsiders may be tempted to assume that the official Iranian position is the one expressed by Defence Minister Mostafa Mohammad Najar in the spring of 2006: 'The United States has been threatening Iran for 27 years and this is not new for us. Therefore we are never afraid of US threats.'

Javad Zarif, the Iranian ambassador to the UN, has also endlessly relayed the official position. Iran's nuclear programme is peaceful; there is no proof given by the International Atomic Energy Authority (IAEA) of a military development; the religious leadership opposes atomic weapons, and Iran has not invaded or attacked any nation for the past 250 years. The power spheres in Iran seem to bet that even in the event of a 'Shock and Awe' assault of B-2s, guided missiles and bunker busters, that simply is not enough to snuff out accumulated Iranian nuclear know-how.

A key question is *which* Iranian leadership will have its final say on the nuclear matter. There are at least four main factions in the complex Iranian game of power politics.

The first faction is a sort of extreme right, closely aligned from its formation to the Egyptian Muslim Brotherhood and involved with a *rapprochement* with Sunni Arabs in general, while opposing even a tactical *rapprochement* with the US. This faction includes the dreaded *hojjatieh* fanatics and may even include the Hezbollah, who of course support both the Lebanese Hezbollah and the Arab nationalism of Moqtada al-Sadr in Iraq. (The difference between the Iranian and the Lebanese Hezbollah groups is that in Beirut and southern Lebanon Hezbollah is comparatively much more active, pushing to be at the heart of political life and improving people's living conditions.) Former Defence Minister Chamkhani, from Khuzestan province (where Iranian oil lies) is very close to this faction. They are very conservative religiously and have a socialist leaning economically.

The role of President Ahmadinejad – a former Pasdaran middle-rank official – in moulding this first faction has been crucial. In 2005 Supreme Leader Ayatollah Khamenei had the support of former president and Machiavellian master of ambiguity Hashemi Rafsanjani at the highest levels of power – the Expediency Council. But as a balancing act the Supreme Leader also decided to boost the profile of Ahmadinejad, who happened to be totally opposed to the pragmatist Rafsanjani. To add more arabesques to this Persian miniature, Khamenei's favourite candidate in the 2005 presidential elections was actually Qalibaf, a former chief of police – basically a conservative but in favour of a controlled opening of political life, the Supreme Leader's own policy.

What this all ultimately means is that Ahmadinejad – even winning against Rafsanjani and Qalibaf – and as the new leader of the extreme right, is not really in charge of the government. An anti-Ahmadinejad coalition runs from Qalibaf supporters to – believe it or not – pro-secular intellectuals close to former President Khatami, such as Soroush and the journalist Akbar Ganji, released from prison in the spring of 2006.

The Supreme Leader knew that Ahmadinejad would revive the regime with his populist rhetoric, very appealing to the downtrodden masses. But the ruling ayatollahs may have miscalculated that since they control everything – the Supreme National Security Council, the Council of Guardians, the *bonyads* (foundations), the army, the media – they could also control the 'street cleaner of the people'. That was not the case, so plan B – restraining the president, and the powerful Pasdaran (the Revolutionary Guards) – went into effect by early 2006.

The second key power faction in Iran is composed of provincial clerics, whose master is none other than the Supreme Leader himself. These are pure conservatives, attached to the purity of the Islamic Revolution, and even more patriotic than the first faction. They are not that interested in more integration with Sunni Arabs. Faithful to the Supreme Leader, they want to keep both progressives and extremists in the same house, *Ahl al Bait*, with the *velayat-e-faqih* – the role of the Islamic jurisprudent – as the supreme law of the land. Ever since the 2004 parliamentary elections – largely boycotted by the Iranian population – an association of clerics totally dominates the Majlis (Parliament).

But there are huge problems behind this appearance of unity. Iranian money from the bonyads badly wants a reconciliation with the West. They know that the relentless flight of both capital and brains – which is being actively encouraged by the Rafsanjani faction – is against the national interest. But they also know this can hurt Ahmadinejad's power. Some Western-connected Iranians even started comparing the Ahmadinejad era to the Gang of Four in China a little while before the death of Mao in 1976.

The Pasdaran for their part want to keep up their fight against Zionism and go all the way with the nuclear programme. This would entail the extra-ordinary possibility of an American attack against Iranian nuclear sites counting on the complicity of a great deal of the mullahcracy – which does not hide its desire to get rid of Ahmadinejad and his Pasdaran gang.

The third power faction is the left – initially former partisans of the son of Ayatollah Khomeini, Ahmad Khomeini, who died in mysterious circum-stances in the 1990s. After that they spectacularly mutated from Soviet-style socialism into some sort of religious democracy, which found its icon in former President Muhammad Khatami of 'dialogue of civilizations' fame. They became the so-called 'progressives' – and even if they lost the 2004 and 2005 elections they are still a force, although already debilitated by the slow awakening of a younger, more secular and more radical opposition.

The fourth and most unpredictable power faction is Rafsanjani's. The consummate Machiavellian masterfully retained his own power during the late 1990s and into the early twenty-first century, juggling between Supreme Leader Khamenei and President Khatami. He may be the ultimate centrist, but Rafsanjani is and will always remain a supporter of the Supreme Leader. What he dearly wants is to restore Iran's national might and regional power, and reconcile the country with the West, essentially because of one reason: he knows an anti-Islamic tempest is already brewing among the new generations in Iran's big cities, who dream of integrating with the nomad elites of global liquid modernity. As head of the Expediency Council, fully supported by the Supreme Leader, and in his quest to 'save' the Islamic Revolution, Rafsanjani retains the best possible positioning.

Meanwhile, Ahmadinejad holds as much power as his predecessor – the urbane, enlightened and sartorially impeccable Khatami: that is, not much. What Ahmadinejad's constantly over-the-top performances (always for internal consumption) did was to solidify the support the Rafsanjani faction receives from the intelligentsia as well as the urban youth, not to mention the 'enlightened police' faction of Qalibaf. But none of this means a Velvet Revolution is around the corner.

Apart from these four factions, there are two others who are outside the ironclad circle of Supreme Leader power: the revolutionary left and the secular right. Clerics call them *biganeh* (eccentric), and the denomination may be correct to a point, as both these groups are quite disconnected from the majority of the population, although they also support the nuclear programme out of patriotism. The extreme left hates the mullahcracy but has also derided Khatami's moderately progressive agenda. As for the Westernized liberals, which include former supporters of deposed Prime Minister Mossadegh and members of the Freedom Movement of Iran, an opposition party, they are becoming increasingly popular with Tehran students, who are more and more pro-American (if not in foreign policy at least in behaviour and cultural preferences).

The Iranian regime may be essentially unpopular – because of so much austerity and the virtual absence of social mobility. But for millions it is still bearable. What is actually happening is the slow emergence of a common front – bent on the restoration of the power of the Iranian state through an alliance with Shiism in Iraq, Bahrain and Lebanon. This may be interpreted as a Shiite crescent by alarmist Sunni Arabs, but there's no military, expansionist logic behind it. The common front is also in favour of moving towards a more market-oriented economy and a progressive liberalization of morals and public opinion. This is what we hear in Tehran from young people, women, workers in the cultural industry and philosophers – and it is Tehran that always sets the agenda in Iran.

***

All these tensions between the four factions came to a head in the 15 December 2006 municipal elections and in the election for the Council of Experts. Rafsanjani's moderate faction scored a stunning victory over the extreme right for the 86-member Council of Experts. 'Hashemi' (as he is known in Tehran), as well as Ayatollah Mesbah Yazdi – *éminence grise* and spiritual leader of President Ahmadinejad – managed to be among the 16 clerics representing Tehran in the Council of Experts, but Rafsanjani received almost double the number of votes for Yazdi.

The Council of Experts (86 clerics only; no women allowed) is key because it is the only institution in the Islamic Republic capable of holding the Supreme Leader to account and even of removing him from office. It is the system's Holy Grail. As is well known, the Supreme Leader – not the President – is where the buck stops in Iran.

Once again, this election was a case of the extreme right against the moderate/pragmatists: the recluse Ayatollah Mesbah Yazdi – aka 'the crocodile' (in Farsi) – against the eternal insider, relative 'friend of the West', former president (1989–97), opportunist and king of the dodgy deal Rafsanjani.

Yazdi is the dean of the Imam Khomeini Educational and Research Institute in Qom, a hardcore *hawza* (theological school) that has prepared and configured the worldview of key members of the Ahmadinejad presidency. It's impossible, especially for foreign correspondents, to interview Ayatollah Yazdi, officially because of 'government rules', unofficially due to his own volition.

Rafsanjani, a.k.a. 'the shark', remains the chairman of the Expediency Council and virtually the regime's Number Two, behind the Supreme Leader and ahead of President Ahmadinejad. Iranian pop culture, with a tinge of Discovery Channel, delighted in describing this as the battle between the crocodile and the shark.

It was heavily symbolic that the moderate Rafsanjani and another former president, the progressive, well-dressed Mohammad 'dialogue of civilizations' Khatami, voted together in the Jamaran mosque, where Khomeini used to deliver his speeches. Iranian reformist papers did not fail to publish the emblematic photo sealing the alliance on their front pages the day after the election.

Hashemi's victory was sweeter not only because he had lost to Ahmadinejad in the second round of the 2005 presidential elections. Yazdi is none other than the Leader of the Supreme Leader himself. There had been rumours in Tehran all through 2006 that Yazdi and his followers were making a naked power grab. They had won city and village council elections, then parliamentary elections and the presidency (with Ahmadinejad), and were ready to conquer the Council of Experts and thus be in position to choose the next Supreme Leader. By December 2006 there were unconfirmed rumours that Ayatollah Khamenei might be seriously ill.

Saudi Wahhabis may complain there are 'no free elections in Iran' (as if there were any elections in Saudi ...). Anyway, popular participation in these Iranian, and we might say 'relatively free', elections was a healthy 60 per cent.

Clerics running for the Council of Experts must pass a difficult theological exam – and must be approved by the Council of Guardians which, as with anything that really matters in Iran, is controlled by the Supreme Leader. The six key mullahs out of the Council's twelve jurists are directly appointed by the Supreme Leader. So inevitably the election for the Council of Experts was Supreme Leader-controlled. No wonder Ayatollah Khamenei described it as the most important in the whole country, stressing that candidates 'should comprise honest, wise, competent, benevolent and trustworthy people'. The Council of Experts is bound to remain under the ironclad dominance of Ayatollah Khamenei's conservative block.

On municipal elections nationwide the extreme right – clustered on Ahmadinejad-endorsed lists – also lost. The absence of a sweep by the extreme right meant a relative surge by the reformists, mixed with Ahmadinejad-faction allies plus a coterie of technocratic conservatives.

Ayatollah Yazdi and his followers have always stressed they want to implement 'real Islam'. They view the Rafsanjani camp as a bunch of filthy rich, morally and legally corrupt decadents, totally oblivious to the concerns of 'ordinary people', whose self-styled key symbol happens to be President Ahmadinejad. Yazdi is also the spiritual mentor of the Hojjatieh, a sort of ultra-fundamentalist sect whose literal interpretation of Shiite tradition holds that chaos in mankind is a necessary precondition for the imminent arrival of the Mahdi (the twelfth 'hidden' Imam – see below). Ahmadinejad may not be a Hojjatieh himself, but he totally understands where they are coming from.

Yazdi's 'real Islam' has absolutely nothing to do with Western democracy. He wants a *kelafat* – a caliphate. Ayatollahs like Yazdi are simply not concerned with worldly matters, foreign policy, geopolitical games or Iran's nuclear programme; the only thing that matters is to work for the arrival of the Mahdi. Yazdi is on record saying he could convert all of America to Shiism. But some in Tehran accuse him of claiming a direct link to the Mahdi, which in the Shiite tradition would qualify him as a false prophet.

Even facing a relative defeat at the polls, the Ahmadinejad faction – known as *Isaargaraan* ('the self-sacrificers') – still maintains a huge, countrywide popular base in the military-security establishment, in the tens of millions, ranging from the Revolutionary-Guard Pasdaran to the Bassijis, the hardcore paramilitary militia, also known as 'the army of 20 million', and expanding to the pious, apolitical, downtrodden masses, mostly rural but also urban (in sprawling south Tehran, for instance). But the defeat at the Council of Experts signals that their efforts for an all-out power grab have been thwarted.

It's always important to remember that Ahmadinejad, more than a politician, is fundamentally a believer in the Mahdi – the twelfth hidden Shiite imam whose Great Occultation began in the tenth century and whose return is imminent to, in essence, save mankind from itself. Ahmadinejad even has his own roadmap for the return of the Mahdi; he drew it himself. According to Shiite tradition, the Mahdi will rise in Mecca – not in Qom – where he will preach to his close followers (Jesus Christ puts in a guest appearance), draw up the armies of Islam and finally settle down in Kufa, Iraq.

The only crucial policy the Council of Experts has implemented since the beginning of the Islamic Revolution has been to appoint Ayatollah Khamenei as Khomeini's successor and new Supreme Leader, in 1989. It was in fact a white coup – because according to the constitution at the time the Supreme Leader had to be a *marja* (source of imitation and top religious leader). Ayatollah Khamenei was not up to standard. Khomeini died while the constitution was being revised; so Khamenei was in fact appointed by a law ratified only after he was already installed as Supreme Leader.

Yazdi has been trying a different strategy: to take over the Council of Experts from the inside and then overwhelm Khamenei. It is fair to argue the Supreme Leader has played a very deft hand. He firmly supported Yazdi before the 2005 presidential election, but then discreetly rallied his followers – and the full machinery of the system – to keep Yazdi and his protégé Ahmadinejad under control. Over the years Ayatollah Khamenei has been politicizing the religious system non-stop, to the point of the Islamic Republic nowadays being neither a democracy nor a theocracy: rather, it's a clerical autocracy.

Once again, neo-cons and the Washington establishment should not jump to hasty conclusions. There won't be regime change in Tehran anytime soon. Throughout 2006 there was a serious crackdown on the reformist press, the Internet, personal blogs, satellite dishes and academia – where more than fifty reformist professors were targeted. What is happening now is the moderates/pragmatists reaching a more solid position allied with the reformists – with the extreme right held in check by a Supreme Leader more supreme than ever. The crocodile may have been rocked. But the Islamic Republic's fierce internal power play is far from over.

***

To succeed, the regime must open up. If it does not, the Iranian economy will never create enough jobs over the next few years to fight unemployment among its overwhelmingly young population. A great deal of the non-oil dependent private sector is controlled by the bonyads, whose managers are usually incompetent and corrupt clerics. Any reasonably informed Iranian knows that an economic crisis, high oil prices notwithstanding, will rip the heart out of the lower-middle class – the regime's base – and more crucially the industrial working class, which used to be aligned with the Tudeh, Iran's communist party.

The key of keys to 'liberate' Iran of most of its problems would lie in finding a nuclear compromise with the West – with the EU, but especially with the US. For all his vocal, popular support in the provinces, if Ahmadinejad and his Pasdaran hardliners go against this national desire for stability and progress, they are doomed.

Demonizing Western parallels of Iran enriching a few grams of uranium to Hitler's march into the Rhineland are positively silly. The uranium enrichment programme may be under the operational control of the Pasdaran, but Ahmadinejad does not set Iran's nuclear policy: the Supreme Leader – who else? – does, his guidelines followed by the Supreme National Security Council, which is led by the Leader's protégé Ali Larijani. The point is not that Ahmadinejad is a suicidal nut bent on confronting the 'Great Satan' by all means available. The point is that he leads just one of four key factions in a do-or-die power play, and he is following an agenda which is not necessarily the Iranian theocratic leadership agenda.

It is as if Ahmadinejad has been playing the typical Bonapartist – using a political deadlock to try to go all the way towards dictatorship. Rafsanjani may also be a closet Bonapartist – but the difference is that he is not interested in dictatorship. The ideal outcome of this whole 'nuclear crisis' would be an Iran moving to a moderately liberal alliance between eternal pragmatist Rafsanjani – the only one capable of subduing the Pasdaran – and the semi-secular left which still regards Khatami as the least bad of all possible models. This is what emerged from the 15 December 2006 polls. It may not be Paradise, but it certainly beats war.

One day before the fifth anniversary of 9/11, Khatami delivered a speech at Harvard; the Iranian proponent of the 'dialogue of civilizations' addressing the temple where the American proponent of the 'clash of civilizations' is a professor may have been the equivalent of Imam Ali giving a speech at the Vatican. Samuel Huntington's belligerent mish-mash remains a neo-con foreign policy Bible, legitimizing the clash between Western civilization and the Sino-Muslim civilizations. As Edward Said always noted, Huntington based most of his speculation on a 1990 article by famed Orientalist Bernard Lewis; for both Lewis and Huntington, the West is the West and Islam Islam, and no complex internal contradictions apply. Khatami for his part fought belligerence with dialogue. His concept was presented at many global forums, including the UN, which even declared 2001 – of all years ... – the Year of Dialogue Among Civilizations.

US corporate media did not even bother to debate what Khatami had to say to Harvard. Now this is what dialogue is all about.

It is impossible to deal with Iran without understanding the complex dialectics behind the Iranian religious leadership. In their minds, the concept of nation-state is regarded with deep suspicion, because it detracts from the *umma* – the Muslim community. The nation-state is just a stage on the road to the final triumph of Shiism and pure Islam. But to go beyond this stage it is necessary to reinforce the nation-state and its Shiite sanctuary, which happens to be Iran. When Shiism finally triumphs, the concept of nation-state, a heritage from the West, will disappear anyway, to the benefit of a community according to the will of Prophet Mohammad.

Reality often contradicts this dream. One of the best examples was the 1980s Iran–Iraq War. Saddam Hussein invaded Iran first. Iranians reacted culturally – this was a case of Persians repulsing an Arab invasion. But Tehran at the same time also expected Iraqi Shiites to rebel against Saddam, in the name of Shiism. It did not happen. For the Shiites in southern Iraq, the Arab nationalist impulse was stronger. And still is. This fact in itself destroys the neo-con charge that Tehran fuels a guerrilla force in southern Iraq with the intention of breaking the country up. The Ba'athist idea of integration of Iraqi communities under a strong state, in the name of Arab nationalism, persists. Nobody in the Shiite south wants a civil war – or the break-up of Iraq. What they want is more autonomy.

***

Now let's examine Shiitestan at large. Azerbaijan – where 75 per cent of the population is Shiite – could not be included in a Shiite crescent by any stretch of the imagination. Azerbaijan, by the way, is a former province of the Persian Empire which Russia took over in 1828. Azeris speak a Turkic language, but at the same time they are kept at some distance by the Turks because the majority of Azeris are Shiites. Unlike Iran, the basis of modern, secular Turkey is national – not religious – identity. To complicate matters further, Shiism in Azerbaijan had to face the shock of a society secularised by seven decades of Soviet rule. Azeris would not be tempted – to say the least – to build an Iranian-style theocracy at home. It is true that Azeri mullahs are Iranified. But as Iran and Azerbaijan are contiguous, independent Azerbaijan fears too much Iranization.

At the same time, Iran does not push too hard for Shiite influence on Azerbaijan because Azeri nationalism – sharing a common religion on both sides of the border – could embark on a reunification of Azerbaijan to the benefit of Baku, and not of Tehran. And if this was not enough, there is the Nagorno-Karabakh conflict, where Iran supports Armenia for basically two reasons: to reduce Turkish influence in Azerbaijan and to help Russia counteract Turkey – perceived as an US-backed Trojan horse – in the Caucasus.

A fair summary of this intractable equation would be that Azerbaijan is too Shiite to be totally pro-Turkish, not Shiite enough to be completely pro-Iranian, but Shiite enough to prevent itself from becoming yet again a satellite of Russia.

On Iran's eastern front, we find the Hazaras of Afghanistan, the descendants of Genghis Khan. In the seventeenth century the Hazarajat, in central Afghanistan, was occupied by the Persian Empire, and the Hazaras converted to Shiism. They have always suffered the most in Afghanistan – totally marginalized in political, economic, cultural and religious terms. Under the Taliban they were persecuted and massacred in droves – as the Taliban were surrogates of Saudi Wahhabism: this was a graphic case of the rivalry between Iran and Saudi Arabia being played out in the heart of Afghanistan, as much as a case of pro-Pakistan Pashtuns against pro-Iranian Hazaras. The Iran–Saudi Arabia rivalry is now being bloodily replicated inside Iraq as well.

Hazaras compose a significant 16 per cent of the Afghan population. As far as Tehran is concerned, they must be supported as an important political power in post-Taliban Afghanistan. But once again it's not a case of the Shiite crescent. Iranian military aid flows to the Shiite party, Hezb-e-Wahdat. But there are more important practical issues, like the road linking eastern Iran with Tajikistan that goes through Mazar-e-Sharif and bypasses Hazara territory. And there is the strong Iranian political influence in Herat, in western Afghanistan – the privileged fiefdom of warlord Ishmail Khan. When Khan was jailed by the Taliban in 1997 in Kandahar, he was liberated thanks to Iranian mediation. He is now Energy Minister in Hamid Karzai's government, but he still controls Herat. The road linking Herat to the Iranian border – previously a nightmare – was rebuilt and paved by Iranian engineers. People in Herat cannot get a single television programme from Kabul, but they get three Iranian state channels. Western Afghanistan is as much Afghan as Iranian.

Now for Shiism in South Asia: The Moghul empire in India was heavily Persianized. Since the fourteenth century, the Moghuls had been speaking Persian; it was the administrative language of the sultans and the empire's high officials in Delhi, and later carried as far away as Malacca and Sumatra. India – as much as Central Asia – was extremely influenced by Persian culture. Today, Shiites are concentrated in northern India, in Uttar Pradesh, around Lucknow and also in Rajasthan, Kashmir, Punjab, the western coast around Mumbai and around Karachi in Pakistan. Most are Ismailis – not duodecimal, like the Iranians. Pakistan may have as many as 35 million Shiites, with a majority of duodecimal. India has around 25 million, divided between duodecimal and Ismailis. The numbers may be huge, but in India Shiites are a minority inside a minority of Sunni Muslims, and in Pakistan they are a minority in a Sunni state. This carries with it a huge political problem. Delhi sees the Shiites in Pakistan as a factor of destabilization. That's one more reason for the close relationship between India and Iran.

The Gulf may be a case of Trojan horses. Seventy-five per cent of the population of the Persian Gulf – concentrated in the eastern borders of Saudi Arabia and the Emirates – is Shiite, overwhelmingly members of a rural or urban proletariat. Hasa province, in Saudi Arabia, which stretches from the Kuwaiti border to the Qatar border – and where all the oil is concentrated – has been populated by Shiites since the tenth century. Seventy per cent of the skilled workforce in the oilfields is Shiite: by all means a time bomb.

Yet one more historical irony rules that the bitter rivalry – geopolitical, national, religious, cultural – between Iran and Saudi Arabia must be played out in Saudi territory as well. A Shiite minority in the land of hardcore Sunni Wahhabism – and the land that spawned Al Qaeda – must be the ultimate Trojan horse. What to do? Just as in Iraq under Saddam, the Saudi royal family swings between surveillance and repression, with some efforts at integration: not so much promoting Shiites in the kingdom's ranks but heavily promoting the immigration of Sunnis to Hasa. Deeper integration must be the solution, as the access to power of Shiites in Iraq will certainly motivate Saudi Arabian Shiites.

Kuwait lies north of Hasa. Twenty-five per cent of Kuwaitis are Shiite – natives or immigrants – and they provoke the same sort of geopolitical quandary to the Kuwaiti princes as they do to the Saudis. Although they are a religious, social and economic minority as well, Shiites in Kuwait enjoy a measure of political rights. But they are still considered a Trojan horse. South of Hasa, in Qatar, where also 25 per cent of the population is Shiite, is the exact same situation.

And then there's Bahrain. Sixty-five per cent of Bahrain is Shiite. Basically they are a rural proletariat. It's the same pattern: Sunnis are urban and in power, Shiites are poor and marginalized. For decades, even before the Islamic Revolution, Iran has insisted that the Shiites in Bahrain are Iranians because the Safavid dynasty used to occupy both margins of the Persian Gulf. Tehran still considers Bahrain as an Iranian province. The Shiite majority in Bahrain is prone to turbulence. Repression has been inevitable, and Bahrain is helped in the process by – who else? – Saudi Arabia.

But there are some encouraging signs. The small Bahrain archipelago is separated from Saudi Arabia by just a bridge. Every weekend in the Muslim world – on Thursdays and Fridays – Saudis abandon Wahhabi suffocation in droves to relax in the malls of Manama and its neighbouring islands. Women in Bahrain are closer to women in Tehran than those in Saudi. They wear traditional clothes but not a full black chador; they drive their own SUVs – nobody stops them or questions them; they meet boys and men in restaurants, shops or cinemas. For them, there are no forbidden places or professional activities.

The locals tend to believe this is due to the relative modernity of the Al-Khalifa family in power. Even the South Asians are treated far better than in the neighbouring corporate dream Dubai. Bahrain is not particularly wealthy – compared to the other Emirates – and unlike Dubai it does not strive to become an economic powerhouse. There are plenty of schools and a good national university – although most women prefer to study in the US or Lebanon. But all this can be illusory. Shiites in Bahrain will not stop fighting for more political participation. Both Grand Ayatollah Sistani and Supreme Leader Ayatollah Khamenei are extremely popular in Bahrain.

In the ultra-wealthy United Arab Emirates, only 6 per cent of the populations is Shiite. But they can present a problem as acute as in Kuwait or Qatar because of the enormous trade and business of Iranian influence in Dubai.

The whole equation of Persian Gulf Shiites has to do with a tremendous identity problem. The key argument in favour of them *not* being an Iranian Trojan horse is that first and foremost they are Arabs. But the question hangs in the air: are they most of all Arabs who practice a different form of Islam, which the Sunni majority considers heretic? Or are they Shiites bound to pledge allegiance to the motherland of Shiism, Iran? The multi-layered answer is not only religious; it involves social and political integration of Shiites in regimes and societies which are basically Sunni. Shiism in the Arab Gulf may be 'invisible' to the naked eye. Only for the moment. Sooner or later the sons of Imam Ali will awaken.

***

Syria, Lebanon and Iraq are the key protagonists in the spectre of a Shiite crescent, according to the House of Saud, King Abdullah of Jordan, the emir of Kuwait and right-wing American think-tanks. Once again, the facts on the ground are much more complex than a simplistic formula.

Syria, although 86 per cent Muslim, is a multi-ethnic and multi-confessional country. The Sunni majority cohabits with 13 per cent of Alawites (who are Shiites), 3 per cent of Druze and 1 per cent of Ismailis. The Alawites derive from a schism in the ninth century around the eleventh imam, al-Askari, whom they consider the last legitimate descendant of Prophet Mohammad. Sunnis as well as Western scholars consider them Shiites. But many serious Islamic scholars are still in doubt.

Since the early twentieth century, Syrian nationalists have never accepted the creation of Lebanon, Jordan and much less Palestine – which became Israel. Alawites – a persecuted minority for centuries - have reached their current enviable position in Syria thanks to the Ba'ath Party ideology, which has always been secular and nationalist. Ba'ath ideology exalted Arabism. So Alawites joined en masse both the Ba'ath Party and the army. The result was inevitable: at the end of the 1960s they took over power in Syria. The incarnation of this process was strongman Hafez al-Assad. Sunnis in Syria always felt they had been 'robbed' of power. But Assad never feared the Sunnis as much as he feared Islamic fundamentalism.

Damascus is, of course, close to Tehran. In Lebanon – to counteract Christian Maronite power – Syria has always supported the Shiites. Does that mean that Alawite-controlled Syria is part of the Shiite crescent? Not necessarily. Lebanese Shiism is practically the same as in Iran. But for the Iranian ayatollahs in Qom, Alawites themselves are heretics. During the 1980s, in Damascus, there was plenty of official talk about a Shiite International from the Mediterranean to Pakistan. But Assad – coming from a sect considered heretic by the duodecimal – could never be the head of such an entity.

The point now with Hafez's son Bashar is if he will be able to keep the Alawites in power by modernizing the Syrian state. Regime change in Syria may remain a priority in Washington. But no one knows how Syrian unity would be affected – the country could become 'Lebanonized', or even worse, 'Iraqified' – or what the consequences would be over the stability of Lebanon and the Israeli–Palestinian conflict. Who needs an Iraqified Syria?

Shiites in Lebanon are predominant in two non-contiguous regions, the south and the north-east near the Syrian border. Lebanese Shiites finally achieved political representation as they became the predominant Lebanese community (no definitive statistics, but they could be as many as 60 per cent). They woke up from decades of political and social torpor, their political consciousness determined by the fact that they were Shiites. This extraordinary, painful process has served as an example for Shiites in Iraq, and may serve as an example for Shiites in the Persian Gulf.

Lebanese Shiites essentially want to be able to co-direct the country along with Christian Maronites, who possess the financial power in Lebanon. This could only happen in a Lebanon free from the current, corrosive, confessional institutional model, something that is unlikely in the short term. The only possible solution for Lebanon would be a broad agreement between the Maronites (the financial power), the Shiites (the demographic power) and the Sunnis (the link with Saudi financial power, and until recently with Syria as well). With the powerful business-oriented Hariri clan – known as 'Hariri Inc.' – stressing the Saudi connection that seems unlikely to happen. The point is that for Lebanese Shiites, Lebanon the motherland is the most important thing, not a Shiite crescent.

Under whoever was in charge – the Ottoman Empire, the Hashemites, the British, the Ba'ath Party, Saddam Hussein – Shiites in Iraq were always marginalized and denied political influence. That was the main reason, in the end of the 1950s, for the creation of the Da'wa Party – which became the expression of Shiite specificity. In the end, History delivered the goal: the current set-up, with Shiite religious parties in power, is what Iran had wanted in Iraq since the Islamic Revolution in 1979.

The Ba'ath Party and Saddam wanted to create a strong, secular, Arab Iraqi nation. They had everything they needed: a sea of oil, lots of water (unlike any other Arab country) and a significant population. In this ambitious project there was no room for religious or ethnic affirmation. So Kurds as well as Shiites were immolated on the altar of this concept – a modern and secular Iraq. During the 1980s – because of the appeal of Khomeini's Islamic Revolution – Saddam Hussein's ultimate nightmare was seeing Iraq break up into three weak statelets: a Kurdistan, a 'Shiitestan' and a Sunni centre with lots of desert and no oil. That nightmare was a key reason for Saddam to launch the Iran–Iraq War. The pretext, according to Saddam himself, was to recover what Iraqis call 'Arabistan' – the Iranian province of Khuzestan wherein lies most of Iran's oil.

President George Bush senior, as is well documented, decided to keep Iraq intact. He knew that the inevitable consequence of an implosion of Iraq would be a Kurdistan and a Shiiteistan near the Gulf. That spelled the death sentence for the Shiite uprising after Saddam's armies were defeated in early 1991. Sunni repression was horrendous: more than 40,000 Iraqi Shiites were killed and hundreds of thousands had to flee to Iran. In 2002, in a Basra still under Saddam, I was convinced that it was Western wishful thinking to believe that Iraqi Shiites would ever forget this betrayal. In the early 1990s the Americans, the 'international community', Arab regimes, no one wanted to see the break-up of the Iraqi state. By another cruel historical irony, the Bush junior administration's terrible blunders may produce exactly this outcome.

Iraqi Shiites for their part always suspected that Al Qaeda wants civil war. By the summer of 2005, Grand Ayatollah Sistani was saying that even if half of Iraq's Shiites were killed, there would be no civil war. They were determined not to succumb to provocation – because they knew they had the numbers to seal their arrival to power. So this is not about religion – or a Shiite crescent. The Holy Grail is power. The US neo-cons dreamed of power over the whole Middle East. The Sunnis don't want to lose the power they thought was theirs in Iraq by divine will. Other Sunni Arab regimes in the Middle East obviously tremble at the sight of a Shiite renaissance. The Shiites reached power after centuries of suffering. And Al Qaeda in the Land of the Two Rivers wants power as well, in the form of an Islamic Emirate of Iraq, Taliban-style (which they virtually have, in Iraq's al-Anbar province).

There was a time, up to the autumn of 2005, that neo-cons were dreaming of a Washington–Najaf axis. It would fit in a pattern of divide and rule, splitting the Arab world between Sunnis and Shiites, who would be perpetually at each other's throats. This would include, of course, Shiites fighting Sunnis in Hasa, in Saudi Arabia. That's a graphic case of neo-con thinking encouraging the rise of a Shiite crescent as a means to weaken the Arab world. But it didn't work. The Americans had to leave holy Najaf and security went to the Badr Organization, the paramilitary wing of the Supreme Council for the Islamic Revolution in Iraq (SCIRI), which rules the whole Najaf province. The neo-cons wanted exactly what Al Qaeda wanted: civil war in Iraq leading to mini-civil wars in Saudi Arabia and in Syria, and ultimately regime change, but to the benefit, from Al Qaeda's point of view, of Salafi-jihadist regimes.

No Shiite crescent – and no Shiite International – to speak of may exist because the Shiite galaxy, with the exception of Iran, remains fragmented, polymorphous, an archipelago. Even duodecimal Shiism itself can be fragmented in many factions – Iranian or Arab, with or without a powerful clergy. The only thing that unifies Shiite communities everywhere – and this had been the case for almost 1400 years – is opposition to 'illegitimate' Sunni Islam, and rejection of other religions.

Of course there is the Iranian Shiite 'sanctuary', sophisticated Iranian diplomacy and still a pan-Shiite Iranian dream. But national and theological antagonisms prevail. The best example is the renewed rivalry between Qom and Najaf. Iranian ayatollahs are extremely concerned by Shiite ramifications opposed to the concept of *velayat-e-faqih*, the Khomeini-concocted base of the Islamic Republic's political system.

This is why the renaissance of Najaf – the site of Imam Ali's tomb, the holiest city of Shiite Islam – can be so problematic. Grand Ayatollah Sistani, arguably the most important religious authority in Shiism today, although an Iranian, sits in Najaf. If the centre of gravity of Shiism goes back to where it was before – in Iraq – Iran's influence will be tremendously reduced. And Shiism – traditionally apolitical – will be back to where it was before the Islamic Revolution.

Rumours about an imminent Iranian bomb have been circulating since at least 1995. What would be the meaning of a hypothetical Shiite bomb? Shiism in this case will have not only a political sanctuary but a nuclear sanctuary. With Iran practically invulnerable to an outside attack, would the religious leadership be tempted to again start exporting its vision of pan-Shiism?

Meanwhile the Shiite dream embodied by Iran, or at least the ayatollahs in Qom, keeps burning – the revolutionary power, the aspiration to be the flag-bearers of the misery of the world, a kind of beggars' banquet, or the ticket for the beggars to finally accede to a banquet, the last hope for the damned of the earth. No wonder Sunnis fear the power of an incandescent idea that for Shiites rises straight from the bottom of their hearts.

Pepe Escobar is the roving correspondent for Hong Kong-based Asia Times online. This is a modified version of the 'Shiiteistan' chapter included in his book Globalistan: How the Globalized World is Dissolving into Liquid War, published in January 2007 in the US by Nimble Books. The Amazon.com link for the book is <http://www.amazon.com/Globalistan-Globalized-World-Dissolving-Liquid/dp/0978813820>.

In the name of God

To the editor of 'Geopolitical Affairs'

Dear Sir,

Thank you for your e-mail of 27.08.1385. We are happy
to inform you that you may publish speeches by the
President of the Republic, providing that you specify the
exact date and the source.

It would be judicious to use the content of the letter
from the President of the Islamic Republic to the
American President, as well as his recent speech to the
United Nations.

Cordially,

Office of the President of the Islamic Republic of Iran.

In accordance with the suggestion from the President's office, Geopolitical Affairs *is
happy to reproduce below extracts from the two documents mentioned.*

**Address by His Excellency Dr. Mahmoud Ahmadi-Nejad, President of
the Islamic Republic of Iran, Before the 61st Session of the General
Assembly, New York, 19 September 2006**

Madam President,

Distinguished Heads of State and Government,

Distinguished Heads of Delegation,

Excellencies, Ladies and Gentlemen

I praise the Merciful, All-Knowing and Almighty God for blessing me with
another opportunity to address this Assembly on behalf of the great nation of

Iran and to bring a number of issues to the attention of the international community.

I also praise the Almighty for the increasing vigilance of peoples across the globe, their courageous presence in different international settings, and the brave expression of their views and aspirations regarding global issues.

Today, humanity passionately craves commitment to the Truth, devotion to God, quest for Justice and respect for the dignity of human beings. Rejection of domination and aggression, defense of the oppressed. And longing for peace constitute the legitimate demand of the peoples of the world, particularly the new generations and the spirited youth, who aspire a world free from decadence, aggression and injustice, and replete with love and compassion. The youth have a right to seek justice and the Truth; and they have a right to build their own future on the foundations of love, compassion and tranquility. And, I praise the Almighty for this immense blessing.

Madame President, Excellencies,

What afflicts humanity today is certainly not compatible with human dignity; the Almighty has not created human beings so that they could transgress against others and oppress them.

By causing war and conflict, some are fast expanding their domination, accumulating greater wealth and usurping all the resources, while others endure the resulting poverty, suffering and misery.

Some seek to rule the world relying on weapons and threats, while others live in perpetual insecurity and danger.

Some occupy the homeland of others, thousands of kilometres away from their borders, interfere in their affairs and control their oil and other resources and strategic routes, while others are bombarded daily in their own homes; their children murdered in the streets and alleys of their own country and their homes reduced to rubble.

Such behaviour is not worthy of human beings and runs counter to the Truth, to justice and to human dignity. The fundamental question is that under such conditions, where should the oppressed seek justice? Who or what organization defends the rights of the oppressed, and suppresses acts of aggression and oppression? Where is the seat of global justice?

A brief glance at a few examples of the most pressing global issues can further illustrate the problem.

A. The unbridled expansion of nuclear, chemical and biological weapons

Some powers proudly announce their production of second and third generations of nuclear weapons. What do they need these weapons for? Is the development and stockpiling of these deadly weapons designed to promote peace and democracy? Or, are these weapons, in fact, instruments of coercion and threat against other peoples and governments? How long should the people of the world live with the nightmare of nuclear, biological and chemical weapons? What bounds the powers producing and possessing these weapons? How can they be held accountable before the international community? And, are the inhabitants of these countries content with the waste of their wealth and resources for the production of such destructive arsenals? Is it not possible to rely on justice, ethics and wisdom instead of these instruments of death? Aren't wisdom and justice more compatible with peace and tranquillity than nuclear, chemical and biological weapons? If wisdom, ethics and justice prevail, then oppression and aggression will be uprooted, threats will wither away and no reason will remain for conflict. This is a solid proposition because most global conflicts emanate from injustice, and from the powerful, not being contented with their own rights, striving to devour the rights of others. People across the globe embrace justice and are willing to sacrifice for its sake.

Would it not be easier for global powers to ensure their longevity and win hearts and minds through the championing of real promotion of justice, compassion and peace, than through continuing the proliferation of nuclear and chemical weapons and the threat of their use?

The experience of the threat and the use of nuclear weapons is before us. Has it achieved anything for the perpetrators other than exacerbation of tension, hatred and animosity among nations?

B. Occupation of countries and exacerbation of hostilities

Occupation of countries, including Iraq, has continued for the last three years. Not a day goes by without hundreds of people getting killed in cold blood. The occupiers are incapable of establishing security in Iraq. Despite the establishment of the lawful Government and National Assembly of Iraq, there are covert and overt efforts to heighten insecurity, magnify and aggravate differences within Iraqi society, and instigate civil strife.

There is no indication that the occupiers have the necessary political will to eliminate the sources of instability. Numerous terrorists were apprehended by the Government of Iraq, only to be let loose under various pretexts by the occupiers.

It seems that intensification of hostilities and terrorism serves as a pretext for the continued presence of foreign forces in Iraq.

Where can the people of Iraq seek refuge, and from whom should the Government of Iraq seek justice?

Who can ensure Iraq's security? Insecurity in Iraq affects the entire region. Can the Security Council play a role in restoring peace and security in Iraq, while the occupiers are themselves permanent members of the Council? Can the Security Council adopt a fair decision in this regard?

Consider the situation in Palestine:

The roots of the Palestinian problem go back to the Second World War. Under the pretext of protecting some of the survivors of that War, the land of Palestine was occupied through war, aggression and the displacement of millions of its inhabitants; it was placed under the control of some of the War survivors, bringing even larger population groups from elsewhere in the world, who had not been even affected by the Second World War; and a government was established in the territory of others with a population collected from across the world at the expense of driving millions of the rightful inhabitants of the land into a Diaspora and homelessness. This is a great tragedy with hardly a precedent in history. Refugees continue to live in temporary refugee camps, and many have died still hoping to one day return to their land. Can any logic, law or legal reasoning justify this tragedy? Can any member of the United Nations accept such a tragedy occurring in their own homeland?

The pretexts for the creation of the regime occupying Al-Qods Al-Sharif are so weak that its proponents want to silence any voice trying to merely speak about them, as they are concerned that shedding light on the facts would undermine the *raison d'être* of this regime, as it has. The tragedy does not end with the establishment of a regime in the territory of others. Regrettably, from its inception, that regime has been a constant source of threat and insecurity in the Middle East region, waging war and spilling blood and impeding the progress of regional countries, and has also been used by some powers as an instrument of division, coercion, and pressure on the people of the region. Reference to these historical realities may cause some disquiet among supporters of this regime. But these are sheer facts and not myth. History has unfolded before our eyes.

Worst yet, is the blanket and unwarranted support provided to this regime.

Just watch what is happening in the Palestinian land. People are being bombarded in their own homes and their children murdered in their own streets and alleys. But no authority, not even the Security Council, can afford them any support or protection. Why?

At the same time, a Government is formed democratically and through the free choice of the electorate in a part of the Palestinian territory. But instead of receiving the support of the so-called champions of democracy, its Ministers and Members of Parliament are illegally abducted and incarcerated in full view of the international community.

Which council or international organization stands up to protect this brutally besieged Government? And why can't the Security Council take any steps?

Let me here address Lebanon:

For thirty-three long days, the Lebanese lived under the barrage of fire and bombs and close to 1.5 million of them were displaced; meanwhile some members of the Security Council practically chose a path that provided ample opportunity for the aggressor to achieve its objectives militarily. We witnessed that the Security Council of the United Nations was practically incapacitated by certain powers to even call for a ceasefire. The Security Council sat idly by for so many days, witnessing the cruel scenes of atrocities against the Lebanese while tragedies such as Qana were persistently repeated. Why?

In all these cases, the answer is self-evident. When the power behind the hostilities is itself a permanent member of the Security Council, how then can this Council fulfil its responsibilities?

C. Lack of respect for the rights of members of the international community

Excellencies,

I now wish to refer to some of the grievances of the Iranian people and speak to the injustices against them.

The Islamic Republic of Iran is a member of the IAEA and is committed to the NPT. All our nuclear activities are transparent, peaceful and under the watchful eyes of IAEA inspectors. Why then are there objections to our legally recognized rights? Which governments object to these rights? Governments that themselves benefit from nuclear energy and the fuel cycle. Some of them have abused nuclear technology for non-peaceful ends including the production of nuclear bombs, and some even have a bleak record of using them against humanity.

Which organization or Council should address these injustices? Is the Security Council in a position to address them? Can it stop violations of the inalienable rights of countries? Can it prevent certain powers from impeding scientific progress of other countries?

The abuse of the Security Council, as an instrument of threat and coercion, is indeed a source of grave concern.

Some permanent members of the Security Council, even when they are themselves parties to international disputes, conveniently threaten others with the Security Council and declare, even before any decision by the Council, the condemnation of their opponents by the Council. The question is: what can justify such exploitation of the Security Council, and doesn't it erode the credibility and effectiveness of the Council? Can such behaviour contribute to the ability of the Council to maintain security?

Excellencies,

A review of the preceding historical realities would lead to the conclusion that regrettably, justice has become a victim of force and aggression.

Many global arrangements have become unjust, discriminatory and irresponsible as a result of undue pressure from some of the powerful;

Threats with nuclear weapons and other instruments of war by some powers have taken the place of respect for the rights of nations and the maintenance and promotion of peace and tranquillity;

For some powers, claims of promotion of human rights and democracy can only last as long as they can be used as instruments of pressure and intimidation against other nations. But when it comes to the interests of the claimants, concepts such as democracy, the right of self-determination of nations, respect for the rights and intelligence of peoples, international law and justice have no place or value. This is blatantly manifested in the way the elected Government of the Palestinian people is treated as well as in the support extended to the Zionist regime. It does not matter if people are murdered in Palestine, turned into refugees, captured, imprisoned or besieged; that must not violate human rights.

Nations are not equal in exercising their rights recognized by international law. Enjoying these rights is dependent on the whim of certain major powers.

Apparently the Security Council can only be used to ensure the security and the rights of some big powers. But when the oppressed are decimated under bombardment, the Security Council must remain aloof and not even call for a ceasefire. Is this not a tragedy of historic proportions for the Security Council, which is charged with maintaining the security of countries?

The prevailing order of contemporary global interactions is such that certain powers equate themselves with the international community, and consider their decisions superseding that of over 180 countries. They consider themselves the masters and rulers of the entire world and other nations as only second class in the world order.

Excellencies,

The question needs to be asked: if the Governments of the United States or the United Kingdom, who are permanent members of the Security Council, commit aggression, occupation and violation of international law, which of the organs of the UN can take them to account? Can a Council in which they are privileged members address their violations? Has this ever happened? In fact, we have repeatedly seen the reverse. If they have differences with a nation or state, they drag it to the Security Council and as claimants, arrogate to themselves simultaneously the roles of prosecutor, judge and executioner. Is this a just order? Can there be a more vivid case of discrimination and more clear evidence of injustice?

Regrettably, the persistence of some hegemonic powers in imposing their exclusionist policies on international decision making mechanisms, including the Security Council, has resulted in a growing mistrust in global public opinion, undermining the credibility and effectiveness of this most universal system of collective security.

Excellencies,

How long can such a situation last in the world? It is evident that the behaviour of some powers constitutes the greatest challenge before the Security Council, the entire organization and its affiliated agencies.

The present structure and working methods of the Security Council, which are legacies of the Second World War, are not responsive to the expectations of the current generation and the contemporary needs of humanity.

Today, it is undeniable that the Security Council, most critically and urgently, needs legitimacy and effectiveness. It must be acknowledged that as long as the Council is unable to act on behalf of the entire international community in a transparent, just and democratic manner, it will neither be legitimate nor effective. Furthermore, the direct relation between the abuse of veto and the erosion of the legitimacy and effectiveness of the Council has now been clearly and undeniably established. We cannot, and should not, expect the eradication, or even containment, of injustice, imposition and oppression without reforming the structure and working methods of the Council.

Is it appropriate to expect this generation to submit to the decisions and arrangements established over half a century ago? Doesn't this generation or future generations have the right to decide themselves about the world in which they want to live?

Today, serious reform in the structure and working methods of the Security Council is, more than ever before, necessary. Justice and democracy dictate that the role of the General Assembly, as the highest organ of the United Nations, must be respected. The General Assembly can then, through appropriate mechanisms, take on the task of reforming the Organization and particularly rescue the Security Council from its current state. In the interim, the Non-Aligned Movement, the Organization of the Islamic Conference and the African continent should each have a representative as a permanent member of the Security Council, with veto privilege. The resulting balance would hopefully prevent further trampling of the rights of nations.

Madame President, Excellencies,

It is essential that spirituality and ethics find their rightful place in international relations. Without ethics and spirituality, attained in light of the teachings of Divine prophets, justice, freedom and human rights cannot be guaranteed.

Resolution of contemporary human crises lies in observing ethics and spirituality and the governance of righteous people of high competence and piety.

Should respect for the rights of human beings become the predominant objective, then injustice, ill-temperament, aggression and war will fade away.

Human beings are all God's creatures and are all endowed with dignity and respect.

No one has superiority over others. No individual or states can arrogate to themselves special privileges, nor can they disregard the rights of others and, through influence and pressure, position themselves as the "international community".

Citizens of Asia, Africa, Europe and America are all equal. Over six billion inhabitants of the earth are all equal and worthy of respect.

Justice and protection of human dignity are the two pillars in maintaining sustainable peace, security and tranquillity in the world.

It is for this reason that we state:

Sustainable peace and tranquillity in the world can only be attained through justice, spirituality, ethics, compassion and respect for human dignity.

All nations and states are entitled to peace, progress and security.

We are all members of the international community and we are all entitled to insist on the creation of a climate of compassion, love and justice.

All members of the United Nations are affected by both the bitter and the sweet events and developments in today's world.

We can adopt firm and logical decisions, thereby improving the prospects of a better life for current and future generations.

Together, we can eradicate the roots of bitter maladies and afflictions, and instead, through the promotion of universal and lasting values such as ethics, spirituality and justice, allow our nations to taste the sweetness of a better future.

Peoples, driven by their divine nature, intrinsically seek Good, Virtue, Perfection and Beauty. Relying on our peoples, we can take giant steps towards reform and pave the road for human perfection. Whether we like it or not, justice, peace and virtue will sooner or later prevail in the world with the will of Almighty God. It is imperative, and also desirable, that we too contribute to the promotion of justice and virtue.

The Almighty and Merciful God, who is the Creator of the Universe, is also its Lord and Ruler. Justice is His command. He commands His creatures to support one another in Good, virtue and piety, and not in decadence and corruption.

He commands His creatures to enjoin one another to righteousness and virtue and not to sin and transgression. All Divine prophets from the Prophet Adam (peace be upon him) to the Prophet Moses (peace be upon him), to the Prophet Jesus Christ (peace be upon him), to the Prophet Mohammad (peace be upon him), have all called humanity to monotheism, justice, brotherhood, love and compassion. Is it not possible to build a better world based on monotheism, justice, love and respect for the rights of human beings, and thereby transform animosities into friendship?

I emphatically declare that today's world, more than ever before, longs for just and righteous people with love for all humanity; and above all longs for the perfect righteous human being and the real saviour who has been promised to all peoples and who will establish justice, peace and brotherhood on the planet.

O, Almighty God, all men and women are your creatures and you have ordained their guidance and salvation. Bestow upon humanity that thirsts for justice, the perfect human being promised to all by you, and make us among his followers and among those who strive for his return and his cause.

An open letter to Mr George Bush, President of the United States of America, 5th August 2006.

For sometime now I have been thinking, how one can justify the undeniable contradictions that exist in the international arena – which are being constantly debated, especially in political forums and amongst university students. Many questions remain unanswered. These have prompted me to discuss some of the contradictions and questions, in the hopes that it might bring about an opportunity to redress them.

Can one be a follower of Jesus Christ (PBUH), the great Messenger of God, Feel obliged to respect human rights, present liberalism as a civilization model, announce one's opposition to the proliferation of nuclear weapons and WMDs, make "War on Terror" his slogan, and finally, work towards the establishment of a unified international community – a community which Christ and the virtuous of the Earth will one day govern, but at the same time, have countries attacked. The lives, reputations and possessions of people destroyed and on the slight chance of the presence of a few criminals in a village, city, or convoy for example, the entire village, city or convoy set ablaze. Or because of the possibility of the existence of WMDs in one country, it is occupied, around one hundred thousand people killed, its water sources, agriculture and industry destroyed, close to 180,000 foreign troops put on the ground, sanctity of private homes of citizens broken, and the country pushed back perhaps fifty years. At what price? Hundreds of billions of dollars spent from the treasury of one country and certain other countries and tens of thousands of young men and women – as occupation troops – put in harms way, taken away from family and loved ones, their hands stained with the blood of others, subjected to so much psychological pressure that everyday some commit suicide and those returning home suffer depression, become sickly and grapple with all sorts of ailments; while some are killed and their bodies handed to their families.

On the pretext of the existence of WMDs, this great tragedy came to engulf both the peoples of the occupied and the occupying country. Later it was revealed that no WMDs existed to begin with. Of course Saddam was a murderous dictator. But the war was not waged to topple him, the announced goal of the war was to find and destroy weapons of mass destruction. He was toppled along the way towards another goal; nevertheless the people of the region are happy about it. I point out that throughout the many years of the imposed war on Iran Saddam was supported by the West.

Mr. President,

You might know that I am a teacher. My students ask me how can these actions be reconciled with the values outlined at the beginning of this letter and duty to the tradition of Jesus Christ (PBUH), the Messenger of peace and forgiveness?

There are prisoners in Guantanamo Bay that have not been tried, have no legal representation, their families cannot see them and are obviously kept in a strange land outside their own country. There is no international monitoring of their conditions and fate. No one knows whether they are prisoners, POWs, accused or criminals.

European investigators have confirmed the existence of secret prisons in Europe too. I could not correlate the abduction of a person, and him or her being kept in secret prisons, with the provisions of any judicial system. For that matter, I fail to understand how such actions correspond to the values outlined in the beginning of this letter, i.e. the teachings of Jesus Christ (PBUH), human rights and liberal values.

Young people, university students, and ordinary people have many questions about the phenomenon of Israel. I am sure you are familiar with some of them.

Throughout history many countries have been occupied, but I think the establishment of a new country with a new people, is a new phenomenon that is exclusive to our times. Students are saying that sixty years ago such a country did not exist. They show old documents and globes and say try as we have, we have not been able to find a country named Israel. I tell them to study the history of WWI and II. One of my students told me that during WWII, which more than tens of millions of people perished in, news about the war, was quickly disseminated by the warring parties. Each touted their victories and the most recent battlefront defeat of the other party. After the war they claimed that six million Jews had been killed. Six million people that were surely related to at least two million families. Again let us assume that these events are true. Does that logically translate into the establishment of the state of Israel in the Middle East or support for such a state? How can this phenomenon be rationalized or explained?

Mr. President,

I am sure you know how – and at what cost – Israel was established:
   Many thousands were killed in the process.
   Millions of indigenous people were made refugees.
   Hundreds of thousands of hectares of farmland, olive plantations, towns and villages were destroyed.
   This tragedy is not exclusive to the time of establishment; unfortunately it has been ongoing for sixty years now.
   A regime has been established which does not show mercy even to kids, destroys houses while the occupants are still in them, announces beforehand its list and plans to assassinate Palestinian figures, and keeps thousands of Palestinians in prison. Such a phenomenon is unique – or at the very least extremely rare – in recent memory.
   Another big question asked by the people is "why is this regime being supported?"
   Is support for this regime in line with the teachings of Jesus Christ (PBUH) or Moses (PBUH) or liberal values? Or are we to understand that allowing the original inhabitants of these lands – inside and outside Palestine – whether they are Christian, Moslem or Jew, to determine their fate, runs contrary to principles of democracy, human rights and the teachings of prophets? If not, why is there so much opposition to a referendum? The newly elected Palestinian administration recently took office. All independent observes have confirmed that this government represents the electorate. Unbelievingly, they have put the elected government under pressure and have advised it to recognize the Israeli regime, abandon the struggle and follow the programs of the previous government. If the current Palestinian government had run on the above platform, would the Palestinian people have voted for it? Again, can such position taken in opposition to the Palestinian government be reconciled with the values outlined earlier? The people are also asking "why are all UNSC resolutions in condemnation of Israel vetoed?"

Mr. President,

As you are well aware, I live amongst the people and am in constant contact with them – many people from around the Middle East manage to contact me as well. They do not have faith in these dubious policies either. There is evidence that the people of the region are becoming increasingly angry with such policies.
   It is not my intention to pose too many questions, but I need to refer to other points as well.

Why is it that any technological and scientific achievement reached in the Middle East region is translated into and portrayed as a threat to the Zionist regime? Is not scientific R&D one of the basic rights of nations? You are familiar with history. Aside from the Middle Ages, in what other point in history has scientific and technical progress been a crime? Can the possibility of scientific achievements being utilized for military purposes be reason enough to oppose science and technology altogether? If such a supposition is true, then all scientific disciplines, including physics, chemistry, mathematics, medicine, engineering, etc. must be opposed.

Lies were told in the Iraqi matter. What was the result? I have no doubt that telling lies is reprehensible in any culture, and you do not like to be lied to.

Mr. President,

Don't Latin Americans have the right to ask why their elected governments are being opposed and coup leaders supported? Or, Why must they constantly be threatened and live in fear? The people of Africa are hardworking, creative and talented. They can play an important and valuable role in providing for the needs of humanity and contribute to its material and spiritual progress. Poverty and hardship in large parts of Africa are preventing this from happening. Don't they have the right to ask why their enormous wealth – including minerals – is being looted, despite the fact that they need it more than others?

Again, do such actions correspond to the teachings Of Christ and the tenets of human rights?

The brave and faithful people of Iran too have many questions and grievances, including: the coup d'état of 1953 and the subsequent toppling of the legal government of the day, opposition to the Islamic revolution, transformation of an Embassy into a headquarters supporting the activities of those opposing the Islamic Republic (many thousands of pages of documents corroborate this claim), support for Saddam in the war waged against Iran, the shooting down of the Iranian passenger plane, freezing the assets of the Iranian nation, increasing threats, anger and displeasure vis-à-vis the scientific and nuclear progress of the Iranian nation (just when all Iranians are jubilant and celebrating their country's progress), and many other grievances that I will not refer to in this letter.

Mr. President,

September Eleven was a horrendous incident. The killing of innocents is deplorable and appalling in any part of the world. Our government immediately declared its disgust with the perpetrators and offered its condolences to the bereaved and expressed its sympathies.

All governments have a duty to protect the lives, property and good standing of their citizens. Reportedly your government employs extensive security, protection and intelligence systems – and even hunts its opponents abroad. September eleven was not a simple operation. Could it be planned and executed without coordination with intelligence and security services – or their extensive infiltration? Of course this is just an educated guess. Why have the various aspects of the attacks been kept secret? Why are we not told who botched their responsibilities? And, why aren't those responsible and the guilty parties identified and put on trial? All governments have a duty to provide security and peace of mind for their citizens. For some years now, the people of your country and neighbours of world trouble spots do not have peace of mind. After 9.11, instead of healing and tending to the emotional wounds of the survivors and the American people – who had been immensely traumatized by the attacks – some Western media only intensified the climate of fear and insecurity – some constantly talked about the possibility of new terror attacks and kept the people in fear. Is that service to the American people? Is it possible to calculate the damages incurred from fear and panic? American citizens lived in constant fear of fresh attacks that could come at any moment and in any place. They felt insecure in the streets, in their place of work and at home. Who would be happy with this situation? Why was the media, instead of conveying a feeling of security and providing peace of mind, giving rise to a feeling of insecurity? Some believe that the hype paved the way – and was the justification – for an attack on Afghanistan. Again I need to refer to the role of media. In media charters, correct dissemination of information and honest reporting of a story are established tenets. I express my deep regret about the disregard shown by certain Western media for these principles. The main pretext for an attack on Iraq was the existence of WMDs. This was repeated incessantly – for the public to finally believe – and the ground set for an attack on Iraq.

Will the truth not be lost in a contrived and deceptive climate? Again, if the truth is allowed to be lost, how can that be reconciled with the earlier mentioned values?

Is the truth known to the Almighty lost as well?

Mr. President,

In countries around the world, citizens provide for the expenses of governments so that their governments in turn are able to serve them. The question here is "what has the hundreds of billions of dollars, spent every year to pay for the Iraqi campaign, produced for the citizens?" As Your Excellency is aware, in some states of your country, people are living in poverty. Many thousands are homeless and unemployment is a huge problem. Of course these problems exist – to a larger or lesser extent – in other countries as well. With these conditions in mind, can the gargantuan expenses of the campaign – paid from the public treasury – be explained and be consistent with the aforementioned principles? What has been said, are some of the grievances of the people around the world, in our region and in your country. But my main contention – which I am hoping you will agree to some of it – is:

Those in power have a specific time in office and do not rule indefinitely, but their names will be recorded in history and will be constantly judged in the immediate and distant futures. The people will scrutinize our presidencies.

Did we mange to bring peace, security and prosperity for the people or insecurity and unemployment? Did we intend to establish justice or just supported especial interest groups, and by forcing many people to live in poverty and hardship, made a few people rich and powerful – thus trading the approval of the people and the Almighty with theirs'? Did we defend the rights of the underprivileged or ignore them? Did we defend the rights of all people around the world or imposed wars on them, interfered illegally in their affairs, established hellish prisons and incarcerated some of them? Did we bring the world peace and security or raised the specter of intimidation and threats? Did we tell the truth to our nation and others around the world or presented an inverted version of it? Were we on the side of people or the occupiers and oppressors? Did our administrations set out to promote rational behaviour, logic, ethics, peace, fulfilling obligations, justice, service to the people, prosperity, progress and respect for human dignity or the force of guns,

Intimidation, insecurity, disregard for the people, delaying the progress and excellence of other nations, and trample on people's rights?

And finally, they will judge us on whether we remained true to our oath of office – to serve the people, which is our main task, and the traditions of the prophets – or not?

Mr. President,

How much longer can the world tolerate this situation? Where will this trend lead the world to? How long must the people of the world pay for the incorrect decisions of some rulers? How much longer will the spectre of insecurity – raised from the stockpiles of weapons of mass destruction – hunt the people of the world?

How much longer will the blood of the innocent men, women and children be spilled on the streets, and people's houses destroyed over their heads? Are you pleased with the current condition of the world? Do you think present policies can continue?

If billions of dollars spent on security, military campaigns and troop movement were instead spent on investment and assistance for poor countries, promotion of health, combating different diseases, education and improvement of mental and physical fitness, assistance to the victims of natural disasters, creation of employment opportunities and production, development projects and poverty alleviation, establishment of peace, mediation between disputing states, and extinguishing the flames of racial, ethnic and other conflicts, were would the world be today? Would not your government and people be justifiably proud? Would not your administration's political and economic standing have been stronger? And I am most sorry to say, would there have been an ever increasing global hatred of the American government?

Mr. President, it is not my intention to distress anyone. If Prophet Abraham, Isaac, Jacob, Ishmael, Joseph, or Jesus Christ (PBUH) were with us today, how would they have judged such behaviour? Will we be given a role to play in the promised world, where justice will become universal and Jesus Christ (PBUH) will be present? Will they even accept us?

My basic question is this: Is there no better way to interact with the rest of the world? Today there are hundreds of millions of Christians, hundreds of millions of Moslems and millions of people who follow the teachings of Moses (PBUH). All divine religions share and respect one word and that is "monotheism" or belief in a single God and no other in the world. The Holy Koran stresses this common word and calls on all followers of divine religions and says: [3.64] Say: O followers of the Book! come to an equitable proposition between us and you that we shall not serve any but Allah and (that) we shall not associate aught with Him, and (that) some of us shall not take others for lords besides Allah; but if they turn back, then say: Bear witness that we are Muslims. (The Family of Imran)

Mr. President,

According to divine verses, we have all been called upon to worship one God and follow the teachings of divine Prophets.

> **"To worship a God which is above all powers in the world and can do all He pleases ... the Lord which knows that which is hidden and visible, the past and the future, knows what goes on in the Hearts of His servants and records their deeds."**

"The Lord who is the possessor of the heavens and the earth and all universe is His court" "planning for the universe is done by His hands, and gives His servants the glad tidings of mercy and forgiveness of sins" "He is the companion of the oppressed and the enemy of oppressors" "He is the Compassionate, the Merciful" "He is the recourse of the faithful and guides them towards the light from darkness" "He is witness to the actions of His servants" "He calls on servants to be faithful and do good deeds, and asks them to stay on the path of righteousness and remain steadfast" "Calls on servants to heed His prophets and He is a witness to their deeds" "A bad ending belongs only to those who have chosen the life of this world and disobey Him and oppress His servants" and "A good end and eternal paradise belong to those servants who fear His majesty and do not follow their lascivious selves."

We believe a return to the teachings of the divine prophets is the only road leading to salvation. I have been told that Your Excellency follows the teachings of Jesus (PBUH) and believes in the divine promise of the rule of the righteous on Earth.

We also believe that Jesus Christ (PBUH) was one of the great prophets of the Almighty. He has been repeatedly praised in the Koran. Jesus (PBUH) has been quoted in Koran as well: [19.36] And surely Allah is my Lord and your Lord, therefore serve Him; this is the right path. Marium Service to and obedience of the Almighty is the credo of all divine messengers. The God of all people in Europe, Asia, Africa, America, the Pacific and the rest of the world is one. He is the Almighty who wants to guide and give dignity to all His servants. He has given greatness to Humans.

We again read in the Holy Book: "The Almighty God sent His prophets with miracles and clear signs to guide the people and show them divine signs and purify them from sins and pollutions. And He sent the Book and the balance so that the people display justice and avoid the rebellious".

All of the above verses can be seen, one way or the other, in the Good Book as well.

Divine prophets have promised:

The day will come when all humans will congregate before the court of the Almighty, so that their deeds are examined. The good will be directed towards Haven and evildoers will meet divine retribution. I trust both of us believe in such a day, but it will not be easy to calculate the actions of rulers, because we must be answerable to our nations and all others whose lives have been directly or indirectly affected by our actions.

All prophets, speak of peace and tranquillity for man – based on monotheism, justice and respect for human dignity.

Do you not think that if all of us come to believe in and abide by these principles, that is, monotheism, worship of God, justice, respect for the dignity of man, belief in the Last Day, we can overcome the present problems of the world – that are the result of disobedience to the Almighty and the teachings of prophets – and improve our performance? Do you not think that belief in these principles promotes and guarantees peace, friendship and justice? Do you not think that the aforementioned written or unwritten principles are universally respected? Will you not accept this invitation? That is, a genuine return to the teachings of prophets, to monotheism and justice, to preserve human dignity and obedience to the Almighty and His prophets?

Mr. President,

History tells us that repressive and cruel governments do not survive. God has entrusted the fate of men to them. The Almighty has not left the universe and humanity to their own devices. Many things have happened contrary to the wishes and plans of governments. These tell us that there is a higher power at work and all events are determined by Him. Can one deny the signs of change in the world today?

Is the situation of the world today comparable to that of ten years ago? Changes happen fast and come at a furious pace. The people of the world are not happy with the status quo and pay little heed to the promises and comments made by a number of influential world leaders. Many people around the world feel insecure and oppose the spreading of insecurity and war and do not approve of and accept dubious policies.

The people are protesting the increasing gap between the haves and the have-nots and the rich and poor countries. The people are disgusted with increasing corruption.

The people of many countries are angry about the attacks on their cultural foundations and the disintegration of families. They are equally dismayed with the fading of care and compassion. The people of the world have no faith in international organizations, because their rights are not advocated by these organizations.

Liberalism and Western style democracy have not been able to help realize the ideals of humanity. Today these two concepts have failed. Those with insight can already hear the sounds of the shattering and fall of the ideology and thoughts of the Liberal democratic systems. We increasingly see that people around the world are flocking towards a main focal point – that is the Almighty God. Undoubtedly through faith in God and the teachings of the prophets, the people will conquer their problems. My question for you is: "Do you not want to join them?"

Mr. President,

Whether we like it or not, the world is gravitating towards faith in the Almighty and justice and the will of God will prevail over all things.

Vasalam Ala Man Ataba'al hoda
Mahmood Ahmadi-Nejad
President of the Islamic Republic of Iran

The Politics of Iranian Oil:
Posing a Challenge to America

ROGER HOWARD

Whenever fears of a global energy crisis grow, the balance of political power inevitably tilts in favour of oil and natural gas producers at the expense of energy importers. In the course of the past two years, politicians in Washington have accused the Kremlin of using their vast energy reserves as 'tools of intimidation and blackmail' against some of their markets, notably the Ukraine and Western Europe, while Venezuelan president Hugo Chavez has been confidently voicing a stridently anti-American rhetoric with a vehemence that has been fuelled by the sharp rise in the price of his key export, oil.

Since 2003, dramatic increases in energy costs and growing insecurity about future sources of supply have inevitably had powerful political repercussions on the second largest producer of oil within OPEC, Iran. Pumping out around 4 million barrels of crude every day, and exporting about 2.6 million, Tehran has found itself holding a weapon of highly destructive diplomatic power, one that it has already used to undermine the political influence of its chief antagonist, the United States.

In an age of tight oil supply, Iran's output of both oil and natural gas buttress its political power in a number of different ways. At one level, the mullahs have reaped huge financial rewards from the recent increases in the price of energy, and in the first half of the financial year that began on 21 March 2006 the export of oil earned them a staggering $29 billion.[1] Of course such vast sums could eventually destroy an overspending government that creates unsustainably high inflation, but in the short term they have allowed the Tehran regime to stave off economic crisis, buy large quantities of military equipment and pursue a vastly expensive nuclear programme of uranium enrichment that could be used to create not just civilian energy, as the Iranians claim, but a nuclear warhead, which the United States and other countries particularly fear.

The mullahs have also been able to use Iran's petroleum reserves to strike up close relations with other energy-hungry countries that are inimical towards, or rivals of, the United States. The new and rapidly growing political alliance between Tehran and Beijing that has been forged only in the course of the present decade is based on several different considerations – such as a common suspicion of American foreign policy and its motives[2] – but there can be no doubt that at its heart lies China's desperate need for new sources of oil and natural gas supply: if these reserves did not exist, then it is highly unlikely that any such relationship would have come about. Such a relationship has considerably shored up Iran's political power, not least because it has given the mullahs a very powerful ally in the UN Security Council.

With so much cash in hand, and with new friends standing at its side, an emboldened Iranian regime has been increasingly defiant of an outside world over the single issue that, more than any other, divides Tehran from its critics: the nuclear dispute. In the spring of 2003 Tehran offered to strike up a new dialogue with Washington and make some concessions over its nuclear programme in return for security guarantees and the lifting of sanctions by the United States, but found its overtures rebuffed by the White House. And in October the same year, Iranian negotiators suddenly and unexpectedly caved in to international pressure by granting extra powers to the inspectors of the International Atomic Energy Agency and by immediately halting uranium enrichment. But just two years later the same regime was willing openly to defy the threat of referral to the United Nations, its subsequent deadlines and the passage of condemnatory resolutions. Of course the contrast can partly be explained by the ever-deepening military quagmire into which the US military had stepped in Iraq, but at least as important is the advent of a tight oil market which has brought Tehran the support of their new and very powerful international Chinese ally, one that has hitherto not shied from vetoing, or threatening to veto, UN resolutions that are critical of Tehran.[3]

But oil is not just a driving force behind Iran's new alliances with some of America's global rivals. It also has powerful repercussions upon the political ties that bind Washington and her allies. In the past few years, Washington's attempts to isolate Iran from foreign investors and to build a united front with which to confront its nuclear ambitions have been made considerably more difficult by the lure of these natural resources. Confronted by a growing domestic demand for oil and gas that they cannot readily ignore, numerous countries throughout the world have greater reason than ever to sidestep or even openly defy Washington's wishes and instead prioritize their links with Tehran. The result is a growing tension between the US and its international allies such as the European Union, Japan and Pakistan, a tension that is already posing a clear challenge to American political power and, barring some dramatic and seemingly miraculous change of political course in the near future, is set to continue doing do in the years ahead.

The Challenge to America

There are two distinct ways in which this unbending policy of isolating Tehran is poised to undermine American power. Most obviously, some US allies will be forced to do their own thing and disregard Washington's lead on issues that the White House and Congress regard as vitally important foreign policy issues. American policy towards Iran is, of course, all about nuclear non-proliferation and 'terrorism' throughout the Middle East, as well as the survival of Israel. To disregard US policy on what are considered to be such fundamental issues would mean making a fairly clear transatlantic break and siding with a regime that Washington considers its key Middle Eastern enemy.

Any such breach would be much more pronounced if the Iranians should ever use their oil weapon imaginatively, deliberately trying to engineer political splits between the United Sstates and its allies. Remember the Arabs' tactics back in 1973, when they withheld supplies of oil to countries deemed to be 'unfriendly' to their position on the Israeli–Palestinian dispute. It was not long before cracks started to appear, first as the Japanese and then the French governments publicly disassociated themselves from Washington's Middle East policy. Tehran could in the future conceivably try a similar thing, awarding contracts to develop its oil and gas fields to Western oil companies on the condition that their governments openly and markedly shift their political positions, just enough to create a clear transatlantic gulf, over the same issue.

The likelihood that, in the years ahead, the Iranian government could manipulate its own energy resources in a similar manner, at the expense of the global political power of the United States, reflects the tension that exists between two highly conflicting influences: Washington's policy of isolating Tehran on the one hand, and the increasing global demand for Iranian oil and gas on the other.

The US Policy of Isolating Iran

Since the mid-1990s, the United States has not only stopped its own businesses from trading with Iran but – much more ambitiously – has also tried to dissuade its friends and allies across the world from doing so. Heavy economic investment in the Iranian economy, runs the argument, not only provides the Tehran regime with the spare cash it needs to pursue this dangerous course but also sends out a clear message to other miscreants that such wrongdoings do not go unnoticed and unpunished but always come at a heavy price: 'all trade with Iran must stop so we don't provide terrorists with hard currency', as Senator Alfonse D'Amato put it in 1996, when congressional concern about alleged Iranian links with Palestinian insurgency against Israel was at fever pitch.

Without the support of its allies, the unilateral efforts of the United States are regarded as inadequate.

To deter other countries from trading with Tehran, Washington has a variety of different powers at its disposal. Since the enactment of the Iran-Libya Sanctions Act (ILSA) in 1996, the US president has had legal powers to sanction any foreign entity that invests more than $20 million in Iran's energy sector. Should any do so, then the president can impose up to two of six possible sanctions: a ban on its imports of goods and services into the United States; a federal government ban on the purchase of its goods and services; the imposition of a loan ceiling of $10 million by all US financial institutions; a prohibition on the sanctioned business from acting as a primary dealer of US treasury bonds; a ban on US export-import assistance, and a denial of licences that approve the export of controlled technology to that business.

Neither ILSA nor its legislative successor, the Iran Freedom and Support Act (IFSA), which passed through Congress in the summer of 2006, have as yet been enforced, although on one occasion, in the fall of 1997, it was invoked against the French oil giant Total, which had signed a $2 billion contract with the Tehran authorities to develop part of the massive South Pars natural gas field. But the mere threat of its imposition has had a powerful effect on many international energy companies, including British Petroleum whose chairman, Lord Browne, decreed in January 2005 that 'politically Iran is not a flyer … because 40% of BP is in the US and we are the largest producer of oil and gas in the US.'

Washington has some other legal powers at its disposal to enforce its secondary sanctions. Any foreign-owned company with a presence in the American market can fall foul of domestic legislation that outlaws doing business with individuals, firms or governments that are deemed to have 'links with terrorism'. In the course of 2006, the spectre of such laws has particularly haunted the international banking sector, which falls wholly outside the scope of IFSA. In January, the Dutch banking group ABN Amro, the UBS bank of Switzerland and Credit Suisse announced that they would be curtailing their business operations inside Iran, knowing that they could easily be devastated by US retaliation: nearly one-third of UBS's total invested assets, for example, belong to American clients.

There are several different reasons why US pressure on European firms to sanction Tehran has been increasing of late. Undoubtedly the single most important reason is heightened concern about the sophistication of the Tehran regime's nuclear programme, and its greater willingness to defy foreign pressure over the issue. Although Iran is still reckoned to be some years away from developing a warhead,[4] revelations in August 2002 of its vast enrichment plants at Natanz demonstrated that its nuclear programme was far more developed than almost any foreign observer had previously realized.

The Bush administration's post-9/11 preoccupation with defeating 'terrorism' has played straight into the hands of Iran's enemies on Capitol Hill, who have argued to great effect that it is supremely well qualified to be a 'terrorist state'. In particular, Israel's strongest supporters point to Iran's association with an organization that many influential American politicians have always wanted to be in the firing line of the 'War on Terror' – the Lebanese movement Hezbollah – while since 2003 Tehran has also been widely blamed for sponsoring a good number of the Iraqi insurgents that have spilled so much American blood.

A final reason is the harsh, uncompromising rhetoric of Iran's president, Mahmoud Ahmadinejad, who was elected on 24 June 2005. While Ahmadinejad is not known to exert any influence over Iran's foreign affairs, which are determined by the Supreme Leader and the Supreme National Security Council, his belligerent and inflammatory talk about 'wiping Israel off the map' has caused alarm, outrage and indignation on Capitol Hill.

Yet while the strength of Washington's political and economic power is pulling its allies in one direction, Iran's highly seductive natural resources are pushing them firmly in the other, tempting them to defy the American policy of isolation.

Iranian Temptations

Iran's challenge to American global hegemony stems from its possession of outstanding natural resources. Its proven oil reserves are undoubtedly vast and widely estimated to hold at least 95 billion barrels,[5] meaning that they are outsized only by those of Saudi Arabia, whose deposits are estimated to contain 260 billion barrels, by Canada's 170 billion barrels, and perhaps by Iraq's, which are thought to contain around 115 billion. While its infrastructure remains in dire need of massive investment, Iran's attractiveness to foreign investors also reflects the relative ease with which these supplies of oil can be moved to foreign markets, not just by pipeline but also by tanker from Iranian ports in the Gulf Straits.

Besides oil, Iran also holds vast deposits of another commodity that has immense value to the outside world: natural gas. Because Iranian natural gas reserves are reckoned to total around 940 trillion cubic feet (cf), second in size only to those in Russia, it clearly has huge potential as a key exporter of natural gas. In particular, one of the great jewels in Iran's energy crown is the massive gasfield at South Pars in the Persian Gulf whose reserves, which are really just an extension of Qatar's North Field, amount to somewhere between 280 and 500 trillion cf.

Its current production, only of around 2.7 trillion cf each year, will also be considerably boosted if yet more important reserves are discovered, as most independent experts expect: Tabnak, a supergiant gas field containing 15.7 trillion cf of gas and 240 million barrels of condensate, was found only in April 2000 and, as recently as June 2004, the Iranian news agency announced that two new natural gas fields had been discovered at Balal and Lavan Island in the Persian Gulf.

Developing such vast reserves not only offers energy companies highly lucrative contracts but also benefits their respective national governments. This is because the 'buyback' contracts offered by the Iranians to develop an oil or gas field will allow the contractor to take possession of an agreed quantity of oil or gas that enables them to recoup the expenses incurred on the project. Although the contractors, or their agents, are then free to sell this wherever they like, it is usually the contractor's domestic market that is particularly likely to benefit. The reason for this is simply that the contractor's refineries, and the network that takes the refined oil to the high-street petrol pumps, are likely to be based in its country of origin. This means that even a privately owned oil or gas company can help its respective national government solve any pending or existing energy crisis.

So, when in February 2004 Tehran granted a Japanese consortium the exclusive negotiating rights to develop the massive South Azadegan field, the government in Tokyo was also able to secure much of the oil that the field would eventually produce. Under the terms of the buyback contract, the consortium partners could recoup their expenditure in the course of six years following the completion of the project by taking delivery of the field's output, which the partners were then able to sell straight to the Japanese market. Since Japan is already a big importer of Iranian oil, the Azadegan project was always viewed in Tokyo as a means of securing future supplies.

During the tight oil market of recent years, Iran's petroleum reserves have of course been increasingly tempting to prospective foreign investors. This is because any sharp increase in the price of oil, reflecting an imbalance between supply and demand, typically generates concern about where future supplies are to be found. Such increases are easily viewed as validating the expectations of some organizations and bodies such as the US Department of Energy, which has argued that between 2001 and 2025 major Middle Eastern oil producers will have to double their total daily output to satisfy growing demand.[6] This is partly because there is much greater demand in the developing world, whose populations and economies are rapidly expanding and whose consumers have higher expectations of standards of living than ever before. A classic case in point is India whose annual rate of population growth averages around 3–4 per cent, roughly the same as Pakistan, and whose fast-expanding economy has created a new 'middle class' with a sophisticated Western-style taste for comfort.

Since the beginning of the millennium, such fears have been heightened by the highly predatory tactics of the Chinese government, which has hitherto not hesitated to satisfy its own fast-growing energy needs by striking deals with regimes that Washington shuns or sharply disapproves of. Beijing has struck up such ties with the governments of Sudan, Cuba, Venezuela and Iran, filling every void that the abstinence of the US and its allies creates. This means that many foreign governments and businesses circles, as well as many American companies, can only view the US policy of isolating Iran with trepidation: such a policy is instead merely seen as providing Beijing with a golden opportunity for China to drive a stake into Iran's oil and gas fields, one that may prove extremely difficult, or even impossible, to dislodge.

The Balancing Act

The daunting task of reconciling these two conflicting pressures — Washington's policy of isolating Tehran versus the lure of Iranian natural resources — has hitherto prompted the United States' allies, such as Japan, Pakistan and the member states of the European Union, to perform a very delicate balancing act.

Since first showing an interest in the development of the South Azadegan oil field, Tokyo has striven hard to strike such a reconciliation. When in February 2004 the deal was formally signed in clear defiance of strong American opposition, the US State Department's Richard Boucher declared that because 'our policy has been, with respect to Iran, to oppose petroleum investment there ... we remain deeply concerned about deals such as this and disappointed that these things might go forward.' This prompted a mixed reaction from the Japanese. Some Tokyo officials brushed aside the criticism, claiming caustically that 'of course the US had to say they were "disappointed" with the deal due to their strong attitude against Iran, but we have continually kept them informed and updated on the Azadegan situation.' But at the same time they claimed that the deal was always dependent on Tehran's nuclear cooperation with the IAEA (International Atomic Energy Agency): so when on 17 March 2004 chief Iranian nuclear negotiator Hassan Rowhani gave assurances that Tehran 'will continue cooperating with the IAEA so that the international community will have no concern over Iran's peaceful use of atomic energy', Japanese premier Junichiro Koizumi moved quickly to reassure the watching world. 'Iran is trying to respond sincerely to the IAEA resolution', he argued, and Rowhani's efforts to do so 'are very important for developing ties between Japan and Iran'.

By mid-September 2006, very strong US opposition to the Azadegan deal appeared to have finally pushed Tokyo off the balance towards Washington.

Because the Japanese had still refused to firmly commit themselves to the project, NIOC reduced their 75 per cent stake to a mere 10 per cent, while Tokyo instead looked to Iraq as a possible source of oil supply. It seems quite possible, however, that if the security situation in Iraq remains dire, then the Japanese may soon be forced to resume negotiations with Tehran.

A similar balancing act has also been performed by the Pakistani government, which has planned to build a $3 billion pipeline that could move huge quantities of Iranian natural gas into Pakistan. The prospect of such a pipeline, which would feed the Tehran regime with considerable quantities of foreign exchange and help cement its political ties with a government that had long been a key American ally in the region, has of course deeply alarmed Washington, which has put very strong pressure on Islamabad to pull the project. On 10 June 2005, the project was discussed at length by Pakistani Foreign Minister Kurshid Mehmood Kasuri and Secretary of State Condoleeza Rice, who pointed out that even if the US administration dropped its opposition there would still be numerous other powerful groups in Congress and the media that were capable of mounting a vigorous campaign of protest and inflicting serious damage upon US-Pakistani relations. Rice particularly had in mind a vociferous number of congressmen and women who had already demanded that the administration invoke ILSA against Pakistani companies and perhaps even cut off the $700 million of US aid that Islamabad receives every year.

To date, such pressure has not prompted Islamabad to steer a different course, or at least admit to doing so. President Pervez Musharraf argued that he would not be persuaded by the United States to drop plans to build a gas pipeline from Iran but would instead take a decision that was based solely on what suited Pakistan, not Washington. 'We are short of energy. We need gas immediately. Our industry is suffering, investment coming to Pakistan is suffering, so our interest is to get gas fast. Iran is the fastest source', he told a British newspaper.[7] During a visit to Moscow to attend the meeting of the heads of the Shanghai Cooperation of Organization (SCO) as an observer, Pakistani Prime Minister Shaukat Aziz also seemed to veer more towards Iran's side: 'we are convinced that Iran's nuclear problem should be settled through dialogue rather than by using force or trying to refer this issue to the UN', especially when 'any state, including Iran, has the right to a peaceful use of nuclear energy.'

An interest in Iranian oil and gas, as well as wider commercial considerations, also help explain marked differences between the US and the member states of the European Union over the question of how to deal with Tehran's nuclear ambitions. These differences have long lurked beneath the superficial show of transatlantic unity on this issue, and have come to the fore even when Iranian negotiators are at their most intransigent. At a conference for EU foreign ministers in early August 2005, a few weeks before a crucial new meeting of the world nuclear watchdog, the IAEA, signs of such dissension had emerged. One envoy said:

> I'd never before seen the Spaniards or Italians look ill at ease with the E3's approach to Iran, but at this meeting there was suddenly a lot of unrest about what would happen, and for the first time their represent-atives made a request to be involved in the diplomatic process with the Iranians and actually help draft an IAEA resolution against them. All of a sudden we had to spend a lot of time discussing the issue to reassure them.[8]

Some EU governments were reported to be wary of possible retaliatory measures by Tehran and looked ready to oppose an immediate referral to the UN Council.

An Iranian Future?

In the future, a number of different influences may swing the balance in Iran's favour, forcing some of the US's allies to side decisively with Tehran.

Most obviously, increasing uncertainty about the availability of future supplies of oil will drive some governments into the arms of those countries that are deemed to have large, untapped energy resources. Such uncertainty is likely to grow not just if the prices of oil and gas remain high but also if the Chinese economy expands at a sharp rate. Such a rapid rate of growth would generate a proportionate increase in energy demand, one that would have strong global repercussions, and prompt China's energy companies to swoop on sources of supply in the same predatory manner as before.

Global fears of Beijing's challenge will also become more pronounced if the Chinese make significant technological advances in the years ahead. Hitherto, the National Iranian Oil Company (NIOC) has prioritized its links with European oil and gas companies purely because they have a clear technological edge over many of their global competitors, one that is of great value for developing Iran's challenging reserves: in 2004 the Japanese oil companies which won the Azadegan contract were forced to look westwards to find a European partner that has such sophistication at its disposal. This means that in the coming years any Chinese advances will make Beijing an even more formidable global competitor than ever before.

Iran's energy sector will also become much more tempting to all its suitors if the Tehran authorities modify the terms on which foreign contractors are employed to develop their oil and gas fields and infrastructure. Hitherto

NIOC has only used a highly restrictive form of 'buyback' contract that is highly unpopular with nearly all foreign energy companies. One of the main grievances is the short lifespan of such contracts: whereas oil companies generally like to have a long-term involvement in such ventures, NIOC has hitherto only offered very short-term deals of around seven years before ownership of the relevant field reverts back to the Iranians.

There have been some recent signs of flexibility by the Tehran authorities. When in September 2006 NIOC prepared to put 24 oil blocks out to international tender, it announced that, in a bid to increase recovery rates, its new contracts would envisage longer terms of involvement by the foreign contractor: this was because the Iranians were 'looking for ways to increase the recovery rate alongside preserving the government's authority on oil reserves', as Mahmoud Mohaddes put it a few weeks before.[9]

An American Response?

For Washington, the only way to meet this challenge is to find some lasting solution to the main source of disagreement and tension with Tehran: the nuclear issue. To lift its own economic embargo on Tehran, or allow its allies to trade freely, without first striking a deal on this matter would of course leave US non-proliferation policy in complete tatters.

Earlier this year, Washington's willingness to talk directly to Tehran on the nuclear issue was made conditional upon a proviso that the Iranians refused to accept: their prior suspension of uranium enrichment. Tehran's obvious determination to ignore such a condition, and its complete disregard of all the various retaliatory threats that have since been made, gives the White House no choice but to give some ground. To find a lasting solution, as well as to even enter initial into talks, the US may have to admit that it is ultimately powerless to force the Iranians to stop enriching uranium. The best that Washington could hope for is their renunciation of just one stage of the complex process of enrichment and acceptance of enhanced powers of UN inspection. The US might also secure such guarantees from Tehran if in return it offered to lift its own economic sanctions against the Iranians whilst also giving them meaningful assurances for their national security.

Whether any American administration is willing to take such a flexible course is ultimately a question of psychology. In the US, the debate on Tehran's nuclear plans has in recent years been coloured by highly apocalyptic language that has exaggerated the dangers posed by a nuclear Iran, and such exaggeration means that any such flexibility is easily regarded as an invitation to nuclear Armageddon.[10] Without first addressing the Iranian nuclear challenge in more balanced terms, it is impossible to imagine any Washington administration showing such flexibility over the issue.

To strike up any such 'Grand Bargain' with Tehran, the United States would also need to acknowledge the realities of its political power in an oil-tight age. The idea of enforcing secondary sanctions against energy-rich countries may in such circumstances be wholly anachronistic: any attempt to economically isolate an energy exporter is likely only to backfire. Just as, half a century ago, the calamities of the Suez venture forced Britain to accept its own post-imperial limits, so too does Iran now look ready to prove where the limitations of American political power lie.

Roger Howard is the author of *Iran Oil: The New Middle East Challenge to America* (IB Tauris, January 2007).

NOTES

1   This was the figure supplied on 11 September 2006 by the Iranian Republic News Agency (IRNA), quoting Hojjatollah Qanimifard, a director of the National Iranian Oil Company (NIOC).
2   See 'Iran's Nuclear Ambitions Test China's Wisdom' by Dingli Shen, *The Washington Quarterly*, Spring 2006.
3   In the autumn of 2006, US-sponsored moves in the UNSC to impose economic sanctions on Iran were blocked by Russian and Chinese opposition.
4   See the report of the IISS *Iran's Strategic Weapons Programmes*, September 2006.
5   In the autumn of 2003, some highly respected independent analysts were very sceptical of unexpected Iranian claims about the size of Bushehr field, which pushed the size of Iran's national reserves up from 95 to 130.8 billion: a leading Honolulu-based consultancy claimed that the Iranians had double-counted existing reserves and assumed a recovery rate that was well above the average figure of 26 per cent. Instead Iran's self-assessment, the analysts concluded, was really just a bid to convince OPEC that Iran should continue with a high export quota that Iraq's newly founded freedoms might imperil.
6   See the US Department of Energy's *International Energy Outlook 2001*.
7   *Financial Times*, 16 May 2005.
8   Interview with the author, London, 1 November 2005.
9   'Iran offers new terms to lure foreign oil explorers', *The Times*, 22 September 2006.
10 On the exaggeration of the Iranian nuclear threat, see the author's articles 'Meeting the Iranian Nuclear Challenge', *RUSI Journal*, October–November 2004; and 'Why Israel Fears an Iranian Bomb', *RUSI Journal*, February–March 2005.

Iran's Gas Vision:
Priorities and Potentials

ALI ARREHCHI

Undoubtedly, the development of the South Pars (SP) energy zone was a positive point in the economic performance of the former president Mohammad Khatami's eight-year administration. It will continue to be a vital sector of the gas industry – if not the whole petroleum sector – in the government of President Mahmoud Ahmadinejad. Nevertheless, the prosperity of SP will depend on the plans of the government.

The development of SP has already provided a promising outlook for the Iranian economy. The ultimate goal is to obtain a major share in the global gas market and to match the country's potential as the second largest holder of gas reserves in the world with its actual performance. Nevertheless, Iran's success will depend on how it will use its opportunities, remove the challenges, satisfy the needs, and promote the strong points.

The following article will try to explain the current priorities of the Iranian government and to highlight the main potentials for foreign investments in this country's gas-sector projects. First, it will embark on a discussion of domestic gas demand, which is posing a serious challenge to policy makers in Tehran. So much so, in fact, that responding to domestic demand has been officially declared a prime objective. Next, the issue of gas injection for enhancing recovery in Iran's ageing oil fields are discussed, as another important priority. Third, we move to the significance of gas exports for Iran, both commercially and strategically. It is believed that the new administration may consider the export of gas – whether through pipeline or in other forms such as liquefied natural gas (LNG) – of lower priority than did the past two presidents. The conclusion section highlights the importance of foreign investment. Iran will need to employ advanced technologies to obtain optimal production at SP. To do that, the Islamic Republic must prepare the conditions needed to encourage strong participation of foreign investors in its projects.

Iran's New Dilemma: Growing Domestic Gas Consumption

Iran holds the world's second largest gas reserves, a point its citizens often recall during cold winters when supplies fail to meet domestic demand. The problem is simple: Iran's gas remains largely under the ground (or sea), and the country faces growing consumption against relatively modest production levels.

Based on the *BP Statistical Review of World Energy 2006*, Iran accounts for about 3.2 per cent of world natural gas consumption and 35 per cent of Middle East consumption. In 2005, Iran had the largest amount of natural gas production in the region. The production stood at 87 bcm (billion cubic metres) which accounted for 3.73 per cent of the world's total. But these figures appear less impressive when we consider the size and population of this country, versus its regional rivals. UAE followed Iran by producing about 50 bcm over the year. Surprisingly, the gas production of Qatar – Iran's main rival producer in the region – stood at 43.5 bcm. In the same year, Iran's total gas consumption was 79.6 million tons of oil equivalent which was 2.5 per cent higher than 2004. This may be shocking when considering that the consumption of China – which has the world's highest consuming population – was at a lower rate of 42.3 million tons. Energy-rich Iran is also a highly wasteful nation, largely due to the presence of heavy subsidies on energy prices in this country.

The government of President Ahmadinejad – which took power on a populist platform in 2005 – will be more determined to address the shortage of adequate gas supplies, particularly to lower-income areas. Two other arguments are fuelling the increase in domestic use of the extant gas supplies. The first is a policy of 'gas replacement'. The idea is simple: by using more of its gas to meet domestic needs, the country will have more crude oil to export and maintain its strategic importance as a second largest exporter in OPEC. Second, in recent years more and more Iranian technocrats have argued in favour of creating 'gas-intensive' industries – such as power plants, petrochemicals, steel, cement, etc. – and gain from the competitive advantage that the possession of cheap energy resources provides, rather than focusing on simple exports of oil and gas. Consequently, Iran has allocated the total production of five producing and four planned SP phases for the domestic grid.[1] It is expected that the government will allow larger reserves from the newly discovered fields of North Pars and Kish.

The Iranian government also wishes to decrease domestic consumption. But these plans are largely 'on paper' and little is being done in terms of concrete steps needed to produce such a result. As mentioned earlier, the large subsidies offered are the main cause for wastage and the high rate of growth in demand. At a mere one cent per cubic meter, Iran offers one of the cheapest gas prices in the world for domestic use. To be fair, tackling the subsidy problem is an overwhelming task and could trigger public dissatisfaction and protests. It is a particularly hard step to take for a government voted in on a populist platform.

On the other hand, the Iranians cannot afford to have such a high domestic consumption volume and must eventually look for a solution. Available opportunities for investors here may then be offering Iran the expertise needed to increase the efficiency of the domestic grid. This could entail advanced pipeline technologies and supply maintenance know-how. Iran may find further motivation in using the help of foreigners when considering that it is currently producing far below its real capacities. Analysts believe that Iran's real natural gas production capacity is five times the current total output.

Injections, Iran's Strategic Priority

Iran – now producing crude at 4.1 million barrels per day (bpd) according to government sources – aspires to increase its crude production to as high as 5 million bpd within the next decade. The increasing depletion of its current oil fields, however, is a serious impediment in reaching this objective. In fact, if policy makers do not act decisively, even maintaining the current level of production may be at risk.

Depletion rates currently stand at an annual of 8 per cent at onshore and 13 per cent at offshore fields.[2] Depletion will continue to be a major challenge unless Iran starts injecting gas into the ageing fields. Iranian officials have already announced that injection will be a top priority from 2006 onward. Besides, there has been a growing determination, particularly among key parliamentarians in the Majlis Energy Committee, that Iran should forsake gas export plans and promote injections to increase crude production and protect reservoirs. Admittedly, the critical comments against exports have diminished recently. There appears to be renewed appreciation for the long-term economic benefits of gas exports, and arguably even more so, for the strategic advantage that they offer. Thus, Iran is not expected to scrap its various export plans, but rather put more effort and emphasis than before on injection schemes.

It is still not clear how much Iran actually needs for injections. Rough estimates vary from 10 to 20 billion cubic feet (bcf) per day. This can be equal to ten SP phases. Phases 6, 7 and 8 have already been allocated for injections into the giant Aghajari oil field. A further source for injections into the field will be provided from SP Phase 12. Other major injection schemes include the three oil fields of Ahvaz, Maroun and Bibi-Hakimeh, and the eight fields of Mansouri, Rag-e Sefid, Maroun (Phase 2), Shadegan, Gachsaran, Kerenj, Parsi and Pazenan. All the fields are located in southern regions and their production provides a major bulk of Iran's total daily output. Nevertheless, the injection plans into these fields are in preliminary stages of study and no source has been earmarked for them yet.

Under the Third Five-Year Development Plan (2000–05), Iran was projected to inject an average of 141 mcm/d (million cubic metres per day) of gas into its oil fields. This objective was not met at the end of the plan and injections hardly reached 80 mcm/d. Under the Fourth Plan (2005–10), Iran is projected to inject as much as 158 mcm/d into its oil fields during March 2006–07. There are no data available to show how the planned injections have been progressing over the past months. There is a consensus among the officials over the need to promote the injection plans. As a result, this can be a lucrative area for international companies which can provide Iran with the latest production enhancement technologies.

Outlook of Power in Gas Exports

As stated above, although exports are lower on Iran's priorities than before, the country is none the less looking at pipeline projects and LNG schemes. There may be several reasons why Iran wants to expand its gas export projects. There is, obviously, the long-term economic benefit of being a key player in the global gas game. Yet, the most important aspect, which has recently become even more pronounced among the officials, is the strategic political significance of export projects in that they promote Iran's stability by increasing the number of international stakeholders. Also, the significance of using gas deals in political bargains may be another incentive for Iran to put the exports on the agenda, even though there may be few short-term economic justifications.

Progress on pipeline projects have been slow, however, due to a combination of factors ranging from price disputes to outside pressure. On the other hand, there has been a surge in Iran's negotiations over its current and future LNG schemes, with Chinese companies receiving a special status in the negotiations.

The pipeline projects to India, Armenia, Georgia and Europe are mostly in the early stages of preliminary negotiations and initial development. The potential areas of work for the existing projects whose fate is almost determined – like the planned pipelines to Iran's northern neighbours – could be maintenance services and the expertise relating to improved pipeline performance. The outlook of the Iran–India project is still plagued by complicated political challenges. Foreign investors can, therefore, take up the project as an international consortium to decrease its political risks and complexities.

Iran is still in early stages of its LNG schemes – Pars LNG, Persian LNG and Iran LNG. There were also serious plans to develop a Gas to Liquids (GTL) project in the South Pars and Iran was at one stage close to a final deal with South Africa's Sasol. The rise of a new government in Tehran, however, changes things, when the new officials maintained that GTL is currently not economical for Iran and may only be pursued in the future. Once again, what complicated the fate of the plan were critical remarks that Iran should first address its growing domestic need and then proceed with other projects for surplus reserves.

Such sentiments came close to also closing the fate of Iran's LNG prospects, before the renewed awareness for the long-term political and economic benefits of these projects breathed new life in these projects. Lucrative areas of investment regarding these projects may be the marketing and shipping of LNG for Iran.

Conclusion

South Pars investment potentials are still huge and a larger part of those potentials are still untouched. This is particularly significant when considering that almost all Iranian gas discoveries have been made during oil exploration operations. In other words, Iran has so far carried out no independent gas exploration projects and experts believe that there is a large potential of successful gas finds in many, particularly the central, areas of the country.

Undoubtedly, Iran's commercial opportunities will always be attractive to international investors. Easy access to international waters and an abundance of natural resources may be only a few remarkable strategic benefits.

Iran is also trying to take steps toward improving its contractual structure to make it more attractive for foreign investment in its oil and gas sector. After much anticipation, the amended buy-back contract were scheduled to be unveiled in Vienna in February 2007. Of course, not all the new terms are likely to work toward the benefit of the foreign company, but improvements are expected overall.

Further, Iranian officials are according a much higher significance than before to gas development projects for several reasons. The main reasons could be the growing domestic demand, the need to promote gas injections into the oil fields, the outlooks of becoming a key player in the future gas market and the significance of involving more stakeholders in terms of gas supplies. These have already made Iran look forward to foreign investment in its gas sector projects. In fact, Iran may today be ready to allocate special benefits to investors who venture to invest in its industries today. These benefits, however, may not be there tomorrow. As always, this is a market for the patient investor.

Ali Arrehchi is a consultant at Atieh Bahar Consulting – Iran's leading strategic consulting company.

NOTES

1   These are SP phases 1–5, which are currently producing, and 9–10 and 15–16 which are planned to come onstream in the near future.
2   Source: FACTS Inc, *Energy Briefs,* April 2005.

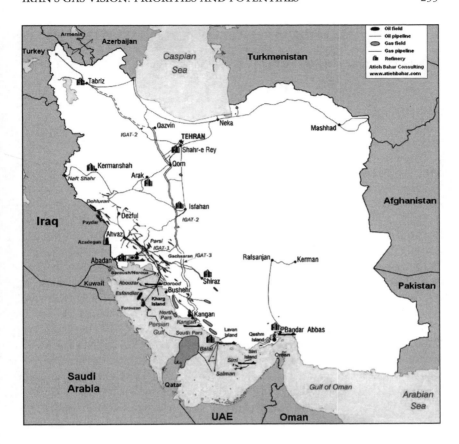

The Abrogation of Government Monopolies and the New Economic Era In Iran

ALINAQI KHAMOUSHI

Finally, after almost 80 years of government monopoly of economic product-ion and distribution, a decree promulgated by the Supreme Leader entitled 'The General Policies of Article 44 Of the Constitution of The Islamic Republic of Iran' removes all government monopolies, except , of course, in oil extraction and gas and thereby initiates a new economic era in Iran. (See the next chapter for the text of Article 44.)

In 1979 just when the expansion of free market economy had been gaining momentum, the reversion to a planned economy – more suitable for the needs of the Revolution – reversed the historical trend, and with the start of the Iraqi-imposed war against Iran, no alternative to full governmental planning and control was conceivable.

However, at the end of the hostilities, it was deemed expedient by the government to begin privatization of economic activities in Iran, and consequently the new outlook and exigencies were incorporated into the country's Five-Year Plans. Yet despite a 6 per cent economic growth rate during this period, it was still considered inadequate.

Based on the experience gained during the implementation of these development plans, especially the Third Plan, it was decided to relinquish as much as possible and only retain those activities the private sector was not capable to undertake.

Finally, in 2005, our Supreme Leader declared that 'in normal conditions, the three government, co-operative, and private sectors shall be dealt with on equal terms.' In other words, the private sector was formally authorized to operate in all economic areas.

Recently the implementation policy of Article 44 of the constitution was declared and the government's economic monopoly was removed. In addition, with the changes made to liberalize economic policies to have a presence in the international markets, and to join the WTO, and despite some opposition

to foreign investment by a small minority, the promotion of foreign investment is moving forward.

Today, because of the cancellation of governmental monopolies in investment and production, the private sector in Iran has more possibilities for
success than the government. The following developments help to clarify the
situation:

- Foreign investment in all fields, whether direct or in partnership with the
  Iranian private sector, is promoted at every level. However, government
  joint projects are limited to the 49/ 51 ratio in favour of the Iranian
  government. But of course private foreign investors may own 100 per cent
  of their capitalization.

- Transparent, simple and very attractive tax conditions are being created
  with the ratification of the amendment to the direct tax law which consists
  of a fixed 25 per cent tax over the annual revenue of companies.

- Private banks and insurance companies have been allowed to start
  operation and so far several have been established and function successfully.

- Unification of the foreign exchange rate, which has been very effective and
  influential for Iran's foreign trade, especially in revenue return and foreign
  investments.

The implementation policies of Article 44 of the Constitution will eventually remove all obstacles for the non-government sectors to take over what
has hitherto been the exclusive privilege and prerogative of the government.

We are convinced that if the proper conditions and the suitable facilities for
the task – not just a transfer of entitlement – are provided by the government,
the policies will eventually bring about what will be known as the greatest
shift in the entire history of Iran's socio-economic administration.

The correct handling of the change required will encourage private-sector
investment, and create new jobs, more manageable inflation and most probably a tremendous increase in foreign trade – in others words, greater economic prosperity.

Moreover, we are convinced in the long run that our high-priority objectives of social security and poverty reduction will have a better chance of
success due to reduced government expenditure and the ultimate increase in
tax revenues that are the inevitable by-products of a growing economy.

However, we should caution, it is a tall order. Any miscalculation of the
severity of the new task and/or underestimation of the new challenges on the
part of the private sector will seriously hamper chances of success. Of the two
new tasks, the substitution of government officials by private managers and

the provision of required financial resources to replace disappearing public funds, the latter will be the greater challenge by far.

In the past, due to mistaken policies, we have been unable to streamline available cash to productive investment opportunities. To remedy the situation in the long and medium term there seems to be no way out of an all-out effort to exploit international capital markets. The recent law passed by the Islamic Consultative Assembly in this respect proves to be of particular relevance. To take the first necessary step, we at the Iran Chamber of Commerce, have already established the first investment holding company (with a final capitalization of more than 500 million dollars) to concentrate capital and expertise to be prepared for the right job at the right moment. But of course the remedy requires a great number of similar solutions. To repeat, unless the government, acting with lots of good will, supports the entire process of the transfer through creation of right facilities, in particular, financial facilities, the successful implementation as well as the fate of the new policies will remain in doubt.

Alinaqi Khamoushi is President of the Iranian Chamber of Trade and Industries.

The Constitution of the Islamic Republic of Iran

ARTICLE 44

The economic system of the Islamic Republic of Iran shall be based on public, cooperative and private sectors, with proper and sound planning.

The public sector includes all large-scale industries, mother industries, foreign trade, large mines, banking, insurance, power supply, dams and large irrigation channels, radio and television, post, telegraph and telephone, aviation, shipping, roads, rails and the like, which are public property and at the disposal of the Government.

The cooperative sector includes cooperative production and distribution companies and institutions established in cities and villages on the basis of Islamic principles.

The private sector includes such activities related to agriculture, cattle-raising, industry, trade and services that supplement the economic activities of public and cooperative sectors.

Ownership in the aforesaid three sectors, insofar as it conforms to other articles of this chapter, does not surpass the limits of Islamic laws, contributes to economic growth and development of the country, and does not harm the society, shall enjoy protection of law in the Islamic Republic.

Details of regulations, scope and conditions of the three sectors shall be determined by law.

In the Name of God, the Merciful and Compassionate

I hereby announce the general policies of Article 44 of the Constitution of the Islamic Republic of Iran. There are a number of observations and remarks in this regard that I should underline.

1. The implementation of these policies requires new legislations or possibly changes in the existing laws, and the government and Majlis need to cooperate with each other for this purpose.

2.   The supervision of the State Expediency Council over the good performance of these policies is essential. This can be achieved by putting in place the required procedures, collaboration of the relevant responsible agencies and presentation of regular annual supervisory reports on a specific date.

3.   The decision regarding 'general policies on development of non-state sector through entrusting activities and ownership of state-owned enterprises' will be made upon receiving reports, documentary evidence, and comprehensive consultative opinions of the State Expediency Council on the relationships between privatization and each of the elements under Article 44, on how different factors can have adverse impact on the efficiency of some state-owned enterprises, the implications of the transfer and ceding activity of the relevant enterprises to the non-state sector under Article 44, on the level of preparedness of the non-state sector and on sanctions and the ways available to the government to exercise its authority.

Enshaallah
Seyyed Ali Khamenei
22 May 2005

In view of the provisions enshrined under Article 44 and in Article 43, general policies of Article 44 of the Constitution of the Islamic Republic of Iran are intended to achieve the following objectives:

- Accelerated growth of national economy.

- Promotion of broad-based public ownership to achieve greater social justice.

- Enhancing the efficiency of economic enterprises and productivity of human and material resources and technology.

- Enhancing the competitive capability of the national economy.

- Reducing financial and administrative burden on the government encumbered as a result of its controlling role in economic activities.

- Increasing the general level of employment.

To achieve the aforesaid objectives, the following guiding principles were agreed upon:

A. General policies concerning development of non-state sector and preventing the unnecessary growth of the government.

1. The government shall not be allowed to engage in economic activities that fall outside those envisioned in Article 44. Moreover, it is obliged to relinquish any activity, including continuation and operation of previous activities that are covered under Article 44, and cede them (at least 20 per cent annually) to the private and cooperative sectors by the end of the Fourth Five-Year Development Plan. Considering that the government has the overall responsibility to ensure good governance, the continuation and initiation of essential activities by the government that fall outside of the main titles of Article 44 are permitted for a definite period of time, upon the proposal of the Council of Ministers and approval of the Islamic Consultative Assembly. Industries that are affiliated to the military, police, intelligence and security services that have confidential character do not fall under this decree.

2. Investment in and management and ownership of those sectors that fall under Article 44 by the non-state enterprises and public institutions, and the cooperative and private sectors are permissible as described below:

    2-1. Large-scale industries, mother industries (including large down-stream oil and gas industries) and large mines (except oil and gas).

    2-2. Foreign trade activities in the framework of trade and foreign currency policies of the country.

    2-3. Banking operations by non-state public enterprises and institutions, publicly held cooperatives and joint stock companies, provided maximum shareholding of each shareholder is determined by law.

    2-4. Insurance.

    2-5. Power supply, generation and importation of electricity for domestic consumption and export.

    2-6. All postal and telecommunication activities, except the main telecommunication grid.

Iran and Azerbaijan: Cousins, Neighbours, Strategic Complexities

MICHEL MAKINSKY

The Azeris are the main ethnic minority in Iran, accounting for 25 per cent of the Iranian population (70 million), and mostly inhabiting poor areas where there is no oil. These areas border Azerbaijan, Armenia and Turkey. The Iranian Azeri region was divided into East and West Azerbaijan in 1994. Azeris are to be found in the same proportion in Tehran, where a substantial number of them are in the civil service and in the army.[1] Indeed, the Supreme Leader, Ali Khameini, is himself an Azeri. Some contend that Turkic-speaking people in Iran (Azeris, Turkmen and Qashqâ'i together) represent 40 per cent of the population, but these data are difficult to verify. Unlike other national minorities in Iran, the Azeris are Shiite, as are the Persians themselves. The Treaty of Turkmanchai in 1828 granted Northern Azerbaijan to Russia (which became an independent state after the dissolution of the Soviet Union), while Southern Azerbaijan joined Persia. This agreement is still regarded as a humiliation by Iranians, for whom nationalism, and national boundaries, are a prickly subject.

The Shah made efforts, especially through the education system, to consolidate Iran's national unity on the basis of past grandeur (making special reference to Persepolis) and on the cultural heritage of Persia. This implied the eradication of local minority cultures. After the Shah's downfall, the Islamic Revolution suppressed all expression of Azeri nationalism, treating demands for language and cultural rights as nothing but a plot conducted on behalf of foreign interests against the integrity of the state. The few committees which celebrate Azeri culture and which look longingly towards Iran's small northern neighbour (the Republic of Azerbaijan) are invariably denounced by Tehran as plotting Azeri unification, and of being agents of pan-Turkic expansionism.[2] However, despite these efforts, most Azeri Iranians feel quite integrated and are not attracted by the idea of belonging to a 'Greater Azerbaijan'.

Nevertheless, for the last fifteen years, these constraints have caused an increase of interest by Iranian Azeris in neighbouring countries. Many watch

Turkish TV while publications in Turkish are mushrooming. The turmoil is discernible. The 1990s saw a transition between cultural revival and political action. In 1993, members of the Iranian Majlis (Parliament) from the Azeri region created a pressure group,[3] the National Movement for the Development of South Azerbaijan (*Gamosh*). The movement – whose leader is a teacher of literature, Mahmudali Chohraganli – is expanding. Although elected in 1995, he has been barred from attending sessions of the Majlis and was instead imprisoned.[4] Gamosh promotes a federal Iran with extensive autonomy for Azerbaijan, as well as its own flag and institutions. The activists are carefully monitored, especially when they travel. Nationalist Azeris believe that the Islamic Republic cannot reform from within, and have become radicalized. Turkey is becoming more attractive for them than the isolation created by the scornful dogma of Persian cultural superiority. Moreover, they resent the fact that Iran supports Armenia in its dispute with the Republic of Azerbaijan over Nagorno-Karabakh.[5]

Turkey and Azerbaijan show some sympathy towards their fellow countrymen in Iran and there are attempts to strengthen mutual ties. But Baku is careful not to add fuel to the fire and it treads a fine line, developing relations without opening itself to the accusation that it is meddling in Iranian internal affairs, let alone fomenting any separatist tendencies. Tehran always expresses its dissatisfaction noisily[6] when its neighbour gives publicity to militant groups, and the Azeris generally respond by taking these groups firmly in hand. Ilham Aliev, who was elected president of Azerbaijan on 15 October 2003, is opposed to any new disputes with Iran and wants to maintain the improved relations with Tehran which he inherited from his father, Heydar.[7] Ilham has personally launched critical initiatives such as the opening of a new Azerbaijan consulate at Tabriz in 2004.

Ethnic tensions have significantly increased since Ahmadinejad's election to the presidency in 2005. All protests are ruthlessly suppressed. Wherever they occur – in Azerbaijan, in Kurdistan, in Arab Khuzestan – the extent of such protests is evidence of widespread popular discontent with economic neglect, low investment and high unemployment. How can a regime which claims to be working for social justice justify keeping the Azeris at such an under-developed level? Azeri demands, indeed, concern economic issues more than ethnic ones,[8] but the ethnic issue has become so explosive that it is now giving cause for concern in Tehran.

Ethnic unrest was at the core of the 2005 presidential campaign, each candidate chasing votes within their client base.[9] The new regime deals with the ethnic issue by closing newspapers, arresting journalists and campaigners, spreading propaganda about 'the hand from abroad' and 'the American-Zionist plot', and by appointing regional officials from the ranks of the Revolutionary Guard. These actions indicate that the president is determined to take control of the situation. He also hopes to extinguish any spark of unrest by spending money from the oil surplus.

However, various phenomena illustrate the extent of the Azeri malaise. On 19 May 2006, the Persian-language newspaper *Iran*, which is closely controlled by the government, published a cartoon of a cockroach speaking Azeri. There were violent demonstrations by students in Tabriz and the unrest spread through the whole region before reaching the Majlis, on 28 May. The resulting repression claimed an unknown number of victims, but the students eventually obtained the closure of the newspaper and the arrest of the editor and the cartoonist. Was it a deliberate provocation organized by a conservative faction? Certainly, the idea that the cartoonist had made a mistake (Azeris are often the butt of Iranian jokes), and the arguments about 'a foreign hand' were unconvincing.[10] The Republic of Azerbaijan kept its distance from the affair, partly for diplomatic reasons and also partly to avoid any movements from getting out of hand on its own territory. Baku treated the matter as an internal Iranian affair and said that it was satisfied by Tehran's assurances that the rights of Iranian citizens of Azeri origin would be protected. Government newspapers attacked the opponents of President Aliev who expressed his support for the demonstrators in 'the South'. Mahmud Chohraganli's presence in Baku was undesirable; those newspapers who in return published cartoons of Ayatollah Khomeini were prosecuted for incitement to racial or religious hatred, which in any case Sheikh Pasharaze declared a shameful act of heresy.[11] The Russian language daily, *Zerkalo* (The Mirror) argued that if Tehran thought that Baku was supporting the demonstrators, then Azerbaijan's geostrategic interests would be affected.[12]

Quarrelsome Neighbours

A shadow is also cast over bilateral relations by differences over the delimitation of zones in the Caspian Sea by the five states which border it: Kazakhstan, Russia, Azerbaijan, Turkmenistan and Iran. Until 1991, the Caspian was bordered only by Iran and the USSR. The juridical status of this 'lake' was previously based on three texts: the 1921 Treaty of Cooperation and Friendship; a 1935 treaty on trade; and a new Treaty on Commerce and Navigation, which was signed on 25 March 1940 and which superseded the 1935 treaty. There are now two opposing approaches to the Caspian question: Russia, Azerbaijan and Kazakhstan want the sea to be divided up into five unequal zones, proportional to the length of their coasts. This solution would give 13 per cent to Iran. The Iranians, supported by the Turkmen, want the sea to be divided up into five zones, each covering 20 per cent of the sea's area. Bilateral accords signed between Russia, Kazakhstan and Azerbaijan in 2002 have in large measure sanctioned a *de facto* partition.[13] Tehran has believed for a long time that a strategic partnership between Russia and Iran would persuade Moscow to acquiesce but it had not understood that Russia's policy was to reconquer the outlying lands of its former empire.[14] Iran has been practically isolated as a resolute opponent of the unequal solution, and it does not know how to accept the inevitable without losing face.

In July 2001, the tensions between Tehran and Baku reached a peak when an Iranian warship and two Iranian aircraft repelled two Azeri exploration units operating for BP in the Alov zone, which Iran has claimed. On 18 January 2006, Iran's North Drilling Company signed an agreement to build an oil exploration platform with a Chinese company based in Hong Kong. The platform is probably intended to explore the Aloz oil field (Aborz in Farsi). Tehran evidently is not going to wait for arbitration on the question of the zones before taking its own initiatives.[15] This will be extremely unwelcome in Baku which will no doubt seek the support of Turkey and the US but which will also try to convince China to withdraw. However, it is likely that Beijing, which is counting on the energy potential of Kazakhstan and whose development depends on the outlet offered by the Baku–Tbilisi–Ceyhan (BTC) pipeline which is to be extended into Kazakhstan, will not want to endanger this future network, to which in any case Azerbaijan devotes enormous importance.[16]

This is without even taking into consideration the power of Russia, which is flexing its muscles. In October 2001, Russia conducted a Russian naval exercise in the Caspian Sea; in August 2002, there were joint Russo-Azeri and Russo-Kazakh manoeuvres. The Iranians regarded these in a negative light.[17] Moscow is trying to include Baku in a system of naval command and coordination, the Casfor,[18] which is a source of great concern in Tehran and which explains the Iranian decision urgently to strengthen its own naval potential in the Caspian.

The election of President Ahmadinejad only complicated further the relations between Tehran and Baku. First, Ahmadinejad's offensive tone towards the West and its allies went down badly in an Azerbaijan which has made a clear pro-Western geopolitical choice and against the Islamization of its society.[19] Secondly, Iran has adopted an aggressive posture towards Israel, a country which Azerbaijan had flourishing relations. Third, Iran's bid for regional power, its intransigent Persian nationalism, and its new religious ideology are all unwelcome in Baku. The major fears of the Azeri leadership concern the consequences of a US military intervention and a real crisis on the nuclear question. Any economic blockade or other measures of intimidation would also be felt in Azerbaijan. Three meetings between Presidents Ahmandinejad and Aliev have permitted a certain *rapprochement*, but mistrust persists. Of course, the threat of a nuclear-armed Iran forces President Aliev to seek a diplomatic solution to the crisis and to place himself in an uncomfortable balancing position. He knows that Azerbaijan's hydrocarbon resources make it indispensable but he also knows that the strongest (and most dangerous) cards are held by other powers.

On 5 May 2006, Azerbaijan hosted the ninth summit of the Organization of Economic Cooperation, based in Tehran, which was born out of the defunct CENTO (Central Treaty Organization). The OEC was initially dominated by the trio of Turkey, Iran and Pakistan, before being enlarged to include the republics of Central Asia. The idea was to create a 'common market' but this has not been achieved. What is important now are the bilateral exchanges between President Aliev and the Turkish prime minister, Recep Tayyip Erdogan, or the Afghan president, Hamid Karzai. But it was above all the meeting between Aliev and Ahmadinejad which attracted people's attention. Aliev was trying to find a middle way between Washington and Moscow and to strengthen his position in the Caucasus and beyond; Ahmadinejad wanted the support of Muslim states and a forum for his bid for leadership in the Muslim world and in the struggle against Israel.[20]

Interferences

Next to Turkey, Azerbaijan is a major issue for US geostrategic policy. In 2002, Washington started to take an interest in the 'ethnic factor' by meeting with Chohraganli, which provoked speculations about a future union between the separatist movements in the Islamic Republic. But President Aliev remained very prudent on this while the American neo-conservatives continued to construct illusionary scenarios about an ethnic dismemberment of Iran.

More decisive was Washington's insistence that Baku adopt a 'positive attitude' towards the idea that Iran should be militarily neutralized by a forward position of troops, installations near its borders, an increase in electronic surveillance stations and, in the case of military operations if the negotiations on the nuclear issue fail, the use of Azeri airspace, waters and territory. Aliev is trying to secure some advantage from these American requests while at the same time trying to avoid a major break with Tehran which would no doubt be followed by reprisals. In 2004, the Azeri Defence Minister, Safar Abiyev, met Donald Rumsfeld to discuss military cooperation. The question of stationing US troops on Azeri territory was raised. Iran reacted violently and threatened Azerbaijan with a pre-emptive strike. Iran is worried since US 'advisers' have been observed at a military base in the Salyan region, while there are persistent rumours that Azeri airfields are being upgraded to NATO standards in Nakhitchevan, Chukhanly and Nasony. Faced with this perceived threat, Tehran has changed its strategy[21] and launched a diplomatic offensive: the consulate was opened in Tabriz, various economic agreements on Iranian investment in Azerbaijan, financial aid and above all a declaration of support for the Azeri position on Nagorno-Karabakh. What the Iranians want in return from the Azeris is for them to forbid the Americans from using Azeri territory for any attack on Iran, and indeed perhaps too for Baku to use its good offices in Washington in the conflict. Baku, however, is not prepared to give firm support to the Iranian position, preferring instead to make vague declarations on the need for a peaceful solution to the Iranian nuclear issue. Meanwhile, Washington's criticisms of the authoritarian nature of the regime in Baku at the time of the legislative elections in November 2005, and the suggestion that there might be a Ukrainian-type 'Orange Revolution' there, will also have an impact. The United States is involved in delicate negotiations on Nagorno-Karabakh and submitted a plan for the resolution of the conflict, which failed to produce an agreement at Rambouillet on 10 February 2006. As the nuclear crisis with Iran intensifies, the US is increasing its dialogue with Aliev in order that he agrees to 'ignore' the stationing of US forces on his territory. It is clear that the Azeri political class is worried, despite its denials. The media insist that it is as a result of 'inevitable' necessity that Baku has an alliance with Washington. No surprise that the Iranian Defence Minister, Mustafa Mohammed Najjar, met both President Aliev and his Azeri opposite number when he led an important military delegation to Baku on 20 April 2006.[22] The president, for his part, said on 26 April 2006 that he would not allow Azeri territory to be used for an attack on Iran.[23]

A Complementary Relationship

The common interests between Baku and Jerusalem became clear at the same time as the partnership between Israel and Turkey was being strengthened. The newly independent Azeri state made much of its relationship with Israel in order to recover after the loss of Nagorno-Karabakh and in order to reconstruct its armed forces. Both countries share a fear of radical Islam. Economic exchanges soon followed, and Israel went from the tenth to the fifth most important trading partner of Azerbaijan.[24] The Iranians, like the Israelis, have deployed widespread networks of informers in Azerbaijan and they miss no occasion to attack Baku's relationship with the Zionist enemy. Azerbaijan wants to diversify its economy away from an undue reliance on hydrocarbons. The announcement of the opening of an Azeri commercial office in Israel in 2007 was carefully presented in such a way as not to irritate Tehran.[25] Jerusalem had been extremely pleased at the construction of the BTC pipeline through Azerbaijan, Georgia and Turkey because it bypassed Iran, even though a pipeline through Iran would have been more reliable and would have cost less. This emphasizes the eminently strategic nature of the American decision in favour of the BTC pipeline.[26] Israel now buys about one-sixth of its oil from Azerbaijan, and Israeli officials have opened negotiations in order to obtain Azeri crude from Ceyhan which would then be transported on the Eilat–Ashkelon pipeline which is being put back into service. A previous project envisaged extending the BTC pipeline under the sea from Ceyhan to Haifa.[27] Some analysts have gone so far as to suggest that the destabilization of Lebanon increases the strategic importance of the BTC pipeline.[28] Certainly, the Israeli invasion of Lebanon affected Azeri public opinion and the opposition has profited from the resentment it generated. On the other hand, Iran is in no way perceived as an attractive model: it is not foreign but is a somewhat unpredictable neighbour, public perception of which can change along with those of Hezbollah, its client. The pro-Israeli positions of the Azeri government were therefore unpopular.

The official inauguration of the BTC pipeline (the contract for which was originally signed in 1999) on 13 July 2006 represented a major strategic failure for Tehran.[29] The first delivery of oil arrived symbolically a few days before the G8 summit which took place 15–17 July 2006 in St Petersburg.[30] It was no surprise, therefore, that on 9 July 2006, the Azeri newspaper *Yeni Musavat* published a new Iranian proposal on Nagorno-Karabakh. The Iranian ambassador in Baku, Asfar Suleimani, suggested that his country be invited to join the Minsk group, which has been tasked with mediating for the Organisation for Security and Cooperation in Europe (OSCE).[31]

Meanwhile, Tehran is continuing to develop energy, trade, security agreements and Memoranda of Understanding with Armenia, adding to Baku's discomfort. However, both Armenia and Azerbaijan are under pressure from the OSCE to find a peaceful settlement. The meeting which took place in Minsk on 28 November 2006 led to some progress but both parties are not still unable to agree on an overall settlement.[32]

At the end of the day, the relationship between Azerbaijan and Iran appears strange: a mixture of realistic complementary interests and of near-paranoiac defiance. Both sides know there are invisible lines which must not be crossed, and they try to use each other as a useful counterweight to the other's neighbours in the fight for influence between the Great Powers. This very delicate chess game has numerous results: due to a reduction in the Russian electricity supply, Azerbaijan will exchange electricity with Iran in 2007. On 27 November 2006,the Iranian state-run daily *Johouri Islami* reported that Supreme Leader Ali Khamenei had threatened Baku, stating that Iran was capable of realizing its historical claims against Azerbaijan.[33] In the meantime, at the beginning of December 2006, the Azeri Minister for Procurement, Yavar Jamalov, welcomed cooperation with Iran when meeting the Iranian

Minister of Defence, Mustafa Mohammed Najjar, in Tehran.[34] Focusing on headlines alone may lead analysts to miss deeper phenomena. The regional balance of power is in a state of perpetual motion. There may be unexpected developments in Iran; Turkey is trying to build a new strategic bloc of Turkophone nations. This is intended both as a response to Europe's hesitations on EU membership for Turkey and also as a means of countering Russia's ambitions in the Caucasus. Such a bloc would also be a means by which Turkey could strengthen her hand in the battle for influence over the resources of the Caspian Sea; Turkey could be a powerful counter-weight to Iran, if it is ever realized. The summit in Antalya on 17 November 2006, where the presidents of Azerbaijan, Kazakhstan, Kyrgyzstan and Turkey decided to explore the idea of creating a Turkish Commonwealth, has produced results beyond what was expected. The idea is that this new 'alliance' will adopt common positions in foreign policy, particularly on the Karabakh conflict, and that it will promote the development of energy routes to the BTC and BTE (Baku–Tbilisi–Ezurum) pipelines.[35] Obviously this new coalition, which may somewhat reflect the old Ottoman legacy, will generate concerns for Iranians who will see that northern neighbours are not perhaps as weak as they were before. A nervous Iranian leadership may eventually feel that this build-up is part of a US-led strategy of encirclement.

Michel Makinsky is Lecturer in Iranian Affairs at the Poitiers School of Business and Management and Special Adviser to the University of Liège.

NOTES

1   Bernard Hourcade, 'Iran,nouvelles identités d'une république', Paris: Belin, 2002, p. 39.

2   See Kaveh Farrokh,'Pan-Turianism takes aim at Azerbaijan: A geopolitical agenda' <http://www.rozanehmagazine.com/NoveDec05/aazarilINDEX.HTML> for an unusual indictment of Iran's policy of 'Turkification' during Khatami's presidency, Olonor, 'The policy of Turkification in Iran' *Persian Journal*, 13 November 2005.

3   See Gilles Riaux, 'La radicalisation des nationalistes azeris en Iran', *CEMOTI*, No. 37, 2004; Brenda Schaffer, *Borders and brethen, Iran and the challenge of the Azerbaijani identity*, Cambridge, MA: MIT Press, 2002, p. 180.

4   See Ali M.Koknar, 'Iranian Azeris : a giant minority,' *Policy Watch*, No. 1111, The Washington Institute for Near East Policy, 6 June 2006,to which this paper is highly indebted.

5   See Svante Cornell, 'Iranian Azerbaijan: a brewing Hotspot Presentation to Symposium on Human Rights and Ethnicity in Iran', Stockholm, Swedish Parliament, 22 November 2004 <http://www.cornellcaspian.com/pub2/0411Iran.pdf>. While positioning itself as a mediator, Iran has in fact favoured Christian Armenia against its Muslim neighbour. Tehran has no wish to see an Azeri victory which, it fears, could boost Baku's nationalists within Iranian territory. Iranians fear that the conflict may spread, generating turmoil and feelings of national solidarity. See Cameron Brown, 'Wanting to have their cake and their neighbour too : Azerbaijani attitudes towards Karabakh and Iranian's Azerbaijan', *Middle East Journal*, Vol. 28, Autumn 2004. Even if it has been unsuccessful, Iran's mediation nevertheless brought some periods of respite periods:

see Abdollah Ramezanzneh, 'Iran's role as mediator in the Nagorno-Karabakh crisis', in Bruno Coppieters (ed.), *Contested borders in the Caucasus*, Brussels: VUB University Press, 1996. Moreover, Turkey, focusing on EU membership, no longer unconditionally supports Azerbaijan and no longer considers the idea of opening diplomatic relations with Armenia to be heretical.

6 See Fariz Ismailzadeh, 'New tensions complicate relations between Baku and Tehran', *Eurasia Daily Monitor* Vol. 3, No. 62, 30 March 2006; 'Iranian expert notes weakness of Tehran's policy on Azerbaijan', *ATURCA*, 16 May 2006 <http://www.aturca.world press.com/2005/O5/16/iranian expert>.

7 Heydar Aliev was Ebulfey Elçibey's successor. The latter was a constant supporter of the Azeri Iranian minority.

8 On the imbalance between conditions in the towns and the country, see B. Hourcade, 'Le fait ethnique en Iran :risque de conflit ou enjeu dépassé par l'urbanisation?', *Géoéconomie*, No. 36, Winter 2005–06.

9 See Bill Samii, 'Iran: Ethnicity and regional interests play out in vote' <http://www.payvand.com>, 23 June 2005.

10 Cf. Bill Samii, 'Ethnic tensions could crack Iran's firm resolve against the world', *Christian Science Monitor*, 30 May 2006; 'Iran :Azeris unhappy at being butt of national jokes', *IRIN*, 25 May 2006; Iason Athanasiadis, 'Foreign plots and cockroaches in Iran',*Asia Times On Line*, 8 June 2006; Nayedeh Tohidi, 'Iran: regionalism,ethnicity and democracy', *OpenDemocracy*, 29 June 2006 <http://www.openDemocracy.net>.

11 Cf. Bill Samii, 'Baku warned against inviting Azerbaijani leader', *RFE/RL Iran Report*, 12 June 2006.

12 Cf. Fatah Abdullayev and Mina Muradova, 'Azerbaijan adopts cautious approach on ethnic Azeri protests in Iran,' *Eurasia Insights*, 1 June 2006 <http://www. eurasianet. org /departments/insight/articles>.

13 Cf. Philippe Sébille-Lopez, *Géopolitique du pétrole*, Paris: Armand Colin, 2006, p. 192. For a summary of the traditional Iranian positions, see Barbara Januz, 'Iran's view on the legal status of the Caspian sea', *Tharwa features*, December 2004 <http://www.tharwa project.com/English/Main-Sec/Features>; and Bahman Aghai Diba, 'The lack of a legal regime in the Caspian sea is a real danger' <http://www.payvand.com/news>, 28 February 2005.

14 Cf. Michel Makinsky, 'Russie/Iran, Partenaires/ Concurrents en quête de stratégie(s)', *Outre-Terre*, No. 4, March 2003.

15 Cf. Taleh Ziyadov, 'Iran and China sign agreement to explore oil in Caspian sea" *Eurasia Daily Monitor*, Vol. 3, No. 22, 1 February 2006.

16 Cf. Svante E. Cornell and Fariz Ismailzade, 'Implications for Azerbaijan', in S.Frederick Starr and Svante E. Cornell (eds), 'The Baku-Tbilisi-Ceyhan pipeline: oil window to the west', *Central-Asia Caucasus & Silk Road Studies Program*, Washington, DC/Uppsala, 2005, p. 79. Kazakhstan's announcement on 16 June 2006 that it would join the BTC pipeline went down very badly in Tehran and will increase Iranian suspicion of Kazakhstan.

17 Cf. Andrew Katen, 'Iran's territorial disputes with its Caspian Sea neighbours', *PINR*, 31 May 2006.

18 Cf. Steven J. Main, 'The bear, the peacock,the eagle,the sturgeon and the black,black oil: contemporary regional power politics in the Caspian Sea', *Conflict Studies Research Centre*, O5/67, December. Casfor, which is based on the agreement of all states which border the Caspian, is a counterweight to the US-Azeri agreement, Caspian Guard, put in place at the end of February 2003. But Azerbaijan would rather not have to make a choice between the two. Cf Rovshan Ismailov, 'Azerbaijan ponders Russian Caspian defence initiative', *Eurasia Insight*, 1 February 2006.

19 As a member of the OSCE, Azerbaijan is not in the same 'camp' as Iran.

20 Cf. Fariz Ismailzade, 'Aliev's recent schedule: balanced foreign policy or bad timing?', *Eurasia Daily Monitor*, Vol. 3 No. 93, 12 May 2006.

21 I follow here the excellent analysis of Arif Yunus, 'Azerbaijan-Between America and Iran', *Russia in global affairs*, No. 3, July–September 2006.

22 'Iran Defense Chief visits Azerbaijan amid nuclear standoff' <http://www.payvand.com/news> 19
    April 2006.
23 'Azerbaijan Leader staying out of Iran fray', Associated Press report, *The Guardian*, 26 April 2006.
24 Cf. Ilya Bourtman, 'Israël and Azerbaijan's furtive embrace', *Middle East Quarterly*, Summer 2006.
25 'Azerbaijan to open trade office in Israel', *Jerusalem Post*, 16 May 2006.
26 Iran's preference for Armenia is probably explained by the Moscow-Baku compromise on the
    division of the Caspian Sea. But it is even more the BTC episode: the isolation of the Islamic
    Republic forced it to seek out allies which are as marginalized as it is. This would explain the
    energy partnership between Tehran and Yerevan, the Irano-Armenian gas pipeline which is to
    enter into operation in 2007 and which will undermine Gazprom's monopoly in Armenia. See
    'Armenia deepens ties with embattled Iran', *Eurasia Insight*, 28 July 2006 <http://www.
    eurasianet.org> and Julien Zafirian, 'À contre-courant' 23 April 2006 <http://www.caucaz.com>.
    The BTC pipeline has the strategic function of bypassing Russia but the political priority, from
    the American point of view, was to exclude Iran. Cf. Enayatollah Yazdani, 'Competition over the
    Caspian oil routes: Oilers' and Gamers' perspective', *Alternatives*, Vol. 5 No. 1–2, Spring–Summer
    2006. In the case of a military conflict with Washington, it would be wrong to rule out an Iranian
    action against the BTC pipeline.
27 'Israel to buy Azeri light and provide passage to eastern market', *APS Review of Oil Market Trends*,
    17 July 2006.
28 Cf. Michel Chossudovsky, 'The war of Lebanon and the battle for oil', Centre for Research on
    Globalisation, 26 July 2006 <http://www.globalresearch.ca/index>.
29 'Iran the only and biggest loser in the BTC pipeline project', *IPS*, 18 September 2002.
30 Cf. Michael Piskur, 'The BTC pipeline and the increasing importance of energy supply routes',
    PINR, 8 August 2006.
31 'Azeri political analysts downplay Iran's Karabakh mediation offer', BBC Monitoring Caucasus, 9
    July 2006.
32 'Azerbaijani, Armenian, Karabakh Officials assess Talks' <http://www.payvand.com/news>, 2
    December 2006.
33 'Iran leader threatens Azerbaijan' <http://www.Today.AZ>, 1 December 2006.
34 'Defense Industry Minister pays tribute to late Imam Khomeyni' <http://www.Today.AZ>, 4
    December 2006.
35 Mevluk Katik, 'Turkish Summit to explore commonwealth possibility', *Eurasia Insight*, 15
    November 2006, and 'Spirit of Cooperation dominates Turkish Summit', *Eurasia Insight*, 20
    November 2006.

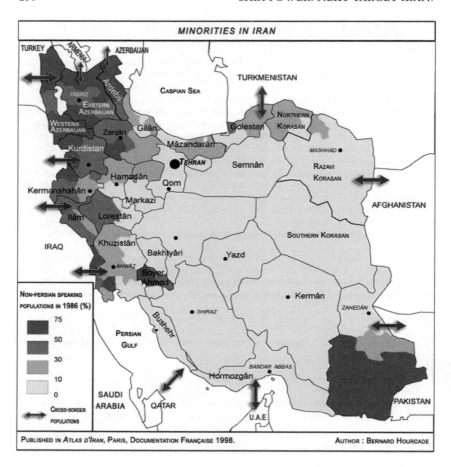

MINORITIES IN IRAN

TURKEY · ARMENIA · AZERBAIJAN · TURKMENISTAN

TABRIZ · EASTERN AZERBAIJAN · CASPIAN SEA

WESTERN AZERBAIJAN · Ardebil · Zanjân · Gilân · Golestan · NORTHERN KORASAN

Kurdistan · Mâzandarân · MASHHAD

Hamadân · TEHRAN · Semnân · RAZAVI KORASAN

Kermanshahân · Qom

Markazi · AFGHANISTAN

Ilâm · Lorestân

IRAQ · Khuzistân · SOUTHERN KORASAN

AHWÂZ · Bakhtyâri · Yazd

Boyer Ahmad

Kermân · ZAHEDÂN

NON-PERSIAN SPEAKING POPULATIONS IN 1986 (%)

- 75
- 50
- 30
- 10
- 0

CROSS-BORDER POPULATIONS

SHIRAZ · PERSIAN GULF · Busheyr

BANDAR ABBAS

Hormozgân

SAUDI ARABIA · QATAR · U.A.E. · PAKISTAN

PUBLISHED IN *ATLAS D'IRAN*, PARIS, DOCUMENTATION FRANÇAISE 1998.   AUTHOR : BERNARD HOURCADE

Kurds in the Islamic Republic: A Survey

SOHEILA GHADERI-MAMELI

More than 15 million Kurds live in Turkey and about 5.5 million in Iraq. During the last two decades, events in these countries, which are notorious for their human, social and economic difficulties, have brought their fate to public attention. But the situation of more than 10 million Kurds in Iran remains more or less unknown.

The Kurds live in the north-west and west of Iran, principally in four provinces: Western Azerbaijan, Kurdistan, Kermanshah and Ilam. There are also Kurds in the provinces of Khorasan, especially in Qootchan and in Shirwan, in Hamadan, in Tehran, in Qazvin and in other towns throughout the country.

According to the 1996 census, the Kurds are estimated to represent about 10 per cent of the country's population. Kurdish political organizations put the figure at between 11 per cent and 12 per cent. About 50 per cent of the 2,500,000 inhabitants of Western Azerbaijan are Kurds, while the province of Kurdistan, which is officially entirely inhabited by Kurds, counts 1,346,000 people.[1] In Kermanshah. there are 1,778,596, and 488,886 in Ilam. Finally, 600,000 Kurds live in other Iranian towns. Just behind the Azeri minority, which is estimated to be 16–20 per cent of the Iranian population, the Kurds constitute the second most important minority in Iran.

The principal debate about Kurds is the following: are they an ethnic minority or are they a people/nation? For some ideologues, the Kurds are a nation divided between the four states of Iran, Iraq, Turkey and Syria. Because of this division, some consider the Kurds to be an ethnic minority in each of the states mentioned above. For others, the Kurds who do not have a state of their own cannot be considered as a nation. This approach makes an amalgam between the notions of people, nation and state. In Iran, the word *qowm*, which means an ethnic group, is used to describe the Kurds, and the Kurdish language is considered to be a dialect of Persian (Farsi).

However, the Iranian Kurds are not satisfied with their situation and they try to demonstrate this dissatisfaction in different ways. In June 2005, very few of them voted in the legislative election and in July, the murder in

Mahabad of seyyed Kemal Afsaram, known as Shwana seyyed Qadir, who was cruelly tortured by the security forces, sparked some big demonstrations in different towns in the whole Kurdish region. Many people were injured and others arrested. Among them was Dr Roya Tooloïi, human rights activist and the editor of *Razan*, paper of the Kurdish Women's Association for Peace.[2]

In November 2005, three Kurdish activists[3] were accused of being members of the Democratic Party of Iranian Kurdistan (DPIK) and were tried by the Islamic Court of Mababad, which sentenced them to between 15 and 20 years' imprisonment. In February 2006, the peaceful demonstration of Kurds in Makoo, Bazargan and Sardasht was violently dispersed by security forces of the Islamic Republic. Eight people were killed, 25 others injured and more than four hundred were arrested.

***

Why did the Iranian Kurds decide again to boycott the elections?[4] What is their political, social and economic situation under the Islamic Republic? What are their demands and what is the government's answer to their claims?

Iran has a centralized political regime. This centralization process began at the beginning of the twentieth century, when Iranian society's feudal organization was replaced by a modern political regime. Reza Khan (1926–41), founder of Pahlavi dynasty, adopted the principle of the nation-state. Persian (Farsi) was chosen as the official language, and the Fars were the favoured ethnic group, which determined the ethnic and linguistic diversity of the country.

His son, Mohammad Reza (1941–79), continued the same policy. Under his reign the Kurds were denied all ethnical specificities and their language was considered a dialect of Persian. Kurds were also deprived of political rights and their rebellions were violently dispersed by the army forces. Many Kurdish leaders were killed and their bodies displayed in public. A very great number of Kurdish activists were sentenced to prison and many of them were exiled abroad. Every political activity was forbidden and the SAVAK (the Organization for Security and Information) was extremely powerful in the Kurdish area.

In this context of persecution, the Kurds very actively participated in the revolutionary events of 1978–79. Mahabad was certainly one of the most agitated towns in Iran.

Once the monarchy was overthrown, the Shiite clergy took power and established an Islamic Republic. This new form of political regime was completely unknown. Despite the anarchy within this new authority, which had at least three centres of decision making,[5] the 'problem of Kurdistan' was the 'problem' of the Republic.[6]

The political situation in Kurdistan was also very confused. Kurdish political groups and organizations were very divided and had no common political programme. The principal and most ancient organization was the Democratic Party of Iranian Kurdistan (DPIK), founded in 1946. The DPIK's main slogan was 'Democracy for Iran and Autonomy for Kurdistan'. The second political group was Komala (The Kurdish Organization of the Communist Party in Iran), which wanted to fight the capitalist system and to create a socialist state. Komala was basically an extremist and Maoist organization. At that time, Komala had no clear project for the future of Kurdistan. Another political organization was the Fedai of Iranian People, a Marxist-Leninist organisation. The Kurdish branch of the Fedai supported a local autonomy statute for the Kurds. There were also two religious personalities: Ahmad Muftizadeh in Sanandaj and Sheikh Ezzedine Husseini in Mahabad.[7]

After thirty years of exile, the DPIK, which wanted to become a political force in Kurdistan, showed a real interest in dialogue with the new regime. But other organizations, especially Komala, had an extremist attitude. They criticized everything and did not propose any other programme or alternative for the future of Kurdistan. Their relationships with the DPIK were strained and sometimes stormy. They accused the DPIK of being a middle-class political organization and criticized its origins in Tudeh, the Communist Party of Iran.

In this confused political context, did Kurdish claims have any chance of being accepted by the new regime? Did the Islamic Republic want to find a political solution to the Kurdish problem?

The new regime made contact with the Kurds at the beginning of the Revolution. The first government delegation was sent to Mahabad on 14 February 1979, in order to ascertain officially what were the Kurdish demands.[8]

By the time the delegation arrived in Mahabad, the population had occupied the military base in the town. Even if, a few weeks previously, in Tehran and other areas of the country, the political and 'revolutionary' organizations had already taken control of the military bases, the new authorities were very disturbed by this development in Mahabad. They asked the Kurdish representatives to end their occupation. But the population did not want to preserve one of the political symbols of repression in the centre of their town any more. The Kurdish representatives proposed to the government delegation that the military base be transformed into a university, and that another military base be built in the suburbs.[9] The government delegation did not make any concessions on this point but it did promise to make the Kurds' demands known in Tehran. The main outcome of this visit was to legitimize the activities of the DPIK.

On 22 March 1979, another delegation came to Kurdistan.[10] This second delegation, headed by Ayatollah Taleghani, recognized the Kurdish people's right to manage their own affairs. However, he insisted that the armed forces, including the Pasdaran (the Revolutionary Guard), maintain a presence in Kurdish areas.[11] That was too much to ask and the Kurdish organizations did not accept it.

However, the Kurds sent three delegations to meet the head of the Republic, Ayatollah Khomeini. He refused to recognize any political rights for the Kurds and asked them to meet with Prime Minister Mehdi Bazargan, who refused to make a political decision until the Constitution was ratified. As a consequence, all the Kurdish parties and organizations decided to boycott the referendum of 31st March 1979, which established the Islamic Republic.[12]

Gradually the relationship between the Kurds and Tehran deteriorated. The situation was strange: while there was no war, there was no peace either. Some tragic events occurred, as in Naghada between 20 and 22 April 1979, where the Azeri militia killed more than 350 Kurds.[13] This event damaged the relationship between Kurds and Azeri, who had lived closely together for a long time.

Despite this conflict, the Kurds decided to take part in the election of the Council of Experts (3 August 1979). The Kurdish candidate in Western Azerbaijan, the secular Dr Abdurrahman Ghassemlou, was elected but he did not attend the Council. [14]

After the events at Paweh,[15] Ayatollah Khomeini decried the Kurds as disloyal and the DPIK as 'a nest of sabotage and corruption' and he appealed for jihad against the Kurds. To solve the Kurdish problem, the Islamic government chose a military solution. This war, as others, had its share of tragedy.[16] Many people were killed in several Kurdish towns such as Sannadaj, Meriwan, Sakkiz and Baneh. The Islamic judge, Ayatollah Khalkhali, sentenced to death a large number of Kurdish activists labelled as 'counter-revolutionary'. The Kurds were accused of being pawns of the Americans and the Israelis. The Islamic government reinforced its diplomatic relations with Turkey, which was opposed to any project of autonomy for the Kurds. They decided to devote more attention to the security of their common borders. Tehran assured Ankara that the Iranian government shared its point of views about the Kurds.[17]

But a lot of Pasdars were killed in Kurdistan, and Iranian public opinion was extremely angry. In Tehran, despite the division between pros and cons, the government decided finally to negotiate with the Kurds. Nearly three months after the beginning of the conflict, on 23 October, a 'special delegation for the solution of the Kurdish problem' was created. On 17 November, Ayatollah Khomeini declared that the war was one that had been imposed by Iran's enemies and promised a solution to the economic and social problem of the Kurds. Three days later, at a very large demonstration in Mahabad, the principal Kurdish leader Abdurrahman Ghassemlou declared that the Kurds would be defending the unity of Iran and that they would accept negotiations.

The Kurds also formed their own delegation, which contained one represent-ative of each political party, with Sheikh Ezzedinn Husseini as an independent personality and a spokesman on behalf of the DPIK.

But the government delegation refused to meet with some political parties it considered 'extremist', especially Komala and Fedai. That was obviously a pretext to avoid negotiation. The government would not accept the Kurdish project of autonomy.[18] The Kurdish delegation never received an official proposal for discussing the future of Kurdistan. On 10 December, in the evening daily paper *Etelaat*, the government published a proposal for 'self-government' of the Kurdish area, which was in fact, a decentralized admin-istrative project.

The Kurds did not accept the government's proposal. They emphasized the fact that there was no mention of political rights, nor of any special measure to prevent discrimination against the Kurds. On the other hand, they did not receive any official document on which the negotiation could be based.

The Kurds were not to have any other occasion to meet with the authorities, which were greatly preoccupied with other problems.[19] They boycotted the referendum for the Constitution (2–3 December 1979) and the presidential election (25 January 1980), but took part in the legislative election (14 February 1980). The Ministry of the Interior cancelled this election in the Kurdish area, officially because of the presence of 'armed groups'.

At the beginning of the spring of 1980, war began in earnest between the Kurds and the government forces,[20] who took control of all the major Kurdish towns. The Kurds were left with some 'liberated zones' in the mountains and villages of Kurdistan in Iran.

At the outbreak of the Iran–Iraq War (22 September 1980), the DPIK declared itself ready to join the Iranian army against Iraq, if the government would accept the autonomy project for Kurdistan and if it would agree to remove the Pasdaran from the whole Kurdish area. But the government made the opposite choice. Several army corps, including Pasdaran units, had bedded down in Kurdistan, which became an interior front, where a low-intensity war was running against the Kurds.

The Kurdish resistance, which had to leave for Iraqi Kurdistan by 1984, received some logistical help from the Iraqi regime. In June 1981, the DPIK jointed the National Council of Iranian Resistance (NCIR) created by the People's Mojahideen (of Iran) and the former Republic President, A.H. Bani Sadr.[21]

Between 1981 and 1989, the political situation in Iran was horrifying. In addition to the negative consequences of the war with Iraq, more than 30,000 Iranian activists were sentenced to death in the prisons by the theocratic regime. The Kurds were not spared this repression. The DPIK's general secret-ary, Dr Ghassemlou, was assassinated in Vienna on 13 July 1989, while he was meeting with the emissary of the Islamic Republic. Three years later, on 17 September 1992, his successor, M. Sadegh Sharafkandi, was also assassinated in Berlin, where he was attending the International Socialist Congress.[22]

In 1993, under pressure from Tehran, the two main Kurdish political parties of Iraqi Kurdistan, the Democratic Party of Kurdistan (DPK) and the Patriotic Union of Kurdistan (PUK) asked the DPIK to leave the Kandil Mountains (located on the Iran-Iraq border) for Koy Sindjak, a small town located between Arbil and Sulaymanieh in Iraqi Kurdistan. Since then, more than three hundred members and sympathizers of the DPIK and Komala have been killed in Iraqi Kurdistan by the Iranian forces with total impunity.

In 1996, under the escort of PUK peshmergas, two thousand Pasdars crossed the border in order to bomb the DPIK's camps. Fortunately, no one was killed because the DPIK had been previously informed of the Pasdaran's plan. Since then, the Iranian Kurdish resistance has continued to go through a period of retreat.[23]

***

What has happened to the Kurdish population in Iran? How have they dealt with the regime? What is their political, social and economic situation?

The Iranian Kurds had to wait until 1997, when Mohammad Khatami, a 'reformist' was elected president of the Islamic Republic. Several Kurdish intellectuals were elected members of the Parliament. They formed the first Kurdish faction of MPs in the Islamic Assembly and asked for the application of Articles 15 and 19 of the Constitution,[24] but the Ministry of Information opposed this demand. Some NGOs were formed, but in reality they are governmental organizations: on the one hand, they depend on public subsidy; on the other, they are under control of the security services. Nevertheless, they have some attraction for young people and women. The Islamic Republic presents these structures as representative of civil society, but in fact all political activities are forbidden and there is no Kurdish political party in Iran. Islamic courts sentenced to death several Kurdish activists, and there are still numerous Kurdish political prisoners in Iran. In 2004, Louis Joinet, a UN expert on torture, who had at least been allowed by the Iranian authorities to visit the prisons and who could speak to some of the prisoners and their family, said that Iran was one huge prison. The election of Mahmoud Ahmadinejad[25] as the president of the Islamic Republic on June 2005 put an end to the reformist 'spring' in Iran. Power is now in the hands of the most fanatical elements of the Republic.

Several Kurdish intellectuals, led by a former member of Parliament, B. Adab, a native of Sanandaj, created the 'Unified Front of Kurds' in January 2006. Their project is based on the Iranian Constitution. They have asked for some reforms in order to improve the cultural, economic and social situation of the Kurdish area, and the application of the Articles 15 and 12 of the Constitution.[26] They emphasize the religious aspect of the Kurdish population and there is no mention of political rights.

The Kurdish population in Iran feels excluded for both national and religious reasons. Like the majority of the Iranian population, the Kurds must endure political repression, but they are also qualified as separatists and accused of being a potential danger to the unity of Iran. Since the collapse of Saddam Hussein's regime in Iraq, Iran has reinforced its relationships with Syria and Turkey. Several meetings have been held between these countries to prevent the creation of a Kurdish state in the north of Iraq. Tehran, Ankara and Damascus continue with their anti-Kurdish politics. According to BBC Persian section, on 4 April 2006, Firouz Dolatabadi, the Iranian Ambassador in Ankara declared that 'to face the danger of an independent Kurdish state supported by the USA, and which threatens the integrity of our two countries, we must take joint measures.'

Since then, Turkey, which had already gathered more than 250,000 solders on the border with Iran and Iraq, added 50,000 others to prevent any incursions by the PKK (Kurdish Workers Party) from Iraqi Kurdistan. On 21 April, the Iranian Army bombed some positions of the PJAK (Party of Free Life in Kurdistan, close to the PKK) in Iraqi Kurdistan.

Even intellectuals very often consider the Kurdish question in Iran a potential danger for the integrity of the country. There is, in fact, a real amalgam between the recognition of the basic rights of the Kurds and the danger of a probable partition of Iran. Some Iranian reviews have published articles about the Kurds. They admit that Kurdistan is one of the most underdeveloped regions in Iran and call for economical measures and some form of freedom. But, actually their main effort is to prevent Iraqi Kurdistan's situation from rubbing off on other Iranians.

But the situation is changing in Iranian Kurdistan. A new generation of Kurdish students is trying to make a scientific and critical analysis of the Kurds' situation in general. They are asking for the recognition of the basic rights of the Iranian Kurds. They follow closely and enthusiastically the situation of the Federal Region of Iraqi Kurdistan.

The two main Kurdish political parties, the DPIK and the two branches of Komala,[27] are heavily penalized by their forced exile in Iraqi Kurdistan.[28] They think that the Islamic nature of the Iranian regime does not permit any pacific and democratic solution for the Kurdish problem in Iran. They want the end of the Islamic Republic and the creation of a democratic and federal Republic. They continue to be part of the Iranian opposition because the Iraqi Kurdish political parties adopted the state logic regarding their relations with Tehran. But the situation is developing positively. Massoud Barzani, the president of the federal Kurdish Region in Iraq, has declared that, from now on, no Kurd will find it acceptable to shoot another Kurd.[29]

As for the Iranian opposition, the fact is that they carefully trying to avoid a discussion of the Kurdish problem in general. They clearly situate it in an Iranian context. Some of them accept that Iranian Kurds have suffered discrimination but the Kurdish problem is very often considered as an economic problem.

The Iranian Kurds, who live close to the Azeris, also have some local problems of their own. Azeri nationalists are not ready to accept that a part of Kurdish territory should be included in the province of Western Azerbaijan.[30] They consider this province Azeri, and this is already a problem as regards the Kurdish population.

On the whole, the political situation is very critical. The people are unsatisfied. A minor local problem can generate a huge consequence. Political life is empty. The traditional Kurdish political parties are prohibited. This situation pushes some people to join the most radical branch of Islam, the Salafis. Drugs and prostitution are spreading into Kurdistan, where social structures have previously been extremely traditional.

As regards the economic situation, one can say that Iranian Kurdistan is one of the less developed areas in Iran. This is the consequence of a deliberate political choice, which was made by the monarchy.[31]

Under the Islamic Republic, the economic situation of Kurdistan has not changed. The rate of public investment is extremely low in the Kurdish region. As a result, few people work in industrial and mining sectors whereas the tertiary sector is flourishing. This is an indication of the imbalance of the economic situation.[32] For example, in 1995, the amount of money spent on 77 projects in the province of Kurdistan corresponded to the amount spent on only 17 projects in the province of Isfahan. Unemployment is one of the highest of Iran. In 1999, when the average rate of unemployment in Iran was about 12.5 per cent, it was 21.5 per cent in Kurdistan province, 18.9 per cent in Western Azerbaijan, 16.5 per cent in Kermanshah and 15 per cent in Ilam.[33]

As a consequence, Kurdistan is also one of the poorest regions in Iran. The province of Kurdistan occupies the rank of 24 in the index of human poverty (IHP), just before the provinces of Sistan and Baluchistan and Kohgiluyeh and Boyer Ahmad. One of the negative consequences of this situation is the high rate of suicide, especially among women, in the Kurdish region. In 2004, Tehran had 404 cases of suicide. The Kurdish province of Ilam was in second place with 381, 212 of whom were women. Ilam retained the first place in relation to the number of its inhabitants.[34]

Few Kurdish executives are employed in Kurdistan. The government has a security approach to the Kurdish area and the Kurdish people. The Kurds are officially considered to be the defenders of their borders, but in reality they are accused of being separatists. Fifty-three per cent of the inhabitants of Sanandaj estimate that the government does not respect the principle of equality between the ethnic groups in Iran.[35] From 1980 to 1997, no Sunni Kurdish executives participated in the administration of affairs in the Kurdish area. In 1997, one Shia Kurdish governor was nominated and a few other Kurdish executives were employed in the province of Kurdistan. There are two possible explanations for this: either there is a lack of Kurdish executives, which would denote a lack of public investment to train them, or there are enough Kurdish executives, but they are not being employed on any large scale in their own area.

President Ahmadinejad's government does not seem to want to change anything in Kurdistan. Some members of Parliament accuse the government of not meeting the real needs of the most underdeveloped regions.[36] It would be interesting to find out what percentage of the 2006 budget has been dedicated to the Kurdish region.

***

In spite of the lack of public investment, the Kurdish cultural situation is excellent. Faced with the suppression of political activities, Kurdish society is concentrating its efforts in the cultural sector. The Kurdish language is not taught as a regional language at school despite Article 15 of the Constitution, which decides that Persian is the official language but provides also the teaching of regional languages in public schools.

However, books, reviews, magazines and papers are published in Kurdish[37] although in Iran all publication is censored. The editors must present published books to the Ministry of Information. To avoid problems, they practise self-censorship. If publishers fail to pass the censor, they will lose their investment, and very often, they must destroy their books. As a result, some Kurdish writers therefore publish their books in Iraqi Kurdistan.

Publications in the Kurdish language have incontestably helped journalists and writers to publish very complicated texts, and Kurdish students have their own publication.[38] However, there is a lack of public investment, of training centres for journalists, syndicates or committees of writers. Thus, for an evaluation of the quality of these publications, only comparative studies in the next fifty years will permit a scientific and critical approach.

Recently the DPIK and the two branches of Komala established their own television channel, while Iranian public television also has a Kurdish channel. Each of them tries to inform the Kurdish public with its own vision of things. Iranian Kurds, who already watch other Kurdish television channels,[39] ignore the official channel.

Music is an important part of Kurdish life. Kurdish music is rich and varied.[40] Several Kurdish music groups exist in Iran, the most well-known being *Kamkar, Youssef Zamani* and *Andalibi*. Singers such as Shahram Nazeri and instrumentalists such as Ali Akbar Moradi and Keyhan Kalhor give concerts in Iran, and also in Iraqi and Turkish Kurdistan, as well as in Europe and the US.

Iranian Kurds are also very interested in cinema. One of the most well-known Iranian directors, Bahman Ghobadi, is a Kurd. [41]

The Iranian Kurdish Diaspora is also very keen on intellectual and cultural activities, publishing dual-language dictionaries in some European languages (English, German, Swedish, Finnish, Danish, etc.), dubbing films and translating European literature into Kurdish.[42]

***

In conclusion, one can say that, like other Kurds, Iranian Kurds have a very clear notion of their identity. They know that they are part of the Kurdish nation. Most of them reject violence and desire a peaceful solution to the Kurdish problem. But neither political nor identity problems seem to have a quick resolution. The government tries to impose Islamic rule and refuses to recognize the political rights of either Kurds or other Iranian minorities. This regime considers that the entire Iranian population is part of the *Ummah* (Muslim nation). It estimates that what distinguishes people from each other is virtue. All society actors capable of opening up this society to tolerance and to respect for individual and collective rights must kept under control. Their situation is getting more and more difficult. Between October and November 2006 several Kurdish people, including journalists, teachers, trade unionists and human rights activists, were arrested.[43]

A portion of the Iranian population actually thinks that only foreign military intervention can change the situation, even if they do not measure the consequences. Others support the Islamic government, which monopolizes almost all the economical, political and military power in Iran.

Whatever the future will be, two questions must be answered. Will Iranian public opinion, including political activists and citizens, accept the existence of the Kurdish problem and the necessity of finding an adequate solution? Will Kurdish representatives be in a political mature mind to be able to have a discussion based on equality, solidarity and freedom with the central authorities?

Soheira Ghaderi-Mameli has a PhD in international relations from the Sorbonne.

NOTES

1   Actually 10 per cent of the population of this province are not Kurds. This is the result of a deliberated political decision, which tends to mix the population in the Kurdish area, which was the case in Iraqi Kurdistan under Saddam Hussein's regime.

2   She was arrested on 2 August at his home in Sanandaj and was accused of 'undermining the national security' and 'disturbing the public order'. When she was released in October, she revealed that she was been tortured and raped in prison. She left Iran and became a political refugee in the United States.

3   Reza Amini, Halmet Azadpour and Abdolah Mohammadi.

4   In 1979, the Kurds boycotted the referendum for the establishment of the Islamic Republic and the first presidential elections.

5   These were Ayatollah Khomeini in Qom, the temporary government of Mehdi Bazargan in Tehran and the Council of the Revolution.

6   Hashem Sahabian, *'Hey'at-é vijéy-é hal-é masa'l-é kordostan'* ('The special delegation for the problems of Kurdistan'), in *Tcheshmandaz-é Iran*, special edition 'Kurdistan', April 2003, p. 51.

7   Ahmad Muftizadeh didn't have any religious function, but Sheikh Ezzedine Husseini was the imam of Mahabad's mosque.

8   The Kurdish political organization submitted a proposal, which contained eight items. Seven of them were related to the Kurdish problem in Iran, and the last one asked the government to expel the Kurdish Democratic Party of Iraq from Iran. This organization was founded by Mustafa Barzani, and after the defeat of 1975, it was located in Iran. The relationship between this organization and the Iranian Kurdish political parties, especially, the DPIK, suffered for many years. Since its creation, Komala was supported by the Patriotic Union of Kurdistan, led by Jalal Talabani.

9   One of the Kurdish leaders, Dr Abdurrahman Ghassemlou, proposed to call it the University of Imam Khomeini.

10   From 18–22 March, the Peshmergas (the Kurdish militia) opposed the security forces in the military base of Sanandaj. Iranian Army helicopters and artillery fire killed 450 people.

11   The Pasdaran (the Guardians of the Republic) are the Islamic militia. This army corps, which later became an important economic force in Iran, contains the most fanatical partisans of the Islamic Republic of Iran.

12   The Kurds considered that the wording of the referendum question ('Do you support the Islamic Republic, yes or no?') prevented a truly democratic choice. They also noted the absence of any information about the nature of the Islamic Republic and wondered about democratic rights.

13   The Azeri militia headed by Mullah Hassani used the pretext of the presence of the Peshmergas in the first DPIK's meeting in Naghada.

14   The Central Committee of the DPIK, which was informed about the hostility of the new authorities, decided to not allow their General Secretary to go to Tehran. Ayatollah Khomeini was very disappointed because he wanted 'to retain' him there.

15   Paweh is a small town located in the north of Kermanshah province. Lethal conflict broke out between the Pasdaran, headed by Mustafa Tchamran, and the Peshmerga of the DPIK between 11–18 August. Twenty people, including the DPIK's representative for Paweh, were killed.

16   At the beginning of the conflict, the Pasdaran killed 56 inhabitants of the village of Qalatan and the whole of the inhabitants of Qarna. These two villages are located close to Naghadeh. The Kurdish opposition described this massacre as the Sabra and Chatila of the Kurdistan.

17   Dr Ahmad Sadr Hadj Seyyed Djawadi, Minister of Justice in the Bazargan government, in *Tcheshmandaz-é Iran*, April 2003, p. 43.

18   The Kurdish eminent jurist and lawyer, S.S. Vaziri, prepared this project, which called the proposal on 26 items. It contained very large and detailed proposals regarding the economic, social and political issues for autonomy status for Kurdistan.

19   The US embassy was occupied by the 'revolutionary students' on 4 December and the government

of Mehdi Bazargan resigned on the 6th. Iran had also renounced the treaty of the Friendly Relationships with the USSR of 1921.

20 During the fourth Congress (19–24 February 1980), the DPIK was confronted at its first session. Seven members of the Central Committee, supported by Tudeh (ICP), asked to negotiate with the government. In the absence of any concrete official proposition, the majority of the Party was resolutely opposed to this approach.

21 The DPIK broke off this alliance on 30 March 1985, due to the lack of any democratic process. The NCIR reproached the DPKI for tempting fate with the Islamic Republic. On the other hand, from September 1982 and for three months, the DPIK and Komala had engaged in a fratricidal war, which considerably reduced the Kurdish movement and seriously damaged its credibility.

22 The DPIK has a conservative status in International Socialist Movement.

23 On 6 December 2006, the DPIK again split into two factions, due to organizational problems.

24 According to Article 15, the official language of Iran is Persian (Farsi) but other regional languages can be used in schools and by the media. According to Article 19, every ethnic group is considered to be equal in rights and there will be no distinction between them.

25 Mr Ahmadi Nejad is one of the founders of Al-Quds brigade, which is known for some suicide attacks in Lebanon and the murder abroad of some opposition leaders, especially Kurdish ones. He is supported by the ultra-conservative branch of Iranian Shias, the Hojjatiyya, which refuses the principle of the Supreme Leader, and adheres to belief in the immanent reappearance of Mahdi, the hidden twelfth and last imam in the Shia hierarchy.

26 According to Article 12, the Iranian official religion is Shi'a Asna Ashari, but the adepts of the other branches of Islam, primarily the Sunni, must be respected and they are allowed to carry out some civil acts (marriage, divorce, inheritance, etc.) in keeping with their religious beliefs.

27 In July 2000, Komala was divided in two parts: the Communist Party of Iran and its Kurdish branch called Komala, and Komala. Both claim the name of Komala and ask for a democratic and socialist regime in Iran, but only one Komala asks for a federal statute for the Iranian Kurdistan.

28 Iranian Kurds respect these parties because despite their difficulties, they maintain the aims of Kurdish national movement.

29 *Hurriyet*, 6 April 2006.

30 This part of Kurdish territory was once part of the Mokri region. In the territorial reorganization of Iran in the nineteenth century, the Mokri region was divided into two parts: one was included in Western Azerbaijan province and another in the Kurdistan province.

31 Under this regime a huge part of the budget was funded to the area located close to Tehran. So the Fourth Plan for Economic Development (1963–75) provided 46 per cent to the Central province, whereas the provinces of Kermanshah and Kurdistan received just 2.4 per cent, Nahid Kouhshekaf, '*Joghrafiyay-é towsé-é va joghrafiya-é ghomi dar barnamehay-é omrani-é dowlat*' ('The geography of development and the ethnical geography in the government projects for development'), in *Gofto-Gou*, No. 43, p. 44.

32 Khaled Tawakoli, '*Kurdistan va vaghé-é dowom-é khordad*' ('Kurdistan and the events of the 2nd Khordad'), in *Gofto-Gou*, No. 43, p. 39.

33 Massoud Sofi Majidpour, '*Negahi bé chakheshay-é towsé dar Iran*' ('Regards on development investments in Iran'), in *Gofto-Gou*, No. 43, p. 85.

34 *Iran, Statistical yearbook, 2004* (Tehran: Markaz-é Amar-é Iran).

35 Majidpour, '*Negahi bé chakheshay-é towsé dar Iran*', p. 86.

36 *Le Monde d'économie*, 21 March 2006.

37 In Sanandaj there are *Sirwan* (weekly), *Rojhalat* (periodical). *Asso* was also a periodical publication, which is now banned. In Mahabad there are *Payami Kurdistan* (weekly) and *Mahabad* (periodical). In Tehran, *Serveh* (periodical) continues to be published, whereas *Ashti* (weekly) is forbidden.

38 In October and November 2006, three Kurdish-Persian student publications of the University of Urmiah (*Manisht*, *Hanaran* and *Trifa*) were banned. This university had already banned two other Kurdish publications, *Rojano* and *Zilan*.

39 Roj TV broadcast from Copenhagen, Kurdistan TV, Kurdsat and Zagro TV from Iraqi Kurdistan.

40 There exist four principal genres in this music: the music of song and dance (*Bazm va Taghazol*),

the music of fight and epic (*Razm va Hemaseh*), the music of heart and mysticism (*Del va Erfan*) and finally the music of conjecture (*Monasebatha*). Interview with A.A. Moradi about Kurdish music, November 2005.

41 Ghobadi's films have been in international festivals and he has won several awards.

42 In 2005, the Iranian Kurds translated more than ten bilingual books (English-Kurdish) for children. They also dubbed two films, *Shrek* and *Madagascar*.

43 Mohammad Sadiq Kaboudwand, Director of the Kurdistan Human Rights organization, who was arrested on 1 May 2006, was sentenced to jail for one year. Loqman Mehri, who is also a member of this organization was sentenced to jail for five years. He was accused of political activities against the Islamic regime. Shirko Jahani, a journalist and a member of the Kurdistan Human Rights organization, was accused of informing foreign journalists about the murder of Shwaneh seyyed Qadir, and again arrested in November. Human rights activists Hemin Weissi and Ibrahim Salehi were also arrested two months ago. Mahmoud Salehi, a Kurdish trade unionist from Sakkez, who was accused of exhorting the workers to attend the 2006 May Day demonstration, was sentenced to jail for four years. Majed Khaledian, Eqbal Jahanmardi, Asaad Khani, Korosh Ranjbar, Sorray Ghassemian (a woman), all teachers in a secondary school in Sanandaj, were accused of political activities against the regime and arrested. Farzad Kamangar, a teacher from Kamyaran and member of Kurdistan Human Rights organisation was arrested in September 2006 and his relatives have had no news of him. In *Rooz*, 30 November 2006.

One, Two or Three Baluchistans?

DELPHINE LECLERCQ

The traditional cultural region of the Baluch people lies in the territories of Iran, Afghanistan and Pakistan. The Baluch are Sunni and speak principally Baluchi and Brahui, both languages of the Persian family. The term 'Baluch' defines members of the second largest tribal group in the western mountainous zone of the Indian subcontinent; it also denotes the inhabitants of Baluchistan, the south-western province of the Islamic Republic of Pakistan, which represents 43 per cent of the total territory of Pakistan. Baluchistan as the land of the Baluch is a colonial construction created by the British in 1846 when they conquered the Brahui Kingdom. The frontiers of this province, to which the British did *not* give the name Brahuistan, does not correspond to the area where the Baluch are distributed in the Iranian Highlands, Sindh and the Punjab.

On 26 August 2006, 'The Tiger of Baluchistan', Akbar Shahbaz Khan Bugti was killed in Kohlu, near Quetta, the capital of Pakistani Baluchistan, where he had taken refuge.[1] As the public face of the movement for the greater autonomy of Baluchistan, he was a pacifist hero and a martyr. As a disloyal Pakistani, accused by the federal government of waging guerilla warfare by militia groups associated with the Baluchistan Liberation Army (BLA),[2] he was Islamabad's public enemy number one. General Pervez Musharraf welcomed his death as a victory. The killing of Bugti resulted in riots that were countered by Rangers and paramilitary forces in major cities of Baluchistan. A curfew was imposed in Quetta. Pakistani and international media have labelled Bugti's murder the '[Pakistani] military's second biggest blunder after Bhutto's execution'[3] and a political nightmare. Such an event as the murder by the government of a leader, who had served in high official positions, resurrects the traumatic Pakistani memories of transformation of eastern Pakistan into Bangladash in 1971. Moreover, his burial under governmental supervision was perceived as a provocation and brought criticism in the Punjab against the rulers in Islamabad. In Baluchistan, a direct consequence of Bugti's death is the renewal of widespread disaffection against the central government and an opportunity for a *Loya Jirga* (traditional court), the first traditional Baluch national Jirga since 1878. Held on 21 September 2006, under the leadership of the Khan of Kalat, the Jirga conferred upon the Khan a symbolic but pertinent revival of power over the tribal assembly, which is composed of seventy Baluch *sardars* (tribal chiefs) from western Iranian and eastern Pakistani Baluchistan, Sindh and the Punjab. The sardars speak different languages, belong to rival tribes and defend different political objectives, but the Loya Jirga was significant because its members share the same pride of being Baluch.

	Iran	Pakistan	Afghanistan
Total Population	68,688,433	165,803,560	31,056,997
Baluch Population	1,370,000	6,000,000	620,000

Source: *CIA World Factbook 2006* (Estimation in July 2006).

The 'great awakening'[4] which took place in Kalat led to a public declaration for an appeal to the International Court of Justice in order to clarify the violation of the 31 March 1948 Autonomy Pact signed on the accession of the independent state of Kalat to the Republic of Pakistan. By making their own position as an 'oppressed nation', the sardars, along with groups and individuals, asserted their common will to attract the attention of international community.

An Idea of National Identity

The idea that Baluchistan could exist as an independent state for the Baluch people is marked by long-term ramifications and a modern definition. The Baluch share the memory of sporadic moments of common rule, such as that of the legendary leader Mir Chakar in the fifteenth century or the Khanate of Kalat in the seventeenth century. After 1947 as traditional Iranian tribal living spaces were destroyed by arbitrary frontiers, the strategic border location of Baluchistan within British India put the Baluchs at a severe disadvantage. The profound and strong sense of individual Baluch identity which has developed inside Pakistan's borders has become a national issue. Self-appointed leaders want to continue putting pressure on the Pakistani government with their demands for a Greater Baluchistan. This would encompass the present Iranian and Pakistani provinces of Baluchistan and portions of southwestern Afghanistan and Sindh. An alternative would be that of an independent Pashtunistan with East Afghanistan and the Pakistani North West Frontier Province and Baluchistan. To maintain their identity in their homelands,

Baluch nationalists claim their rights through a movement which, at times, can be armed. Their grievances concern military domination in Iran and Pakistan, the *sardari* system, the unfair allocation of resources, the lack of decision making at regional and national levels,[5] and the repression of the Baluch language as medium of communication and instruction.[6]

In eastern Baluchistan, during more than thirty years of conflict, 5,000 rebels have been killed as well as 3,000 Pakistani soldiers. A fifth military operation is still attempting to suppress the armed struggle which was reinvigorated in the summer of 2004. Between 1978 and 1994, military rule was in place in the Pakistani province after a gloomy period in the 1970s. Hopes had been raised by the 1970 independence of provinces, resulting in a revival of separatist activities. However, the 1973 Constitution was a disappointment, as it did not give any more autonomy to the provincial governments, and between 1973 and 1977, the guerilla movement grew into a strenuous armed insurrection.

In 1974, 4,000 Baluchi tribesmen were killed when 100,000 men were sent by Bhutto, supported by the Iranian Air Force, to Baluchistan. The struggle had taken the form of a planned resistance for Baluch interests after 1962 under the influence of Marxist-Leninist liberation movements. In 1963, between Mengal and Marri tribal territories, camps were set up which seem to be the seedbeds of the future Baluch People's Liberation Front, whose post-1973 younger generation had opted to struggle for outright independence.

Regional Involvements

In Pakistan, tribal conflicts have spilled over tribal boundaries and have spread to the coast. Attacks are on the increase in Gwadar where the Baluch National Movement (BNM) is popular among the middle class. With a younger, educated leadership, the movement imposes itself as the arbitrator of rivalries, which Islamabad has been unable to handle despite arresting leaders, patronage and disinformation. Pakistan's imperialist military rule has facilitated separatism among the Baluch, who are aware of the strategic and economic importance of the province.

In Iran, the Baluchis are in the majority in the south-eastern frontier region of Sistan-Baluchistan; they are also present in Kerman and Khorasan provinces. As in eastern Baluchistan, the region is the least developed in Iran in spite of its natural resources and geographical advantages. The people are largely illiterate, less urban, and eager to maintain their cultural and traditional heritage. Under the secular Pahlavi government, close relationships with tribal leaders had improved limited self-government in Sistan-Baluchistan. However, after the Islamic Revolution, in 1980, a non-Baluchi Shia governor was appointed and any resistance to the dominant rule was curbed violently.[7] Ever since, the western Baluchis have been active in occasional armed resistance, which is quite difficult to identify owing to the absence of any defined political parties and illegal organizations. Moreover, many refugees and guerrillas in the region are linked to the Afghan war.

On the vast and permeable Iranian-Pakistani border, drug trafficking is a major industry which generates lucrative profits. Zahedan, capital of the Iranian Sistan-Baluchistan province, is a centre for worldwide drugs trading. According to the 1997 report of the *Observatoire Géopolitique des Drogues*, the region is the location *par excellence* to observe the geopolitics of the drug trade. Every day, Baluchis go to Afghanistan to exchange petrol for Afghan opium from the Pashtun provinces of Helmand and Nangarhar. The opium is transformed into heroin in laboratories set up on the border by Afghan leaders and local businessmen under the protection of Inter-Services Intelligence (ISI), the Pakistani military intelligence service. The drugs then pass into Iran via Zahedan and in the north via Taybad in Khorasan. Profits from the southern opium trade route compensate for the lack of traditional economic activities in Baluchi society. According to Interpol, a hundred tonnes of heroin per year cross between the north and south of Pakistan to be smuggled on to Europe. This southern axis is potentially better than that of Central Asia, because it requires only one or two border crossings between Afghanistan and Iran. The traffickers, being well armed and with a perfect knowledge of the region, have the ways of crossing into Iran despite a secure border guarded by a strong Iranian surveillance.

Presence of arms among the tribesmen is a recurrent issue in the Pakistani media. In the Pakistani press, questions are raised as to how rebels can be in possession of sophisticated arms. Pakistan accuses India, Iran and the United States of America for this proliferation of weapons. In August 2004, the Baluchistan Chief Minister said that external elements, including the Indian intelligence agency Research and Analysis Wing (RAW), played a role in the increased trouble in the strategically important zone of Gwadar. Islamabad believes Delhi to be active in Baluchistan in order to divert attention from Kashmir where a low-intensity war has been going on for nearly sixty years. Security and stability in the region that is a bridge to the Indian subcontinent, is essential because it is a potential-crossing point for a natural gas pipeline to India from Iran and Turkmenistan. This facility would have an impact on both regional and global energy needs, and Pakistan and Iran have fundamental financial and geopolitical interests in the project. In addition to which, the absence of American involvement in the project – due to the change in their attitude towards Afghanistan at the end of 1990s – leaves them with more room to manoeuver. Unocal Company has ended its activities in the pipeline project across Afghanistan. President George Bush is still opposed to it because of an intended ramification of the project, which would connect Gwadar to China.

The Strait of Hormuz is a crucial route for international oil distribution. The port of Gwadar on the Baluchistan belt, between the Strait and Persian Gulf, is one of the three Pakistani naval bases and would become the most important because it would serve more than twenty countries. Built and financed by the Chinese, the first phase of construction has been accomplished with limited-capacity installations. By 2010 it will be accessible to 200,000-tonne oil tankers. As a consequence, the economic centre of the region will move to the south and will generate economic activities with railway networks and roads connections to Afghanistan and Central Asia.

However, in March 2005, widespread strikes and protests forced General Musharraf to cancel his visit to Gwadar with the Chinese Prime Minister. Failure to consult the Baluch people about these momentous developments helps the Baluchi nationalist movements to maintain their rhetoric against Islamabad's attitude as an alien power that develops Baluchistan in pursuit of its own interests. The central government squeezes out wealth from the province while denying any royalties from mineral resources to the Baluchis. It becomes all the more important because Baluchistan's natural resources represent 20 per cent of all Pakistan's mineral and energy resources and 36 per cent of Pakistan's gas production. Through the decades-old controversy over natural gas by the Sui company,[8] independence movements call for land repossession and the sharing of natural gas revenues at the National Finance Commission (NFC) Award. Considering their extracted resources as an import substitute, they demand the return of more than $100 billion to the Baluchistan government. Moreover, Baluchis own 2 per cent of the Siandak Copper and Gold Project and their objective is to obtain revenues and taxes from the federal government. In 2004, the Chief Minister of Baluchistan made the demand for a share in the NFC Award on the basis of revenue generation, as had been done in Sindh. If fact, billions of rupees are allocated to the Gwadar Development Authority. According to the Pakistani Information Minister, 60 per cent of the country's development expenditure will be concentrated in that province.

Future Implications for World Politics

The United States is already conducting military operations in Afghanistan from bases in Pasni (Las Bela) and Dalbandin (Mekran) in Baluchistan. At the same time General Musharraf has failed to produce results in Waziristan. Afghanistan and the US accuse Quetta of being a base for Taliban resurgence. In this context it is possible to imagine that if the Afghan situation veers out of control for Washington, could the Baluch Nationalist Movement be considered as a potential tool of influence in the region by the US? At best the Americans could use the BNM as a measure of putting diplomatic pressure on Islamabad and Teheran. Without considering the Afghan question, could the Americans, already present in Baluchistan on the western Iranian border, envisage it as a strategic point for an eventual military intervention in Iran? As Frédéric Grare[9] points out: 'Some Pakistanis suspect that Washington would like to use Baluchistan as a rear base for an attack on Iran ... They do not make clear which side the Americans are on: whether they are opposing the Baluch nationalists because they are supported by Iran or whether they are supporting the Baluch because they are hostile to the Chinese ... So far nobody has been able to prove any of these accusations.' Nevertheless, *The New Yorker*[10] confirms that US commandos have launched penetration initiatives across Pakistani Baluchistan into Iran. Regarding the US presence in the region, the following question becomes more relevant: what could be their real ambitions or agenda in Central Asia? Effectively, they may be trying to rein in Chinese ambitions in Central Asia, while at the same time, looking at the prospects for their own oil supply from the Middle East, with special attention on Gwadar. On its side, Iran is afraid of Pakistan's interest in Central Asia, linked, among others, to interest in the pipeline and in India.

In Pakistan, can Baluchistan irredentism set the precedent for other provinces where there is a feeling of a lack of national integration? *Muttahidda Qaumi Mahaz* (MQM) – a nationalist movement of *Mohajirs*, principally present in urban Sindh – has already held a Jirga. There is the fear that the Baluch nationalist movement could degenerate into what we could call the 'Bengali syndrome' of 1971.[11] There is little possibility that the denial of Baluch rights will be put on the international agenda, though there is an option of involving an international forum, such as the International Court of Justice or the United Nations but Pakistan has ways of countering this. In fact, old pacts as that of Kalat are less relevant in the present geopolitical situation and leave too little a room for manoeuvring. In Pakistan, as in Iran, there is a need to engage the discontented population in politics instead of militancy. Nationalist and regional parties must be brought into the mainstream to balance out Punjabi domination and to create a wider sense of national inclusion as a safeguard against the threat of disintegration. There is a real danger of this because of the presence of a large Baluch community in Sindh, especially in Karachi, the economic backbone of Pakistan.

We can conclude by stating that while we focus on Baluchistan, we also have the USA, India, Central Asia, Afghanistan and Iran – Pakistan in mind. The complicated and ambiguous interactions within the region are linked, more or less with western Baluchistan and even more so with eastern Baluchistan. All such interactions have consequences on what is considered in

Baluchistan as the Baluchi national question and in Islamabad, as that of national law and order.

Delphine Leclercq is a PhD student in geopolitics at the Sorbonne.

NOTES

1   Akbar Shahbaz Khan Bugti (1927–2006). Educated in Oxford, he was the *Tumandar* of the Bugti tribes of Baluchistan in Pakistan. Elected to the National Assembly of Pakistan in May 1958 and appointed as a State Minister, his government was deposed by Iskander Mirza in October 1958. After being barred from public office, he supported his brother's campaign for the National Awami Party in 1970 but tensions led to the dissolution of Baluchistan Provincial Assembly by the then President, Zulfiqar Ali Bhutto, on 14 February 1973. He then became Governor of Baluchistan until he resigned in January 1974 during the military intervention in the province. In 1988, he joined the Baluchistan National Alliance and was elected Chief Minister in February 1989. He created his own political party, the *Jamhoori Watan Party* (JWP), the largest single provincial party in Baluchistan, which was introduced in the National Assembly in 1993. Bugti had led several armed struggles during the1950s, '60s and '70s. Since 2005, he had been targeted by air attacks, which forced him to leave his fiefdom in Dera Bugti.

2   In Islamabad, the BLA is banned as being a 'Great Threat' to law and order in Baluchistan, The party is also banned in London. Active since the early 1980s, this clandestine militant group was supported indirectly by Moscow until 1991.

3   'Media slams killing of Nawab Bugti', *The Indian Express*, 29 August 2006.

4   Kachkol Ali Baluch, the opposition leader in Baluchistan Assembly Press Conference on <www.Balochwarna.org>.

5   National Assembly 1971 (4 of 300 seats for Western Pakistan), National Assembly 2002 (11 of 272 seats) in. Talbot Ian, *Pakistan, A Modern History*, London: Hurst & Compagny, 1998, 2005.

6   Speaking Baluchi is forbidden in formal and public places. No press freedom exists in Baluchistan.

7   Amnesty International has put Baluchis on a list of groups especially subject to human rights violations in Iran in 1993.

8   In February 2005, the rape of a woman in Sui, the principal gas-producing center in Baluchistan under the control of Akbar Bugti, incited attacks on the gas fields which brought retaliation from General Musharraf.

9   Frédéric Grare, *Pakistan: The Resurgence of Baluch Nationalism*, Carnegie Papers No. 65, January 2006.

10 Seymour Hersh, 'The Coming Wars: What the Pentagon can now do in secret', *The New Yorker*, 24 January 2005.

11 The 'Bengali syndrome' is the traumatic experience of western Pakistanis in 1971 when the eastern side of Pakistan seceded to become Bangladesh. Present-day west Pakistanis are haunted by memories of this event, and remain fearful of new secessions.

PART IV
The Shiite Empire

Iran's Role in the Radicalization of the Sunni–Shia Divide

ELY KARMON

The war in Iraq has produced a tremendous change in the Middle East and in the Muslim world at large. For the first time in history, an Arab country is controlled by the Shia. The West does not grasp yet the full meaning of the Shia revival and the potential for deep change in many of the countries in the region and their regimes where Shiites represent the majority or an important minority.

In a concise and persuasive article, Vali Nasr examines the background to the Shia revival in Iraq after the fall of Saddam Hussein and its implications for the larger Middle East. He stresses the role of the Iranian revolution of 1979 in mobilizing the Shia identity and pushing for specifically Shia agendas by supporting financially and politically groups such as Amal in Lebanon, al-Da'waa al-Islamiya (the Islamic Call) in Iraq, Hizb-i Wahdat (Party of Unity) in Afghanistan, and Tahrik-i Jafaria (Shia Movement) in Pakistan. The Tehran–Damascus axis is part of Iran's Shia expansionist agenda and enabled it to establish Hezbollah in Lebanon, supporting the organization throughout the 1980s and 1990s to confront the US presence in Lebanon and entrench Iranian influence among Lebanese. According to Nasr, revolutionary Iran failed to alter the balance of power between the Shia and Sunnis across the region and ultimately gave up trying to do so, while the Saudis became the defenders of Sunnism and the symbol of its resistance to Shia 'usurpers'.[1]

According to this view, Saudi Arabia for its part was motivated by the desire both to control its own Shia minority and to thwart Khomeini's challenge to the Islamic legitimacy of the kingdom. Riyadh's investment in Sunni militancy did not raise much concern in the West in the 1980s and the 1990s, for during that period Iran and its brand of Shia militancy were viewed as the most dangerous face of Islam and the main threat to Western interests. The Shia were then associated with anti-Americanism, revolution, terrorism, hostage taking, and suicide bombing. Nasr considers that after Khomeini's death in 1988, Shia militancy ceased to be the ideological force that animated Islamic activism and was replaced by Sunni militancy following the 1991

Gulf War, at least partially if not primarily as a response to the Shia activism that followed the Iranian Revolution.[2]

Saddam's fall has radically changed that balance by empowering the Shia majority, and the Shia–Sunni competition for power has emerged as the greatest determinant of peace and stability in Iraq directly influencing the broader region from Lebanon to Pakistan. However, the Shia revival and the decline in Sunni power in Iraq had not created Sunni militancy; it has invigorated and emboldened it. The anti-Shia violence that plagues Iraq today was first manifested in South Asia and Afghanistan in the 1990s by militant groups with ties to the Taliban and Al Qaeda. The bombings in Baghdad, Kerbala, Najaf and other Shia strongholds in Iraq have claimed many lives but these attacks closely resemble acts in Mashad, Karachi, Quetta, and Mazar-i Sharif since the early 1990s. The current sectarian threat in Iraq is therefore more the product of a deeply rooted rivalry in the region than the direct result of recent developments in Iraq.[3]

Finally, Nasr claims that today Sunni militancy and Wahhabi activism, not Shia revolutionary fervour, pose the greatest danger to US interests, because it is an ascendant, violent, ideological force that is not only anti-Shia but also virulently anti-American. He considers Shia revolutionary activism as essentially a spent force with Iran 'currently a tired dictatorship teetering on the verge of collapse'. Shiism, he claims, no longer produces the kind of ideological politics that Sunnism continues to generate. Moreover, he considers the Shia-dominated countries of Iran and Iraq are better positioned to achieve economic growth and democracy than their Sunni neighbors (with the exception of Turkey).[4]

The problem is that Nasr's article was published in the summer of 2004, before the election of Mahmoud Ahmadinejad as president of Iran, before the radicalization of Tehran's policy on the nuclear issue and the clash with the UN and the international community, and before the latest violent crisis against Israel initiated by Hamas and Hezbollah in the clear framework of an Iranian destabilization strategy of the Middle East.

The Sunni–Shia Divide

The numerous religious, political, socio-economic and sometimes ethnic conflicts between Sunni and Shia communities throughout the Muslim world impact on the behaviour of the more radical organizations and also the supportive state players, which can use these conflicts for ideological or tactical reasons to increase the solidarity with allied groups. The existence of two parallel Islamist trends, the revolutionary Iranian Shia model as opposed to the radical Sunni Wahhabi or Salafi one, affects the ideology and strategy of the numerous violent groups active in the Muslim world, as clearly proved in the open terrorist war between Sunni and Shia groups in Pakistan, Afghanistan and in Iraq and these days on the issue of Hezbollah's war against Israel.

According to the Syrian poet Ali Ahmad Said Isbir:

> The history of the Muslims since the inception of the Islamic State [is] a continuous endless war, with the aim of negating pluralism inside Islam on the basis of a single simple power center with its sources in a unique religion. This war has never ended: in a way or another its flames were never spent, not only among the two antagonistic groups, the Sunni and the Shia, but also among other less known and less involved ones.[5]

The Shia number around 130 million people globally, some 10 per cent of the world's 1.3 billion Muslims. The overwhelming majority of Shia (approximately 120 million) live in the area between Lebanon and Pakistan, where they constitute the majority population in Iran, Iraq, Bahrain and Azerbaijan, as well as the single-largest community in Lebanon, and sizeable minorities in various Gulf emirates, Saudi Arabia, Pakistan, and Afghanistan (and in neighbouring countries such as India and Tajikistan and in East Africa). From the marshes of southern Iraq to the ghettoes of Karachi, the Shia have been the underdogs – oppressed and marginalized by Sunni ruling regimes and majority communities.

Pakistan's Bloody Sectarian War

The Pakistani Shia community representing 15 to 20 per cent of the population, that is, about 25 million people and traditionally linked to the ulema of Najaf, stayed away from politics till the mid-1970s. The Iranian Revolution, the Iran–Iraq War, the transposition on Pakistani soil of the rivalry between Iran and Saudi Arabia and the Islamization policy launched by General Zia ul Haq from 1979 with the aim of transforming Pakistan into a Sunni state, all these factors contributed to a religious and political mobilization of the Shia community. The *Tehrik-e Nifaz-e Fiqh-e Jaafria* (TNFJ) later renamed *Tehrik-e Jaafria Pakistan* (TEJ), a religious movement founded in 1980, became more radical from 1985 on and under the leadership of Allama Arif Hussein al Husseini transformed itself into a political party in 1987. His assassination in 1988 marked the start of widespread sectarian violence which has continued since the early 1990s.[6] To counter the growing political assertiveness of the Shias and their political party the TEJ, Zia-ul-Haq, Pakistan's military dictator of the 1980s, encouraged and assisted Sunni extremist organizations such as the *Sipah-e-Sahaba Pakistan* (SSP).

The anti-Shia campaign and violence in Pakistan have been largely the work of the militant Deobandi-Wahabi, who are a minority in Pakistan, but enjoy tremendous influence because of the support of the military-intelligence establishment and the seemingly inexhaustible flow of funds from Saudi Arabia.[7]

The bloody sectarian war between Pakistan's Shiites and Sunnis caused a total of 1,784 Pakistanis casualties and another 4,279 injured persons across the country between January 1989 and 31 May 2005. And there are indications that the trends may worsen. Thus, 187 persons were killed and another 619 were injured in 19 incidents of sectarian violence in 2004. Within the first five months of 2005, 120 Pakistanis have lost their lives, and 286 have been injured in 30 incidents of sectarian violence.[8]

An aggravating feature of this sectarian violence has been the growing number of suicide bombings in or near mosques or holy shrines and mutual assassinations of major religious leaders. Thus, on 19 March 2005, fifty people were killed and over a hundred others injured during a bomb explosion near the shrine of a Shia saint at Fatehpur village in the Baluchistan province; on 27 May 2005, at least 25 people were killed and approximately a hundred others injured during a suicide bombing at the Bari Imam Shia shrine in the capital Islamabad; on 9 February 2006, forty people were killed and fifty others wounded in a suspected suicide attack on a Muharram procession of Shia Muslims in the Hangu town of North West Frontier Province.[9]

Al Qaeda groups and affiliates were directly involved in this sectarian conflict. Pakistani Sunni, Taliban and Al Qaeda combatants fought together in military campaigns in Afghanistan, most notably in the capture of Mazar-i Sharif and Bamiyan in 1997, which involved the widescale massacre of Shiites. Pakistani Sipah-i Sahabah fighters did most of the killing, nearly precipitating a war with Iran when they captured the Iranian consulate and killed eleven Iranian diplomats.[10]

According to Indian sources, Ramzi Yousef, now in jail in the US for his involvement in the New York World Trade Centre explosion of February 1993, Maulana Masood Azhar of the *Jaish-e-Mohammad* (JEM), Fazlur Rahman Khalil of the *Harkat-ul-Mujahideen* (HUM) and Abu Musab al-Zarqawi, started their career as terrorists as members of the SSP and participated in many of its anti-Shia massacres in Pakistan, Iran and Afghanistan. The suspicion that the arrest of Khalid Sheikh Mohammad (KSM) by the Pakistani authorities in Rawalpindi in March 2003 and his handing over to FBI was a result of the betrayal of the Hazaras (Shias) of Baluchistan provoked several deadly attacks against Shias. The massacre of the Shias in Quetta in March 2004 was in reprisal partly for their suspected collaboration with the Americans in their hunt for bin Laden and partly for the murder of Maulana Azam Tariq, the leader of the SSP, allegedly by Shia extremists.[11]

Saudi Arabia

Already in November 1979, almost parallel to the occupation of the Mecca sanctuary by radical Sunnis under the leadership of Muhammad al-Utaybi and Abdallah al-Qahtani, Shia demonstrations in the eastern province of Saudi Arabia marked a new activism which degenerated in their first intifada, the spontaneous uprising.[12] Saudi Hezbollah, known locally as the Followers of the Line of the Imam [Khomeini] (*Ansar Khat al-Imam*), was founded in 1987 by several prominent clerics, including Sheikh Hashim al-Shukus, Sheikh Abdulrahman al-Hubail and Abduljalil al-Maa, from the Eastern Province. The organization espouses Khomeini's principle of *vilayat-e-faqih* (the rule of the Islamic jurisprudent, which is the basis for the Islamic Republic's theory of the state), and most members emulate *marja'iyya* ('the source') – Iran's Supreme Leader Ayatollah Khamenei. The Followers of the Line of the Imam wholly distrust the ruling family and government. For the most part, that sentiment has translated into isolation, though it reportedly slipped into periodic violence.[13] Interestingly, the extent of Wahhabi hostility toward the Shia is expressed by the dissemination since the beginning of the nineteenth century of a myth according to which the founder of Shiism was a Jew named Abdallah ibn Saba.[14]

The truck bombing in June 1996 of the Khobar Towers apartment complex in Dhahran, Saudi Arabia, where 19 members of the US Air Force personnel were killed and hundreds of other Americans were injured, has been the main terrorist attack by Shia radicals in Saudi Arabia. According to the US indictment against the perpetrators, Iranian officials and Lebanese Hezbollah operatives were involved in the plot. The government cracked down on Saudi Hezbollah in the wake of the Khobar bombing but there are some indications Hezbollah/The Followers of the Line of the Imam may have increased their presence and influence of late by focusing on social and cultural activities to the exclusion of politics.[15]

The war in Iraq and the concomitant empowerment of the country's Shiites again fuelled anti-Shiite hostility. Posters on a popular web-forum stressed that 'they are the enemy, they are the enemy, they are the enemy', adding 'God damn the rafida [dissenters].' Acts of violence against Shiites have risen over recent years, uncorroborated rumours of planned or failed attacks have spread rapidly within the community. Over the past two years, incidents with an apparent sectarian connotation include the burning of Shiite mosques in Qatif and community centers in Tarut, as well as vandalism against a Shiite cemetery at Annak. Sunni–Shiite issues are taking on greater public importance in Saudi Arabia. Of particular concern for the future of Sunni–Shiite relations has been the alarming rise in the number of Saudi jihadi militants drawn to Iraq. Hostility to Shiites and their growing role in Iraq also is important as many

Saudi jihadis went to Iraq 'to kill Shiites'. The prospect of the eventual return of several hundreds of battle-tested Saudi mujahideen from Iraq raises the possibility that – like their predecessors returning from Afghanistan – they will look for a new battlefield and so pose a potential threat to the Shiite minority.[16]

Bahrain

The Shia Muslims of Bahrain are a disadvantaged majority, widely dispersed within the 35 islands in the Persian Gulf that make up the state. They share other Bahrainis' ethnic Arab background and Arabic language, but they have distinct religious beliefs from the minority Sunni Muslims, and the Sunni royalty that rules the country.[17]

During the 1980s, opposition to the regime took the form of small-scale acts of sabotage carried out by small, well-organized, groups. After the death of ruler Sheikh Isa bin Sulman al-Khalifa in March 1999, and after Shia activists provoked unrest sporadically from 1994–99, the opposition declared its willingness to cease its protests. This more conciliatory approach reduced tensions and although smaller rallies continued in recent years the new leader, Sheikh Hamad, adopted a new constitution in late December 2000. The country officially became a constitutional monarchy in 2002, and in October more than half of the eligible voters participated in the first elections since 1973, electing forty members of the Council of Deputies (the lower house of the national assembly). The new body included a dozen Shia MPs, though this is not close to a proportional representation of their group population.[18]

Bahrain is often seen as a bellwether of Sunni–Shiite relations, as Shiite influence in the region continues to grow. Some see it as an enclave that mimics the heavily Shiite demographics of Iraq, heavily affected by what happens in Iraq and Iran. Sunni extremists in Bahrain paint the country as the edge of a Shiite crescent controlled by Iran and threatening to menace the vastly larger predominantly Sunni Arab world.

Since December 2005, when an Iranian cleric was arrested at the airport, organized confrontations between Shiite youth and Bahraini security forces have become almost weekly events. Shiite politicians claim they only want jobs, equal opportunity and greater representation in government. But Shia demonstrators held up pictures of Iranian leaders and the leaders of the Iranian-backed militant group Hezbollah. The Unemployed Youth Movement has adopted a yellow flag that resembles Hezbollah's trademark banner, and photographs of Hezbollah leaders hang prominently on the walls of Shia family homes. Even moderate Sunnis note that the Shiite opposition itself is fighting for control more than reform.[19]

The Sunni–Shia violent conflict in Iraq

Al Qaeda From the September 2003 assassination of Ayatollah al-Hakim and up to his death on 8 June 2006, Abu Musab al-Zarqawi made the utmost effort to provoke the Shia of Iraq to retaliate against the Sunnis and thus trigger a civil war. This strategy, reflecting the common Wahhabi doctrine, became obvious after US authorities leaked a letter written by him in January 2004. The Shia were described as 'the most evil of mankind ... the lurking snake, the crafty and malicious scorpion, the spying enemy, and the penetrating venom'. Their crime was 'patent polytheism, worshipping at graves, and circumambulating shrines'.[20]

Zarqawi's position contradicted bin Laden and Al Qaeda's views concerning the Shia. It should be noted that in his audio message of February 2003, bin Laden stressed the importance of the Sunnis and Shia fighting united against the Americans. He even cited Hezbollah's 1983 suicide bombing of the US Marine barracks in Beirut as the first 'American defeat' at the hands of Islamist radicals.[21]

The victorious image in the Arab and Muslim world achieved by the Shia Hezbollah movement and its leader Hassan Nasrallah after the Israeli unilateral withdrawal from southern Lebanon in May 2000 and, more recently, the exchange of prisoners (including many Palestinians) between Israel and Hezbollah in January 2004, created much resentment and criticism in Saudi jihadi-Salafi elements. Moreover, the presentation of Nasrallah as the 'New Salah al-Din' put the role of the global vanguard of Islam played by Qa'idat al-Jihad at risk for a takeover by the Hezbollah. Since the process of establishing a new government in Iraq, with a clear Shia majority, Salafi web-sites and forums have stepped up their attacks against the Shia, Iran and Shia doctrines.[22]

In a video aired on Al-Jazeera, in what appears to be a response to Grand Ayatollah Ali al-Sistani's call on his Shia followers to vote en masse and decree that those who boycott the elections are 'infidels', bin Laden warned against the participation in elections in Iraq: 'Anyone who participates in these elections ... has committed apostasy against Allah.' He also endorsed the killing of security people 'in Allah's name'.[23]

It is of note that in the end it was bin Laden who accepted the strategy of Zarqawi and the Saudi jihadists, recognizing the predominance of the leaders who continued the fight on the ground rather than that of the nominal leadership which was hiding somewhere in Pakistan. This process took a whole year (from December 2003 to December 2004) and resulted in the nomination of Zarqawi as the 'emir' of Al Qaeda in Iraq.[24]

However, bin Laden's attack on the Shia has been cautious, without referring directly to their leaders. Interestingly, in a book which includes most of his statements, there is not one reference to the Shia as such, let alone an attack on the Shia.[25]

This important issue continued to trouble the relations between the Al Qaeda leadership and al-Zarqawi, as evidenced in the letter sent to the latter by Ayman al-Zawahiri in July 2005. In this major document Zawahiri acknowledges 'the extent of danger to Islam of the Twelve'er school of Shiism ... a religious school based on excess and falsehood', and 'their current reality of connivance with the Crusaders'. He admits that the 'collision between any state based on the model of prophecy with the Shia is a matter that will happen sooner or later'. The question he and 'mujahedeen circles' ask Zarqawi is 'about the correctness of this conflict with the Shia at this time. Is it something that is unavoidable? Or, is it something can be put off until the force of the mujahed movement in Iraq gets stronger?'

Moreover, Zawahiri reminds Zarqawi that 'more than one hundred prisoners – many of whom are from the leadership who are wanted in their countries – [are] in the custody of the Iranians.' The attacks against the Shia in Iraq could compel 'the Iranians to take counter measures'. Actually, Al Qaeda 'and the Iranians need to refrain from harming each other at this time in which the Americans are targeting' them.[26] This is indeed evidence of a new kind of *realpolitik* on the part of Al Qaeda leadership!

However, this did not change Zarqawi's position. In his last audio message before his death he blasted Iraq's top Shiite cleric, Ayatollah Ali Sistani, as the 'leader of infidelity and atheism', accused Shiite groups and government forces of being responsible for numerous attacks on Sunnis and suggested that Shiites themselves were behind the February bombing of the Shiite shrine in Samara. He also criticized the militia of the radical Shiite cleric Moqtada al-Sadr for stopping the fight against American forces.[27]

In a recent interview with Al Qaeda's media production unit on the fifth anniversary of the September 11 attacks, Ayman al-Zawahiri suggested for the first time that Zarqawi's murderous behaviour toward the Shiites had not been sanctioned by bin Laden: 'The instructions of Sheikh Osama, may God protect him, to the brothers in Iraq, chief among them Abu Musab ... were that they focus their efforts on the Americans and neutralize the rest of the powers as best they could.' Al-Zawahiri dismissed the interviewer's claim that many thought Al Qaeda initiated the Shiite–Sunni fighting, saying that 'Al Qaeda has not done anything to them [the Shiites] because Al Qaeda in Iraq is too busy with jihad against the Crusader occupation.'[28]

The Shia

For a year and a half, from August 2003 until February 2005, Sunni attacks met with barely a response from most Shiites. The only ones accused of meting out revenge from the outset were members of the Badr Organization, allegedly responsible for the assassination of former regime officials and suspected Baath party members, in addition to suspected insurgents, but for a long time these actions did not reach critical mass. However, once the Shiite parties, brought together in the United Iraqi Alliance, won a simple majority of votes in the January 2005 elections and, in alliance with the Kurdish list, gained power three months later, the Supreme Council of the Islamic Revolution in Iraq (SCIRI) took over the Interior Ministry, allowing the Badr Corps to infiltrate its police and commando units. Soon, Iraqis witnessed a steep rise in killings of Sunnis that could not be explained by the fight against insurgents alone.[29]

Arab Shiites have been increasingly polarized by the Sunni suicide attacks on Shia targets, kidnappings, and disappearances which have intensified since the January 2005 elections. They are all too aware that figures like Zarqawi have threatened jihad against Shiites and have said they are not legitimate followers of Islam. Although the CPA tried to establish legal barriers to maintaining militias the Supreme Council for the Islamic Revolution in Iraq (SCIRI) and the faction of Abdul Aziz al-Hakim still have large militia elements. These are forces that Sunni groups have increasingly accused of committing atrocities against them since the spring of 2005. Sunnis feel particularly threatened by the Badr Organization, created by SCIRI and trained by the Iranian military. Sunnis assert that members of the Badr group are the ones responsible for the targeting and assassination of a number of senior Sunni clerics, many from the Muslim Scholars' Board. Some of the killings of an estimated 700 Sunnis between August and November 2005 involved men who identified themselves as Ministry of Interior (MOI) forces. US sources also noted that large number of members of the Badr Organization had joined the MOI forces, including the police and commando units, since the new government was formed in April 2003, and the lines between some MOI units and the Badr Organization had become increasingly blurred.[30]

Moqtada al-Sadr has played a divisive role in Iraq since the first days after the fall of Saddam Hussein. He has been accused of playing a role in the murder of rival Shiite clerics like the Grand Ayatollah Abd al-Majid al-Khoi on 10 April 2003. In October 2003 al-Sadr's men attacked supporters of the moderate Shiite Grand Ayatollah Ali al-Sistani near the Imam Hussein shrine. He attacked the US presence in Iraq almost immediately after the fall of Saddam Hussein. His Mahdi Army presented a serious threat to Coalition and government forces in Najaf, in Sadr City in Baghdad, and in other Shiite areas in the south during much of the summer and early autumn of 2004. Since the elections Sadr revived the Mahdi Army, which again began to be openly active in parts of Southern Iraq such as Basra, Amarah and Nasiriyah, and still has cells in Najaf and Qut as well. Since the autumn of 2005, his organization and other Shiite groups with similar beliefs have been accused of political assassinations and kidnappings.[31] Some Iranian leaders appear to view Sadr as a useful potential ally with whom they might cooperate in the same way they have worked with the leadership of the Lebanese group; Sadr's movement has parallels with Hezbollah, and Tehran may view the Hezbollah model as instructive to Iraq under current circumstances.[32]

The Mahdi Army and the Badr Brigades compete with the Iraqi police for control in Iraq's largest cities, Baghdad and Basra, are well organized and gain popular support with their religious character and their ability to provide security and certain social services. Some police and army units within the Iraqi Security Forces (ISF) have moved away from their original training and developed independent and often problematic methods of operation.[33]

According to the book published in mid-2005 by the Jordanian journalist Fuad Husayn, who spent time in prison with Zarqawi, Abu-Mus'ab thought that the US–Israeli confrontation with Iran is inevitable and could succeed in destroying Iran's infrastructure. Accordingly, Iran is preparing to retaliate by using the powerful cards in its hands. The area of the war will expand, pro-US Shia in Iraq and Afghanistan will suffer embarrassment and might reconsider their alliances, and this will provide Al Qaeda with a larger vital area from which to carry out its activities, including Lebanon.[34]

But a document published after Zarqawi's death describes a 'bleak situation' of the Islamist insurgency in Iraq, which led Zarqawi to conceive a replacement strategy to provoke a 'delegated war' the best of which would be

> ... the one between the Americans and Iran, because it will have many benefits in favor of the Sunni and the resistance, such as: freeing the Sunni people in Iraq, who are [30 per cent] of the population and under the Shia Rule; drowning the Americans in another war that will engage many of their forces; the possibility of acquiring new weapons from the Iranian side, either after the fall of Iran or during the battles; to entice Iran towards helping the resistance because of its need for its help; weakening the Shia supply line.

The document ends with some operational proposals for how to provoke this war.[35]

Lebanon

During the last year there seemed to be a possible change in Al Qaeda's and Zarqawi's strategy in relation to Iran and its proxy organization the Lebanese Hezbollah. It is possible that the rocket attack by Zarqawi's men from southern Lebanon on northern Israel in December 2005 was a first step in some kind of understanding between the two sides – Al Qaeda and Iran – which permitted the attack from a territory notably known to be under the rigorous control of Hezbollah.

It took two weeks for Hezbollah to deny its knowledge of the attack and to caution against the use of territory considered under its responsibility: 'There are some [operatives] in Lebanon,' said Sheikh Naim Qassem, Hezbollah's deputy secretary-general. 'We don't know how many and we don't know their plans or if they intend to do [military] operations here … [and] it's important to caution everyone not to make Lebanon an arena for settling scores.' He claimed it is indeed possible to act without Hezbollah's knowledge and that the organization is still investigating the Al Qaeda claim.[36]

The Lebanese authorities arrested 13 Al Qaeda suspects in different parts of the country and charged them with 'establishing a gang to carry out terrorist acts, forging official and private documents and possessing unlicensed arms'. Among these Al Qaeda suspects were seven Syrians, three Lebanese, a Saudi Arabian, a Jordanian and a Palestinian. Beirut's *Daily Star* reported an alleged Al Qaeda statement that warned the Palestinians camps of Sabra and Shatila in Lebanon that they would face attacks from Al Qaeda if they did not conform to their ideology.[37]

Interestingly, in April 2006 nine men were charged with plotting to assassinate Hezbollah's secretary-general Sheik Hassan Nasrallah. They were presented as 'Salafists who saw in Sheik Nasrallah a good Shiite target to avenge the death of Sunnis in Iraq'.' Nasrallah himself declared that he would not blame Lebanon's Sunnis if the conspirators were shown to be motivated by Sunni militancy.[38]

It is of note that several days before his death Zarqawi called for the disarmament of Lebanon's Hezbollah, according to an audio message posted on the Internet. He accused Hezbollah of serving as a 'shield protecting the Zionist enemy [Israel] against the strikes of the mujahideen in Lebanon', in a reference to Sunni Arab militants loyal to the Al Qaeda network. In reaction, a Hezbollah spokesman dismissed Zarqawi's call, accusing him of trying to 'distort the image of the resistance and its leaders', through the media.[39]

Possibly, this *volte-face* of Zarqawi's after the attempt to operate from southern Lebanon under the benevolent neutrality of Hezbollah is a result of his intricate relationship with Iran.

On 2 June 2006, Hezbollah organized riots in Beirut protesting the broadcast of a sketch on an LBC television programme ridiculing the Shiite militia's position on disarmament, implying that Hezbollah would make any excuse to avoid laying down its weapons. The show's producer apologized, but the demonstrations did not end until Nasrallah himself appeared on Hezbollah's own al-Manar network and appealed for calm. The Hezbollah demonstrations were intended to support the group in the framework of the Lebanese National Dialogue, because Hezbollah is in no hurry to give up its weapons. Not only do the weapons support the party's 'resistance' credentials, the Shiite party also likely sees its arms as an insurance policy against the possible entrenchment of Al Qaeda in Lebanon. Nasrallah acknowledged the danger of the 'Zarqawi phenomenon' during interviews in February and June 2006. According to this view, the presence of anti-Shiite Al Qaeda forces will only stiffen Hezbollah's resolve to retain its weapons, which it sees as essential to defending the Shiite community.[40]

The Shia Crescent

According to Jordan's King Abdullah, Iran's meddling in the Iraqi elections was an attempt by Tehran 'to create a Shiite crescent from Iran to Syria and Lebanon'. Some Arab analysts don't believe this strategic project is viable. According to this view a divided Iraq may lead to a change in the regional balance of power, but not necessarily noticeably in favour of Iran while a united Iraq with a balance of power between the three communities will serve Iran better but curb its influence. In any case, there are important differences within the various Shia communities. Iraqi Shiites are Arabs and culturally closer to Iraqi Sunnis than to Persian Shiites. The Allawis are a small sect within Shia Islam, and Syria's Muslims are in any case 85 per cent Sunni. Lebanon's treacherous ethnic and religious mix is volatile at the best of times and Shiites there are as little interested in a flare-up of inter-communal violence as anyone else.[41]

Zaman, the Turkish Islamist newspaper, notes with some concern that Iran is now extending itself economically, militarily and religiously, even though the latter does not have the connotations of a revolution. This extension is achieved through 'centripetal' force towards Iraq with its holy Shia cities Najaf and Kerbala, with the potential to make radical changes to the Shiite theological structure, and towards Lebanon, where Hezbollah has as much potential as Iraq by taking advantage of its conflict with Israel and championing the cause of the oppressed. Significantly, the author evaluates that after the war in Lebanon Hassan Nasrallah has better chances than Sheik Mohammed Hussein Fadlallah to lead the Lebanese Shiites. The expansion of the Shiite axis towards the west finds expression in both the east and south. There's now a more concrete and politically active Shiite presence in Pakistan, Tajikistan and Azerbaijan. The predominantly Shiite population in Bahrain is already making its influence felt throughout the society and efforts are being made to set up organizations in Saudi Arabia.

The Iranian military exercise in late August 2006, codenamed 'Zulfikar Coup', was intended as a warning to US and British forces in the Middle East that they should not enter Iran under any circumstances. However, notes *Zaman*, it's evident from the row between the Shiite and Sunni worlds that the coup did not only target the Western occupiers.[42]

Abd al-Rahman al-Rashed, an Arab journalist, argues that the most likely target of Iran's nuclear weapons is the Arab countries of the Persian Gulf. 'It is incomprehensible that Iran will bomb Israel, which has a shield of missiles, tremendous firepower and nuclear weapons artillery sufficient to eradicate every city in Iran,' he wrote. 'This means that if this destructive weapon is used, the only option for a target is the Arab Gulf.'[43]

From an Iranian perspective, Tehran indeed would like this crescent since for 25 years it harboured, organized, trained and armed Iraqi Shia groups opposed to Saddam Hussein. The integration of Iraq into the alliance between Tehran, Damascus and Beirut will also influence the balance of power, provide more political, financial and military support and greater strategic depth to Syria. The alliance is also likely to provide more support for Islamic groups such as Hezbollah, Hamas and Islamic Jihad. However, Iranian leaders hold that the regime in Syria is not a Shiite regime, and its foreign policy is not geared to serving Shiite interests. Rather, the current regime in Syria ascribes to Arab nationalism and its primary foreign policy goal is furthering Arab interests as defined by Damascus. For Iran, the alliance with Damascus is based on opposition to the US and Israel and has nothing to do with Shiites. Therefore, while the Middle East is not going to witness a 'Shiite crescent', the coming to power of a Shiite-dominated government in Iraq will have important consequences in support of Shiite political rights: an Iran–Iraq alliance against the GCC (the Gulf Cooperative Council), and strengthening the position of Syria and Islamic groups *vis-à-vis* Israel.[44]

The effects of 'the second Lebanese War'

This author has evaluated that the escalation on Israel's borders in June–July 2006 was set off by actors supported by Iran – that is, Hamas, Hezbollah and Syria – and meant to take the pressure off Iran by triggering a major military clash in the Middle East, which will divert international attention from Iran's nuclear programme. At the same time it served the major strategic interests of the other three actors. Specifically, the Hezbollah intervention in the conflict at this moment, prepared strategically by Iran during the last six years by arming it with long-range artillery and rockets, was meant to give a clear signal to the US, the West and Israel of what would happen if serious international sanctions would be decided against Iran or if Iran's nuclear facilities would be destroyed by a US or Israeli attack.[45]

Actually, Israel's indecisive strategy during the war and Hezbollah's resistance on the ground during the three weeks of the Israeli military offensive has strengthened Hezbollah's image and standing in the Arab and Muslim world. While the main Sunni regimes of Saudi Arabia, Egypt and Jordan indirectly supported Israel's attempt to quell Hezbollah, the Arab masses in these countries, including movements like the Egyptian Muslim Brothers, supported the Shia Lebanese radical movement. Hassan Nasrallah came to be considered a new Salah al-Din who regained lost Arab and Muslim honour, a highly significant element of Arab and Islamic culture, and Hezbollah, a model for the Islamist warfare.

In July 2006, the Saudi Salman al-Awdah issued a *fatwa* in support of Hezbollah and even considered this support a duty, despite the disagreements with Hezbollah. His position was strongly opposed by scholars of global jihad. One of them accused al-Awdah of creating an internal plot (*fitnah*) among the Muslims by supporting the apostate Shia movement.[46]

In a message broadcast on Al-Jazeera on 27 July 2006, bin Laden's deputy Ayman al-Zawahiri said Al Qaeda would not stand by while '[Israeli] shells burn our brothers' in Lebanon and Gaza. He called on Muslims to join forces and fight what he called the 'Zionist-crusader war' against Muslim nations.[47]

According to Reuven Paz, Zawahiri's message circulated in Jihadi forums sparked a hot debate among the Sunni jihadists. One of the salient analyses on the subject was published by the Egyptian Sayf al-Din al-Kinani on the website Global Islamic Media Front (GIMF) under the title 'The Puzzle of the Oppressed and the Red Lines'. In it Zawahiri's message was interpreted as the necessity for Muslims to fight for Palestine and Lebanon, while only Sunnis are considered true Muslims. As Shiites are not Muslims according to this view, their fight against Israel is not regarded as jihad and serves only foreign interests. One of the leading clerics of the Saudi Salafi clerics, Abdallah bin Jaberin, renewed his April 2002 popular fatwa against Hezbollah.[48] Another Salafi scholar, Khubab bin Marwan al-Hamad, stated on the Nur al-Islam website that the Jewish attack against the Lebanese Muslims was part of a test by Allah as a result of their disbelief and corrupted culture adopted from the West. However, for him too, any support for Hezbollah and the Shia was prohibited, as a result of their long series of sins.

Paz evaluates that by the end of the war the vast majority of jihadis considered that the sacred principle of *Al-Wala' wal-Bara'* (loyalty and rejection) prevented any form of support for Hezbollah, Nasrallah, or Iran, even though the Shia movement was fighting the Jews, protected Hamas and the Palestinian Jihad and caused the image of Israeli defeat. Hezbollah was widely nicknamed *Hizb al-Shaytan* (Party of the Devil) and Hassan Nasrallah was named only Hassan Nasr, in order not to add Allah to his name. In many ways, it looks as if the victorious image of Hezbollah has created even more anti-Shia rage among the Sunni Jihadis.[49]

The Kuwaiti jihadi-Salafi cleric Sheikh Hamed al-'Ali has led the attack against the Shia and negated any possibility of support to the Hizb al-Shaytan. In a fatwa published in August 2006, he attacked the 'Iranian organized campaign to destroy the Muslims' as 'a Safawi imperialist racist conspiracy similar to [the one] in Iraq'. In another fatwa published after the cease-fire between Israel and Hezbollah, he claimed that the Israeli–Hezbollah war created a chaos that will be solved only by a much broader war with Iran. Iran's policy was presented as a 'Safawi/Irani project more dangerous than the Zio-Crusader one'. He actually called for a jihad 'against Iran ... in addition to [the jihad against] the Jews and the Christians'.[50]

On the background of the Arab opposition to Hezbollah, led by Saudi Arabia and Egypt, the conservative Iranian daily *Jomhouri-ye Eslami* published a scornful editorial blasting the heads of Saudi Arabia and Egypt, as well as the head muftis. The paper accused these muftis of betraying Islam by serving the pro-Western Sunni Arab kings, as well as the US and the Western infidels.

According to the analysis of a liberal Saudi observer one of the more interesting results of the Israel–Hezbollah war has been the sidelining of the global jihadi movement and the broader Salafi currents that sustain it, which despite their rhetoric were reduced to mere spectators as Hezbollah, once again, dealt a serious blow to Israeli prestige. While some analysts interpreted Ayman al-Zawahiri's latest message as an olive branch to Iran, Hezbollah and Shia militants more broadly, it in fact was not a departure from the terror network's stance on sectarian relations in Islam, according to the same Saudi journalist. In any case, Al Qaeda is increasingly a marginal component of the Salafi-jihadi movement, and its ideological influence on the new generation of radicals is nowhere near as strong as is often assumed.[51]

Hezbollah's success has indeed faced the Sunni Islamist movements with a challenge. The fact that the small Shia organization managed to inflict upon Israel what the Sunni Arab armies have failed to do could be seen as a proof that true Islam is the one practised by the Shia, those very Shia whom the Sunni jihadists in Iraq and their spiritual mentors label as infidels or apostates. The Sunni Islamists must therefore demonstrate that Sunnis too can fight the Israelis. At the least they must make sure that Hezbollah is not seen as fighting Israel alone, while the Sunnis let it down, and that they are not inferior to the Shia in defending Islam and Arab honour.[52]

Arab observers argue that galvanized by Hezbollah's stand, by Hamas' undiminished capacity to launch rockets into Israel, by the Shia Islamists' electoral achievements in Iraq, the Palestinian authority and Egypt, by Iran's defiance of the West and of Israel and by Iran's nuclear potential, Arab opinion appears now to tilt back towards the old rejectionist approach, which seeks Israel's elimination and considers it achievable. That is seen as a serious threat not only to Israel, but also the Arab regimes. However, because Hezbollah has successfully downplayed its Shia identity and its obedience to vilayat al-faqih Ayatollah Ali Khamenei, Iran's role behind Hezbollah and its increasing influence in the Middle East are carefully hidden.[53]

In a speech on 19 November 2006, Hassan Nasrallah, the secretary-general of Hezbollah (who is also the personal representative of Iran's spiritual leader Ayatollah Ali Khamenei in Lebanon),[54] called on his followers to take to the streets and to topple the Lebanese government of Fuad Siniora. A daily newspaper close to Hezbollah promised that if the government did not fall within 40 days, it would receive a 'decisive blow' that would topple it. Senior figures in the '14 March Forces' warned that Lebanon was on the verge of a political *putsch*, and that it was Syria and Iran that had ordered Hezbollah to create the crisis. Against the backdrop of this crisis, the Christian Lebanese Minister of Industry Pierre Gemayel was assassinated on 21 November.[55]

As in the case of the recent war in Lebanon, the timing of the current crisis serves the interests of Iran, which is facing a UN Security Council discussion on proposed sanctions against it. On November 8, 2006, the conservative Iranian daily newspapaer *Kayhan* cited Iranian Supreme Leader Ali Khamenei, stating that in light of the new strategic order that has emerged in the Middle East, the Shiites in Lebanon must receive the largest representation in the Lebanese government institutions because 'they constitute 40% of the [Lebanese] population, and occupy 40% of the Lebanese territory. They are the most united [group in Lebanon], and their security-military forces have become the most significant forces in that part of the Arab region.' For his part, the Shia Lebanese Parliament Speaker Nabih Beri declared during a meeting with Iranian President Ahmadinejad in Tehran that 'the Arab states must take special steps to thwart the enemies' plot of [instigating] strife [and] the Islamic Republic of Iran has a leading and essential role in this regard.'[56]

The sit-down demonstration in the heart of Beirut, which was declared by Nasrallah on 30 November 2006, continued during the first week of December. On the background of rioting and clashes between supporters of the opposition and supporters of the 14 March Forces, the term 'intifada' has begun to be used for the Beirut demonstration. The Lebanese National Opposition issued a communiqué calling for participation in a mass rally on Sunday, 10 December 'to prepare for new forms and ways of protest and nonviolent expression'. The Iranian newspaper *Sobh-e Sadeq*, the mouthpiece of Iran's Supreme Leader Khamenei, claimed that Hezbollah's success 'in holding early elections or changing the composition of the political [structure] of the Lebanese government will mean … the defeat of Western policy and the Zionist regime in Lebanon'.[57]

But Iranian interests in Lebanon go far beyond supporting the 'resistance' against Israel. The recent events in the region confirm that Iran is using Hezbollah as a tool to increase its regional power and counter Western interests. The popularity of Iran and Hezbollah in Lebanon is not based mainly on Hezbollah's military capability, but rather on Iran's economic support through public service institutions and charities. Without those economic mechanisms, Hezbollah's guerrillas could not have become a political force in the country.[58]

Some analysts evaluated before the war that Hezbollah could transform Lebanon through a democratic process into an Islamic Shiite republic. In an article published following the war in Lebanon, the Jordanian-American reformist intellectual and researcher Dr Shaker al-Nabulsi warned of Hezbollah's intent to set up such a republic based on the principles of the current Iranian regime. Al-Nabulsi said the greatest concern relates to the possibility of Hezbollah's ideology spreading through the entire Arab world in such a way that there would no longer be a need to 'export' Ayatollah Khomeini's revolution. The danger to democracy and freedom lies in a possible triumph of Hezbollah ideology rather than in the group's military accomplishments, he said.[59]

Conclusion

It is interesting to note that even from the autumn of 2002 Iran and its allies Syria and Hezbollah had accepted the inevitability of US intervention in Iraq and planned for the emergence of a post-Saddam era in which the United States would figuratively sink in the region's sands; Iran and its allies would exploit their historical and religious ties to Iraqi Shiites while at the same time call for Sunni/Shia unity in the face of Western aggression. They seemed to believe that, given the difficulties US forces would inevitably encounter in post-war Iraq, the Bush administration would be neither willing nor able to take forceful responsive action against them in the short term. For this reason they decided not to open a second front at Israel's northern border at the height of the lethal Palestinian intifada.[60] For the same reason Iran strongly opposed Nasrallah's short-lived proposal at the beginning of February 2003 for an 'Iraqi national accord' between Saddam Hussein and the Iraqi opposition that should 'set principles for national reconciliation and a mechanism for holding free and fair elections that bring to power a government enjoying the support of the Iraqis'.[61]

Mohsen Rezai, secretary of the powerful Iranian Expediency Council recently acknowledged the role of the US in helping Iran to become the regional superpower:

America's arrival in the region presented Iran with an historic opportunity. The kind of service that the Americans, with all their hatred, have done us - no superpower has ever done anything similar. America destroyed all our enemies in the region. It destroyed the Taliban. It destroyed Mr. Saddam Hussein. It imprisoned the hypocrites [Mojahedin-e Khalq] in France. It did all this in order to confront us face to face, and in order to place us under siege. But the American teeth got so stuck in the soil of Iraq and Afghanistan that if they manage to drag themselves back to Washington in one piece, they should thank God. Therefore, America presents us with an opportunity rather than a threat – not because it intended to, but because its estimates were wrong.[62]

Through its ties with Hezbollah, Iran has also managed to fill the power vacuum left by Syria's withdrawal from Lebanon. At the same time, Iran has taken advantage of the cut in international funding to the Hamas-dominated Palestinian Authority to make up its economic shortfall, thus gaining an even firmer foothold in the Palestinian territories. Iran therefore might finally see some of the long-awaited fruits of the 1979 Islamic Revolution and project its power throughout the Middle East. The political losers include the leaderships of the Arab Gulf states, Egypt, and Jordan among others. The Middle East could also see the marginalization of Saudi Arabia as the religious leader of the Muslim world; sectarian conflicts, between Shiites and Sunnis, are bound to increase, as witnessed every day in Iraq.[63]

Mahmoud Ahmadinejad represents on the regional level the 'Second Islamic Revolution' which strives to export the revolution beyond Iran's borders while he sees himself as walking in the path of the architect of the Islamic Revolution, Ayatollah Khomeini, who made the export of the revolution one of the fundamental elements of his vision.[64]

In a recent article Nasr finally admits things have changed, and quickly: Ahmadinejad, the militant president, confidently rallies the Third World under the banner of anti-Americanism, and the Iranian regime is bold and assertive. Not only has Iran an important role in Afghanistan and Iraq, says Nasr, but lately it has managed to influence developments in Lebanon and the Palestinian territories: 'Egypt and Jordan fear that Iran will overshadow them regionally, while Saudi Arabia and the Persian Gulf monarchs – all of whom are Sunnis ruling over sizeable numbers of Shiites – worry about the spread of an aggressive Iranian hegemony over their domains.'[65]

According to a more optimistic view, as presented by the US analyst Martin Indyk, the foundations for a 'new Middle East' may emerge from the ashes of the conflict between Israel and Hezbollah. Indyk evaluates that there is the possibility of a 'tacit alliance' developing between Israel and the Sunni Arab leaders of Egypt, Jordan, Saudi Arabia, the Palestinians and Lebanon. 'A common interest has emerged from the conflict,' he said at a talk at the University of Sydney Conservatorium. 'We are beginning to see scared leaders.' Sunni fears had been raised by the potential growth of a Shiite axis, dedicated to waging war with Israel, that included Iran, Iraq, Syria and the Hezbollah in Lebanon: 'Many Sunni leaders are concerned and now seem to be emerging with an opposing view which argues that peace with Israel is the way forward for the Arab world.'[66]

The challenge for Ahmadinejad is how to prevent the emergence of this anti-Iranian American-Israeli-Arab alliance. Nasr evaluates that his rhetoric suggests that he does not understand 'the complexity of the challenges facing Iran, or the delicate touch that is needed if Iran is to realize its interests. This may be good news, or not.'[67]

At present at least, it seems that Iran is leading the game in the growing conflict between Shia and Sunni Islam, at a state level as well as that of radical terrorist movements and groups.

Ely Karmon is Senior Research Scholar at the Institute for Counter-Terrorism, and the Institute for Policy and Strategy at the Interdisciplinary Centre, Herzliya, Israel.

NOTES

1   It seems Nasr's article has also influenced the debate in the US establishment and academia on this important issue. See Vali Nasr, 'Regional Implications of Shia Revival in Iraq', *The Washington Quarterly*, 27 (3), Summer 2004.

2   Ibid.

3   Ibid.

4   Nasr, 'Regional Implications of Shia Revival in Iraq'.

5   Adonis, 'Le Chiavi del Islam', *L'Espresso*, 29 June 2006.

6   'The Ottoman Policy toward the Shia community of Iraq in the late 19th century', *Images, Representations and Perceptions in the Shia world, Conference at the University of Geneva*, 17–19 October 2002 <http://www.unige.ch/lettres/meslo/arabe/shiawor.html>.

7   B. Raman, 'Islamabad Blast: Gilgit-Related', *South Asia Analysis Group Paper*, No. 1393, 29 May 2005.

8   Amir Mir, 'Pakistan. Sectarian Monster', *South Asia Intelligence Review (SAIR)*, 3 (47), 6 June 2005.

9   See 'Major incidents of terrorist violence in Pakistan, 1988–2006', *South Asia Terrorism Portal* <www.satp.org/satporgtp/countries/pakistan/backgrounders/index.html>.

10   Nasr, 'Regional Implications of Shia Revival in Iraq'. The crisis passed when the Taliban apologized and turned over the bodies.

11   B. Raman, 'Massacres Of Shias In Iraq & Pakistan – the Background', *South Asia Analysis Group Paper*, No. 941, 3 March 2004.

12   Yitzhak Nakash, *Reaching for Power. The Shia in the Modern Arab World* (Princeton, NJ: Princeton University Press, 2006), pp. 50–51.

13   Nasr, 'Regional Implications of Shia Revival in Iraq'.

14   Nakash, *Reaching for Power*, p. 45.

15   'The Shiite Question In Saudi Arabia', *The International Crisis Group, Middle East Report*, No. 45, 19 September 2005 <http://www.crisisgroup.org/home/index.cfm?l=1&id=3678>.

16   Ibid.

17   'Assessment for Shi'is in Bahrain', *The Minorities at Risk (MAR) Project*, Center for International Development and Conflict Management, University of Maryland, 31 December 2003 <http://www.cidcm.umd.edu/inscr/mar/assessment.asp?groupId=69201>.

18   Ibid.

19   Hassan M. Fattah, 'Ripples from Iraq disturb Bahrain', *The New York Times*, 15 April 2006.

20   Nimrod Raphaeli, 'The Sheikh of the Slaughterers: Abu Mus'ab Al-Zarqawi and the Al-Qa'ida Connection', *MEMRI Inquiry and Analysis Series*, No. 231, 1 July 2005.

21   Reuven Paz, 'Global Jihad and the Sense of Crisis: al-Qa'idah's Other Front', *The Project for the Research of Islamist Movements (PRISM) Occasional Papers*, 1 (4), March, 2003 <http://www.e-prism.org/pages/4/index.htm>.

22   Reuven Paz, 'Hezbollah or Hizb al-Shaytan? Recent Jihadi-Salafi Attacks against the Shiite Group', *PRISM Occasional Papers*, 2 (1), February, 2004 <http://www.e-prism.org/images/PRISM_no_1_vol_2_-_Hizbullah_or_Hizb_al-Shaytan.pdf>.

23   Nimrod Raphaeli, 'Iraqi Elections (III): The Islamist and Terrorist Threats', *MEMRI Inquiry and Analysis Series*, No. 202, 18 January 2005.

24   See Ely Karmon, 'Al-Qa'ida and the War on Terror – After The War In Iraq', *MERIA Journal*, 10 (1), March, 2006 <http://meria.idc.ac.il/journal/2006/jv10no1a1.html>.

25   See Bruce Lawrence, *Messages to the World. The Statements of Osama bin Laden* (London and New York: Verso, 2005).

26   'Letter from al-Zawahiri to al-Zarqawi', *ODNI News Release*, No. 2-05, 11 October 2005 <http://www.dni.gov/letter_in_english.pdf>. The Office of the Director of National Intelligence released the letter dated 9 July 2005, obtained during counterterrorism operations in Iraq.

27   '"Zarqawi tape"demands that Hizbullah lay down its arms. Head of Al Qaeda in Iraq lashes out at "infidel" Shiites', Beirut *Daily Star*, 3 June 2006

28   Michael Scheuer, 'Al-Zawahiri's September 11 Video Hits Main Themes of Al Qaeda Doctrine', *Terrorism Focus*, Jamestown Foundation, 3 (36), 19 September 2006.

29   'The Next Iraqi War? Sectarianism and Civil Conflict', *International Crisis Group Middle East Report*, No. 52, 27 February 2006.

30   Anthony H. Cordesman, 'The Iraqi Insurgency and the Risk of Civil War: Who Are the Players?', *Center for Strategic and International Studies, Working Draft*, revised, 1 March 2006.

31   Ibid.

32   W. Andrew Terrill, 'Strategic Implications of Intercommunal Warfare In Iraq', *The Strategic Studies Institute*, February 2005 <http://Www.Strategicstudiesinstitute.Army.Mil/Pubs/ Display. Cfm?Pubid=595>.

33   For a detailed report on the Shiite anti-Sunni units see Cecile Zwiebach, 'The Confused Security Situation in Iraq: Some Less Publicized Units', *PolicyWatch*, No. 1114, The Washington Institute for Near East Policy, 21 August 2006.

34   Fuad Husayn, *The Second Generation of Al-Qa'ida* (Part 13), a serialized book on al-Zarqawi and Al Qaeda published by the London *al-Quds al-'Arabi*, 11 July 2005.

35   'Text of a document discovered in terror leader Abu Musab al-Zarqawi's hideout. The document was provided in English by Iraqi National Security Adviser Mouwafak al-Rubaie', *Associated Press*, 15 June 2006.

36   Ilene R. Presher and Nicholas Blanford, 'Al Qaeda takes aim at Israel', *The Christian Science Monitor*, 13 January 2006.

37   Steve Schippert, 'Al Qaeda Branching into Lebanon, Hezbollah Unimpressed', *ThreatsWatch*, 14 January 2006 <http://inbrief.threatswatch.org/2006/01/alqaeda-branching-into-lebanon/>.

38   Hamza Hendawi, 'Hezbollah Links Plot to Clashes in Iraq', *Associated Press*, 15 April 2006.

39   '"Zarqawi tape" demands that Hizbullah lay down its arms'.

40   David Schenker, 'One Year after the Cedar Revolution: The Potential for Sunni-Shiite Conflict in Lebanon', *Policywatch*, No. 1114, The Washington Institute for Near East Policy, 20 June 2006.

41   Mourhaf Jouejati, 'Much ado about nothing. Shi'ite crescent', *bitterlemons-international.org*, 4 (3), 3 February 2005.

42   Kerim Balci, 'Zulfikar Coup', *Zaman*, 14 September 2006 <http://www.zaman.com/?bl= columnists&alt=&trh=20060914&hn=36501>.

43   Abd al-Rahman al-Rashed, 'Why We Fear Iran', *Al-Sharq Al-Awsat*, 22 April 2006.

44   Kamran Taremi, 'Shi'ite crescent. An Iranian perspective', <http://www.bitterlemons-international.org>, 4 (3), 3 February 2005.

45   See Ely Karmon, 'The Axis of Destabilization of the Middle East', *Institute for Counter-Terrorism*, 18 July 2006 <http://www.ictconference.org/s119/apage/2803.php>.

46   Reuven Paz, 'Hotwiring The Apocalypse: Jihadi Salafi Attitude Towards Hezbollah And Iran',

PRISM Occasional Papers, 4 (4), August, 2006.

47   'Al-Zawahiri urges attacks on Israel' <http://english.aljazeera.net/NR/exeres/1D608570-C11E-4AEB-B14B-84B47DC401E7.htm>.

48   Paz, 'Hezbollah or Hizb al-Shaytan?'.

49   Paz, 'Hotwiring The Apocalypse'.

50   Ibid.

51   Mahan Abedin, 'Al Qaeda eclipsed by rise of Iran as Islamists bask in success against Israel', 18 August 2006 <http://www.saudidebate.com/index.php?option=com_content&task=view&id=268&Itemid =123>.

52   Israel Elad Altman, 'Some Regional Implications of the Hizbullah-Israel War', *PRISM*, 4 August 2006, at <http://www.e-prism.org/images/Some_regional_effects_of_the_Hizbullah-Israel_war_-_4-8-06.pdf>.

53   Bernard Haykel, 'A Hizbullah "Victory"?', *Al-Sharq al-Awsat*, 5 August 2006.

54   When he met with Iranian Supreme Leader Khamenei in 2001, Nasrallah publicly kissed Khamenei's hand, which implied that he had accepted Khamenei as his leader.

55   Pierre Gemayel was the son of former Lebanese President Amin Gemayel, and he served as the representative of the Phalangist party in the Siniora government and was a senior figure in the '14 March Forces' political" alliance. See H. Varulkar, 'Lebanon on the Brink of Civil War (3)', *MEMRI Inquiry and Analysis Series*, No. 302, 23 November 2006.

56   See H. Varulkar, 'Lebanon on the Brink of Civil War (2)', *MEMRI Inquiry and Analysis Series*, No. 301, 21 November 2006.

57   'Lebanon on the Brink of Civil War (6): Beirut, December 10 at 3 PM – A Mass Rally for a "Second Phase" and Escalation of Actions to Topple the Government', *MEMRI Special Dispatch Series*, No. 1385, 8 December 2006.

58   'Iran's Shadow Government in Lebanon', *PolicyWatch*, No. 1124, Washington Institute for Near East Policy, 19 July 2006.

59   See Beirut newspaper *Al-Mustaqbal*, 17 September 2006.

60   See Ely Karmon, 'Fight on All Fronts?: Hezbollah, the War on Terror, and the War in Iraq', *Washington Institute for Near East Policy, Policy Focus*, No. 46, December 2003.

61   See Nasrallah's interview in 'Hezbollah's Nasrallah on Iraq Initiative, Israeli Mock Raids, Intifadah', Beirut newspaper *Al-Safir*, 10 February 2003 and Zvi Bar'el, 'Nothing like spending the war in Beirut', *Ha'aretz*, 19 February 2003.

62   Excerpts from an interview with Mohsen Rezai, Secretary of the Iranian Expediency Council, aired on Iranian Channel 1 on 11 November 2006. Transcript by *MEMRI, Clip*, No. 1321.

63   Reza Aslan, 'A giant awakes', *The Guardian*, 3 June 2006.

64   Y.Carmon, A. Savyon, N. Toobiyan and Y.Mansharof, 'The Middle East Crisis – Local, Regional, and Global; Conventional and Nuclear (2): The War in the Perception of Iran, Syria, and Hizbullah', *MEMRI Inquiry and Analysis Series*, No. 289, 24 July 2006.

65   Vali Nasr, 'The New Hegemon', *The New Republic*, 12 December 2006.

66   Richard North, 'Common interest emerging in the Middle East', *The University of Sydney News*, 24 August 2006 <http://www.usyd.edu.au/news/84.html?newsstoryid=1235>.

67   Nasr, *The New Hegemon*.

Iranian-Arab Relations: A Persian Perspective

MEHRDAD KHONSARI

Historically, Iran-Arab relations – in particular their perceptions of one another since the termination of colonial rule, as well as the way in which those perceptions have translated themselves into policies – is a very complex issue.

Prior to the start of this analysis, it is important to point out that in the case of Iran's interlocutors, namely the Arab states, one is not talking about one country or one region. It thus follows that Iranian relations and percept-ions of its Arab neighbours in the Persian Gulf should differ from those of Arab countries that are more distant or less engaged with Iran. Hence, Iran's more distant Arab countries – distant in both geographic and political relations, say with Syria or Lebanon – are vastly different to Iran's relations with countries like Egypt and Jordan, let alone those much further away in places like Sudan or the various North African states. Today, the Iranian government's vocal and material support for hard-line Palestinian elements, as a consequence of its uncompromising attitude towards the State of Israel, has an inevitable bearing on Iran's overall relations with all Arab governments. There is the additional dimension that perhaps for the first time in a major way, the anti-Israeli, pro-Palestinian message of the current Iranian leadership – something that the more measured, more media-conscious Arab leaders cannot match – is resonating in a most effective way with the Arab public across the board. Therefore, there is yet another distinction that now needs to be made between perceptions of the 'State' and those of the 'Public' in any consideration relating to Iran-Arab relations.

Iran's relations with the Arab world and, in particular, with many of its immediate neighbours, have over the years been mainly governed and affected by issues in five separate areas:

- Divergent ethno-religious backgrounds
- Divergent views on oil

- Unresolved territorial disputes

- Reaction to outside influences in the region

- Arab perceptions and reactions to the Islamic Revolution.

Divergent Ethno-Religious Backgrounds

The primary source of divergence between Iranians and Arabs stems from the ancient hostility between ethnic Persians and Arabs – of the Shia and Sunni sects of Islam. The bases for these attitudes have existed long before Western powers – either Britain in the past or the US today – ever thought of entering the region.

Shia ideology, perhaps more than any other factor, assisted the rise of modern Iran to power. Contrary to conventional wisdom, the role played by Shiite leaders did not start in 1979, given that this ideology has always played an important role in all aspects of Iranian political thinking. Here, one can easily point to the part that was played by the Shia *Ulema* (Islamic scholars) in the constitutional movement of 1906, and the role that they later played in preventing Reza Shah from declaring a very secular Republic, along the lines of Ataturk's newly established Turkish Republic. On the other hand, most Arabs adhere to the tenets of Sunni Islam. The basic difference between the two sects lies primarily in the Shiites' refusal to recognize the spiritual legitimacy of the first three Caliphs of Islam, whom according to the Sunnis were the true inheritors of Mohammad's mantle. Shiism supported the cause of Iranian nationalism against Arab occupiers, and by the sixteenth century the sect had manoeuvred its way into becoming the state religion of Iran – a position it has retained to this day. None the less, significant numbers of Shiites have also flourished within the peripheral boundaries of Iran and beyond, most notably in Iraq, Bahrain and Lebanon – countries in which they either constitute a majority or a substantial minority – as well as in Afghanistan, Saudi Arabia and the GCC (Gulf Cooperative Council). However, until the recent political transformation of Iraq, it was only in Iran that the majority Shiites were actually in power. In other countries, they have at best had some representation, while in some instances; it has been known that they have been persecuted.

Without doubt, this split in religion has been a negative factor in Iran-Arab relations. Its importance has varied throughout history. But, as we see so clearly today, this is an issue that can easily be revived or resurrected. It is also pertinent to note that race and language differences also pose communication problems of considerable magnitude. Unfortunately, a stereotypical image of Arabs in Iranian minds is something that has been reinforced throughout history by Iranian scholars, administrators and artisans. Therefore, as long as concrete steps are not taken by Iranians in the direction of projecting Arabs in a different light, this highly one-sided negative perception will remain an obstacle to better Iran-Arab ties. However, a step of this nature requires political and cultural socialization at a grass-roots level, which obviously requires the national will of the nation – something that has simply never been properly tended to in Iran. The advent of the Islamic Revolution could conceivably have helped to change this entire milieu, but the opportunity was wasted, principally by factors such as the devastating eight-year-long Iran–Iraq War, where the majority of Arab countries rallied behind Iraq on the one hand – and on the other, by the desire in some quarters in Islamic Iran to export Khomeini's revolution to the Arab and Islamic world.

Divergent Views on Oil Policy

Rivalry within OPEC between Iran and Arab producers, has also been a defining barometer in Iran-Arab relations. While the key areas of contention between them in 1970s, 1980s, and in more recent times, may have varied, they have consistently been factors that have affected Iran-Arab relations as whole. While in the past, issues such as the price and the production output of oil dominated areas of disagreements between Iran and the major Arab producers, today given the 'high oil price milieu', the emphasis has switched to arguments that pit 'boosting production capacity' – a position favoured by the Saudis – against 'maximizing oil revenues' – something that is of more interest to Iran. This crucial issue is augmented by other factors such as continuous rivalries, in addition to unresolved problems concerning ownership of assets and the division of spoils regarding fields that are located between Iran and some of its Arab neighbours in the Persian Gulf. While disputes of this nature could potentially multiply should major expansions in the Iraqi petroleum sector ever become a reality, the most prominent bone of contention at present lies with what the Qataris call the 'North Dome' and what Iran calls the 'South Pars' field. However, it should be said that while friction within OPEC as a result of high oil prices as well as Saudi-Iranian entente is very contained in present circumstances, there has nevertheless been a great deal of resistance as well as friction on the part of the Arab members of OPEC, when it has come to accepting an Iranian Secretary General on rotation.

Unresolved Territorial Disputes

Two important, but as yet unresolved territorial disputes, are without question a source of tension as well as pressure on better Iran-Arab relations.

The most prominent of these is the age-old dispute between Iran and Iraq over conflicting claims to navigation rights in the Shatt-al Arab waterway at the mouth of the Tigris-Euphrates. This dispute was supposedly resolved in the course of the March 1975 OPEC Summit meetings in Algiers (which coincidentally also quelled the Kurdish rebellion which had raged in Iraq since 1974). Since then, Saddam Hussein first abrogated the Algiers Treaty when he wanted to attack Iran in 1980, and then re-ratified it, when he was trying to fend off Iran from joining the coalition of military forces that had gathered to force him out of Kuwait a decade later. None the less, it is important to point out that to this day, there has been no formal treaty between Iraq and Iraq, that would officially bring the Iran–Iraq War to an end and settle all the relevant outstanding issues. Both the reaffirmation of the 1975 Algiers Treaty as well as the whole issue of reparation that is owed to Iran by Iraq because of its aggression in 1980 are very sensitive issues that will require careful attention in the future. How events actually proceed on these sensitive issues are critical to the whole thrust of Iran-Arab relations. It is difficult to predict how Iran will actually resolve these outstanding issues with the new supposedly 'Iran-friendly' Shia-dominated government in post-Saddam Iraq, given the extent of strong domestic feelings and expectations that exist on both sides.

The ongoing dispute over the ownership of the two Tunb Islands ('Lesser Tunb' and 'Greater Tunb') and Abu Musa in the Persian Gulf, has also been a major bone of contention between the small sheikdoms of Ras Al-Kheimeh (claiming the Tunbs) and Sharjah (with claims on Abu Musa) on the one hand, and Iran (having occupied all three on 30 November 1971) on the other. Since the British withdrawal from all areas 'East of Suez', and the creation of the United Arab Emirates, consisting of a number of small sheikdoms, inclusive of Ras Al-Kheimeh and Sharjah, the UAE has claimed the mantle of pursuing the former claims against Iran.

Despite the hue and cry during the past 35 years, little has been achieved in a way of resolving the dispute. Indeed, during the past 35 years, each party has, at various times, claimed 'beyond a shadow of a doubt, that based on authentic documentation', the islands were a historic part of their respective territories. However, in all this time, there has been a *de facto* recognition by the UAE, that Tunb Islands are under the full control of Iran, and that Iran's presence in Abu Musa is governed by a 'Memorandum of Understanding' (MOU) signed by the government of Iran and the then Sheikh of Sharjah some 35 years ago.

Here, it is worth noting that the Memorandum of Understanding agreed between Iran and Sharjah in 1971 has provided both parties with a pragmatic *modus vivendi* on the only island which has local inhabitants. Moreover, contrary to certain Arab rhetoric which has condemned Iran as yet another 'occupier of Arab land', it is crucial to emphasize that the exercise of Iranian sovereignty over the Tunb Islands has not resulted in any serious displacement of the Arab population (which numbers a few hundred at most), and as such, the dispute should not be taken out of context.

Moreover, for sake of overall Iran-Arab relations, it is unhelpful for Arabs to attempt to utilize this disagreement with Iran to jeopardize regional security, for the sake of promoting nationalism or displaying Arab unity in order to shield some of their other perhaps more pressing problems. Here, in light of Iran's own experience, it is important for some of the region's Arab leaders not to become beguiled by certain supporting gestures which they might witness on the part of some of the major Western powers, due primarily to their existing differences with the current Iranian regime. They should note that these same powers had, in fact, provided tacit support and approval for the positions proposed by Iran at the start of this dispute in 1971. Given the extent of domestic sensitivities that exist, it would be most prudent for all the disputing parties to settle their differences amongst themselves. Also, given the importance of arriving at some form of a permanent agreement, neither Iran or nor its Arab neighbours in the Persian Gulf stands to gain by attempting to settle the final outcome of this dispute by looking for any external power to tilt the ultimate balance in their favour.

Reaction to Outside Influences in the Region

It is obvious that due to its economic-strategic significance, the Persian Gulf cannot remain free of external pressures, influences and interventions. The overriding concern of all external players, be they the US, Western Europe, Japan or China, lies in the continued availability of Persian Gulf oil at bearable prices. However, both Iranian and Arab perceptions of one another are hugely affected by the interrelationship that they each have with these key external players. Needless to say, in present circumstances, the troubled nature of Iran's relations with the P5 over the pursuit of its nuclear policy is not without diplomatic flak of its own with all Arab governments and in particular, Iran's Arab neighbours to the south.

Here, on another note, it is perhaps also important to state that historically the whole region has suffered so long from outside intervention that the main oil producers, whether Sunni or Shiite, generally regard foreign oil companies with a great deal of suspicion. For example, Saudi Arabia, while relying on Western technology, refuses to open its oil fields to foreign oil companies. Iran has opened up a bit via the so-called 'buyback' system but refuses to allow direct foreign oil equity investments.

Arab Reaction to the Islamic Revolution

Initial Arab response to the success of the Iranian Revolution was one of welcome both at the 'state' and 'public' levels. At a state level, with perhaps a few exceptions such as Egypt, Jordan and Morocco, the removal of a seemingly overpowering regional strongman was viewed with a sigh of relief, while at a public level, his removal at the behest of a simple and empty-handed holy man gave the promise that perhaps armed with 'Islam', ordinary Muslims, too, might one day replicate the Iranian experience. However, the provocative nature of the pronouncements from Tehran and their attempts at politicizing Islamic rituals such as the Haj, coupled with the start of the Iran–Iraq War soon brought those earlier feelings of euphoria to an abrupt end. More recently, things again looked promising for enhanced Iran-Arab relations, due to factors such as the death of Khomeini and the 'mellowing' of the Iranian Revolution under Rafsanjani and Khatami. As yet, it is unclear how the election of Ahmadinejad, with his radical and provocative references to the kind of revolutionary dogmas initially raised by Khomeini, may affect Iran-Arab relations at both the state and public levels. In a perhaps deepening climate of mistrust, the only certainty is the fact that the new Iranian administration has challenged the 'compromising stance' of the Arab League towards the Israel–Palestine dispute. While the crux of the Arab League's proposal, initially made by the current Saudi ruler, promises to recognize Israel if the latter should accept the formation of a Palestinian state on the basis of the June 1967 borders, the Iranian president has advocated a much harder stance that calls for an altogether elimination of the State of Israel.

In conclusion, for Iran-Arab relations to move beyond their present limited scope, it is essential that both sides should endeavour to become much better acquainted and familiar with one another. This requires bold policies by the Iranian state as well as its Arab counterparts.

Cultural exchanges, promotion of tourism, trade, investments and other economic activities – much like the booming business life between Iranians and Arabs that has, out of necessity, erupted in Dubai – can help promote better understanding at both the 'state' and 'public' levels. Unfortunately, while the priorities for better relations are very clear, progress in attaining them has been slow. Until such time as clear forward steps are initiated through bold action on both the Iranian and Arab sides, old suspicions will not give way to a new agenda that is much more suited to the future needs and security of all Arabs and Iranians alike.

Mehrdad Khonsari is Senior Research Consultant at the Centre for Arab and Iranian Studies in London.

Review of Vali Nasr's
The Shia Revival: How Conflicts within Islam Will Shape the Future

TURI MUNTHE

Vali Nasr's latest book, *The Shia Revival*, is a political manifesto of genius. Its title doesn't so much describe as aspire; it is advocacy, not history or political theory, and advocacy of the most convincing kind. It must be: Nasr's objective is to convince a West traumatized by Khomeini, a hostage crisis, three decades of Iranian revolutionary zeal, Ahmadinejad's nuclear ambitions, and Shia death squads, not to mention Hezbollah and the Marine barrack bombings of 1983, that Iran and the Shia are their only true partners for peace in the Middle East.

'In March 2003,' he suggests, 'the United States not only changed the regime in Iraq but also challenged the regime – call it "the Sunni ascendancy" – that had long dominated the region as a whole.' Arab nationalism – the cement that would bind the region together has failed – and as the identity-crisis that has rocked the Middle East and Arab world since the last days of the Ottoman Caliphate only intensifies, sectarianism has become the new game: 'In the coming years Shias and Sunnis will compete over power first in Iraq but ultimately across the entire region ... The overall Sunni–Shia conflict will play a large role in defining the Middle East as a whole and shaping its relations with the outside world." And as that happens, Nasr contends, the West has no options in its choice of partners.

Fully aware of the degree of cultural revulsion the West experiences in relation to Iran (Nasr's previous books answer to it), Nasr's Shia manifesto is foremost an exercise in suggestion. He goes to great lengths to make Shiism Christian, 'Even the more extreme practices of some Shias, such as shedding one's own blood [during the *ashura* – the Shiite feast of atonement – celebrations] ... resemble rituals such as those of the Penitentes, a lay Catholic brotherhood originally formed on the Iberian Peninsula', while the ashura ceremony in Lucknow 'brings to mind the festival of Corpus Christi in Cuzco'. But Nasr is not exclusive.

Nasr would have Shias Sufi – that cuddly California-friendly brand of Islamic mysticism – and he also makes them Jews: 'treated as the enemy within, they were the first to come under suspicion when there was an external threat to the ruling establishment.' The point is to make Shias Western, or Judeo-Christian, with a particular dialectic in mind: 'The Shias' historical experience is akin to those of Jews and Christians in that it is a millennium-long tale of martyrdom, persecution and suffering. Sunnis, by contrast, are imbued with a sense that immediate worldly success should be theirs.' And here's the rub. To a Western political class most of whom have not the foggiest idea that any distinctions exist amongst Muslims, Nasr has turned with a group that looks far more like 'us' than 'them', and the great thing is that they're almost as many of them – in the Middle East proper – as the 'others'.

Nasr, where the combined intelligence-fixing of the US and UK secret services failed, again plays up the Saddam–Al Qaeda connection (p. 230). And in a final display of chutzpah, he even goes so far as to make Khomeini's revolution Sunni: 'the current excessive legal-mindedness of Iran's ayatollahs is in some ways a "Sunnification" of Shiism', with the one objective of making common cause between the West and his team. The focus – the 'my enemy's enemy' principle – is pointed: 'Shiism has found much to fear from the kind of puritanical righteousness that Wahhabism ... and Salafism ... promote ... The brand of radical Islam that began spreading across Central Asia and the Caucasus in the 1990s ... was a Sunni radicalism born of the deliberate Saudi policy of containing Iran.' And we, all along, thought Al Qaeda only hated us...

Nasr makes the point that Shias alone have benefited from the war in Iraq, suggesting this 'makes them in principle more likely to work with the United States. Greater democracy serves Shia interests across the region, and hence Shia revival is favorably disposed toward democratic change' and the 'Freedom Agenda'. The Shia are the 'New Europe' (p. 21). In the very first chapter, he tells us that 'the Sunnis are the real problem.' Nasr believes that a democratic Iraq will be the model for Iran (p. 177), and has Grand Ayatollah al-Sistani – whose approach represents 'the most compelling and most credible challenge that fundamentalism and other forms of authoritarianism have ever had to face' – as the new, much improved Khomeini, and face of the Shia future, a future geared (as he would have Sistani) towards tolerance, democracy and spiritually inspired ethics.

***

Not so long ago, Vali Nasr would have been laughed back to what, because of the large Iranian diaspora there, is affectionately known as 'TehrAngeles', where he is from. Instead, upon publication of *The Shia Revival*, he spent the summer and autumn as talking-head nobility in the major think-tanks of

Washington and Europe. The indescribable horror (and unintelligible mess) that Iraq has become, has prompted a rethink so fundamental of US policy in the Middle East as to render the notion of a West–Iran alliance possible and, to some, even desirable. And it has, if the Iraq Study Group Report is anything to go by, taken root. While Iraq shatters, Lebanon is splitting at the seams, Afghanistan slips beyond our grasp, Syria regroups, the Palestinian–Israeli conflict remains explosive, and Al Qaeda grows from strength to strength. In each case, the Shia and Iran play a part. Does it really, Nasr's pleading aside, make sense to engage?

Iraq

Western use of the Shia and/or Iran in Iraq takes two forms. Iran has been asked to help 'harmonize' the country: stop supplying weapons and training, and do its bit to ensure the territorial entity remains intact and that a slow and equitable drive towards full participation of all sects and ethnicities can take place. The Iraq Study Group Report claims, somewhat optimistically, that this is in Iran's interests since 'worst-case scenarios in Iraq could inflame sectarian tensions within Iran, with serious consequences for Iranian national security interests' (Recommendation 9). Most observers would probably say Iran has no interests at all (historical, short-term or medium-term) in aiding the Sunni factions in Iraq, nor any political will to do so (as the ISGR actually concedes).

The West's other option is to attempt to stabilize Iraq by 'prioritizing' the Shia, in effect establishing a Shia Saddam to rule the country from on high. Given Iraq today, where Prime Minister Nuri al-Maliki is himself allegedly implicated in the running of the Shia death squads patrolling Baghdad, it is hard to imagine that scenario doing much to stem the sectarian cleansing taking place today. Nor is that scenario imaginable without the direct intervention (in financing and personnel) of Saudi Arabia, Jordan, Egypt and Al Qaeda, which would in turn bring Iran directly into the fray.

Lebanon

Greater engagement with the Shia in Lebanon could help the situation there but only by cleaving Hezbollah from Iran. Tehran has no interest in alleviating the pressure on Israel it exerts through Hezbollah, nor, ultimately would it be served by a settlement in Palestine. Iran, like many countries in the region, uses the Palestinian plight as a useful distraction, pulling a critical domestic eye away towards external evils. Unlike Arab countries, Iran has the added incentive of destabilizing Israel to garner support amongst Arabs and Sunnis who traditionally regard Persian Shia Iran as outside the cause.

But how would the West achieve that cleavage? Negotiation, recognition and a distant diplomatic pardon might be held out as incentives, and might regardless be a sensible step to take. But any more aggressive tampering with Lebanon's gossamer-fragile political settlement – a new demographic survey, a push to rewrite Taba – and Lebanon risks going up in flames as the Christian-Druze-Sunni camp sees itself sold down the river to 'Iranian' interests and Israel balks.

Afghanistan

Iran certainly has a vested interest in blocking the rise of the Taliban, Sunni extremists who harbour as much or more hatred for Shias than they do for the West. But what can they do in Afghanistan. Notwithstanding the fact that up to a fifth of the Afghan population is Shia, and that the majority of the country speak Dari (a sister to Farsi), Iran has so far been incapable of even stopping the trade of opium into Iran, where over 4 million heroin addicts make Iran the world's top consumer. This, despite the most stringent controls across the entire patrollable Afghan–Iran border.

Syria

Vali Nasr's thesis proposes that Shias benefit from the Freedom Agenda. The Alawite Assads might beg to differ, ruling a country that is 80-per cent Sunni since 1970. But regardless, resting more heavily on the proto-Shiite Assad regime, which a promotion of Shia interests elsewhere would necessitate, means acquiescing to a noxious meddler that stands contrapuntally against the West's most cherished dreams for the region: stability in Lebanon, peace in Palestine and safety for Israel.

Al Qaeda

Al Qaeda's great battle, as Ayman al-Zawahiri's now-famous pamphlet 'Knights Under the Banner of the Prophet' makes clear, is with the infidel within – the apostate royal family of Saudi Arabia, amongst others, the apathetic assimilating Muslim citizens of the modern world, and of course the Shia (as Nasr emphasizes). It is hard to imagine how siding with the Shia in the region's power struggle would serve to calm Al Qaeda's anti-Westernism.

The Gulf

On the face of it, support of the Shia of the Gulf looks like the easiest sell. They represent large minorities in most of the region – Kuwait, Saudi, Yemen, the UAE, Oman and Qatar – and a majority in Bahrain, yet they remain politically excluded. But as the tempers unleashed by Gamal Abd al-Nasser's renaming of the region itself show – *al-Khaleej al-Arabi* (Arabian Gulf) for *Khaleej e-Fars* (Persian Gulf) – any outside fiddling with the power balance in that most vital oil route will set the region on the brink of war. Sunni authority in the Gulf *should* deal with expanding Shia power as a fact, and aim – for everyone's benefit – at inclusion, but nothing suggests that it will.

***

In practical terms, therefore, Vali Nasr's cajoling pitch offers neither grounds for optimism for a Shia revival in the region, nor convincing grounds to suggest the West would benefit from early investment in it.

Yes, those of us who still buy the idea that the fundamental problem of the whole bloody area is political and economic exclusion (at a local and regional level), and that stability will only ultimately come with political enfranchisement and some form of greater democratic participation, must certainly think of the Shia revival – in the long term – as an excellent development.

And yes, in thinking about Iran itself, there is little debate amongst US and European scholars and think-tankers that engagement is the only option. Not because that nebulous and fractured 'Shia Crescent' which so terrifies the Kings Abdullah of Jordan and Saudi Arabia could serve immediate Western interests in the region, but because, as Robert Gates recently explained to Senator Byrd of West Virginia at his Senate Armed Services Committee confirmation on 5 December 2006, Iran is far too strong. While Iran currently poses no symmetric threat to the West, it holds most of the cards in the region. We can no longer bully – Iran may not be able (or in any way willing) to help our interests in the region, but it can certainly harm them more.

But perhaps this brings us to the two fundamental flaws of Nasr's analysis. The first, as suggested above, is that while the Shia and Iran are rising, they are by no means the regional hegemon that – on board – provides the blanket fix to our nightmares in the area. And the second, and greatest problem with Nasr's analysis, is his deliberate mischaracterization of today's Iran.

Deeply divided it certainly is, bordering on the brink of social revolution it might conceivably be, but about to become a US stooge in the region it is certainly not. And the current president, whose mandate extends until mid-2009, is a millenarian, proto-socialist revolutionary busy turning the clock back to the early fevered years of the Khomeini regime, and intent – for sound political reasons relating to the problems at home – on blustering confront-ationalism in external relations. There may well have been a window of opportunity under ex-President Khatami to woo Iran onto the international stage in a pliant role. But we played our cards abominably. After mass demonstrations calling for greater freedoms in May 2003 saw 4,000 student activists locked up, Bush included Iran in the Axis of Evil and ensured the country snapped immediately back behind their Supreme Leader. That window is now closed. Add to Ahmadinejad's personal politics the hellhole of Iraq, the growing power of Al Qaeda, the political concerns of today's Saudi Arabia, Jordan and elsewhere, and the window looks bricked in.

Nasr's *The Shia Revival* is a manifesto for a different time. It has a great deal to recommend it beyond even its fundamentally sound view that only inclusion (political and economic) will solve the riddle of the region. Its long chapter on Iraq represents the clearest and most concise description of inter- and intra-sectarian war I have yet seen. But Nasr's greatest contribution is in marking a qualitative shift in our understanding of the region today. He writes:

The concepts and categories that are often cited in order to explain the Middle East to Western audiences – modernity, democracy, fundamentalism, and secular nationalism, to name a few – can no longer satisfactorily account for what is going on. It is rather the old feud between Shias and Sunnis that forges attitudes, defines prejudices, draws political boundary lines, and even decides whether and to what extent those other trends have relevance. (p. 82)

It may not be all, but in a period of spiralling identitarian conflict, we forget that old rivalry at our peril.

In November 2006, I spent a week in Amman with some high-level Sunni escapees of the civil war next door. They were there with one misconceived objective in mind – to convince the coalition forces to back a return to Sunni power, even suggesting Saddam himself. The British, whose *divide et impera* first installed a Sunni monarch over a predominantly Shia people, were time and again held up as the only voice of reason on Iraq. I was told that, if given power, the Sunnis would and could kill a million militarized Shia in a month, and would take their Shia containment responsibilities so far as to carry the war directly to Iran. The plan is plainly absurd, of course, not least because power is not ours to give in Iraq anymore. But the principle underlying it unfortunately finds echoes in Nasr, for both he and my Sunni activists seem happier calling in the most destabilizing force in the region to gain the upper hand over their 'fellow' Muslims, Arabs and Middle Easterners.

In 1996, Massoud Barzani, leader of the KDP in Iraqi Kurdistan at the time and current president of the Autonomous Kurdish Government, called Saddam's forces in to oust Jalal Talabani's rival PUK forces from Irbil. It worked. Nasr seems to call for a similar play in the broader Middle East today, with Americans against Sunnis rather than Arabs against Kurds. The idea is misguided not simply for its delicate treachery, but because the difference between Saddam in his case, and America in this one, is that Saddam had real power.

Vali Nasr, *The Shia Revival: How Conflicts within Islam Will Shape the Future*, (New York: Norton, 2006) ISBN-13: 978-0-393-06211-3

Turi Munthe is a Fellow of the Royal United Services Institute.

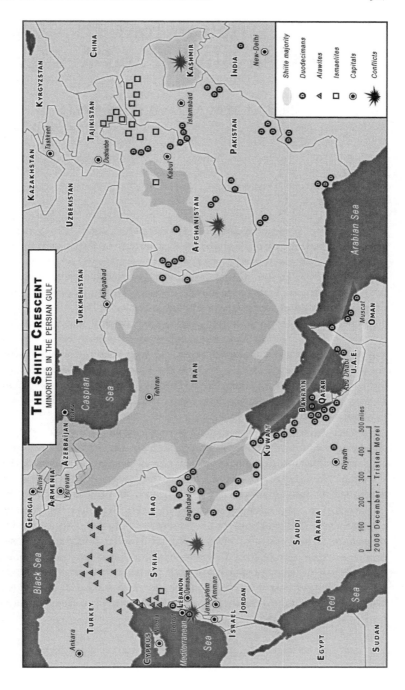

THE **SHIITE CRESCENT**
MINORITIES IN THE PERSIAN GULF

| | Shiite majority | Duodecimans | Alawites | Ismaelites | Capitals | Conflicts |

2006 December - Tristan Morel

Iran in Iraq:
Between Illusion and Reality

MUHAMMAD SAID SAHIB

Introduction

Iran has been present in Iraq for thousands of years. The great city of Ctesiphon, 30 km east of Baghdad, the capital of the Parthian Empire, prospered more than one hundred years before the foundation of Abbassid capital at Baghdad. Near to the ruins of Ctesiphon is the tomb of Salman the Persian, who was a famous companion of the Prophet Mohammad. For Iraqis, this tomb is a symbol of continuity of Persian presence in Iraq.

In the modern history of Iraq, the Iranian Safavid and Qajari dynasties (sixteenth to eighteenth, and eighteenth to twentieth centuries respectively) competed with the Ottomans to dominate Iraq. The Ottomans finally took control of Iraq from 1534 to 1917. These four centuries continue to have a large impact on modern Iraqi society. But the people of Iraq were themselves seldom involved in the struggle between the Ottomans and Persians for the domination of their country.

In fact, the Iraqis did not make any social demarcations according to this struggle. A significant example was the Iranian currency which circulated in the Iraqi markets in the nineteenth century. In spite of the efforts of the great Ottoman Wali of Baghdad, Medhet Pacha, to eradicate this currency, it continued to circulate on the market. However, in present-day Iraq, Iran and Turkey still try to influence Iraqi politics, but Iran is more present on a popular level. This is because of the presence of holy Shiite shrines in Iraq and because of Iran's hostility to the regime of Saddam Hussein. Because of its previous domination of Iraq, Turkey's influence on the Iraqi population is less great. It has influence primarily through the Turkmen minority. The Iranian influence in Iraq is still a subject which creates a good deal of confusion. In order to understand this situation, we will examine the different issues of the Iranian presence in Iraq.

Iran and the Dislocation of Iraq

For different reasons, media analysts discuss the question and often tend to agree that Iran wants to dismember Iraq. In reality, Iran has no interest in such a dislocation or in the creation of a Shiite state in the south of Iraq. First, such a state would be regarded by the Arab peoples as a Persian plot against them, whereas the whole of Iranian foreign policy is directed to wooing the Arabs in order to try to obtain their sympathy and support. Secondly, any collapse of Iraq would necessarily entail the creation of a Kurdish state, which Iran considers a great danger for its own national security. Third, in terms of the 'Great Game' of foreign policy, Iran would lose more than it would gain. Present-day Iraq is dominated by Shiites, who represent 60 per cent of the population (more than 15 million people). Six million Shiites live in what would be the 'Sunni' zone, especially in the capital Baghdad, Dyala in the north-east, or Samarra in the North. With a Shiite state, the Iranians would 'gain' a smaller state, which would be unrecognized or boycotted by its neighbours, and whose policies would not necessarily be pro-Iranian, and 'lose' the rest of the country. Indeed, the Shiite political forces who would dominate such a state might throw their lot in with the Americans. Currently, these forces have more interest to be on good terms with Iran. Finally, in the present context of struggle with the West, in particular with the US and Israel, the Iranians currently have greater room for manoeuvre with Kurdish forces, especially with the Patriotic Union of Kurdistan of the President Talabani (for historical reasons), and with Sunni factions, especially some radical anti-American leaders in present-day Iraq.

In other words, the present situation is easier for Iran than it would be if it faced hostile Kurdish and Sunni states and a problematic Shiite state. For all these reasons, I think that Iran is not in favour of dislocating Iraq and hopes instead to realize its interests in a unified Iraq.

Shiite Political Parties in Iraq

On the whole, the foreign influence on Iraqi political parties became much more important with the installation of the Ba'ath party in power in 1968 and especially since 1979, when Saddam Hussein eliminated his 'father leader' Bakr and took power himself. The Kurds looked to Russia and the Soviet Union, Arab nationalists to Egypt and Nasser; Muslim Brothers received support from Jordan and some of the Gulf States, while the Shiites looked to Iran. This paper looks in some detail at this last category.

The Islamic Dawa Party

In 1979, the most important Shiite political party in Iraq was the *Dawa* ('the call') party. It declared itself an Islamic party, but its members and its direction were Shiite. It was founded by the famous writer and philosopher from Najaf, Sayyid Muhammed Baqir al Sadr, killed by Saddam in 1981. He was supported by many young scholars, for instance by two Lebanese *ulemas* (Islamic scholars) from Najaf: M.H. Fadhlullah (later the spiritual guide of Hezbollah) and M. Mahdi Shams al Deen, a moderate and non-violent thinker, who was for many years the head of the Superior Shiite Council of Lebanon. The writings and the strategy of this party indicated a real orientation to have Sunni allies, notably activist sheikhs like A.A. al Badri, the imam of the Adila Khatoun mosque in Baghdad, who was killed in prison in 1970. Other Shiite parties like *Al Shabab al Muslim* (Muslim Young) and *Al Hizb al Aqa'idi* (Ideological Party) which formed in the 1960s were already moribund by 1979.

The paradox is that many members of the Dawa party were imprisoned or killed as was the party's leader, Muhammed Baqir al Sadr, who proposed a draft constitution draft for a new Islamic Republic of Iraq. However, Dawa militants and leaders who went into exile in Iran were also badly treated by the Iranian authorities – so badly that, in 1982, the party newspaper *Al Jihad* (The Struggle), published in Tehran at this time, was deprived of all resources. Dawa's independent position within Iran cost it dearly, to the point that the Iranian regime decided to create the Supreme Council of Islamic Revolution in Iraq (SCIRI), which was supposed to assemble all Shiite Islamic organizations. The real purpose of SCIRI was to reduce the role of the Dawa party, which explains why many Dawa leaders decided to leave Iran for Britain (for example, Ibrahim al Ja'fari and Walid al Hilly) or for Syria (Nuri al Maliki). At present, Dawa has no militia.

The Supreme Council for the Islamic Revolution in Iraq (SCIRI)

The Supreme Council for the Islamic Revolution in Iraq rapidly became an organization aligned with and financed by Iran. Its first leader was Mahmud al Hashimi; later it was led by Sayyid Mahmud Shahrudi, chief of the Judiciary Authority of Iran. Its speaker and strongest personality was the deceased Muhammed Baker al Hakim, assassinated after his return from Iran to Iraq by Al Qaeda in August 2003.

The main creation of SCIRI is the Badr Division, a paramilitary body which has undertaken some military operations against Saddam's forces. In democratic Iraq, this militia is said to be a civil society organization. Meanwhile, there is much evidence that the Badr militias kill Sunnis; others say that they assassinate only people who participated in the war against Iran, like the pilots who bombed Iranians towns in that war.

At any rate, SCIRI is the Iraqi organization which is the most closely linked to Iran. However, Iranians officials know that after the fall of Saddam, SCIRI leaders are no longer part of the opposition but are instead in power, and have started to establish their own relations with the United States and with European countries. Adil Abdul Mahdi, SCIRI's vice-president, has had excellent relations with the American and French authorities for many years. For this reason, the Iranian authorities are now devoting their efforts to cultivating further privileged relations with other organizations.

The Islamic Action Organization

The Islamic Action Organization is a local organization created in the holy city of Kerbala in the 1970s. Its spiritual chief was the well-known Sayyid M.M. al Shirazi. The group had some links with Iran, especially in conservative religious circles. Now there are two organizations, the second with the suffix 'general command'. Both are still strong in the area of Kerbala.

Muqtada al-Sadr and the Mahdi Army

In theory, this young firebrand does not have good relations with Iran. When his father was killed by Saddam, his death was not correctly commemorated in Iran. Moreover, the Badr brigades are the enemies of Sadr and his supporters, for these latter reject federalism and are suspicious of Iran's intentions in Iraq. Sadr's Mahdi Army has become very popular following the destruction of a holy tomb in Samarra. Sadr City in Baghdad is a bastion of support for Muqtada al-Sadr and the Madhi Army.

Al-Fadhila (Islamic Virtue) Party

This was created following a split with Sadr's organization. It is led by Sheikh Al-Yakubi. It has many armed young people, especially in Basra and the South. It stands for traditional tribal and religious values, and its popularity is an expression of the resentment of those tribes against the central power in Baghdad and against urban power generally.

Iraqi Hezbollah

This was created after the fall of Saddam in April 2003. It has no militia but its leaders have military training and have fought Saddam's forces in the South.

The explosive situation in Basra

About one year after the fall of Saddam Hussein, Basra was dominated by the partisans of Muqtada al-Sadr, in competition with supporters of SCIRI. In 2005, Sadr's movement accepted the political process and representation in the government. Following the creation of Al-Fadhila, its popularity is even greater. The southern tribes hated Saddam's regime and now they want their revenge, not only against the central government in Baghdad but also against the religious hierarchy in Najaf. The leader of Iraq's Shiites, Ayatollah Sistani, is himself an Iranian who has lived in Iraq for many years. In the tradition of Najaf, open debate is encouraged and new ideas are welcomed. Najaf also encourages the view that it is right to oppose a despotic power, albeit only by ideas. Shiites therefore tend to be oppositionists rather then wielders of power themselves. To overturn this tradition was the main innovation of Ayatollah Khomeini in his book *Vilayet-e Faqih*, and by the Islamic Revolution generally. This explains why Sistani encourages people to participate in the political institutions of democratic Iraq.

Conclusion

Iraqi Shiites are very proud of their independence and they have no hostility towards Iranians, the ancient competition between Najaf and Qom (in Iran) notwithstanding. Iraqi Shiites may sympathize with their Iranian co-religionists but it is not obvious that they would fight for them. Iran's influence in Iraq is therefore neither permanent nor uniform.

Dr Muhammad Said Sahib is with the IRI Programme/College of Law in Sulaimaniya, Iraq.

Syria and Iran in a Middle East in Transition

LORENZO TROMBETTA

'Syria hopes to attract Iranian investments in support of the deep political relations which link our two countries.' On 23 November 2005, Amir Husni Lufi, the Syrian minister of economics made this declaration in Damascus addressing a commercial delegation from Iran. 'Our doors are open to Iranian investments into our economy to the tune of hundreds of millions of dollars,' Lufi continued. 'The strategic alliance with Iran has always been extremely fruitful for Syria and we are not afraid to pay the political price for Iranian investments on our territory.'[1].

Only a few days previously, on 19 November, it was reported that the Syrian secret services had arrested in Damascus, on the request of Tehran, a group of Arab-Iranian activists from the Khuzestan/Arabistan region of Iran. They had been accused of 'attacking the national security of the Islamic Republic' and condemned to death in Iran. At least three of the members of this Organization for the Liberation of Ahwaz were promptly extradited to Iran by Syria.[2]

These are just two of the reports broadcast almost every day by Arab news outlets and which, in the context of the Middle East today, show the extreme political, strategic and economic proximity between the Syria of Bashir Al-Assad and the Iran of Mahmoud Ahmadinejad. But the Syrian-Iranian axis is also often mentioned in the North American and European media. In the majority of cases, these media prefer to describe the alliance between the two countries as the principal threat to the stability of the region which extends from the Mediterranean coast of the Levant deep into Central Asia, via the Persian Gulf.

The first embrace between Syria and Iran dates from 1979 and since then the two countries have entertained the closest and most stable alliance in the contemporary Middle Eastern history.[3] Throughout the turbulent events in the Middle East of the 1980s and 1990s, this mutual understanding has survived numerous tests of solidarity in different geographical scenarios.

Different Ideologies and an Iron Alliance

In the post-war period and throughout the 1960s, relations between Damascus and Iran were dominated almost permanently by an attitude of mistrust. Syria, which had been governed by the nationalist pan-Arab Ba'ath party since 1963, and which was more and more in the Soviet orbit, was perceived by the Shah's Persia, which was by contrast closely linked to the Western powers, as a potential threat to its regional interests. For its part, Damascus regarded Tehran's policies as nothing but an instrument in the hands of the United States. With the arrival to power of Hafez Al-Assad in the autumn of 1970, and with the adoption of a more pragmatic Syrian policy, there was a period of temporary thaw which led to Assad's first visit to Tehran in 1975. Iran then wanted to use Syria to counter Iraq, while Syria wanted to use Tehran's good offices to intercede with the United States and win political points in its conflict with Israel.

With the overthrow of the monarchy in Iran and the creation of the Islamic Republic, Syria was the first Arab country to recognize the new regime, on 12 February 1979, when it declared its own support for the Islamic Revolution. Since then, the Middle East has changed considerably but the understanding between the two countries has remained constant. Even today, it continues to contribute to the overall political balance in the region.

In the light of the last two decades of political events in the region, and of the choices made over this long period by the leaders in Syria and Iran, it is possible to identify the principle factors which have caused this strategic alliance to be so durable. The first, as political scientists emphasize, is that this is an alliance of only two countries and, in comparison with alliances containing several members, the risk of a break-up is smaller: 'The smaller the alliance, the more cohesive and effective it is, and the more important the contribution of each member.'[4].

Secondly, the alliance has been and largely remains essentially defensive, directed against the threats from Iraq and Israel and intended to impede encirclement by the United States. This too would seem to confirm the political science model according to which 'alliances with set and limited objectives are more stable and durable.'[5]

Furthermore, the interests of the two allies lie in different geographical regions in which they can, none the less, cooperate. Iran dominates the region of the Persian Gulf, while Syria projects its power towards the control of Lebanon. Over the years, Damascus and Tehran have therefore coordinated their acts and initiatives according to their respective strategic requirements: Syria has been preoccupied mainly with the political and military conflict with Israel, while Iran was concerned more directly with the regional ambitions of Saddam Hussein's Iraq.

Finally, another extremely important factor which has contributed to the strength of these links is the fact that the two regimes have different political ideologies: on the one hand, the secular pan-Arabism of the Syrian Ba'athists, forged by the 'father of modern Syria', Hafez Al-Assad (who governed from 1970 to 2000), on the other the pan-Islamic fundamentalism conceived by the leader of the Iranian Revolution, Ayatollah Ruhollah Khomeini. In a region such as the Middle East, in which authoritarian regimes use ideology as an instrument by means of which to shore up their political legitimacy, an alliance between two partners who are not in ideological competition with each other seems to be more durable.[6]. Neither member of the alliance has an interest in claiming supremacy over the other. Iran, which is not an Arab country, has never aspired to be the champion of Arab nationalism in the way that Syria under Assad father and son did and does. For its part, Damascus has never wanted to guide the reawakening of Islam, leaving this to Tehran.

Different Arenas, Common Enemies

The relationship between Syria and Iran has developed in various phases; it has manifested itself in different geographical areas and it has been partially determined by alliances concluded between rival regional actors.

Iran and Iraq, 1979–82

In the first phase, between 1979 to the summer of 1982, the first positive results of the understanding between the Damascus and Tehran became clear during the Iran–Iraq War which broke out in September 1980. After the *rapprochement* of February 1979 which followed Khomeini's arrival to power in Iran, the two countries had initiated various projects for military and political cooperation at a time when both saw their relations with the United States deteriorate and their relations with the Soviet Union improve.

In the same year, there was no thaw in relations between Damascus and Baghdad which continued its bitter conflict with Iran in order to try to obtain pre-eminence in the Gulf. It was inevitable, therefore, that Assad's Syria responded to the call for help from its Iranian ally which had been 'attacked by an expansionist Saddam'. A few days after the official opening of hostilities, on 22 September 1980, Damascus opened an air bridge to supply Tehran with arms, logistical equipment and medical supplies.[7] On 8 October, Assad himself flew to Tehran to sign a pact of friendship and cooperation with the Soviet Union and in order to convince the Kremlin to supply the Iranian Army against an Iraq which was then close to the United States.

In these same years, the Syrian-Iranian alliance was reinforced by the emergence of axes of strategic rivals. Egypt under first Sadat and then Mubarak (from October 1981) allied itself ever more closely with the US and against Arab countries. The alliance between Iraq and Jordan therefore extended to Cairo in the West, threatening to encircle Syria. Syria was viewed badly by these countries, not only because of its support for Iran but also for its unpopular intervention in the Lebanese conflict (1975–91).

At the beginning of 1982, the agreement between Damascus and Tehran was formalized by the signature of a series of economic-commercial and military agreements between the two countries. In March of that year, the then Syrian minister of foreign affairs led a delegation of fifty businessmen and high-level politicians to Tehran where he signed a protocol with the Iranian authorities which indicated that the Islamic Republic would export nine million tonnes of crude oil a year at a reduced price ($28 per barrel instead of $34) in return for four hundred thousands tonnes of Syrian phosphates used for the petrochemical industry in Iran. The agreement also provided for the exchange of large quantities of arms to be used, respectively, against Iraq in the Gulf War and in Lebanon against anti-Syrian militias. Another measure which Damascus adopted in favour of its Iranian ally and against Iraq was to seal its eastern borders in April 1982 and to close the Kirkuk–Baniyas–Tripoli pipeline which brought crude oil from Northern Iraq to the Mediterranean coast. This caused Saddam Hussein's regime to lose $17 million per day (approximately $6 billion per year).

Lebanon and Israel, 1982–85

With Israel's massive invasion of Lebanon in June 1982, a new phase in the relationship between Syria and Iran began. In the first three years, Damascus's support for Iran in its war with Iraq had made the Islamic Republic too dependent on aid from its Arab ally. Later, when the Syrian Air Force and Army found themselves in extreme difficulty against the supremacy of the Israel Defence Forces in the Beqaa Valley and in West Beirut, Iran's intervention on the side of Syria re-established some balance in the relationship between the two countries.

After the initial losses of the Syrian military and its Lebanese allies (Palestinian militias, Amal's Shiites, Jumblatt's Druze) against the advances of the Israeli Army, Damascus started a war of attrition in Beirut and in other parts of the country which were occupied by Israeli soldiers and which were under the control of rival Christian militias. In this context, Iran's logistical, military, intelligence, economic and ideological support was decisive, especially in those parts of the country where there was already a strong local Shiite presence.

As a first emergency measure, at the beginning of June 1982, immediately after the Israeli invasion, Tehran sent numerous fighters to Damascus who were then sent into Lebanon.[8] On 17 June 1982, a delegation, led by the Iranian Minister of Foreign Affairs Ali Akhbar Veliyati, travelled to Syria to discuss the details of the support Iran would provide and suggested sending a massive contingent of volunteers (some 40,000) and members of special units (10,000) to be used alongside the Syrian Army and the Shiite militias of Amal. But Assad preferred for the time being to decline the offer, afraid that such a generous act by the Iranians would have undermined the future sovereignty of Damascus in the Lebanese scenario, given the possible future military and ideological expansionism of Tehran.

Later, from September 1982 onwards, after having suffered heavy losses in Lebanon and after having seen Syria's positions in the Beqaa Valley and West Beirut withdraw, the Syrian president turned to his Iranian ally with the idea of using a small number of Iranian combatants in a non-conventional war against Israel and its allies. At least 2,000 members of the Iranian Revolutionary Guard were sent to Baalbeck, the stronghold of the Beqaa Valley controlled by pro-Syrian forces, while Amal's forces saw their numbers swell to 10,000 well-armed and well-trained men.

In the two years from 1983 to 1985, after a series of victories in key areas of Lebanon (the Druze Shuf, the mountains to the east of Beirut, the motorway from Damascus to Beirut, the north of Mt Lebanon),[9] Syria managed to impose its rule, directly or indirectly, on large parts of Lebanon. It was against this background that the Shiite party Hezbollah emerged, born with the aim of resisting the 'Zionist' occupation and closely linked to certain Iranian leaders.[10]

But in the same period, the front of Arab countries close to the United States was reorganized around Egypt, above all in reaction to the Iranian invasion of Iraq in July 1982. Saddam Hussein's regime was very clever in asking for the support of 'Arab brothers' at this point, and in consolidating its alliance with Washington thanks to the good offices of Saudi diplomacy. Meanwhile, Syria did not manage to take complete control of Lebanon and found itself ever more encircled by the axis of Egypt, Jordan and Arafat's PLO. This stalemate reinforced yet again the Syrian-Iranian alliance, which was again perceived as a defensive alliance against the threats of hostile actors.

In the second half of the 1980s, and until the outbreak of the Gulf War in 1990, the two partners consolidated their alliances, recognizing each other's supremacy in their respective areas: once one or two tensions were resolved over the control of the Shiite Party of God, Damascus was definitely considered by Tehran to be the main power in Lebanon. Iran supplied indispensable military and ideological support to the Shiite militias of Amal and to Hezbollah. In the Gulf, meanwhile, Syria supported Iran both in its military and economic conflict with Iraq and also by putting itself forward as a mediator, in the interests of Iran, in various crises between the Islamic Republic and other Arab countries in the region.

Ahmadinejad and Assad in a Middle East in transition

Since then, the Middle Eastern political landscape has changed, as have the dynamics in the region. This is partly a reflection of the changes which have occurred in the wider world. After the collapse of the USSR, the US became the only superpower and arbiter in the region and, from the autumn of 2001, the interventionism of the Bush administration in Afghanistan and Iraq, together with the diplomatic initiatives by Washington and Paris in Lebanon, isolated Syria and Iran from the Western bloc.

Today, however, their alliance is reinforced by the direct and indirect support of diplomatic and energy powers like China and Russia, but also by Venezuela and North Korea. Both the Iranian and the Syrian presidents, whose images appear side by side to illustrate the alliance, have declared themselves keen to pursue their relations and to emphasize the solidity of their alliance. This was recently strengthened by the signature of an agreement in October 2006 between Iran, Syria and Hugo Chavez's Venezuela for the creation of a tripartite consortium which will manage the new refinery of crude oil on the outskirts of Damascus.[11] The economic and commercial links between the two countries is only one aspect of the strategic relationship which is destined to keep Syria and Iran united, at least in the short and medium term. The two points of reference, the Gulf and the Levant, continue to preoccupy the leaders in Tehran and Damascus even if matters there are less volatile than in the past.

Syria-Iran and Iraqi temptations

In post-Saddam Iraq, which has been subject to more than three years of foreign occupation and which is ever more torn to pieces by internal violence in a territory now divided along ethnic-confessional lines, Ahmadinejad's Iran and Assad's Syria are trying to play their own cards with different objectives in mind. On the one hand, they want to accredit themselves, directly or indirectly, with the United States as 'stabilizing forces' in certain sensitive regions of Iraq (the Shiite south of Iraq for Iran, the central area inhabited by Sunni tribes for Syria); on the other, they want to prevent hostile elements from operating within Iraq to threaten Syrian or Iranian territory.

This is the sense of the recent report by the bipartisan Iraq Study Group in the US on possible solutions to the Iraqi crisis. The 'wise men' of the committee speak of the need to establish a constructive dialogue with Syria and Iran, thereby giving each country the role of firemen called to put out the flames in Mesopotamia.

Here the relationship between Damascus and Tehran become more delicate. The Sunni tribes in the centre of Iraq have for centuries maintained blood links ('*asabiyya*) with their Syrian 'relatives' beyond borders drawn up only eighty years ago, but no one can be sure that they will allow themselves to be subject, directly or indirectly, to the regime in Damascus. By analogy, the inhabitants of Southern Iraq share their Shiite religion with the Iranians but this does not mean that Tehran can impose its own protectorate there, even an informal one.

Presented as theoretical zones of influence for Syria and Iran, these two regions of Iraq could instead turn out to be dangerous traps, both for Assad and for Ahmadinejad. In the vacuum created by the dislocation of the Iraqi state, the Sunni tribes in the centre of the country and the Shiite populations in the South, which for decades were controlled by the regime of Saddam Hussein (the former favoured, the latter repressed), could well now decide that they do not want to lose their autonomy by becoming instruments in the regional power game.

In addition, there is another traditional factor of instability in the region, namely the Kurdish presence in territory divided between Turkey, Syria, Iran and Iraq. Since the creation of the autonomous Kurdish zone in Northern Iraq in 1991, but especially since the fall of Saddam in April 2003, the Iranian and, even more so, the Syrian Kurds have been watching the 'Iraqi solution' with extreme interest, in which their 'brothers' over the borders are now living.

In Lebanon it is now Tehran which dominates

From the Gulf to the Mediterranean, the other front of the Syrian-Iranian alliance continues, even today, to be Lebanon. Here Damascus and Tehran seek to maintain their respective influence manoeuvring against the United States and France. From the summer of 2004 the clash between the two blocks has become ever sharper with a series of victories and defeats for both formations.

Damascus replied to UN Resolution 1559 initiated by Paris and Washington in September 2004 but extending the mandate of its faithful lieutenant, Emile Lahoud, until the end of the autumn of 2007. After the massive street protests and the strong international pressures brought to bear after the assassination of Rafiq Hariri in February 2005, Syria was forced to withdraw its troops after fifteen years in Lebanon.

However, hopes have not been fulfilled that the international commission of enquiry into Hariri's murder would turn into a battering ram with which to destroy the Syrian regime. For the time being, the enquiries are continuing without any senior official from Syria having to answer for the crime, while the war in the summer of 2006 between Israel and Hezbollah has, *de facto*, reinforced the Lebanese parties supported by Syria and Iran and weakened those supported by the United States and France which are today represented by the precarious government of Fouad Siniora. The current crisis in Lebanon which sees the opposition to the anti-Syrian government coalesce around the Party of God should in fact been seen as the umpteenth manifestation of a far greater clash which extends over time and place.

In this context, the Syrian-Iranian relationship is currently without any doubt in favour of the Islamic Republic. Its principal ally in Lebanon, the Party of God (Hezbollah) led by Sayid Hassan Nasrallah, while being a Lebanese party, does maintain the closest links with the upper echelons of the Iranian regime. Damascus' role is limited to providing its own logistical support to Hezbollah's armed wing, allowing major arms supplies to transit its own territory in order to reach the Beqaa Valley. In the past, Syria seemed to be able to influence decisions made by Hezbollah using it as an instrument of pressure against Israel; today, by contrast, it seems that it is Syria's own decisions which are secondary to the agenda set by Tehran and Nasrallah.

In the war between Hezbollah and Israel, Bashir Al-Assad expressed his own support for the 'Islamic resistance' of Nasrallah's men[12] and recently senior officers in the Lebanese Army have implicitly confirmed that arms were supplied directly to the Shiite militias in Lebanon via Syrian territory.[13] But Damascus' role seems to be limited to these aspects, while it is the emissaries of Tehran in Lebanon who coordinate Hezbollah's actions against Israel.[14]

It is in this context that Syria's effort to keep open the possibility of dialogue with the United States and the European Union should be understood – as an attempt to avoid Syria's foreign policy becoming subject to that of its ally, Iran. From the middle of September 2006, there have been intense efforts by Damascus to reopen contacts with the principal European countries and with the Bush administration.

Recalling the agreement reached in 1990 with President George Bush Senior, when Syria gave military support to the Western anti-Saddam coalition in return for acceptance of the Syrian presence in Lebanon, Syria today might hope once again to count for something in Lebanon by finding a compromise with Washington.

This might be why on 27 November 2006 Bashir Al-Assad, together with his Iraqi opposite number Jalal Talabani, declined an Iranian invitation to visit Tehran. A week previously, when the first leaks from the Baker-Hamilton report suggested that Iran and Syria be involved in solving the Iraqi crisis, President Ahmadinejad invited both Assad and Talabani to Tehran 'in order to try to stop the spiral of violence in Iraq'. Analysts interpreted his gesture as an attempt by Ahmadinejad to prevent the United States from regaining control of Iraq by using the good offices of Damascus. At the end of November 2006, with the visit to Baghdad of Syrian Minister of Foreign Affairs Walid Al-Mu'allim, a historic *rapprochement* occurred, after a quarter-century of tensions, between Syria and Iraq.

In any case, the lasting image of the relationship between Syria and Iran surely remains the warm handshake between Ahmadinejad and Assad on 1 December 2006 at the Olympic stadium in Doha at the opening of the 15th Asian Games.

In a Middle East in transition, the balance of power in this alliance, which has lasted nearly three decades, might undergo changes in the short term. However, the strategic bases of the Damascus-Tehran axis seem destined to remain unchanged. The longest bilateral alliance in the modern history of the region seems set to last.

Lorenzo Trombetta is the author of Siria. *Nel Nuovo Medioriente* (Syria in the New Middle East) (Rome:Editori Riuniti, 2004). He is writing a thesis on modern Syria at the Sorbonne and at La Sapienza in Rome.

NOTES

1   *Tishrin*, 24 November 2006, Damascus, p. 1. The daily explained that the new Iranian investments were in industry, public transport, construction and agriculture. According to the Chamber of Commerce in Damascus, quoted by the London-based pan-Arabic daily, *Al Hayat*, on 19 November 2006, in 2004 Iran exported goods to Syria to a total value of $56 million, while every year some 200,000 Iranian businessmen go to Syria on business.

2   *Levant News – Akhbar ash-Sharq*, 'Damascus extradites to Iran a group of Ahwaz Arabs', 19 November 2006, London <http://www.thisisyria.net/2006/11/19/syriatoday/03.html>. Since uprisings started again in April 2005 among the Ahwaz of Khuzestan, according to Irin, the humanitarian information service of the United Nations, Iran has intensified its repressive campaign against its citizens of Arabic ethnicity in the region. The Ahwazi Human Rights Organization, based in the United States, claims that from April 2005 more than 25,000 people have been arrested, at least 131 executed and some 150 'disappeared'. The Syrian authories claim that 'no prisoner of conscience has been extradited from Syria to Iran.' They claim that for other crimes there exist extradition agreements between the two countries. See Irin, 'Syria: Ahwazis in fear after news of deportation and death sentence', 11 December 2006).

3   M. Goodarzi Jubin, *Syria and Iran – Diplomatic Alliance and Power Politics in the Middle East*, London, 2006, p. 2. This is the most comprehensive and most up-to-date account of the alliance between the two countries, and it has an excellent bibliography. The quotations from specialists below come from Goodarzi.

4   E.H. Fedder, 'The concept of alliance', *International Studies Quarterly*, No. 12, 1968, pp.65–86, p.83; O.R. Holsti, P.T. Hopmann and J.D. Sullivan, *Unity and disintegration in international alliances*, Lanham, MD: University Press of America, 1985, p. 21.

5   H. Dinerstein, 'The transformation of alliance systems' in *American Political Science Review*, No. 59, 1965, pp. 589–601, p.599.

6   One thinks for example of the fierce ideological war fought between the two Ba'athist regimes in Syria and Iraq throughout the 1970s, 1980s and 1990s, and of the battle between the leaders in Damascus and Cairo for the leadership of the pan-Arab movement in the 1950s and 1960s.

7   Syria supplied Iran with Sam-7 ground-to-air missiles, 'Sagger' anti-tank missiles and RPG rockets.
8   Damascus spoke of 400 men, European diplomatic sources claimed at the time that the true figure was about 3,000.
9   The Western press and Western commentators attribute numerous attacks in these years to the Syrian-Iranian connection. Among the most famous are: the attack against Lebanese President Bashir Gemayel, in September 1982 in East Beirut, who had only recently been elected and who was supported by Israel; and the attacks of 18 April and 23 October 1983, respectively against the US embassy in Beirut and against French and American barracks near the Lebanese capital. A total of 361 persons died in these three attacks.
10   There is a large bibliography of Hezbollah, the Party of God. See for instance Judith Palmer Harik, *Hezbollah: The Changing Face of Terrorism*, London: I.B. Tauris, 2006; Naim Qassem, *Hizbullah: The Story from Within*, London: Saqi Books, 2005; Ahmad Nizar Hamzeh, *In The Path Of Hizbullah*, Syracuse: Syracuse University Press, 2004; Amal Saad-Ghorayeb, *Hizbu'llah: Politics and Religion*, London: Pluto Press, 2002.
11   *Arabicnews*, 'Iran, Venezuela, Syria oil refinery project', 31 October 2006. According to press sources, the project would cost $1.5 billion but the parties still have to agree on their respective investment quotas. The refinery could produce 140,000 barrels per day. <www.arabic news.com/ansub/Daily/Day/061031/2006103101.html>.
12   Ansa (Italian press agency), 'Israele-Libano: Assad, Hezbollah ha vinto battaglia militare', Cairo, 14 August 2006.
13   Ansa, 'Libano: capo esercito smentisce Nasrallah su blocco armi', Beirut, 8 December 2006. In the communiqué of the armed forces of Beirut, it was stated that, 'Throughout the war sufficient measures were taken to prevent the transfer of weapons and munitions from abroad, with the exception of those delivered directly to the resistance in the South.'
14   Ansa, 'Libano-Iran: Tehran apre ufficio a Tiro per ricostruzione – Un centro studi e ricerche per potenziare il sostegno iraniano', Beirut, 16 November 2006. At the inauguration of the office in Tyre were present, among others, Husam Khoshnovest, the personal representative in Lebanon of the Iranian president, Mahmoud Ahmadinejad, and Abd al-Majid Salih, a Hezbollah deputy elected by a local college. 'This office,' Khoshnovest said, 'will serve as a centre for study and research to assist the Republic of Iran's reconstruction programme in the south of Lebanon.'

Interview with Majed Bamya

What is the perception of Hezbollah among Palestinians?

Hezbollah is admired, as is its Secretary-General Nasrallah. It is the model of successful resistance. Hezbollah became a regional actor, especially after the Israeli withdrawal from southern Lebanon in 2000. The Lebanese resistance had not only been successful in liberating Lebanese territory from Israeli occupation but also in doing so without concessions, without interminable negotiations. The Palestinians negotiated with the Israelis without tangible results for seven years, while Hezbollah liberated the territory without even negotiating an agreement with them. The unacceptable Israeli proposals made at Camp David, which consisted, for example, of Palestinians having sovereignty mostly in the suburbs of East Jerusalem; of Israel keeping most of the city; of a Palestinian state in four pieces; and of a 'right of return' for refugees deprived of any substance, gave the impression that negotiations were useless. We were asked to legitimize what international law condemns, to renounce willingly our rights. All that, added to Sharon's provocation on the esplanade of mosques, led to the second Intifada.

This image of a solid, organized and efficient resistance was renewed by Hezbollah during the recent Israeli war against Lebanon. After the withdrawal of Syrian troops and a rather good result at parliamentary elections for the forces of 14th of March which demanded this withdrawal, analysts asserted the loss of influence of the movement. By attacking Israeli soldiers, Hezbollah was trying to reinvest both the national arena, by allowing the Lebanese prisoners' release, and the regional scene by supporting the Palestinians who were undergoing one of the worst attacks the Gaza Strip had ever known, which developed following the capture of an Israeli soldier. This act, as well as the resistance which followed, and the well-elaborated speeches of Nasrallah, led to undeniably wide support for the movement and its leader in Palestine and in the Arab world.

How is the Shiite movement perceived in the Arab world?

It is feared by governments and adored by the people. It seems that the attempt to characterize this movement as a Shiite movement did not succeed in frightening the Sunnis. Hezbollah is a national liberation movement, now guardian of Arab honour, the only force able to stand up to Israel. Arab governments in general, and Saudi Arabia and Egypt in particular, have another perception of Hezbollah: they consider it as a Shiite force instrumentalized by Iran, a factor of regional destabilization, and an Islamic force which could inspire similar forces in the Arab world. These two countries hold Hezbollah responsible for the war. That was a monumental error. It was obvious that the capture of both soldiers served only as a pretext for the Israelis and the Americans to put an end to any form of military resistance in the region and to any force able to defy them.

Another American objective for the war was to deprive Iran of one of its major assets in this regional confrontation with the United States and inflict on it an important defeat.

The forces of 14th of March will continue pleading for Lebanon not to be a war ground for other countries, considering this war irresponsible and that it only served the interests of Syria and Iran. Nevertheless, such an interpretation is misleading since Israel was accustomed to negotiate exchanges of prisoners in this kind of situation and that this time it preferred to choose war. That opened the gap between two Lebanons, more than ever visible and dangerous, with forces mutually accusing each other of having submitted to the Israeli-American diktat or, on the contrary, to be subjected to the Iranian and Syrian alliance. This internal war, these reciprocal charges of treason are an error. Hezbollah defended Lebanon, counting on those ready to support this resistance. The forces of 14th of March wanted to put an end to the war and the instrumentalization of Lebanon. Those two national agendas are not so incompatible as some may think or may want us to think. They become incompatible by the interference of other regional and world actors. Asking for the withdrawal of the Syrian troops was legitimate. Wanting to counter the influence of Iran and Syria is legitimate. But that is only possible, if one wants to avoid the break-up of Lebanon, if there is no other interference, and I mean thereby American and Israeli interference.

By attacking Lebanon, Israel gave credit to Hezbollah's analysis according to which it is the only force able to defend the country. Israel must withdraw from all Lebanese territory, including the Chebaa Farms, release all the prisoners and commit itself to no longer attacking Lebanon, providing solid guarantees. Lebannon's internal division will then dissipate, whereas they reached a paroxism following this war. We will thus be able to reconcile two visions of Lebanon.

In this confrontation, the Arab world, such as numerous states, was a factor of tension and not appeasement, supporting openly the forces of 14th of March, that is, opposing Hezbollah, considering it to be under Iranian influence, while continuing to ignore Hezbollah's national agenda and legitimacy. Currently the Arab countries are trying to find exits to the crisis. A change of reading of the origin of the present crisis and its implications is the only way to put an end to it.

How was the Israeli campaign of the summer of 2006 viewed by the Palestinian population?

There were two Israeli campaigns, in Gaza and in Lebanon, with the objective of showing that attacking Israel will not go unpunished and that there can be no resistance to the American project for the region. The war was a failure, leading to the humiliation of Israel and the strengthening of Iran's regional stature. The countries which sought a negotiated exit to the Israeli–Arab conflict lost their credibility.

In addition, the Palestinian population, like the Lebanese population, endured in its flesh this campaign which caused hundreds of dead on the Palestinian side, and more than a thousand on the Lebanese. It was clear that Israeli impunity did not have any limits. Impunity leads to irresponsibility and Israel's irresponsibility will lead the region to chaos. The United States and some European states opposed the ceasefire, the Security Council could not call for such an end of hostilities for the first time in its history. Thus, the credibility of the international community was largely undermined. The Palestinians lost any remaining trust in this international community which mobilized itself to release three Israeli soldiers made prisoners of war, while it had done nothing for years for the 10,000 Palestinian prisoners or to obtain Lebanese prisoners' release.

Will one draw finally the lessons of this war on the two fronts, Lebanese and Palestinian, namely that there is neither a military solution, nor a unilateral solution to the conflict?

Only a vigorous condemnation and a determined action to end the Israeli occupation and the colonial policies led behind the security folding screen would return to the states which had called for the negotiations with Israel some of their credibility and legitimacy. I point out here that Israel refused the Arab states' proposal made at the Beirut Summit of 2002, of a regional solution for the conflict. This proposal called for the liberation of all Arab occupied territories in 1967, that is, the establishment of a Palestinian state based on the June 1967 borders, the liberation of the Golan Heights and Chebaa Farms, and finding a just solution for the Palestinian refugees in accordance with Resolution 194 of the United Nations General Assembly, in exchange for the recognition of Israel.

The Israeli refusal to negotiate final-status issues by hiding behind preconditions, its will to trace its borders unilaterally to annex more Palestinian land, to consolidate its occupation in Jerusalem and in the West Bank are not only a factor of tension but are also the main obstacle to peace. Security measures often hide colonial interests and Israel must understand that it cannot continue its occupation and enjoy peace.

Ahmadinejad talks about the destruction of Israel while the Israeli acts destroy any prospect for a Palestinian state on the ground, not in words, with no leading European state or the US to effectively condemn such policies. This double standard is undermining international credibility and any constructive approach in the region.

Is there an Iranian presence in Palestine?

Iran is a regional actor and the cold war which prevails in the Middle East between Iran and certain Arab states may intensify this role. Iran is a firm supporter of Hezbollah and has links with the Palestinian movements of Islamic Jihad and of Hamas. The latter could count on its financial support after the decision of some governments, especially the United States and the European Union, to suspend aid to the Palestinian government. A number of elements must therefore be pointed out.

First of all, concerning the suspension of aid, it left the field open to Iran to play a more important role in Palestine where it had only a minor presence. This suspension not only produced a catastrophic humanitarian situation, it also accentuated tensions and threatens to cause chaos. These sanctions against Palestinian democracy must cease. The right to vote means the right to choose. The Palestinians chose and the international community should have heard their dismay to see that electing Abbas had no real positive consequences. Even more, occupation intensified in the West Bank with the construction of the wall and of new settlements while the world was applauding a unilateral withdrawal from Gaza, transforming in fact this narrow piece of land into a prison. The international community supported Abbas only in words and did not allow him to show that the way of negotiations was open and that it led to freedom and to recognition of the Palestinians' rights.

The second pivotal point is that the Iranian regime, feeling threatened by the new American policy, became more radical. This policy must be re-examined after having proved a failure in Iraq, Palestine, Lebanon, Syria and, even further away, in North Korea. It weakened the region and caused instability, which often announces chaos.

Instead of addressing the reasons leading to terrorism, the United States chose violence and escalation, ignoring the sometimes legitimate claims of the people concerned, and confusing national struggle and international terrorism. Iran drew from this policy new strength and a true influence, especially after the war on Iraq, and then during the war on Lebanon.

However, the Iranian presence remains weak in Palestine, but the escalation of the confrontation with the United States leaves only little space for those who have an independent national agenda. Indeed, the Arab world must not be subdivided between moderates on the one hand and Islamists on the other. Such a reading is not only simplistic, it is apocalyptic. Similarly, there are not on one side traitors and on the other fanatics. The present American policy leads all the forces to define themselves through their acceptance or refusal of this policy. Some believe that they cannot oppose the United States, even in their country's best interest. Some believe resisting American policy is the only choice, to preserve the regime or even sometimes to preserve their national interests. The fact that American policies are seen as aggressive, imperialistic and one-sided (pro-Israeli) strengthens these forces. Therefore the United States must take a firmer position against the Israeli occupation and abandon the will to redefine the Middle East. A better understanding of the people of the region, who should be able to express their will by themselves, is the only way out. The United States does not have the necessary legitimacy to choose for them or to pretend to help them to choose. Then, and only then, will we be able to resist any other external influence and that is our responsibility, especially when other states use our struggle to defend their own interests.

What do you think of the project of a Shiite crescent?

The attitude of a number of governments encourages the recrudescence of an old war between Sunnis and Shiites that will lead to the explosion of the Middle East. We have a duty to avoid such a tragedy at all costs. The US war on Iraq exacerbated these divisions. Al Qaeda also used these divisions and launched a war against the Shiites, even though a number among them were also opposed to the US occupation. Undeniably, the civil war opposing two of the principal components of the country, Shiites and Sunnis, not only threatens the future of Iraq but also that of the region. Indeed, this confrontation could expand to Lebanon and continue spreading to other countries.

The countries of the region gave body to this religious division which seems absurd and suicidal to me. The Saudi position, since denied by the authorities, is inspired by the idea of such a confrontation. The regime would have stated that the Sunnis of Iraq will be under its protection if the Americans were to withdraw. Iran sometimes plays this card, in Iraq as in Lebanon, but maintains its influence in other countries by its alliance with Syria and its support for movements like Hamas.

Hezbollah acted in a responsible manner on the matter by considering that one of the achievements of the war was uniting Sunnis and Shiites (as well as Christians) in the Arab world. That makes all the more irrelevant the current reading of the Lebanese crisis as a confrontation between Shiites on the one hand and Christians, Sunnis and Druzes on the other. Indeed, General Aoun, a Christian leader, is Hezbollah's ally.

This crisis must be placed in a particular Lebanese context that is not just characterized by religious diversity, which is often the only template used by the Western countries and even sometimes by the states of the region. This crisis must also be analysed in a regional and international context which is not that of the confrontation between moderate and radicals. Nevertheless, it must be acknowledged that the fact that the Shiite in Iraq were kept away from the power and those of Lebanon were socially, economically and even politically disadvantaged led to the affirmation of a Shiite identity. But a leader like Nasrallah does not misuse this identity; he places himself and his movement in a dual belonging, to the Arab world and to the Muslim world. He should therefore not accuse his opponents of treason while calling for a national unity government. The same applies to Hamas. That would make not only the union impossible but also civil war inevitable.

This confrontation between several forces in the region, as for example the confrontation between Hamas and Fatah, must be explained in something other than a religious context. I choose this example not only because these confrontations threaten my people's future and undermine their struggle but because they contradict the religious thesis. The majority use then the distinction between radicals and moderate. I challenge this division. It is impossible to understand the region and conceive its future if one refuses to recognize the forces emanating from political Islam. In the same way as those who want to negotiate with Israel are not all traitors, those who consider their faith as a source of their political beliefs and those who resist military occupation are not all fanatics. They draw their legitimacy from their resistance to occupation and from their work on a social level. Wars do not weaken them but strengthen them. Ending the occupation will make it possible to better distinguish these forces, know their actual weight, their social project. People will be then in a position to choose peacefully and without fear.

The true division in the Middle East takes place elsewhere and this division was transformed into a gap by the post-11 September American policy. The division is linked to each force's attitude towards the policy of the United States or in a broader way towards the West. There are the forces which at regional level find that to be able to serve their interests, whether it is to preserve their own regime or to ensure their independence and the well-being of their people, they need to comply with the political line wanted by Washington. They join therefore the so-called 'moderate' forces which combat terrorism and which are not opposed too openly to the United States. However the popular discontent with the results of the American policy is seen, this perception is today more accurate than ever, as aggressive and openly pro-Israeli, reflected very negatively on these forces. Opposition forces, to preserve their own regime or to guarantee the national interests, choose to resist the political agenda determined by Washington and these forces therefore ride on this popular discontent. There is not on the one hand the axis of virtue and on the other hand the axis of evil. On both sides, certain leaders seek only to preserve their places. Similarly, there are dictatorships on both sides, democracies on both sides, fundamentalist regimes and secular ones on both sides. The template which is often proposed to us is therefore outdated.

Thus, the American policy is dangerous because it undermines any reconciliation between forces in the various states of the region and threatens to exacerbate tensions and threats. This policy leads to polarization and delegitimizes the forces it intends to support. A more constructive attitude for overall peace in the region and an in-depth change of the so-called 'war against terrorism' are essential to open prospects in a region where such prospects lack cruelly. The United States must understand and address the legitimate aspirations of the people of the region. It needs to distinguish between the means which sometimes need to be condemned and the cause that must be supported. If we do not want the gap endangering the future of the region to grow, then it is time to tackle the causes of violence. It is also time for the forces of the region to draw up a common strategy and refuse to enter into the present model decided by Washington. Finally, European countries must not submit to the present policy at the same time when the Americans are recognizing its failure.

The concept of the Shiite crescent is only one of the consequences of this policy. There are always spheres of influence and Iran probably conceives this area as an expansion of their country to southern Lebanon, passing through Iraq. But Syria, a non-Shiite country, also regards these countries as an area where it exerts influence. One must cease simply fearing the implementation of such a project, that of the Shiite crescent, and instead face the factors which can lead to such a division. The realization of this project would mean the break-up of Lebanon and Iraq. If we want to avoid this tragedy, one must come out from this sterile opposition. It is the responsibility of the United States, Europe, but also of the states and the forces of the region, not to accept this division and not to use it. Such a division jeopardizes the essential interests of our nations.

Is it possible to speak about a 'radical corridor' from Iran to Gaza?

The answer is no. The radical corridor crosses the Arab and Muslim world. The radical corridor crosses the world. There are extremists and different extremisms everywhere and in recent years they enjoy all the conditions needed to flourish: fear, tensions, racism, rejection of the other. They feed each other. But today, all attention is concentrated on Muslim extremism. Some may respond that it is the most deadly one. But the war on Iraq was also deadly and totally unjustified. It was the expression of American extremism. And this war fed extremism in the region. It is time to address people's legitimate aspirations, to end the occupation, to cease making of the Middle East a zone of influence. It is time to prove concretely to the people of the region that dialogue, the relation with the rest of the world, can guarantee their rights, protect their interests, and fulfil their aspirations. Maybe then, the idea that a confrontation is not needed can prevail without dividing the countries of the region. Maybe then we will have a restored legitimacy for a better partnership with other countries without looking as though we were in submission to them. In short, addressing the causes of violence is the only way to end it.

With all that, the United States preferred a dogmatic, monolithic approach to a complex region, rich in history and in diverse cultures, which does not cease shouting its desire for freedom and dignity. Democracy became an instrument in the Americans' hands, to undermine the legitimacy of those who fought to install it in the region. Countries were summonned to choose between the axis of virtue and that of evil. Under the cover of partnership, one guessed easily the diktats which always brought about rejection.

There is no radical corridor going from Iran to Gaza, there is a boiling and burning Middle East. If we want to avoid all that exploding, people must have prospects. Those who embody the people's aspirations, whatever their beliefs, must be heard. Racism must be fought to avoid the conflagration of the clash of civilizations. For the moment the radical corridor grows, in each region, each country, each individual. If the policy of upholding double standards continues, if one does not answer the injustices, this radical corridor will grow and its extension will be ensured. There is urgency to end the current American policy, to end the Israeli colonial policy, to re-examine the European policy. The countries of the region will also have to be more responsible, more able to address their people's aspirations. All will have to assume their historical mission, that of avoiding the explosion of this region, that of avoiding the division of the world.

Geopolitical Affairs interviewed **Majed Bamya**, former president of the Union of Palestinian Students in France, in December 2006.

Iranian-Egyptian Relations: The Shiite Factor and the Muslim Brotherhood

AHMAD RASEM AL-NAFIS

It is well known that Muslims are divided into two major subdivisions, Shiites and Sunnis. Both faiths agree that the holy Koran and the statements of the Prophet Mohammad (Hadith) are the principal sources of Islamic legislation, but they differ about the proper way of documenting the Prophet's statements and hence about the correct and orthodox understanding of Islam.

The divisions between these two strands of Islam go back to the very beginnings of the Muslim faith. However, in modern times, the conflict has become perhaps even sharper than before, especially with the rise of a virulent and manic strain of anti-Shiism, invented by the Sunni cleric, Mahammad ibn Abdul Wahhab. Wahhabism was exploited by British intelligence as a useful tool with which to stir up trouble in the Ottoman Empire.

Wahhabis consider that all other Muslims are infidels, especially Sufis and Shiites. Today, there are thousands of Wahhabi establishments all over Egypt, which are funded by Saudi money and which are allowed to operate without any interference from the Egyptian government.

Political Sunnism, which is now under the leadership of Saudi Arabia, considers any Shiite political entity as an existential threat that should be ended as early as possible. This idea has been a constant one since the end of the Fatimi State 800 years ago.[1] It is this idea which explains why all Arab regimes supported Saddam Hussein in his eight-year war with Iran.

The manic Arab Sunnism, with its long-term experience in plotting and conspiracy, was able to convince the West that Iran poses a terrorist threat against them, in spite of the fact that Wahhabi terrorism is just an extension of Sunni Islam and is not at all different from it.[2]

The present crisis between the Arabs and Iran was never a result of the alleged Iranian support of terrorism. Instead, its roots lie in the existential threat posed against that political Sunnism which enabled these absolute monarchies to survive all these centuries. The present situation in Iraq is a clear example of this refusal to coexist with a Shiite Arabic state, and that is why many Sunnis accuse the Arab Shiites of Iraq of being Iranians (Safawis).

Most Arabic regimes now support Al Qaeda operatives in Iraq, recruiting them with money, personnel and logistics in the hope of ending the Shiite nightmare.

When most of the terrorist organizations working in Egypt in the past decades were funded by Saudi money and supplied by Wahhabi decrees, the Egyptian authorities put the blame on Iran, saying not a word against their Saudi friends.

The Saudi (Wahhabi) alliance with the Egyptian rulers reached a peak during the Israeli aggression on Lebanon last summer, when the Wahhabi speakers were given free rein to attack Shiites and Hezbollah, describing it as an apostate movement, more dangerous for Islam than Israel itself.

This manic Sunni, anti-Shiite mindset was the driving factor behind statements by Abdullah, king of Jordan, against what he called the threat posed by the 'Shiite crescent'. The same mindset also explains the statements of President Hosni Mubarak of Egypt, who denied the Shiites' Arabic nationality[3] – as if Arabic nationality should be restricted only to Sunnis!

The fact that the Israeli attack on Hezbollah came only three months after Mubarak's speech suggests that his statement was giving permission in advance for Israel to do its job.

Many of the Iranian envoys who met with President Mubarak received the same message: there would be no objection against political or financial relations, but Iran should not take advantage of these ties to propagate the Shiite faith among Egyptians.

Late in 2003, at the same time of the meeting held between Mubarak and Khatami in Switzerland, the Egyptian authorities were upholding their annual tradition of arresting a Shiite group in a city near the Red Sea. This was not an isolated practice but a constant policy aimed at terrifying people from converting to the Shiite faith. I personally experienced the results of this manic behaviour by being imprisoned three times, in 1987, 1989 and 1996.

What is more important is that the Egyptian authorities have failed to find any solid proof of the alleged Iranian support for Egyptian Shiites.

At the same time, Iran's strategic priorities do not include support for Shiite minorities abroad. Instead, in the face of the threat from Israel and the United States , they support the Hamas movement in Palestine, in spite of the fact that it is not Shiite but a branch of the Egyptian Muslim Brotherhood.

The Egyptian authorities ban and confiscate Shiite books sent from Iran or from any other place, while putting no restrictions on any amount of Wahhabi terrorist books sent from Saudi Arabia without limits.

The Situation of the Muslim Brotherhood

The Muslim Brotherhood's situation is an ambiguous one. It considers itself to be a leading Sunni party, committed to defending the Sunni faith against all kinds of apostasies, including of course Shiism. The Wahhabi connection has a vital role in formulating their beliefs. This is evident to those, like me, who approached the society – I was a member of the Muslim Brotherhood for nine years (1976–85).

A clear example of their view towards the Shiite faith was the statements of their ex-chairman, Omar Al-Telmesany, who, in an interview with *Al-Mosawar* weekly magazine,[4] said that the conflict between Shiites and Sunni was due to Shiites not Sunnis.

It is a deep and serious conflict. When Khomeini instigated the Islamic Revolution, we supported him in spite of this serious and deep conflict over our faith. We supported the Iranian people because they were oppressed by their ruler. We gave them political support because we felt we had a moral obligation to help the oppressed win their freedom, not because they were Shiites.

Relations between Iran and the Muslim Brotherhood have had their ups and downs, according to the Iranian researcher Abbas Khamiar. There are in fact numerous points of convergence between the two sides. The most important is their common belief in Islamic unity. In spite of the movement's hostility to Shiism, the founder of the Muslim Brotherhood, Hassan Al-Banna, believed that there were good chances of accord between Shiism and Sunnism. Another point of agreement was their hostility to nationalism, since the Muslim Brotherhood thinks that the occupation of Palestine is the fault of Arab nationalists. They of course also agree on the overall question of Jerusalem and Palestine.

The main differences between them stem from the Brotherhood's fears that Shiism will extend into their zone of influence. These fears were expressed by the Tunisian Rashed Al-Ganoushy, who said that Iran should invite non-Muslims to become Muslims instead of inviting Sunnis to be Shiites.[5] This political support to the Shiite movement, Hezbollah, during the Israeli war on Lebanon in the summer of 2006, was evident when the present leader of the Muslim Brotherhood declared his readiness to send 10,000 men to fight beside Hezbollah against Israel.[6] At the same time, speakers of the Brotherhood denounced the anti-Shiite decrees made by those Wahhabi clerics who said that Shiites were more dangerous for Islam than Israel.[7]

Permanent Lines of Partition

Immediately after the Israelis' failure to achieve their goals in Lebanon, there was a pan-Arabic state of panic because of the rising popularity of the Shiite

Hezbollah and its leader Sayed Hassan Nasrallah. He was the only Arabic leader not defeated by Israel, indeed the only one among all Muslims, not only Shiites.

This means one thing: the collapse of the imaginary lines of partition between Shiites and Sunnis which, it was once believed, were unbreachable. One manifestation of this fever was the statement by Sheikh Al-Qaradawi, a prominent Sunni and Brotherhood cleric, to a group of Egyptian journalists in late August 2006. He condemned Shiite attempts to convert Sunni communities to Shiite thought, describing Sayed Hassan Nasrallah as a Shiite fanatic and wondered how a Shiite Egyptian writer — myself — could dare to issue a book replying to one of his books.

He added that Egypt is the homeland of Sunni Islam and that we should never allow Shiites to penetrate the country.[8] He made similar remarks to the Egyptian newspaper *Al-Masry Al-Yoom* on 26 November 2006, when he called for respect for the final lines of partition between Sunnis and Shiites, and attacked Nasrallah's attempts to use his victory over Israel to expand Shiism and Shiite influence among Sunni Muslims.

Similar arguments were also expressed by another Islamic leader close to the Brotherhood, Mohamad Saleem Al-Awa. He called for Shiites to stop proselytizing among Sunnis, especially in Egypt and Morocco, saying that this would only deepen divisions between the two sects.[9]

In conclusion: there are no great differences between Iranian-Egyptian and Brotherhood-Iranian relations. Both have the same fear that Sunnis will convert to Shiism. Both seek to preserve the atavistic version of Sunni Islam founded by the monster, Moawia Ibn Abi Sofian. The Brotherhood is thus in substantial agreement with the Egyptian state and in conflict with Iran. The Brotherhood's proposals for political reform in Egypt in 2004 were more ambiguous about religious freedom than the present Egyptian constitution, which does not even mention the concept.[10] It is therefore unlikely that the Brotherhood will help Egypt restore its severed relations with Iran. There are points of convergence between Iran and the Brotherhood, mainly on Palestine but also on political Sunnism and fears of its continued dominance over the Muslim world.

Dr Ahmad Rasem Al-Nafis is an Egyptian Islamic thinker and writer.

NOTES

1   The Shiite Fatimi State, with its capital in Cairo, included vast areas of the Islamic world extending from Morocco in the west to Syria in the east; and their spiritual position was very influential because they controlled the holy pilgrimage places of Mecca and Medina.

2   Ahmad Rasem Al-Nafis, *Islamic parties, colonization of Islamic Umma*, Beirut: Dar AlMahja, 2005.

3   <http://www.alarabiya.net/Articles/2006/04/08/22686.htm>.
4   <http://www.shiaweb.org/shia/Shia_in_Egypt/pa48.html>.
5   <http://www.alkashf.net/vb/showthread.php?t=3076>.
6   <http://www.alarabiya.net/Articles/2006/08/03/26287.htm>.
7   <http://www.albawaba.com/ar/news/250508>.
8   *Al Qabas* newspaper, Kuwait, 2 September 2006.
9   <http://www.alarabiya.net/Articles/2006/11/20/29251.htm>.
10   Ahmad Raeem Al-Nafis, in *Al Qahera* newspaper, 23 March 2004.

Islam in Post-Soviet Azerbaijan: A Brief Outline

BAYRAM BALCI

Introduction

Islam as a political and social issue is a new phenomenon in independent Azerbaijan, even though Azerbaijan shares a long border with the Islamic Republic of Iran and has maintained close relationships with Islamic civilization.

Islam was imported into today's Azerbaijan as early as 639, when the Arabs, under the command of Hudayfa Ibn al-Yamdu, were aspiring to take over the whole of the Caucasus. By 652 the Arabs had reached as far as Derbent (in today's Dagestan), but from 639 to 693 control was loose; at times Arab occupation of the region was effective, but at other times the Arabs retreated to more central regions of their empire. The strongest resistance to this Arab expansion was that of the Khazars, a relatively small but powerful Turkic Jewish kingdom, located around the Caspian Sea, in the north of today's Azerbaijan. After the fall of the Umayyads and while the Abbasids were consolidating their power, foreign control over the Caucasus remained weak. Land claims brought Khazars into opposition with Arabs for a long time and Derbent soon materialized as the borderline.

From the eleventh century, energetic invasion by the Seljuk Turks boosted the process of Islamization, even though not all the inhabitants were converted by the new rulers (Constant, 2002). In the thirteenth century, when Mongols invaded the region, the process of Islamization was totally disrupted; it started again in 1502, when Safavid Persia took over all the territories that are part of today's Azerbaijan. For some time the Caucasus had been the battlefield of fierce competition between Sunni, supported by the Ottomans and their Crimean vassals, and Shiite, supported by the shahs of Iran; one of the latter, the famous Abbas Shah, heavily defeated the Ottomans at Tabriz in 1605 (Sellier and Sellier, 1997). This defeat resulted in the weakening of Sunni Islam throughout the region and, conversely, the strengthening of Shia Islam. Azerbaijan was divided along a north–south axis. The northern population was predominantly Sunni, while the southern population, being closer to Iran and the authority of the shah, was predominantly Shia. This centuries-long confrontation between the Ottoman and Persian Empires shaped Islam in Azerbaijan and crystallized a definite division between Sunni and Shia communities, even if the frontier between the Sunnite region and the Shia region is not very clear. Subsequently Russian and then Soviet rule damaged Islam in the area.

Islam Under Pressure during Russian and Soviet Rule

Scholars agree on 1828 as a turning point in the history of Shia Islam in Azerbaijan. The Treaty of Turkmanchai made the Araxes River the new border between Russia and Persia, and Azerbaijan, which until then had been a group of small khanates more or less subject to Safavid Persia, found itself divided into two separate entities, belonging to two different empires. South of the Araxes border line the Shia Azeri populations remained under the control of the Shia rulers of Iran, while those north of the Araxes were incorporated into Russia and cut off from major Shia cities like Qom, Mashad and Tabriz. The Islamization process continued in southern Azerbaijan, but northern Azerbaijan was already experiencing a secularization process. The political division thus also involved a deep religious division. The centuries-old struggle for influence between Sunni and Shiite changed into a competition between Muslim and Christian rulers.

However, if foreign intrusion favoured their coming together, it did not smooth out dogmatic and pragmatic barriers. In the north, colonization, together with other social and political phenomena like the Russian cultural and political influence resulted in the decline of Islam (and especially of Shia Islam since 75 per cent of the population were Shiites).

The most important factor bringing pressure to bear on Islam (Shia and Sunni) was undoubtedly the secularization process and the ever-growing influence of modern intellectual trends, like the Enlightenment, brought by the Russian settlers or others imported by young intellectuals from the Ottoman Empire (Volker, 2001). From the very beginning of the nineteenth century, for example, newspapers like *Ekinçi* and *Molla Naäsriddin* offered open platforms for numerous secular Azeri intellectuals educated in Moscow, St Petersburg, Istanbul or elsewhere in Europe. One of these, Ali Merdan Topçubaşı (1895–1981), was one of the greatest politicians in Azerbaijani history. Others, equally respected, like Ali Bey Huseyinzade (1864–1941) or Ahmet Ağaev (1869–1939), also played a significant role in the struggle against Shia rituals in people's everyday life (especially against the important ceremony of *ashura* – the Shiite feast of atonement) and thus contributed to the decline of Islam in their country.

Shia Islam also declined under the influence of Pan-Turkism, which had reached its apogee. From Istanbul to Baku, intellectuals spoke almost the same language (the Azeri language being close to Ottoman Turkish) and were united in their fear of Shia Islam as an obstacle to the building of a greater Turkic world (Altstadt, 1993, pp. 50–73).

The third factor contributing to the decline of Shia Islam was the successful spreading of Pan-Islamism. This political and religious ideology, developed in the nineteenth century by the charismatic Jamal al Din Afghani, aimed at putting an end to all factions and conflicting trends within Islam that were perceived as weakening the Muslim world. In this context Al Afghani paid particular attention to the Sunni–Shia division. In Azerbaijan, his ideas found the support of Sheikh-ul-Islam Akhund Abdulsalam Akhundzade, the highest religious authority in the country from 1880 to 1907, and who subsequently proclaimed the unity of Islam, while tensions and conflicts between Azeris and Armenians facilitated reconciliation amongst Azeris 'against their common enemy' (Volker, 2001).

The fourth factor contributing to the decline of Shiism was the establishment of the Soviet regime, even though in its early years at least it appeared to be favourably disposed towards Islam (albeit out of self-interest): in a speech in Baku in 1920, for instance, the Komintern representative, Zinoviev, spoke of 'the *ghazavat*[1] against imperialist forces'. In 1923 the country's religious leaders claimed that the Soviet authorities had saved all Muslims of the Turkic world from British imperialism. By August of that year Yemel'yan Yaroslavsky – the leader-to-be of the 'Union of the Godless' which would take up the fight against religion in the USSR – advised the highest political authorities to act with the greatest caution towards Islam. No frontal assault was launched on Islam until 1924, by which time the Soviet authorities had consolidated their control in the USSR. The first targets were Islamic rituals. In 1924 local Soviets, the Communist Party and affiliated media denounced the *ashura* as a barbaric practice from another age (Lemercier-Quelquejay, 1984). In 1925 a Union of the Godless was established in Baku and the property of religious foundations was confiscated. Attacks against Islam intensified during the following years. By 1932 the Union of the Godless had 70,000 members and its impact on society increased. An anti-religious museum was opened in Baku. Soviet anti-Islamic policy did not distinguish between Sunni and Shiite, and thus unintentionally contributed to the smoothing out of differences between the two doctrines; indeed one may speculate that one result of Soviet policy was to pave the way for the rise of a national non-confessional Islam which has become a tool for the post-Soviet leadership in Azerbaijan in its new state-building strategy.

1991 – Independent Azerbaijan: Revival of Shiism or Revival of Islam?

Resisting fierce anti-religious propaganda and repression, Islam never faded away from social life and individual consciousness. Though reduced, Islamic institutions survived, benefiting from the regime's ambivalence towards Islam. Despite their deep-rooted hostility to religion, the Soviet authorities themselves established official institutions in charge of Islam in the shape of regional Muslim Spiritual Boards. The Board for the Caucasus was based in Baku and supervised the activities of all Muslims, Sunni and Shiite alike. Reporting directly to Moscow, this was primarily a propaganda tool aimed at the Muslim world abroad for foreign policy purposes. Functioning mosques were rare and tightly controlled by the Board. No official institution in the Caucasus provided religious education for Muslim clergy; such education was available in the only two official madrassahs in the USSR, located in Tashkent and Bukhara. When Azerbaijan gained its independence, the religious scene was still dominated by this official Islam, but the latter was challenged by what Alexandre Bennigsen has called 'parallel Islam' (Bennigsen, 1985).

Developing on the fringe of official Islam, this 'parallel Islam' expressed itself in Soviet times as kind of popular (Shia) religiosity focusing on pilgrimages to *pir* or *imamzade*, the burial places of saints, descendants of the families of Shia imams or great religious scholars. There are dozens of such popular places of worship throughout the country. The Soviet authorities disapproved of such pilgrimages, but religious consciousness was real and officials knew about the public's attendance at these sites (Bennigsen, 1981). Five of them deserve particular attention as they were the most popular and, surprisingly, those most tolerated by the authorities.

The shrine of Mir Mövsim Ät Ağa is undoubtedly the most important place for parallel Islam. Located in Şüvelen, only 40 kilometres from Baku, it attracts large numbers of people looking for miraculous solutions to their problems, as the saint was well known as a miracle worker. The most interesting feature of this case is that worship and pilgrimage started in the Soviet period, after the death of the saint in 1951, a fact which illustrates how complex the Soviet experience was for Islam, involving both repression and enough freedom to allow the worship of new saints. In 1992 Haci Nizam, a well-respected and charismatic local religious leader, took on responsibility for the site and collected millions of *manat* – the new national currency – to restore and enlarge the mosque and develop charities off the premises. The Spiritual Board considered him a threat and tried to dismiss him, but he found influential support in the highest circles of power, so the Board had to leave him in control at Şüvelen (Motika, 2001)

Located ten kilometres from Baku, on the seashore, amidst roads and oil wells, the tomb of the sister of the Eighth Imam, Bibi Heybet, is somewhat less popular.[2] In this case the most interesting feature is that the site was restored by the government thanks to the personal support of President Heydar Aliyev, whose portrait welcomes visitors at the entrance. Similarly, the shrine of the daughter of Imam Reza, Rahime Hanim, in Nardaran has benefited from popular and official interest since the very beginning of the 1990s. The tomb of *imamzade* (affiliated to the Prophet's family) of Ibrahim, the son of the Fifth Imam Mohamed Bakir, a dozen kilometres outside Ganja, also deserves attention. Pilgrimage to this shrine contributed to the preservation of Islam in the region in Soviet times, as according to the shrine keeper it attracted pilgrims from all over Soviet Union. In Nahçıvan, a *qadem-gâh* (literally, footprint of a holy person) called Ashab-e-Kehf, where several saints left their footprints before going to heaven, has been restored by the post-Soviet authorities.

These places of worship, like other shrines throughout the country, are highly prized by the local populations for practical reasons, since they make religious observance less demanding: one needs only to go to a saint's tombstone in order to say a prayer or make a vow. Moreover, those who worship in this way are not exposed as affiliated to a particular mosque or to any new partisan organization based on Islam, such as the Islamic Party of Azerbaijan, whose charismatic and self-educated leaders are openly hostile to the government.

Since independence, both parallel and official Islam have continued to coexist in Azerbaijan, along with three other marginal trends. The first of these is close to Wahhabism. It is hostile both to official Islam and to saint worshipping, and its leaders are self-taught religious men. It has no real effect on Shia Islam and I shall not therefore cover it in detail (Motika, 2001). The second is the Islamic Party of Azerbaijan, which represents political Islam. Discredited because of its close relationships with Iran, a country with a negative image throughout Azerbaijan, the party has little influence on the population.

The third trend comprises the 'Muslim modernists', as Motika calls them. These are well-known Orientalists who are striving to build bridges between Islam and Azerbaijani society and are deeply influenced by modern western thinking imported under Russian and Soviet rule. The secular authorities support their efforts as they shape a national Islam and contribute to the emerging of a specific national identity, as this serves the new state-building policy. Nevertheless, the authorities again show an ambivalence in their relationship with Islam, on the one hand encouraging its development and on the other hand setting limits to the free establishment of Islamic associations and movements.

Whatever may have been the intentions of the leaders of post-Soviet Azerbaijan, the internal political and social climate in the 1990s favoured a revival of Islam in general and of Shiism in particular, even though the Constitution asserts the secular and lay nature of state institutions and makes no reference to Islam.[3] When he returned to power in January 1993 President Aliyev granted particular attention to Islam and – like the other leaders of former Soviet Muslim states – went on pilgrimage to Mecca. There was a renewed interest in religious literature, and new mosques were built all over the country. Although such projects were local initiatives, they were sometimes supported by the political authorities (Motika, 2001). The most striking initiative by the state in the religious field was however the creation of the Islamic University of Baku (*Bakı Islam Üniversiteti*) , the first of its kind in Azerbaijan. It was opened in 1989 but became fully operational after independence. Two departments – *ilahiyat* (theology) and *sharqshunaslik* (orientalism) – aim to train students as religious officials and specialist in the Arabic and Iranian fields. All graduate students hold official positions in various parts of the country.[4] Although the staff say that the content of the education is close to that of the Turkish Sunni College of Theology (created in Baku by the Turkish authorities) the education is in fact Shia-oriented, as is clear from the available literature in use and from the posters in the corridors and classrooms depicting classical Shia symbols such as Ali or the slaughter in Kerbala.

This state initiative encouraged private Islamic organizations to develop their own institutions. Managed by the dynamic Elçin Eskerov, the Centre for Religious Studies (*Dini Araşdırmalar Merkezi*) is a young non-governmental organization (NGO) working to raise religious awareness among the population. (The term 'NGO' refers more to the Centre's aspiration to independence than to reality, as the state brings pressure to bear on its activities and most of all on its editorial line.[5]) Both of its websites[6] and its journal *Qutb* (*Pole*), reflect its mobilization priorities: the denunciation of Christian missionary movements and extreme Islamic trends such as Wahhabism and the introduction of religious education in secondary schools.

Though less dynamic (published every three months, and without a website), the journal *Kelam*, edited by Qazi Haci Mireziz Seyidzade, one of the managers (teacher and administrator) of the Islamic University of Baku, offers interesting insights into Islam in Azerbaijan. The editorial line is not openly Shia-oriented, but a large number of papers are dedicated to Shiism as the majority trend in the country.

Iran contributed to the renewal of Shiism in Azerbaijan through the activities both of the state and of individuals. When the USSR collapsed, Azeri towns such as Lenkoran, Masalli, Astara, or even Julfa and Ordubad in Nahçivan, developed close economic, cultural and human relationships with Iranian towns on the other side of the Araxes. Aware of this, and somewhat concerned, the Iranian authorities sought to control and influence those exchanges that were already too significant to be stopped. Since the early days of independence, then, some Azerbaijani citizens living near the border have been granted safe conducts allowing them to cross the border easily (this privilege is not extended to Azerbaijani citizens in other parts of the country). Goods imported from Iran include religious literature to supply bookshops in Azerbaijan. Two Islamic shops on Fizuli Avenue in Baku display a large range of Shia literature along with objects such as beads, prayer mats, *muhur* (pieces of clay on which Shia Muslims lay their foreheads when praying), videos and rose water imported from Iran. The Iranian *Al Hoda* bookshop in Baku offers the largest choice of Shia literature, and especially the works – translated into the Azeri language – of the most important past and contemporary Shia thinkers, such as Allame Muhammad Huseyn Tabatabayi (*Islamda Shia –Shiah in Islam*), Seyyid Mujteba Musevi Lari (*Islam ve Gharb Medeniyeti – Islam and Western Civilization*) and Sheikh Abbas Gumi, who wrote the biography of the twelve imams. The author and *marja'a* Ayatollah Fazil Lenkorani, whose many writings, especially his *Risale*, have been translated into the Azeri language, holds a special place in Azeri bookshops. He currently lives in Iran. He is well known for his conservative ideas. It is surprising to meet some of his followers in the secular society of Azerbaijan. His relative prestige among religious people stems from the fact that he is himself an ethnic Azeri; he came from Kirvan, not far from Lenkoran in southern Azerbaijan.[7] Some of his books were translated in Baku by graduates of the Institute of Oriental Studies or the Islamic University of Baku. Others were translated in Iran to be sold in Azerbaijan.[8]

The opening of the border has encouraged not only trade but also the development of particular bilateral relationships in terms of cultural cooperation and education. Azeri students go to Iran and Iranian missionaries come to Azerbaijan. In the early 1990s, numerous Azeri students went to study religion in Tehran or Qom and on pilgrimage to the mausoleum of Imam Reza in Mashad. Each year during *Muharram*, the month of mourning for Shia Muslims, hundreds of pilgrims from southern Azerbaijan visit the shrine. Because of the political situation in Iraq, they are unable to go on pilgrimage to Kerbala, but when they return home they are proud to add to their name the title *Kerbalayi* or *Mashadi*, which brings as much prestige and recognition as the title *Haci*.

In the early days of independence Iranian diplomats encouraged the Shia revival in Azerbaijan, but soon, concerned that the geopolitics of the region was leading to the coming together of Azeri irredentists from both sides of the Araxes river, they began to stress that their moving closer to Azerbaijan was based on religion as the only feature common to both countries. Somewhat awkwardly, this policy was soon stopped, while Iranian diplomacy was allowed to establish two cultural centers in Baku, which provided Persian language and literature courses along with courses on religion, complying with the regime's requirements. Moreover, the Iranian embassy in Baku, as part of its cultural cooperation programme, supports students who wish to study in Iran, and the Islamic University of Baku is partly funded by Iran. In order to spread its message more effectively, the embassy recently issued a new journal in the Azeri language, *Işığa Doğru* (*Towards Light*), a vehicle for religious propaganda and the promotion of Iranian culture. Similarly, the Iranian authorities have directly encouraged another journal, edited in Tabriz in southern Azerbaijan, *Körpü* (*Bridge*), supposedly the 'bridge' between Iran and Azerbaijan.

Last but not least, the Shia revival after independence also affected political life. The Islamic Party of Azerbaijan (*Azerbaycan Islam Partiyası*) emerged in 1992, and although its leaders claim to be above the Sunni–Shia dispute it is obviously Shia-oriented.[9] The authorities reluctantly granted the party legal registration in 1995 but still consider it as an agent of the Iranian state, and consequently the IPA finds itself isolated on the political scene. In December 2003 a split gave birth to the Party of Islam and Democracy (*Islam de Demokrasiya Partiyası*) (*525-ci*, 2003). Its leader, Haci Elikram Eliyev, was released from gaol in November 2003 after several months for alleged participation to the 'Nardaran events' in May 2002, when riots put the police face to face with so-called 'really dangerous Islamist activists threatening public peace'. The latter and their supporters claimed that the riot started because of the deep social unrest experienced in the region since independence. The fact remains that this is the most Shia-oriented political organization and at the same time the most sensitive to the political culture of the Islamic Republic of Iran, even though its leader and advisers try to modify this image by developing relationships with other Muslim states, for example Turkey.[10] However, the favourable context in which Shiism has experienced a revival in Azerbaijan has also benefited parallel religious phenomena and allowed the emergence on the public scene of other Islamic organizations, some of which are hostile to Shiism.

State Policy and Turkish Influence: Holding Back the Expansion of Shiism

The strengthening of Shia Islam and its taking root among the people has met a number of obstacles, as a result of specific features of Azerbaijani society as well as of the activity of foreign and non-Shiite Muslims.

First of all, we should recall that Azerbaijani society has been secularized since 1828, when the Russians took over the region: that is to say, much earlier than Central Asia, where resistance went on until 1881. In Azerbaijan, intellectuals were already looking westwards, borrowing new ideas from

Russia and Europe. Then the arrival of Soviet rule completed the erasure of religion from people's minds, Shia and Sunni alike. A recent poll conducted by an independent scholar shows how little religion affects the day-to-day life of the population (Faradov, 2002).

Moreover, the religious policy of the state today does not encourage the strengthening of Islam, particularly Shiism. Various steps taken by the government, like the establishment in June 2001 of a State Committee for Religious Affairs (*Dini Gruplarla Iş Üzre Devlet Komiteti*), show how eager the secular powers are to control religion, so that all religious groups comply with the official requirements of state policy in this area. Various publications and interviews with some officials from the Committee show that the regime's objective is to shape a national Islam that will not be under Turkish, Iranian or Arab influence.[11] The head of the Committee is a well-respected Arabist, Refig Aliyev.

Since the State Committee was established, all organizations aiming to develop their activities in the country must register with the Ministry of Justice and comply with demanding rules.[12] All requests are processed in the Ministry of Justice. Since missionary movements are judged to have expanded out of control, a secondary role of the Committee, performed together with specialists on religion, consists in controlling the content of all religious materials imported into the country for distribution. The Committee is represented in various districts, which allows a closer control over religious activity, especially in the areas bordering on Iran, such as Nahçıvan and Lenkoran.[13]

The way the Committee functions reveals that it was in fact established to fight religious influence from Iran and from the Arab countries; this shows the degree of government concern about the perceived growing dangers of Iranian Shiism and of Wahhabism. The Committee's duty is to prevent Islam from becoming radicalized. Immediately after its creation, numerous underground madrassahs were closed in the environs of Baku and in the south, close to the Iranian border.[14]

A final (unofficial) function of the Committee is as a power-balancing tool to control the Spiritual Board for Muslims, led by Sheikh-ul-Islam Allahşükür Paşazade. The Spiritual Board is loyal to the secular authorities, and is reproached for this by some Islamic leaders, but the authorities mistrust the Spiritual Board and prefer to entrust religious matters to bureaucrats rather than to religious figures. However, suspicion regarding the Committee's effectiveness is high as even its officials acknowledge that it fails to enforce the registration of all organizations (Information, 2002).

Another factor contributing to the weakening of Shiism is the dynamic Turkish presence in Azerbaijan. This competition with Turkish Islam is not new; it started at the beginning of the twentieth century, when the ideas of Turkic intellectuals prevailed in the country. Ever since the break-up of the

Soviet Union the official policy of the Turkish state and various activities of private organizations originating in Turkey have played a crucial role in the weakening of Shiism.

Although it claims to be secular, the Turkish state is far from indifferent to internal as well as external religious issues. On both scenes, the *Diyanet* (board for religious affairs, under the prime minister) functions as an intervention tool.[15] Until the 1990s the scope of activities of the *Diyanet* was limited to Western Europe, with the aim of keeping Turkish immigrants under the spiritual authority of Ankara; the collapse of the communist bloc provided new opportunities for extending its activity to the whole Muslim and Turkic world from the Balkans to Central Asia via the Caucasus. The *Diyanet* was then entrusted in the context of Turkish diplomacy with assisting the new Turkic republics in their state-building efforts and in strengthening their religious and national identity on the Turkish model (Balci, 2001). In order to 'sell' the Turkish model of governance and in order not to leave Arab and Iranian missionaries a clear field, Turkish imams were sent to Central Asia and the Caucasus to preach the compatibility of Islam, democracy and secularism.

Among the top priorities of the *Diyanet* are educating a new generation of Muslim elites, distributing Islamic literature throughout Eurasia, and bringing together on a regular basis the prominent religious leaders of the area under Turkish patronage. Its publications can easily be found at the entrance to mosques all over the region. The most important of all its functions is to ensure that secondary schools and colleges of theology shape the new elites of Kyrgyzstan, Turkmenistan and Kazakhstan, in the same way that Marmara University in Istanbul shapes the Turkish elite. Each embassy in the region has a special officer is in charge of religious affairs and educational cooperation.

As far as Azerbaijan is concerned, although a large majority of the people are Shiites, while Turks are Sunnis, the *Diyanet* pursues its mission with particular energy. It has opened college of theology, financed the building of several mosques[16] and supported hundreds of students to come and study in Turkey. Important delegations from Azerbaijan are systematically invited to Turkey, and each time the *Diyanet* arranges a conference or colloquium on religious issues.[17]

Perhaps more influential than the efforts of the Turkish state and the *Diyanet* in Azerbaijan are the activities of new brotherhoods which are likely to benefit Sunnism and hold back Shiism. These are the various *Nurcu* groups (named after Said Nursi), but principally the groups of missionaries of Fethullah Gülen, which are all heavily involved in the religious scene in Azerbaijan.[18] They run secondary schools and the *Araz Kurslari*[19] education centres. They do not provide religious courses as such, but teachers from Turkey pass on Islamic and especially Sunni-oriented standards of conduct and morality in student boarding-houses, and speak freely of their spiritual guide, Fethullah Gülen. In addition to the schools, the *fethullahci* newspaper *Zaman*, the television channel *Samanyolu* and the radio station *Burç FM* – all with a high profile in Azerbaijan – also contribute to the spreading of Turkish Sunni Islam.

Another Turkish Islamist movement, led by Osman Nuri Topbaş and close to the Naqshbandiyya brotherhood, is also active in the promotion of Sunni Islam. Influenced by the teachings of Aziz Mahmut Hudayi, spiritual leader of a brotherhood that emerged in the sixteenth century, this group has been developing charitable and missionary activities in Azerbaijan since 1991, via an association, *Azerbaycan Gençlerine Yardim Fondu* (Foundation for Assistance to Azerbaiji Young People), which collects funds and distributes aid to refugees and the destitute. In Baku it provides English, Arabic, Koranic and computer courses for young people, but is also very active in the regions, especially in Sheki, Zakatala and Ağdaş, where the teachings of Osman Nuri Topbaş are conveyed through a Koranic school and two madrassahs. In accordance with the law, all these institutions are registered with the State Committee for Religious Affairs. In this case, as in the case of most public or private Turkish institutions, though they claim to be beyond the Sunni–Shia division, their teachings favour the Sunni position.

The general climate in Azerbaijan is favorable to Sunnism to the detriment of Shiism since the country suffers from a relatively bad relationship with its large and influential neighbour, Iran, the leading Shiite power in the world (Shaffer, 2002). The tension between the two countries is having a significant effect on the specifics of Shiism in Azerbaijan.

As noted above, under Russian and Soviet rule Shiite Islam declined in Azerbaijan, but there was no interruption to the influence of Shiite thinkers in Iran. Azerbaijan was isolated and Azerbaijani Shiites were refused the right to go on pilgrimage and maintain contacts with Iranian Shiite clergy. Soviet antagonism to the pro-American Pahlavi dynasty made matters worse. Anti-Americanism was the driving force of the new regime installed in Iran in 1979, but the new regime was also hostile to the Soviet Union, which like the US was perceived by the mullahs as a 'great Satan'. In order to destabilize Iran, Moscow even manipulated Azeri irredentism and supported reunification plans involving the annexation of Southern Azerbaijan (inside Iran).

When it became independent, Azerbaijan renewed contact with Iran, but relations remain fragile. Several disputes between Tehran and Baku have already tainted bilateral diplomacy.

The first post-Soviet government under Elçibey was nationalist and Pan-Turkic, and Elçibey adopted an aggressive stance towards Iran, demanding a solution to the issue of Southern Azerbaijan. Lacking experience in foreign politics, he called for a reunified Azerbaijan with Tabriz as its capital city. Members of his party still defend this cause in the Azerbaijani media, especially in the columns of the sharply anti-Iranian daily newspaper *Yeni Musavat,* and

support those irredentist organizations which are poisoning Azerbaijani–
Iranian relations. Among these, *Guney Azerbaycan Milli Oyanış Hareketi* (the
Movement for the National Revival of Southern Azerbaijan), founded by Azeris
in Iran who want to join the independent North, and *Dunya Azerbaycanlari
Kongresi* (the World Azeri Congress) contribute to the deterioration of bilateral
relations, claiming that Azeris in Iran are 'victims of Persian chauvinism'.[20]

Elçibey was not in power for long, but although his successor Heydar Aliyev
was more cautious and was ready for conciliation with Iran, relationships did
not improve, as a dispute arose between the two countries over the problematic
and strategic international status of the Caspian Sea and the sharing of its
natural resources. The crisis became so serious that in the summer of 2001 the
countries avoided armed confrontation only at the last moment (Sabahi, 2004).
Tehran also started developing favourable diplomatic relations with Armenia,
which was still occupying Azerbaijani territories; the question of Nagorno
Karabakh was still a bleeding wound (Cornell, 1997). Baku is now on good
terms with the other 'Great Satan', the United States. In December 2003 a visit
to Baku by Secretary of State Donald Rumsfeld aggravated tension with both
Tehran and Moscow on the suspicion that Washington wanted to establish US
bases in Azerbaijan.[21]

Conclusion: Overcoming the Sunni–Shia Division?

The development of Islam in Azerbaijan, and of Shiism in particular, went
through four major periods, determined by three key dates. Long after Islam's
initial rise, 1828 foreshadowed its decline, 1920 marked its repression and
1991 forecast its revival. Its decline and repression under Soviet rule erased
the division between Sunni and Shia. On the eve of independence most
Azerbaijanis were unable to tell the difference between the two, and this
remains the case today. The general lack of religious knowledge has favoured
the peaceful coexistence of both groups, so that Sunni and Shia Muslims pray
in the same mosques and follow the same imams, and Shia *muhur* can be found
at the entrance of all mosques. Sunni and Shia do not differ much in the way
they pray; differences are visible only in small gestures, such as the way they
raise their hands or lay their foreheads on the carpet. Moreover, they show each
other mutual respect in everyday life. The Sunni avoid celebrating weddings
and other festivities during *Muharram,* the month of mourning for Shia
Muslims. However, this somewhat idyllic picture does not apply to some
particular trends within each school. Among the Sunni, Wahhabism has
shown no open-mindedness and no tolerance towards Shiites. A foreign
import, Wahhabism has profited from the openness of Azeri society and is
now placing pressure on the peaceful coexistence of Sunni and Shia. Fearing

that they will damage people's sensitivities, the post-Soviet authorities in Azerbaijan try to limit external influences and to encourage the emergence of a national Islam within the country which will go beyond the Sunni–Shia division. From now on, two alternative scenarios can be envisaged.

The first scenario is that, as the authorities hope, a national Islam will emerge, erasing the already weak borders between Sunni and Shia. Such a development would represent a victory for the government, but it implies a powerful state able to force its religious policy on the people. Against all expectations, however, the state is experiencing the most serious difficulties in establishing its authority over all Islamic leaders and movements. The fear of radicalization is freezing control institutions and motivating state tolerance towards those organizations that do not comply with official requirements and refuse to go through registration.

The second scenario forecasts the implosion of today's Sunni–Shia harmony, as a result of the activity of foreign missionaries, both Sunni and Shia. Turkish religious influence, both public and private, is strengthening Sunnism and undermining Shiism. Some Wahhabi preachers (in the environs of Baku and in some districts in the north of the country) even refuse dialogue with Shia leaders. At the same time, it is likely that Shia influence from Iran will also produce division in Azerbaijan. Such influence is resisted by the secular authorities, and it is difficult to measure its effect on local Islam or its impact on today's fragile harmony. Nevertheless, in the first years of independence, numerous missionaries from Iran certainly contributed to the exacerbation of the Sunni–Shia division, and it is far from clear that they have ceased their activity.

Dr Bayram Balci is Director of the French Centre for Central Asian Studies in Tashkent.

References

The newspaper *525-ci qazet*, 23 December (2003)

Altstadt, A.L. (1992) *The Azerbaijani Turks: Power and Identity under Russian Rule*, Stanford, CA: Stanford University, Hoover Institution Press.

Balci, B. (2003a) 'Fethullah Gülen's missionary schools in Central Asia and their role in the spreading of Turkism and Islam', *Religion, State & Society*, Vol. 31 No. 2, pp. 151–77.

Balci, B. (2003b) *Missionnaires de l'Islam en Asie centrale, les écoles turques de Fethullah Gülen*, Paris: Maisonneuve & Larose et IFEA.

Balci, B. and Buchwalter, B. (2001) 'La Turquie en Asie centrale, conversion au réalisme: 1991–2000', *Dossiers de l'Institut Français d'Etudes Anatoliennes* (Istanbul), Vol. 5, 2001, 110 pp.

Bennigsen, A. (1981) *Les musulmans oubliés: l'Islam en Union soviétique*, Paris: Seuil.

Bennigsen, A. (1985) *Le Soufi et le commissaire: le soufisme en Union Soviétique*, Paris: Seuil.

Constant, A. (2002) *L'Azerbaïdjan*, Paris: Khartala.

Cornell, S.E. (1997), 'Peace or war?: the prospects for conflicts in the Caucasus', *Iranian Journal of International Affairs*, Vol. 9 No. 2, pp. 208–24.

Faradov, T. (2002) 'Religiosity and civic culture in post Soviet Azerbaijan : a sociological perspective', in A.B. Sajoo, *Civil Society in the Muslim World: Contemporary Perspectives*, London: I.B. Tauris, pp. 194–213.

Lemercier-Quelquejay, C.(1984), 'Islam and identity in Azerbaijan', *Central Asian Survey*, Vol. 3 No. 4, pp. 29–55.

Motika, R. (2001), 'Foreign missionaries, homemade dissidents and popular Islam: the search for new religious structures in Azerbaijan', in R. Brunner and W. Ende, *The Twelver Shia in Modern Times: Religious Culture and Political History*, Leiden, Boston, MA, Köln: Brill, pp. 284–97.

Motika, R. (2001), 'Islam in post-Soviet Azerbaijan', *Archives de Sciences Sociales des Religions*, No. 115, pp. 111–24.

Ne'mat, M. (1992) *Azerbaycanda Pirler*, Baku: Dovlet Neşriyati.

Sabahi, F. (2004), 'Oil diplomacy in the Caspian: the rift between Iran and Azerbaijan in summer 2001', in F. Sabahi and D. Warner (eds), *The OSCE and the Multiple Challenges of Transition in the Caucasus and Central Asia*, Aldershot: Ashgate.

Sellier, J. and Sellier, A. (1993), *Atlas des peuples d'Orient, Moyen-Orient, Caucase, Asie Centrale*, Paris: La Découverte, pp. 118–120.

Shaffer, B. (2002) *Borders and Brethren: Iran and the Challenge of Azerbaijani Identity*, Cambridge, MA: MIT Press.

Taş, K. (2002) *Turk halkının gözuyle Diyanet* (*The Diyanet as Perceived by Turkish Public Opinion*, Istanbul: Iz yayıncılık.

Volker, A. (2001) 'Why do they cry? Criticisms of Muharram celebrations in tsarist and socialist Azerbaijan', in R. Brunner and W. Edne (eds), *The Twelver Shia in Modern Times: Religious Culture and Political History*, Leiden, Boston, MA, Köln: Brill, pp. 114–34.

Yavuz, H. (1999), 'Said Nursi and the Turkish experience', *The Muslim World*, No. 89.

NOTES

1   The term *ghazavat*, which fell into disuse, means a holy war against non-Muslim religions. The leader of such a war, the *ghazi*, enjoyed high prestige among Muslims.

2   Above the shrine, across the road, lies a cemetery with a *qadem-gâh*, where a saint left his footprints. The building is a small mausoleum, containing two huge rocks protected by a glass with traces of candles and tiny slots allowing worshippers to leave little notes, pictures, and messages. For an exhaustive study of places of worship in 'parallel Islam' in Azerbaijan, see Ne'mat, 1992.

3   The Constitution of the Republic of Azerbaijan specifies the secular nature of the state in Article 17, the strict separation of politics and religion in Article 18 and freedom of worship in Article 48.

4   Haci Sabir (rector) and Elçin Esenov (professor), Islamic University of Baku, interviewed by the author, Baku, 19 May 2003.

5   Islam's main specialists maintain that the Centre was set up by the Ministry of Youth to fight specific problems among young people such as alcoholism, drug use and conversion to new religions or sects.

6   The most active are <http://www.islam.az> and <http://www.islam.in-baku.com>; another is <http://www.crr-az.org>.

7   Elçin Esenov, professor at the Islamic University of Baku, interviewed by the author, Baku, 23 January 2004.

8   Manager of *Al Hoda* bookshop, Baku, interviewed by the author, Baku, 3 January 2004.

9   Rôşan Ahmatli, member of the Islamic Party of Azerbaijan, interviewed by the author, Baku, 12 May 2003.

10 Kerbalayi Vagif, one of the officials of the Islamic Party of Azerbaijan, interviewed by the author, Baku, 4 January 2003.

11 Samed Bayramzade, secretary-general of the State Committee for Religious Affairs, interviewed by the author, Baku, 29 October 2002.

12 In November 2003 the Committee released an official list of all registered religious organizations. See the official website <http://www.addk.org>. The Committee acknowledged, however, that many organizations, especially foreign ones, were not registered but were still operating.

13 Idris Abbasov, in charge of the State Committee for Religious Affairs in the Autonomous Republic of Nahçıvan, interviewed by the author, Nahçıvan, 10 December 2003.

14 Haji Sedi, imam of the Cuma mosque in Lenkoran and director of the annex of the Islamic University, Lenkoran, interviewed by the author, 14 May 2003.

15 For information on the activities of the *Diyanet* see< http://www.diyanet.gov.tr>.

16 In particular, the construction of three important mosques was funded by the *Diyanet*: Kazim Karabekir in Nahçıvan, the Karabakh Martyrs' Mosque in Baku and the Central Mosque in Sheki.

17 The gatherings are called *Avrasya Din Şurası* (Religious Counsels of Eurasia); they bring together influential religious and political figures from Central Asia, the Caucasus and other Turkic areas, allowing Ankara to exert influence on the religious management of the whole of Eurasia.

18 Said Nursi (1873–1960) is one of the Islamic thinkers who has most affected the Turkish social and religious scene in the last fifty years. He is also well known in Central Asia and the Caucasus through the activism of his followers (Yavuz, 1999). Several infra-communities assert the Nursi legacy. Fethullah Gülen and his followers comprise one of these; they are probably the most active of all in Turkey as well as in all the countries of Eurasia. From his voluntary exile in the US, the charismatic leader rules over a powerful community particularly involved in education (Balci, 2003a, 2003b).

19 The *Araz Kurslari* may be compared to the private Turkish *Dershane*, where students are trained to pass competitive university entrance exams.

20 For information on the activities of the World Azeri Congress, see <http://www.dunyazerbaijanis-congress.com>.

21 For information, see <http://www.eurasianet.org>, December 2003.

Hezbollah America Latina – Queer Group or Real Threat?

ELY KARMON

The Failed Explosive Operation in Caracas: 23 October 2006

On 23 October 2006 the Baruta Municipality Police found two explosive devices near the US embassy in Caracas, Venezuela. One of the bombs was found in a box containing leaflets making reference to the Lebanese radical Islamic group Hezbollah. Local television news network Globovisión reported that one of the devices was in a flowerpot near the embassy, while the other was outside a school, near the diplomatic premises. Wilfredo Porras, acting director of Baruta Police, said they arrested a man carrying a 'backpack with six containers of 100 black powder bases, pliers, adhesive tape, glue and electric leads'. The man declared that 'the devices were set to explode in 15 minutes.'[1] 'The idea was apparently to create alarm and publicize a message,' Borraz told reporters, saying the explosives were made to scatter the pamphlets.[2]

It is possible that the second device was intended to be exploded near the Israeli embassy but the student got nervous and dropped it near the American embassy. The arrested man is Jose Miguel Rojas Espinoza, a 26-year-old student of the state-run Bolivarian University – a school offering free education that was founded by President Hugo Chavez.

An organization calling itself the Hezbollah America Latina (Hezbollah LA) took responsibility on 25 October for the attack on its website and promised that it will stage other simultaneous attacks with the same goal of publicizing the organization. It presented Rojas as 'the brother mujahideen, the first example of dignity and struggle in the cause of Allah, the first prisoner of the revolutionary Islamic movement Hezbollah Venezuela'.[3]

Surprisingly, on 18 August 2006 the organization had already threatened to explode a non-lethal device against an ally of the US in one Latin American city in order to launch its propaganda campaign as a beginning of the war against imperialism and Zionism and to show its solidarity with the Lebanese Hezbollah after the war in Lebanon (see Annex 1). In addition, even before the 18 August announcement, in a programmatic statement under the title 'The

Jihad in America will begin in 2007', Hezbollah leader in Latin America (and Venezuela) Teodoro Darnott announced that two 'Latin mujahideen' had been prepared under orders to place two explosive devices in a Latin American city. The organization promised to announce the event beforehand and stated that the goal of the operation will be to alert the public opinion about the beginning of the war against imperialism and Zionism.

What is Hezbollah in Latin America?

Several months ago, probably in June or July, a website presenting itself as the mouthpiece of Hezbollah LA has began to be active at <http://groups. msn.com/autonomiaislamicawayuu/hezboallah.msnw>. Interestingly, the website is written in Spanish and in Chapateka, a mixture of the Indian Maya language and antique Spanish.

Although the website is claiming activity of Hezbollah LA in El Salvador, Colombia, Venezuela, Argentina, México and Chile, actually the backbone of the organization is Hezbollah Venezuela, the second active group seems to be in Argentina and the others are practically inactive, at least on the Internet. The leader of Hezbollah Venezuela (which presents itself also as Autonomia Islamica Wayuu) is Teodoro Darnott and he also leads the Latin American 'network'.[4]

The group's development has been rather unusual. According to a Venezuelan opposition blogger, Gustavo Coronel, it started about six years ago, in 1999, as a Wayuu community project for micro-farming, in an area north-west of Maracaibo, Venezuela. The leader of the small group, Teodoro Rafael Darnott, was a member of the tribe. It seems that the project failed to gain enough attention from the authorities. In 2001, therefore, Teodoro Darnott made an opportunistic political move: he joined Chávez's political party, MVR (Movimiento Quinta República) and he was given a letter signed by one of the regional leaders of the party describing him as a national authority. Still, the project, now called by Teodoro *Mi Pequeño País* (My Little Country), failed to make the desired headway. Therefore, he changed the name of the group to 'Jehovah Nisi', a name with evangelical overtones, and began to call himself Commander Teodoro. It is not clear when Commander Teodoro decided to switch, once more, to become a follower of Hezbollah. He seems a very uncultured person, certainly not an expert on the Islamic religion or way of life. Coronel evaluates that at some point in time the real 'Islamic fanatics' probably contacted him because 'they saw in Teodoro an ambitious man, looking for a way to make some money, with a group already formed and a certain capacity of leadership over the group, all members of his Wayuu tribe... Teodoro appears as the visible head but he must be coached from the sidelines, effectively controlled by the professionals.'[5] Darnott was arrested by the Venezuelan authorities on 17 November 2006.

Hezbollah Venezuela

What is the short-term objective of Hezbollah Venezuela, asks Coronel? He evaluates 'that they are not interested in a violent stage, although they claim (a bluff, since they openly say it) to be considering a terrorist act "of low intensity," to make themselves known. The main objective of Hezbollah in Venezuela is, most probably, to make a psychological impact, to let the world know they are there ... They are eager for attention.'[6]

This was also the evaluation of Spanish academic researchers at Jihad Monitor which analysed the group's websites, as expressed in. Manuel R. Torres Soriano's article 'The fascination of Success: The Case of Hezbollah in Latin America' (in Spanish). Torres emphasizes the leftist revolutionary background and rhetoric of the group.

Teodoro traces the origins of Hezbollah Venezuela to a small Marxist faction called The Guaicaipuro Movement for National Liberation (*Proyecto Movimiento Guaicaipuro por la Liberación Nacional* – MGLN), which struggled against the oppression of the poor indigenous peasants in the Valle de Caracas region (see Annex 2). Darnott presented himself as Comandante Teodoro, in the clear intention to imitate Subcomandante Marcos, the Mexican guerrilla leader in Chiapas, and the insurgency of the Zapatista movement. According to this account the MGLN did not resist the pressure of the security forces and had to retreat to Colombia. They returned after five years to Venezuela to convert themselves to Hezbollah, without a clear explanation for this metamorphosis.[7]

Torres considers as significant the group's synergy with the so-called 'Bolivarian revolution' in Venezuela. In one of its ideological editorials the group expresses enormous respect and positive appreciation for the achievements of Hugo Chavez's regime: 'Hezbollah America Latina respects the Venezuelan revolutionary process, supports the policies of this process concerning the social benefices for the poor and the anti-Zionist and anti-American policy of this revolution.'[8]

However, the group does not accept Chavez's socialist ideology, not because it opposes it, but because Hezbollah's ideology is 'theocratic and it obeys divine rules'. Therefore, for a new Venezuela to emerge the revolution should aspire 'to the divine and the moral' and should support firmly the Hezbollah 'political-military project'.[9]

The group's strategy 'to change Venezuela' as disseminated via the Internet, includes: total destruction 'of the sex industry'; attacking the upper classes, 'who are the most corrupt'; attacking corruption in government and in the masses, both civilians and military; attacking false idols and satanic cults, as defined by them.[10]

Hezbollah Argentina

A thorough analysis of the website of Hezbollah Argentina shows a strikingly different picture from that of Hezbollah Venezuela.

While the Venezuelan group primarily is composed of indigenous Wayuu Indians with a strong leftist background and revolutionary rhetoric, the Argentinian group seems to include radical rightist mixed with leftist populist elements, the two trends with very close relations with the local Arab Shia community and the Iranian regime.

The *rightist* influence is clear in some of the most anti-Semitic, anti-Israeli and anti-American texts of Norberto Ceresole: The Falsification of the Argentinean Reality in the Geopolitical Space of Jewish Terrorism' and 'The Attacks in Buenos Aires: A Product of the Infiltration of Jewish Fundamentalism in the Service of Israeli Counter-Espionage'. In this vein, on the Hezbollah Argentina website some photos from the suicide bombings in the Israeli embassy (1992) and the Jewish Community AMIA building (1994) are subtitled 'Jewish terrorism'. It is interesting to note that the Ceresole texts are probably downloaded in exact form and fonts from the website of Radio Islam[11] and a Shia website.[12]

Norberto Rafael Ceresole was a sociologist and political scientist, who died in 2003. He identified himself with Peronism, was active in the 1970s in the left-wing Argentinian terrorist groups ERP (Ejército Revolucionario del Pueblo) and Montoneros and later became a neo-fascist, anti-Semite, Holocaust-denier and viscerally anti-Israeli. He was adviser to leftist as well as radical rightist politicians and military leaders in his country, like Aldo Rico, Mohamed Seineldin, a.k.a. 'Carapintada', and Raúl de Sagastizabal, and across Latin America.

According to his own account, Ceresole made contact with the Iranian regime immediately after the bombing of the Jewish AMIA building in 1994 and he accused the Jews and the Israeli secret services of being responsible for the bombing. He visited Iran and Lebanon, where he met an 'important, intelligent Arab movement, a patriotic group active in Southern Lebanon'. He also wrote a book on Hezbollah, published in Spain.[13]

In a 'letter to his Iranian friends', Ceresole tries to prove that there is a parallel between the Shia faith and what he calls the 'minority, pre-conciliar traditional Catholicism' (that is, pre-Vatican II Council), which is theologically irreconcilable with Judaism. He considers Iran since the Islamic Revolution to be 'the centre of resistance to the Jewish aggression' and the only state that has supplanted 'the secular Arab resistance' in fighting the Jewish state. But according to Ceresole, many would like to see the Iranian 'counterstrategy' not only resist Israeli aggressiveness, but systematically destroy every aspect of the Jewish state. Moreover, he states, the struggle against the Jewish state cannot be circumscribed geographically only to the Middle East.[14]

Hezbollah Argentina's *leftist*, or rather *populist*, trend is visible in their cooperation with Quebracho, a small Argentinean militant group. Hezbollah Argentina's website proudly announced in September 2006 that a demonstration by a group of some twenty Quebracho militants had thwarted a protest demonstration of the Jewish community in front of the Iranian embassy.

The Quebracho Patriotic Revolutionary Movement (*Movimiento Patriótico Revolucionario* – MPR) affirms itself be a political organization fighting for a 'socially just, economically independent and politically sovereign country', for the 'National Anti-imperialist Revolution'. Violence, according to MPR's vision, is the violence of the system and its injustice. Therefore the group is not opposed to the violence of the people, who have the right to justice and self-defence. As an example, the group claims that President Chavez of Venezuela, who won democratic elections, is accused by his imperialist enemies to be violent and a dictator. The violent struggle becomes generalized if it is more effective than other forms.[15]

Quebracho militants refuse to define themselves as leftist or rightist. They consider themselves 'revolutionary patriots' in the framework of the Latin-American liberation struggle 'in which the national struggle has however a pre-eminent place'. They are revolutionary because they believe in 'real, profound changes'. Their enemies are 'imperialism and the great capital: the big financial monopolies, the IMF, the World Bank, the Inter-American Development Bank, the US, the EU, Japan and Israel, among others'. They include also the national oligarchies.

The Quebracho MPR came into being on 31 August 1996 as a result of an agreement between various 'popular organizations' and considers itself allied to the ethos of (terrorist organizations) the Peronist Montoneros, the Trotskyite *Partido Revolucionario de los Trabajadores – Ejército Revolucionario del Pueblo* (PRT-ERP) and the struggle of Hebe de Bonafini and the Mothers of the Plaza de Mayo.[16] The group boasts that it has participated in several violent anti-imperialist manifestations in the year 2004 against Citibank, the IMF, the Argentinian Army's participation in the 'invasion of Haiti', etc.

The group clearly presents its cooperation with the Arab-Argentinian Dwelling (*Hogar Árabe Argentino*) organization of Berisso and the Islamic Association of Argentina (*Asociación Argentino Islámica* – ASAI) of La Plata, which are 'permanently attacked by the Zionists'. It also expresses solidarity with the struggle of the Lebanese Hezbollah and the Lebanese and Palestinian peoples against the 'terrorist attacks of Israel and the genocide of thousands of their people' (see Annex 3).

According to a local observer, the Islamic Association of Argentina's membership is mainly people who have converted to Shiism (while there are few Argentinians who convert to Sunnism); the group cooperates closely with the Iranian embassy and therefore is frowned upon by the Argentinian Sunnis. The ASAI and its religious leader Sheikh Abdala Madani clearly identify themselves with the Iranian regime, as evidenced by their website and the Khomeini posters they carry at every anti-Israeli demonstration.[17]

The Islamic Association of Argentina website contains an interview by leftist Turkish journalists with Hezbollah Secretary-General Hassan Nasrallah dated 20 August 2006 in which he praised the socialist movement

> ... which has been away from international struggle for a considerable time' and at last 'has begun to offer moral support for [Hezbollah] once again ... The most concrete example of this has been Hugo Chavez, the President of Venezuela. What most of the Muslim states could not do has been done by Chavez, by the withdrawal of Venezuela's ambassador to Israel. He furthermore communicated to [Hezbollah] his support for [the] resistance. This has been an immense source of moral strength for [Hezbollah].'

Nasrallah saluted 'the leaders and the peoples of Latin America' for their heroic resistance to 'the American bandits'; this resistance led the Lebanese people to 'embrace Chavez and Ernesto Che Guevara' and post 'pictures of Chavez, Che, Sadr and Khamenei together in the streets of Beirut'.[18]

Interestingly, the text appears in a prominent place on the site, although the Hezbollah has flatly denied that Nasrallah has 'given any interviews to any Turkish or other non-Lebanese journalist during the month of August' and the Turkish daily *Evrensel* has declared it a forgery.[19] Do they believe that the opinions expressed in the interview suit their interests in Latin America?

Why Hezbollah Prospers in Venezuela and Argentina

It is probably not by chance that the Latin American Hezbollah seems to flourish in these two countries.

Venezuela was considered for many years one of the bases of the Lebanese Hezbollah in Latin America. Margarita Island, a free-trade zone that is home to a sizeable Arab Muslim community, is especially cited as a potential terrorist base. The alleged threat emanating from Margarita Island is receiving far more attention in Washington, but is as much a product of the tensions between the Bush Administration and President Chavez.[20]

What makes Hezbollah Venezuela worthy of attention is the timing of their activities. The group has attained visibility at a time when 'the strange liaison' between Hugo Chavez and Iranian President Ahmadinejad has become an item of international interest.[21] Chavez has come out in support of Iran's nuclear programme as well as denouncing the war in Lebanon, accusing Israel of a 'new Holocaust'. At the Non-Aligned Movement summit, which was held in Cuba leading up to the Iranian leader's Caracas visit, Venezuela and Iran channelled the tide of global anti-US sentiment into support for Iran's right to nuclear energy.[22]

The recent wave of anti-Semitism in Venezuela, as reflected in analyses at a September 2006 Caracas conference on the Middle East conflict and its local repercussions, made the Jewish community rather nervous. Some at the conference feared that Chavez's attacks on Israel may lead to attacks on local Jews. Already, graffiti is appearing on the Mariperez synagogue with increasing frequency. Some even accused Chavez of bringing in Hezbollah to indoctrinate Wayuu Indians in the west of the country. According to Jewish activists, the wave of anti-Semitism comes from official and pro-government media and Chavez's failure to repudiate these media and the anti-Semitic graffiti represents the 'crux of the problem'. In meetings between Jewish leaders and high-level government officials, including Chavez himself, the government has claimed that its hands are tied. 'We'll do what we can, but we can't deny people freedom of speech', has been the government's response.[23]

This tolerant attitude towards radical personalities and ideologies is well illustrated by President Chavez's conduct towards the famous terrorist of Venezuelan origin Carlos Ilich Ramirez, the famous Jackal, captured by the French and sentenced to life imprisonment in 1997. In 1999, Carlos sent a letter from his prison to the 'distinguished fellow Venezuelan' offering solidarity and support. President Chavez acknowledged the authenticity of the letter while expressing his concern for his 'fellow countryman in disgrace'. The Venezuelan ambassador in Paris was ordered to assist the terrorist and 'to safeguard his human rights'. During his October 2001 visit to Paris, Chavez was hopeful for a positive outcome of his request by signing a pact towards the repatriation of detainees, but the French government stated that agreements could not include repatriation of terrorists.[24] On 1 June 2006, President Chavez referred to Carlos as his 'friend' during a meeting of OPEC countries held in Caracas.[25]

The present Argentinian government is not sympathetic to radical organizations or regimes, but in this country there are many active groups and movements of the radical right and left which have often expressed anti-

Semitic and anti-Israeli, as well as anti-US, views and activities. The difficulties in the long investigation and prosecution of the terrorist bombings of the Israeli embassy and AMIA building which involved at times the arrest and trial of rightist or corrupt elements are evidence of the tolerant background to such radical endeavours.[26]

In late October 2006, Argentine prosecutors asked a federal judge to issue an arrest warrant against former Iranian President Hashemi Rafsanjani and seven others for the 1994 bombing of the AMIA Jewish cultural center that killed 85 people. The Culture and Islamic Guidance Ministry representative in Argentina, Mahsan Rabani, was also involved. In 1993, he began inquiring about renting a commercial van in Buenos Aires, asking specifically for a Renault Traffic, the type of van used by the bomber.[27]

There is also a strange coincidence concerning the special relationship between Hugo Chávez and Norberto Ceresole and Argentinean rightist and anti-Semitic personalities. In 1994 Ceresole founded with the Centro de Estudios Argentina en el Mundo and started to meet with Mohamed Seineldin. It was through this military group that Ceresole met Hugo Chávez and began to function as an adviser to his team. On 15 June Ceresole was detained and deported from the country by the Venezuelan intelligence police (DISIP), accused of trying to forge political links in Venezuela, in particular with Chávez.

By the end of July 2006, the Simon Wiesenthal Center, which had discovered Hezbollah Venezuela's website on the Internet calling for 'Jihad in Latin America', sent a letter to the Executive Secretary of the Inter-American Counter-Terrorism Centre (CICTE), Steven Monblatt, asking for an investigation of the group.[28]

However, it seems that the Venezuelan authorities have not attempted to challenge Hezbollah Venezuela or to explain the government's silence, even after the bombing attempts at the US embassy and the new threats emitted on its website.

Islamization in Latin America

Another factor influencing the growing attraction to radical Islamist terrorist groups could be the successful campaigns of Islamic proselytism in the heart of poor indigene Indian tribes and populations by both Shia and Sunni preachers and activists.

The influence of Muslims in the past was mainly based on major and minor concentrations of Muslim immigrants in different areas of the continent. Major Muslim immigration can be seen in countries such as Argentina and Panama, and also in Guyana, Trinidad & Tobago, which are English-speaking.

Brazil, which has a Portuguese-speaking community, holds the largest Muslim community in South America.

According to Yahya Juan Suquillo, an acting imam in Ecuador, it is a great misconception to think that since there is a very small conversion rate among Christians to become Muslims in Islamic states there might be the same situation for Latin American people. Latin America is searching for its own identity and the common people are clearly looking forward to a totally different spiritual change. Proof of this is that twenty to thirty years ago, Catholicism claimed almost 90 per cent of the total population in Latin America whereas today the numbers are now only between 55 per cent and 65 per cent. Latin America is a fertile area for Islamic *dawah* (preaching to the unconverted) and Islamic values are already present in Latin American culture. Muslim institutions in the past have failed to identify the potential of Latin American people for accepting Islam. Therefore they must work 'with a genuine strategic plan to promote the peaceful way of life that Islam teaches in His book, the Glorious Qur'an'.[29]

According to the website 'Global Terrorism Analysis', Spain's al-Murabitun, which emphasizes the cultural links between the Arab world and Latin America through Spain's Moorish heritage, is believed to be the most prolific missionary movement operating on the continent. The Murabitun are comprised predominantly of Spanish and European converts to Islam.[30] Since 1995 hundreds of Tzotziles tribespeople from Altos de Chiapas converted to Islam.[31] The Murabitun and like-minded movements advocate a collective reversion to Islam, a return to the region's true heritage, as opposed to what many see as conversion to the Muslim faith. The Murabitun also claim that Islam is not tainted by European and Western colonialism and imperialism, but instead serves as a remedy for the oppression and destruction brought about by the Spanish conquest.[32]

The Murabitun's efforts to gain adherents in Mexico include an unsuccessful attempt to forge an alliance with Subcommandante Marcos and his Zapatista Army of National Liberation (EZLN), following the group's armed rebellion in Chiapas in 1994.[33] In an article comparing Zapatism and Islamism, Fausto Giudice tries to present aspects of Islam that are compatible with the Zapatista ideology and strategy: what he calls 'the direct democracy', the principle of consensus, the 'shura' (council) and 'majlis' (parliament) structure. He even asks himself if Subcomandante Marcos could be the incarnation of the Mahdi (the twelfth 'hidden' Imam).[34] Marcos and his popular Zapatista movement seem to have such a symbolic importance in the eyes of the Islamists that a Turkish Al Qaeda publication has even pretended that he has indeed converted to Islam.[35]

The growing number of adherents to the radical Shia ideology, as exempli-fied in the activities of Hezbollah LA illustrates the competition between the two branches of Islam in the continent and could influence the radicalization of the local Muslim communities, both the older original ones and the converted.

Does Al Qaeda bandwagon Hezbollah?

Since 25 October 2006, two days after the failed bombing near the US embassy in Caracas, the Hezbollah Venezuela website has taken a new turn. A spate of Al Qaeda and other Sunni terrorist organizations' announcements, manifestos and videos, mainly from Iraq, have been posted by the Autonomia Islamica Wayuu and a certain Samir237. Strangely, many of the postings are in French and not Spanish.

For instance the Brigade Silahudine Al Ayubi (Military wing of Jaami?) announces nine attacks in Baghdad; announcement of attacks by the Brigade of the Mujaheed Abu 'Ubadah of the Al Qaeda organization in Iraq; material of the Information Centre al Fajir belonging to the Army Ansar al Sunnah; announcement of a new address for the forum al Firdaws (<http://al-firdaws. frbb.net/index.forum>); several preaching audios of Sheikh Abu Qatada; many videos of the sniper Juba and beheadings of kidnapped people, and the announcement of the Rafidayn Center concerning the formation of the Islamic State in Iraq.

Possibly, local sympathizers or activists of al-Qaeda evaluate that the opening of the 'bombing propaganda campaign' by Hezbollah LA presents a good opportunity to begin their own campaign of recruiting and indoctrination in Venezuela and other Latin American countries.

Conclusion

On 2 November 2006, Hezbollah Venezuela announced that 'out of respect for the revolution and its leader', Hezbollah Venezuela will suspend 'the repetition of its presentation until after the elections of December 3, an example of civility, humanity and respect as well as revolutionary condition' (see Annex 4).[36]

It is clear from this statement that Hezbollah Venezuela was referring to the Bolivarian Revolution, the great political project of President Chavez, and to the 3 December 2006 presidential elections. The message conveyed a kind of open solidarity with the regime and an attempt not to hamper it during the last days of the election campaign.

Indeed, on 6 November 2006 a certain Samir237 posted an announcement in the name of Sheidy Teodoro Darnott asking 'to vote on 3-D against the United States, for Chavez, the anti-imperialist candidate of Hezbollah Venezuela'.

The end of this 'episode' in the short history of Hezbollah Latin America does not permit us yet to draw a clear conclusion regarding the real character and goal of the group. It is possible that Israel's war against Hezbollah in Lebanon in the summer of 2006 has given incentive to the leadership of Hezbollah LA to go public and materialize its threats. Darnott, the Venezuelan leader, denies any link to the Lebanese Hezbollah and indeed the religious and ideological substratum of his documents is very poor and superficial. In the case of the Argentinian 'branch' the Shia and Iranian link is quite obvious and could prove more dangerous.

However, in view of the first terrorist attempt, even if it was only for propaganda purposes, several worrying aspects should be stressed.

The special permissive atmosphere in Venezuela may send a message to the group (in the post-presidential election period) and to more dangerous terrorist organizations that their activities on its soil or from its territory might be tolerated or even politically permitted.

There is a growing trend of solidarity between leftist, Marxist, anti-global and even rightist elements with the Islamists. The fact that the Lebanese Hezbollah sponsored a strategic conference of anti-global groups and movements in Beirut in September 2004, already pointed to this potentially dangerous coalition for the future.[37]

Finally, there is the possibility that the Lebanese Hezbollah, and Al Qaeda, may recruit 'converted' Latin American terrorists for their operational terrorist international activity; as they did in the past in the Middle East and Europe.

ANNEX 1

Friday, August 18, 2006

Bismilahi Rahmani Rahim
(En el Nombre de Allah, El Compasivo, El Misericordioso)
Propuesta Política-Militar Integrista, fundamentalista
Islámica Latinoamericana

As salamu aleikum

Noti Hezboallah

Hezbollah Latino América analiza colocar explosivo contra una organización aliada de U.S.A en América Latina. el motivo seria el lanzamiento de Hezbollah Latno América como un movimiento internacional, el difundir el rechazo a los ataques de Israel contra hezbollah Líbano, manifestar nuetra solidaridad y respaldo a Hezbollah en su lucha contra el sionismo y el imperialismo norte americano. El aparato explosivo será de bajo poder y no causara daños humanos ni a la propiedad sino que solo difundirá panfletos con consignas de hezbolla Latino América contra la ocupación y contra el imperialismo de U.S.A, de esta forma Hezbollah se presentara ante la opinión publica nacional e internacional ya como un movimiento revolucionario islámico, que trabaja para establecerse en todos los pises de América Latina y desde estos países abrir un nuevo espacio de la resistencia islámica internacional.

Wa aleikum salam

Hezbollah Latino America

Web site http://groups.msn.com/AutonomiaIslamicaWayuu

ANNEX 2

Teologia De La Liberación Y Opción Por Los Pobres

Movimiento Guaicaipuro Por La Liberación Nacional

ANNEX 3

comunicados y noticias / QUEBRACHO

08-10-06, Bs. As.

LA BANDERA DE HIZBULLAH EN LA FIESTA DEL INMIGRANTE

Desde que comenzó a realizarse en la localidad de Berisso la tradicional Fiesta del Inmigrante, la comunidad islámica, particularmente quienes forman parte del Hogar Árabe Argentino de Berisso y la Asociación Argentino Islámica (ASAI) de La Plata, han sido permanentemente atacados por el Diario El Día y los sionistas.

El stand del Hogar está adornado por una bandera de la organización patriótica Hizbullah, ejemplo de la lucha que todo el pueblo libanés está dando todos los días contra los ataques terroristas del Estado de Israel y sus aliados yanquis. Esto parece que resulta intolerable para el sionismo, genocida de miles de palestinos y libaneses.

Y como si esto fuera poco, estos cómplices del genocidio contra los pueblos que se resisten a perder su dignidad, han vuelto a arremeter, tratando de impedir que en el día de hoy, cuando se realizará el tradicional desfile de todas las colectividades cerrando la Fiesta del Inmigrante, la bandera de Hizbullah participe de la movilización.

Desde el MPR QUEBRACHO queremos expresar nuestro más profundo sentimiento de solidaridad y saludamos la valentía de los integrantes del Hogar Árabe Argentino de Berisso y la Asociación Argentino Islámica (ASAI) de La Plata, quienes, no dejándose amedrentar, llevarán bien en alto el estandarte de Hizbullah, como ejemplo de lucha no sólo del pueblo libanés, sino de todos los pueblos que luchamos día a día contra el imperialismo que pretende sojuzgarnos.

ANNEX 4

Ely Karmon is Senior Research Scholar at the Institute for Counter-Terrorism, and the Institute for Policy and Strategy at the Interdisciplinary Centre, Herzliya, Israel.

NOTES

1 Caracas daily *El Universal*, 23 October 2006.
2 *CNN*, 23 October 2006.
3 See <http://groups.msn.com/justiciadivinavenezuela/general.msnw?action=get_message&mview =1&ID_Message=25>.
4 The Wayuu are a pastoral tribe living on the Guajira Peninsula, on the north coast of Colombia and Venezuela where they live without taking into account the frontier between the two countries. Their territory extends over approximately 15,300 km2, of which 12,000 km2 are in Colombia in the Department of the Guajira and 3,380 km2 are in the state of Zulia in Venezuela. Their territory is hot, dry and inhospitable; the rains are scanty and badly distributed. Merciless sunlight, constant winds and very high evaporation rate are distinctive factors of the Guajira – in short, all the

characteristics of a desert. Human health, agriculture and animal husbandry all suffer from the lack of available water, and as a result the people have few options available for their own livelihoods. The latest census (1993) shows the Wayuu population to be more than 130,000 inhabitants. The Wayuu culture is being gradually eroded, and already many traditional skills have essentially been lost. This loss of culture is also increasingly accompanied by a lack of self-esteem, particularly among the youth. The Wayuu have traditionally had a very loose social structure with few local organizations. In modern times, the clan system has become much weaker than it once was, but has not yet been replaced by alternative social structures. As a result there is a lack of institutional capacity at the local level and a lack of human resources for the development of new associations or other organizational structures. See *The Wayuu Jayuir Foundation*, at http://www.geocities. com/jayuir/ wayuu_en.html.

5   This paragraph is based on Gustavo Coronel, 'The Hezbollah Venezuelan Metastasis', *VenezuelaToday*, 4 September 2006, at <http://venenews.net/gustavo-coronel/hizbula-hezbollah-hizbullah+venezuela+hugo-chavez.html>.

6   Ibid.

7   Manuel R. Torres Soriano, 'La Fascinación por el exito: el caso de Hezbollah en América Latina', *Jihad Monitor Occasional*, Paper No 1, 17 October 2006, at <http://www.ugr.es/~terris/ Hezbollah %20Latino.pdf>.

8   Ibid.

9   *Hezbollah Venezuela*. 'Nuestra posición oficial respecto a la revolución venezolana. Editorial', 3 August 2006.

10   Gustavo Coronel, 'Chávez joins the terrorists: his path to martyrdom', *VenezuelaToday*, 2 September 2006, at <http://venenews.net/gustavo-coronel/hezbollah+venezuela_hugo-chavez_ syria-iran_wmd+ terrorism . html>.

10   See <http://www.radioislam.net/islam/spanish/sion/terror/cap2.htm>. Radio Islam was a Swedish radio channel, now a website, allegedly dedicated to "the liberation struggle of the Palestinian people against Israel", one of the most radical right wing anti-Semitic homepages on the net", which espouses Holocaust denial and praises Adolf Hitler and Nazism.

11   See <http://www.islam-shia.org/>.

12   Alberto Garrido, 'Chavez y la relacion con el mundo musulman', *El Universal*, 13 February 2006, at <http://www.lanuevacuba.com/archivo/notic-06-02-1320.htm>.

14   Norberto Ceresole, 'Carta abierta a mis amigos iranies',"at the Holocaust denial website <http://www.vho.org/aaargh/espa/ceres/arta.html>.

15   See the ideological material at <http://www.quebracho.org.ar>.

16   Bonafini was one of the founders of the Association of the Mothers of the Plaza de Mayo, a protest organization of Argentine mothers who lost their children during the Dirty War, the persecution and suppression of dissident groups by the military regime that ruled Argentina between 1976 and 1983.

17   See <http://www.organizacionislam.org.ar/index.htm>.

18   See Roza Çi∂dem Erdo∂an / Mutlu Pahin, 'Entrevista a Sayyed Hassan Nasrallah, dirigente máximo de Hezbollah Sobre la resistencia contra las tropas de Israel, los regímenes colaboracionistas, el Ché, Chávez, los socialistas y el frente único contra el imperialismo', *Izquierda Punto Info*, at <http://www.organizacionislam.org.ar/conflib/reporsayyed.htm>.

19   Taylan Bilgic Cihan Celik, 'Statement from Evrensel Daily about the Forged Nasrallah Interview', *Foreign News Desk Evrensel Daily/Istanbul Turkey*, 2 September 2006, at <http://green leftbloggers.blogspot.co2006/09/evrensel-statement-re-forged-nasrallah.html>.

20   For a discussion on Lebanese Hezbollah's activity in Latin America see Ely Karmon, 'Fight on All. Fronts?: Hezbollah, the War on Terror, and the War in Iraq', The Washington Institute for Near East Policy, *Policy Focus*, No. 46, December 2003, pp. 9–10 at <http://www.washingtoninstitute. org/pubPDFs/PF46.pdf>. See also Blanca Madani, 'Hezbollah's Global Finance Network: The Triple Frontier', *Middle East Intelligence Bulletin*, 4, no. 1 (January 2002) <ww.meib.org/ articles/0201_l2.htm>.

21   Coronel, *The Hezbollah Venezuelan Metastasis*.

22 Jose Orozco, 'Venezuelan Jews Fear Chavez-Iran Ties', *The Jerusalem Post*, 19 September 2006.
23 Ibid.
24 'Chavez Journeys the World', *Democracia Y Desarrollo*, 16 October 2001, at <http://www. venezuela today.org/01-10-17_in.htm>.
25 *El Universal*, 1 June 2006.
26 Yossi Melman, 'Argentina bombing case moves ahead', *Ha'aretz*, 8 September 2003.
27 Ze'ev Schiff, 'Argentine lawyer asks to jail Iran officials for Jewish center blast', *Ha'aretz*, 25 October 2006.
28 See 'El Centro Simon Wiesenthal urgió al Comité Interamericano contra el Terrorismo la investigación sobre la presencia de Hezbollah en la region' at <http://www.itongadol.com.ar/ shop/detallenot.asp?Noted =15255>.
29 For a detailed description of the strategy of Islamist penetration in Latin America see the transcript of a presentation by Yahya Juan Suquillo, Imam of the Islamic Center of Quito Ecuador, 'Islamic Principles in Latin America' at the Fourth Annual Conference of Latin American Muslim Leaders in Curacao, 16–18 September 2003 in the *Latino Muslim Voice* (November 2003), official newsletter of the Latino American Da'wa Organization at <http://www.latinodawah.org/ newsletter/oct-dec2k3.html#9>.
30 The group is an international Sufi order founded in the 1970s by Sheikh Abdel Qader as-Sufi al-Murabit, a controversial Scottish Muslim convert born Ian Dallas. Aurelino Perez heads the Murabitun's campaign in Chiapas, where he competes with Omar Weston, a British-born Muslim convert who resides in Mexico City and heads the Centro Cultural Islamico de Mexico (CCIM), for adherents in Chiapas and the rest of Mexico. See <http://www.jamestown.org/terrorism/ analysts.php?authorid=311>
31 María Teresa Del Riego, 'Celebran indígenas musulmanes', at <http://groups.msn.com/autono miaislamicawayuu/general.msnw?action=get_message&mview=0&ID_Message=544&LastModif ied=4675592423029140791>.
32 Chris Zambelis, 'Radical Islam in Latin America', *Terrorism Monitor*, Jamestown Foundation,Vol. 3, No. 23, 2 December 2005.
33 Ibid.
34 Fausto Giudice, 'Y si el subcomandante Marcos fuese la encarnación del Mehdi', at <http:// groups.msn.com/autonomiaislamicawayuu/general.msnw?action=get_message&mview=0&ID_ Message= 542&LastModified=4675592299897498067>.
35 '"[El] Kaide" (1) Magazine Published Openly in Turkey!', *MEMRI Special Dispatch Series*, No. 951, 5 August 2005.
36 See <http://groups.msn.com/autonomiaislamicawayuu/general.msnw?action=get_message& mview=1&ID_Message=642>.
37 Ely Karmon, 'Hezbollah and the Antiglobalization Movement: A New Coalition?', *PolicyWatch*, The Washington Institute for Near East Policy, No. 949, 27 January 2005. See <http://www. instituteforcounterterrorism.org/apage/5222.php>.

PART V
Psychoanalysis and Geopolitics

Psychoanalysis and Geopolitics: The Iranian Holocaust Conference

THEODORE DALRYMPLE

Vehemence of expression is not necessarily proportional to strength of argument, quite the reverse: and one of the probable causes of the rise of political Islamism is an awareness of the extreme intellectual vulnerability of the religion to the kind of rationalist criticism that has so weakened Christianity, and destroyed communism. The collapse of Islam would be even more damaging to the Islamic world than the collapse of Christianity has been to the Western world, since it has nothing else of any moral or intellectual significance to offer, and its economic and technical retardation would then be exposed in all its nakedness. Take but Islam away, untune that string, And, hark, what discord follows!

In this, as in so many other cases, an ounce of prevention is better than a ton of cure, and the recent International Conference to Review the Global Vision of the Holocaust, hosted by the Institute for Political and International Studies in Tehran, is best seen as a rhetorical diversion from the need for self-examination and the inadequacy of Islam as a philosophical response to the modern world. In opening the conference, the Iranian foreign minister said that the root cause of the problems of the Middle East was the Palestinian question, an assertion flattering to the self-conception of the region no doubt, but so simplistic that it hardly requires refutation. When the world outlook to which you are deeply attached and which defines you is under threat, the best defence is to blame others for your own deficiencies and throw dust in their eyes.

It is important to recall the context in which the conference was first arranged. Together with a cartoon competition on the subject of the Holocaust, it was a response to the Danish cartoons which, in the estimate of Islamists, insulted Mohammed, and an attempt to forestall further mockery of what, in fact, is very easily mocked. (The extremely muted Islamic response to the vastly wittier and more derogatory cartoons that appeared in the French satirical papers, *Charlie Hebdo* and *Le canard enchaîné*, some time after the Danish cartoon crisis, suggests that the vulnerability to uncowed Voltaireanism was well understood, and that silence was in this instance the better part of refutation.)

One of the most powerful tools in any rhetorical armamentarium is the *tu quoque* argument: you are equally guilty of what you accuse me of. And there is no doubt that this argument has been wielded with considerable cunning by the Iranian government.

Strictly speaking, the conference was not organized straightforwardly to deny the reality of the Holocaust. The presence and speech of Rabbi Aharon Cohen, of the Neturei Karta sect of Judaism, which rejects political Zionism as heretical, served three purposes at once. First, it deflected any possible criticism that the conference was anti-Semitic in intent; second, because Rabbi Cohen asserted that the Holocaust was an historical reality, in which millions of Jews were killed, the conference could be presented as genuinely open-minded, an inquiry after truth, and not just a gathering of Holocaust-deniers; and third, it gave credence to President Ahmadinejad's argument, that even if the Holocaust took place, and was not merely a myth, it did not legitimate Zionism. And, of course, the illegitimacy of Zionism, even if the Holocaust took place, would lend psychological credence to the notion that the problems of the region were all attributable to it.

The fact that there were genuine Holocaust deniers, such as the French former academic, Robert Faurisson, on the same platform as people who accepted the historical reality of the Holocaust gave to the conference that appearance of genuine debate. And the presence of people like Faurisson was essential to the fundamental, *tu quoque*, purpose of the conference.

Faurisson made precisely the same point as David Duke, the former leader of the Ku Klux Clan, who was also at the conference: that Western claims to freedom of speech were bogus and hypocritical, because a number of Holocaust deniers (Faurisson among them) had faced persecution, prosecution and even imprisonment because of their views.

Duke said, *inter alia*: In Europe you can freely question, ridicule and deny Jesus Christ. The same is true for the Prophet Mohammed, and nothing will happen to you, heck you might even star in your own weekly TV show, but offer a single question concerning the smallest part of the Holocaust and you face prison!

And Faurisson said, *inter alia*: In France it is perfectly lawful to proclaim unbelief in God but it is forbidden to say that one does not believe in the 'Holocaust', or simply that one has any doubts about it. This prohibition of any kind of disputing became formal and official with the law of 13 July 1990. The said law was published in the *Journal officiel de la République française* on the next day, that is, 14 July, the day of commemoration of the Republic and of freedom ... Relevant case law specifies that all this applies 'even if [such disputing] is presented in veiled or dubitative form or by way of insinuation' (*Code penal*, Paris: Dalloz, 2006, p. 2059). Thus France has but one official myth, that of the 'Holocaust', and knows but one form of blasphemy, that which offends the 'Holocaust'.

The existence of laws in France, Germany and Austria that do indeed prohibit free speech on this one subject, and that have been used actually to imprison people, lends force to what Faurisson said. It might be argued that these countries have good historical reason to be particularly sensitive on the subject, that makes the laws in them less absurd than they would be in other jurisdictions; on the other hand, they could also be taken to indicate a lack of legislator's trust in the decency and good sense of their electorate. In any case, propaganda is not interested in subtle distinctions, and any person who demands absolute freedom to criticize the religious beliefs of others can be painted a hypocrite when he declares certain other beliefs to be beyond criticism (or, in the case of the cartoon wars, mockery).

What is clear is that the *tu quoque* argument justifies, psychologically if not in strict logic, the suppression of fundamental dissent concerning religious dogma. If everyone can be shown to be dogmatic about something, then it is no criticism of any particular dogma that it is unquestionable, and no one has the right or standing to criticize it as such.

The Iranian authorities have said that they will hold a Holocaust cartoon competition every year, and start an institute devoted to the study of the Holocaust, whose headquarters they say they hope one day to move to Berlin. What I suspect they really hope for, though, is the outlawing of rational criticism of Islam in return for a cessation of their support for Holocaust denial and equivocation.

Dr Dalrymple is a British psychiatrist and a prison doctor.